Kant

and the *Critique of Pure Reason*

'Sebastian Gardner's book is the best introduction to Kant's masterpiece
to have been written in over twenty years. . . . This is a truly useful introduction for every reader of Kant that at the same time genuinely
advances our understanding of the greatest of modern philosophers. I
expect to recommend it for many years to come.'

(Paul Guyer, *University of Pennsylvania*)

'Gardner's argument and analysis are carried out in a tough and vigor-
ous way. *Kant and the Critique of Pure Reason* is valuable for students
who want a clear story.'

(Graham Bird, *University of Manchester*)

The *Critique of Pure Reason* is the cornerstone of Kant's philosophical system
and one of the greatest works in the history of Western philosophy. A proper
understanding of the major philosophical developments of the last two hundred
years – from Hegel to Wittgenstein to Heidegger – presupposes a knowledge
of the *Critique of Pure Reason*.

Ideal for students coming to Kant for the first time, this GuideBook will be an
invaluable guide to his epistemology and metaphysics.

Sebastian Gardner is Lecturer in Philosophy at University College London.
He is the author of *Irrationality and the Philosophy of Psychoanalysis*.

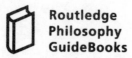

**Routledge
Philosophy
GuideBooks**

Edited by Tim Crane and Jonathan Wolff
University College London

Kant and the *Critique of Pure Reason*
Sebastian Gardner

Mill on Liberty
Jonathan Riley

Mill on Utilitarianism
Roger Crisp

Wittgenstein and the *Philosophical Investigations*
Marie McGinn

Heidegger and *Being and Time*
Stephen Mulhall

Plato and the *Republic*
Nickolas Pappas

Locke on Government
D. A. Lloyd Thomas

Locke on Human Understanding
E. J. Lowe

Spinoza and the *Ethics*
Genevieve Lloyd

LONDON AND NEW YORK

Routledge Philosophy GuideBook to

Kant
and the *Critique*
of Pure Reason

■ Sebastian Gardner

First published 1999
by Routledge
11 New Fetter Lane,
London EC4P 4EE

Simultaneously published in the
USA and Canada
by Routledge
29 West 35th Street,
New York, NY 10001

Reprinted 2000

*Routledge is an imprint of the
Taylor & Francis Group*

© 1999 Sebastian Gardner

Typeset in Times and Frutiger by
The Florence Group, Stoodleigh,
Devon

Printed and bound in Great Britain
by Clays Ltd, St Ives plc

*British Library Cataloguing in
Publication Data*
A catalogue record for this book is
available from the British Library.

*Library of Congress Cataloging in
Publication Data*
Gardner, Sebastian.
  Kant and the Critique of pure
    reason / Sebastian Gardner.
    p.   cm. – (Routledge
  philosophy guidebooks)
  Includes bibliographical
  references and index.
    1. Kant, Immanuel, 1724–1804.
  Kritik der reinen Vernunft.
  2. Knowledge, Theory of.
  3. Causation.   4. Reason.
  I. Title.   II. Series.
  B2779.G27   1999 98–42339
  121–dc 21

ISBN 0–415–11908–1 (hbk)
ISBN 0–415–11909–X (pbk)

For my mother,
Jude, Euan and Benedict,
Emma, Bobby and Jade

We do not deny that the Kantian solution is extremely subtle and is perhaps balanced on the point of a needle, but who would believe that a solution to this problem could be found which was not alarmingly subtle?

(Gottfried Martin)

Transcendental idealism arises in general through a direct inversion of previous modes of philosophical explanation.

(F. W. J. von Schelling)

Contents

10 The reception and influence of the *Critique* 327

Preface

Kant published the *Critique of Pure Reason* (henceforth *Critique*) in two editions, and there are substantial differences between them. They are interlaced in the translation by N. Kemp Smith (2nd edn, London: Macmillan, 1933), where the 'A' numbering in the margin refers to the first edition and the 'B' numbering to the second, corresponding to the pagination of the German originals. Quotations in this book are taken from this edition, which has hitherto been standardly employed in English-language Kant commentary. Two new translations of the *Critique* have appeared very recently, the one by W. Pluhar (Indianapolis: Hackett, 1997), the other by P. Guyer and A. Wood (Cambridge: Cambridge University Press, 1998).

References are also made in this book to Kant's *Prolegomena to any Future Metaphysics* (*Proleg*) (trans. J. Ellington, Indianapolis: Hackett, 1977), *Critique of Practical Reason* (*CPracR*) and *Groundwork of the Metaphysics of Morals* (*Gr*) (trans. and ed. M. Gregor, in Kant, *Practical Philosophy*, Cambridge: Cambridge University Press, 1996), *Critique of Judgement* (*CJ*) (trans. W. Pluhar, Indianapolis: Hackett, 1987) and his *Philosophical Correspondence, 1759–99* (ed. and trans. A. Zweig, Chicago: University of Chicago Press, 1967). Where material from these works is quoted, it is taken from these editions, and all references are to the marginal pagination. The standard edition of Kant's works in German is the Prussian Academy edition, *Kants gesammelte Schriften*, ed. Königlich Preußischen Akademie der Wissenschaften (Berlin: Georg Reimer, subsequently Walter de Gruyter, 1900–). References to this work are given in the form *Ak* followed by volume number and page number. Regarding Kantian terms such as 'First Analogy', 'fourth paralogism', capitals are used when referring to a section of the *Critique*, and lower case when referring to the argument given or discussed there.

It cannot be pretended that the prose of the *Critique* – its 'colourless, dry, packing-paper style' and 'stiff, abstract form', as the poet Heinrich Heine put it – has many immediate attractions. Kant himself was acutely conscious of the work's literary limitations, and excused it on the grounds that what it contains requires quite special technical expression. Kant's philosophical vocabulary is baroque and unfamiliar. It does not strictly consist of neologisms, because the terms Kant employs are drawn from earlier philosophical sources and other (mathematical, juridical) quarters, but their meaning cannot be sought outside Kant's texts. The only remedy for the difficulty presented by the style and terminology of the *Critique* is repeated exposure.

I should at the outset say something about the approach to Kant taken in this book, if only so that readers unfamiliar with the *Critique* and commentary on it should be made aware of how it differs from some of the many other approaches which may be taken.

The book reflects work, most of it in the last two decades, on Kant's theoretical philosophy by Henry Allison, Karl Ameriks, Richard Aquila, Ermanno Bencivenga, Graham Bird, Gerd Buchdahl, Dieter Henrich, Arthur Melnick, Robert Pippin, Ralph Walker, Wayne Waxman and others. These writers do not express a single view of Kant by any means, but they share an outlook to the extent of agreeing that Kant's metaphysic of transcendental idealism is far from being a mere curiosity in the history of philosophy and is instead (at the very least) a highly interesting philosophical project. With a view to providing an introduction to the *Critique* that takes account of this recent work, this book emphasises the basis, content and implications of the doctrine of transcendental idealism, and furthermore seeks to bring out its strengths. It should consequently be emphasised that there is an altogether different line to be found in Kant commentary, according to which transcendental idealism is an incoherent doctrine, and the success of the *Critique* lies in a set of metaphysically neutral but epistemologically forceful arguments which may, with more or less difficulty, be isolated from their idealistic environment. The classic work in this school is P. F. Strawson's *The Bounds of Sense: An Essay on Kant's 'Critique of Pure Reason'* (London: Methuen, 1966). Not dissimilar conclusions have been defended more recently by Paul Guyer. I have paid some attention to this approach, but chiefly for purposes of contrast, and have not by any means attempted to represent all that may be said on its behalf.

A further reason for the approach to the *Critique* taken in this book is provided by its introductory character. Virtually every sentence of the *Critique* presents difficulties. Attempts have been made to provide commentaries comprehensively elucidating each individual section of the work, and some of these run to several volumes without getting near its end. The most that a brief commentary can hope to do is communicate a broad picture of what Kant says in the *Critique* which will provide a framework for the study of individual sections and, more importantly, make this task seem worth pursuing. Highlighting the theme of transcendental idealism again seemed suited to this purpose.

Limitations of space have meant that certain other questions of interpretation could not be pursued. I have ignored what is known as the patchwork theory. In the view of some commentators (most prominently in the English-language commentary by Norman Kemp Smith) the text of the *Critique* should be regarded as a composite of elements written at very different stages of Kant's philosophical development, the upshot being that Kant's mature, 'Critical' view requires a kind of hermeneutical archaeology. This approach to the text is currently not much favoured. More perilously, I have not drawn attention to the possibility of identifying quite different, inconsistent philosophical pictures in the two editions of the *Critique* but instead proceed on the assumption, which should also be recognised as open to challenge, that this is not the case.

One point regarding the organisation of the book. As the contents pages show, transcendental idealism is treated in two different chapters. The first (chapter 5) aims to give the content of the doctrine and Kant's defence of it; the only critical issues discussed are those that pertain to the argument of the Aesthetic. The many further interpretative and critical questions which arise, but which cannot be considered without a grasp of the Analytic, are set out in the second chapter on transcendental idealism (chapter 8), which is more involved, and in which I have made some suggestions as to how Kant's position may be understood, though without wishing to give the impression that such a brief discussion can do any sort of justice to the difficulty of the topic.

My account of the *Critique* has for the greater part been formed by assembling what has struck me as most illuminating in the writings of the authors listed above, particularly Henry Allison's *Kant's Transcendental Idealism: An Interpretation and Defense* (New Haven: Yale University Press, 1983) and Robert Pippin's *Kant's Theory of Form: An Essay on the 'Critique of Pure Reason'* (New Haven: Yale University Press, 1982). These studies make as strong a case as can be imagined for the value of history of philosophy as itself a form of philosophical enquiry. The form of this book has made it impossible to record my indebtedness in any detail; the works included in the Bibliography at the end are selected with a view to providing readers with a route into the secondary literature, and do not necessarily correspond to the material on which my discussion draws.

I would like to thank Jo Wolff for inviting me to write the book, Maria Stasiak and the editorial staff at Routledge for their help in its preparation, and the Philosophy Department at Birkbeck College for providing me with research leave which allowed me to finish it. I am deeply indebted to Mark Sacks for detailed comments on the final version which gave me the opportunity to eliminate many philosophical errors and to attempt to rectify many weaknesses. I am also grateful to Graham Bird, Eric James and Tim Crane for comments and suggestions. Finally I wish to thank my family for their continued support throughout the period spent writing a book without pictures.

The problem of metaphysics

In the Preface to the *Critique* Kant observes that, although metaphysics is meant to be 'the Queen of all the sciences' (Aviii), reason in metaphysics 'is perpetually being brought to a stand' (Bxiv). Ever and again 'we have to retrace our steps' (Bxiv). The degree and quality of disagreement in metaphysics makes it a 'battle-ground', a site of 'mock-combats' in which 'no participant has ever yet succeeded in gaining even so much as an inch of territory' (Bxv). The result is that in the sphere of metaphysics we vacillate between dogmatism, skepticism and indifference. The peculiar instability of metaphysics stands in stark contrast to the security of mathematics and natural science, and leaves us with no choice but to conclude that metaphysics 'has hitherto been a merely random groping' (Bxv).

Against this background, Kant makes his famous announcement of a Copernican revolution in philosophy: 'Hitherto it has been assumed that all our knowledge must conform to objects', but since this

assumption has conspicuously failed to yield any metaphysical knowledge, we 'must therefore make trial whether we may not have more success in the tasks of metaphysics, if we suppose that objects must conform to our knowledge.... We should then be proceeding precisely on the lines of Copernicus' primary hypothesis', this being the hypothesis of heliocentrism (Bxvi).

This chapter traces the route by which Kant arrived at his view that metaphysics constitutes a problem, and his view of what exactly the problem of metaphysics consists in. The next chapter outlines the Copernican revolution, which according to Kant supplies the only possible remedy.

Historical background: the Enlightenment and its problems

The feature of Kant's philosophy most strongly emphasised in synoptic histories of philosophy is its synthetic relation to the two mighty traditions of rationalism and empiricism – specifically, to the philosophies of G. W. Leibniz (1646–1716) and David Hume (1711–76). These Kant may be said to have confronted with one another in such a way as to make the deficiencies of each palpable, and then to have shown how his own, 'Critical' or 'transcendental' philosophy offers a superior alternative. This is a fruitful way of regarding Kant, if only because he frequently describes himself as doing just that. In broader terms, however, overcoming the opposition of rationalism and empiricism is a subsidiary theme in Kant's philosophy: primarily, it is a response to the deep problems bound up with the project of Enlightenment that dominated the eighteenth century.

Like all extended periods in the history of ideas, the unity of the Enlightenment, or Age of Reason, becomes visible only when the detailed doctrines of individual thinkers are allowed to go somewhat out of focus: the epoch was of course far from homogeneous and consisted more in a commonality of approach than subscription to any single set of beliefs. With that qualification, it may be said that the Enlightenment received its chief inspiration from the successes of the scientific revolution in the sixteenth and seventeenth centuries, and was concerned with defending what Western thought now takes for granted: the right of each to make up his own mind on matters of theoretical or practical substance, in place of appeal to established authority or tradition. An identical Reason was held to exist immanently in human nature, needing only to be brought to the light of day through appropriate pedagogic means. Enlightenment thinkers sought to promote civic and political institutions that would respect individual autonomy and foster the growth of knowledge, happiness and virtue. From intellectual emancipation, political emancipation would follow. Enlightenment (*Aufklärung*) is, as Kant put it in an essay which attempts to define the notion, '*man's emergence from his self-incurred immaturity*'; its motto is '*Sapere aude!*' ('Have the courage to use your own reason!'). The programme dictated by this outlook consisted in developing what Hume called 'the science of man', and in submitting all received wisdom and existing practice to the scrutiny of reason. As Kant put it:

> Our age is, in especial degree, the age of criticism, and to criticism everything must submit. Religion through its sanctity, and law-giving through its majesty, may seek to exempt themselves from it. But they then awaken just suspicion, and cannot claim the sincere respect which reason accords only to that which has been able to sustain the test of free and open examination.

(Axi[n])

A further, unrepeatably optimistic belief typical of Enlightenment thinkers was that the process of human self-illumination was already well entrenched: progress in the natural sciences, in particular the awesome achievement of Isaac Newton (1642–1727), the move towards religious toleration and decline in the authority of the Church, the social and political transformations associated with the rise of the bourgeoisie, heralding an end to tyranny and the irrational legacy of the Middle Ages – all seemed to demonstrate that history had, so to speak, turned a corner, and could not fail to continue on the path of progress.

Germany did not participate in the original phase of Enlightenment thinking. Lying directly behind it were the ideas of John Locke (1632–1704) and Newton, and leading figures of the Scottish Enlightenment were Hume and Adam Smith (1723–90). By the middle of the century its centre was firmly located in France, concentrated around the *Encyclopédie* edited by Denis Diderot (1713–84) and Jean d'Alembert (1717–83), contributors to which included the *philosophes* C. de Montesquieu (1689–1755), Voltaire (1694–1778), É. de Condillac (1715–80), P. d'Holbach (1723–89), Jean-Jacques Rousseau (1712–78) and M. de Condorcet (1743–94). In Germany the Enlightenment took hold relatively late, owing to unpropitious (still largely feudal) social and political conditions, and it was strongly associated there with philosophical rationalism. The representative and dominant *Aufklärung* philosophy was that of Leibniz, as propagated by Christian Wolff (1679–1750) and his followers. Wolff had recast Leibniz's philosophy in an explicitly systematic form, and in the first half of the eighteenth century the so-called 'Leibniz–Wolffian philosophy' became standard fare in German universities. It was not, even at is zenith, without its critics, and the German philosophical landscape of course encompassed other trends. C. A. Crusius (1715–75) submitted the Wolffian school to sharp criticism, and it later lost ground to *Popularphilosophie*, an eclectic, intellectually flaccid movement hostile to its esotericism (dismissed by Kant as 'a pretentiously free manner of thinking', Bxliii). But the Leibniz–Wolffian system had no rival of comparable philosophical stature until Kant's Critical philosophy burst upon the scene late in the century. By then, the prestige of the Enlightenment had been tarnished, as over the course of the eighteenth century it became clear that the project of a rational reconstruction of humanity had weaknesses and involved costs.

In the world-view of scholasticism, knowledge of God and knowledge of nature had complemented one another; Thomism had united Christian theology with Aristotelian natural science in a single discourse. In the new sciences this was no longer so; their image of nature – in which mechanism, mathematics and particulate matter replaced Aristotelian substantial forms and final causes – lacked any intrinsic theological dimension. It was not universally held that this created an insuperable problem for, or constituted a deep objection to, religion. With some exceptions, Enlightenment thinkers – few of whom were even genuine materialists, and who for the greater part continued to regard morality as bound up with God's existence, despite some attempts to place it on an independent footing – were not ready to embrace atheism, and stopped short at criticism of the Church. Though the outlook of the Enlightenment had the power to erode religious belief, it could equally be regarded as showing the necessity of making religion a rational affair, and most took the latter view of its agenda. This was particularly so in Germany, where there was no strong reaction against existing religious authority, in contrast with the fierce anti-clerical campaign of the *philosophes*. All the same, the question presented itself as to how knowledge of nature, and knowledge of God, were to be co-ordinated. The favoured Enlightenment solution was natural theology, which exalted the order of nature, in place of revelation, as proof of God's existence, making reason the foundation of religion, since it is reason that cognises order in nature. Natural theology was not ultimately satisfactory, however, since it effectively disposed of biblical authority, and the deism which it supported (God as 'Divine Watchmaker', Supreme Technician) was too austere for the demands of a living faith. The possibility of conflict between science and religion – with morality hanging in the balance – obtruded increasingly. Metaphysics, as guardian of reason and human knowledge as a whole, found itself with divided loyalties.

The tension between the demands of religion and those of natural science was one of several that crystallised in the 'Leibniz–Clarke correspondence', published in 1717. The real protagonists in this extremely important and wide-ranging dispute were Leibniz and Newton, for whom Samuel Clarke (1675–1729) acted as spokesman. Each advocated a different mode of theorising about nature: Leibniz employed a deductive method, derived from René Descartes (1596–1650) and modelled on mathematics, which began with abstract general notions and worked down to concrete nature; Newton by contrast ascended from quantitative measurement of the phenomena to first principles. In the correspondence Leibniz attacked, as incompatible with theology and the principle of sufficient reason, certain key Newtonian tenets regarding space and time and other matters; Clarke defended them, both on scientific grounds and with regard to their theological compatibility. The upshot was that on numerous fundamental points Leibniz's reasoning from the principle of sufficient reason arrived at conclusions about the structure of reality diametrically opposed to those to which Newton had been led by his 'deduction from the phenomena'. This situation was deeply worrying, and not only because the inability to reach agreement might obscure the self-evidence of the authority claimed by the new scientific knowledge: the fact that natural science and metaphysics, both of which could claim to be rational descriptions of reality, should contradict one another, amounted to sheer paradox, and meant that the autonomous exercise of reason in scientific research posed a threat to rational religion. Again, metaphysics found itself compromised.

The most powerful onslaught on the dogmas of the age – though it was conducted in the cause of human self-knowledge, and in that respect qualifies as an unequivocal triumph of Enlightenment thinking – was, of course, Hume's skeptical empiricism. Reason had been intimately associated in eighteenth-century thought with nature. Hume disunited them, to the disadvantage of reason. On Hume's account, our beliefs about the external world have no foundation in reason and repose entirely on 'habit' or 'custom', the operation of associative and other mechanical propensities of the mind. Nature, *qua* ground of our beliefs, consists in nothing but these operations. Furthermore, the non-rational support that nature provides for our beliefs is available only for those that concern matters of experience. Religious belief, and the whole edifice of metaphysical speculation, have no ground whatsoever: every volume 'of divinity or school metaphysics' we should commit 'to the flames', 'for it can contain nothing but sophistry and illusion'. Hume's conclusions might be rejected as merely paradoxical, but showing them to be erroneous was another matter altogether. And it became increasingly clear that Hume demanded a reply.

Rousseau, like Hume, is numbered among the giants of the Enlightenment, though he too can hardly be said to have exalted reason in the standard Enlightenment sense. His alienation from the spirit of the age was signalled by his early, acrimonious break with Diderot and the other *philosophes*. In so far as Rousseau asserted man's natural goodness and potential for regeneration, his vision conformed to the outlook of the Enlightenment. Central to his outlook was a conception of autonomy according to which the individual is fully realised only in a condition where he, in obeying the dictates of his conscience, legislates for himself in a way that gives simultaneous expression to his true self and the will of others. This conception tended to display prevailing Enlightenment conceptions of morality as superficial, but it did not strictly conflict with them. What set Rousseau apart was that he associated human nature, moral consciousness and religious faith, not with man's independent power of reason, but with feeling, *sentiment intérieur*: he denied the priority of reason. And even more importantly, Rousseau grounded his moral vision on an excoriation of the achievements of civilisation, at times ascribing to the artifice of society total responsibility for human vices and misery. The arts, natural sciences and theoretical enquiry in general were included in this attack. The net result of Rousseau's philosophy was, at the very least, to create a doubt: had the activities of reason – including perhaps the metaphysics of philosophers – played a part in corrupting and immiserating humanity, and warping its moral understanding of the world?

To the internal difficulties facing the cause of Enlightenment were added, later in the century, the voices of those comprising what has been called the Counter-Enlightenment. The move to positively break with the Enlightenment had been prefigured to some degree in Rousseau. The three main names associated with the Counter-Enlightenment in Germany, where it was particularly pronounced, are J. G. Hamann (1730–88), J. G. Herder (1744–1803) and F. H. Jacobi (1743–1819). Hamann and Jacobi, though very different, both strove to defend what, in their view, reason is too limited to grasp: what the Enlightenment condemned as valueless because contrary to reason, they regarded as a refutation of reason's claim to supremacy. For Jacobi, this meant the power of feeling that reveals directly the God of theism; for Hamann, it meant poetry, genius and divine revelation through Christian scripture and the particulars of language and history. By taking sides with the victims of reason's hegemony, Jacobi and Hamann committed themselves to an outright anti-intellectualism, if not irrationalism; they were described as *Glaubensphilosophen* or *Gefühlsphilosophen*, 'philosophers of faith or feeling'. Herder, though influenced by Hamann, was more moderate, and offered an intellectual alternative to the Enlightenment: a naturalistic and historicist picture of man that repudiated the autonomy of reason and affirmed its dependence on particular concrete forms of embodiment, above all language. Herder thereby put at least a question mark over reason's universality. Hamann and Herder comprised (with J. W. von Goethe, 1749–1832) the intellectual sources of *Sturm und Drang* (Storm and Stress), the literary movement which paved the way for romanticism in Germany.

The Counter-Enlightenment drew inspiration in part from a force outside philosophy – Pietism, an evangelical Lutheran movement that had originated in Germany towards the end of the seventeenth century as a reaction against Protestant dogmatism. Once established, Pietism tended to fossilise and became dogmatic in turn, but in its inception it was a religion of the inner spirit rather than outward forms, which set store by personal experience of conversion, cultivation of an inward devotional life and the manifestation of a morally good will in charitable works. The anti-intellectualism of the Counter-Enlightenment reflected this religious sensibility. Pietism had, as it were, anticipated the crisis into which the Enlightenment would lead religion, and it lay ready with a solution: the independence of religion from reason. The movement provided a constant source of resistance to the Enlightenment (the arch-rationalist Wolff was temporarily banished from Prussia as a result of charges of godlessness levelled at him by his Pietist colleagues). Hamann, Herder and Jacobi were all deeply influenced by Pietism, as was Crusius. The further significance of Pietism in the present context is that it was the religion in which Kant was brought up.

The conflict between the Enlightenment and its detractors exploded in Germany after the death of Gotthold Lessing (1729–81) – a great cultural figure who had held the banner of *Aufklärung* – with the so-called *Pantheismusstreit* ('pantheism controversy'). Initially it consisted of a heated epistolary exchange between the polemical Jacobi and Moses Mendelssohn (1729–86), a rationalist philosopher. Subsequent to Jacobi's publication of the relevant documents, a public quarrel ensued, into which many others, including Kant, were dragged. Superficially, the topic of dispute was the factual question of whether Lessing had, or had not, secretly been a 'Spinozist', meaning an atheist and fatalist. But the real question was the philosophical one of where reason stood on the subject of religion: Mendelssohn maintained the orthodox Enlightenment position that reason supports faith; Jacobi held that the unbridled exercise of reason necessarily terminates in the faithlessness represented by Spinoza's pantheism. Though it did not take place until the 1780s, the *Pantheismusstreit* gave expression to long-standing concerns.

Eventually, nature itself seemed to put a question to the proponents of Enlightenment. In 1755 an appalling earthquake devastated Lisbon. This event, which appeared to flatly contradict the Enlightenment assumption of the rational purposiveness of nature, ramified spiritually throughout Europe, and added fuel to the debate that already existed concerning Leibniz's theodicy, his claim that this is the best of all possible worlds.

These issues – the growing and seemingly irresolvable tensions within the Enlightenment, and its mounting conflict with those who refused to accept the authority of reason – pervaded the intellectual world inhabited by Kant; several are discussed in his early writings. Kant thus witnessed and participated in the process by which the Enlightenment made itself, over the course of the century, ready for a new development, as it became clear that it had resulted in too much dispute and confusion to survive in its original form; either it had to be rethought, or it must allow itself to dwindle as a spent force. Kant's achievement was to create a philosophy of the Enlightenment in its maturity that took account of the difficulties confronting it, and brought it to a culmination. The Enlightenment was not, in fact, to survive in an overt form as a unified and dominant cultural force; romanticism took its place in cultural history. But Kant provided it with a definitive articulation and equipped it with the strongest possible defence, making explicit the underlying conception that it had had of itself all along.

Kant's life

Kant's life is, famously, characterised by outward uneventfulness. Immanuel Kant was born in 1724 in the East Prussian city of Königsberg, where he spent almost all of his days. Kant's father was a craftsman, and the family poor. Both Kant's family and schooling were Pietist. Kant never lost sympathy with this faith: though he condemned the hollow, mechanical religious observances which filled his schooldays with gloom, he praised those whose Pietism was genuine, among whom he numbered his parents, as 'outstanding', 'having the highest thing men can possess, that calm, that serenity, that inner peace, undisturbed by any passion'.

At the University of Königsberg, Kant studied natural science, mathematics, philosophy and theology, and was exposed to the Leibniz–Wolffian system and Newton's theories. After graduating, he took up, as was usual for those without private means, a series of positions as house tutor, which enabled him to pursue his studies. On presentation of a treatise on metaphysics (a solidly rationalist work) Kant rose to the rank of *Privatdozent*, which entitled him to lecture at the university but provided him with no income other than the fees received directly from his lecture audiences. The astonishing scope of Kant's teaching, to which financial need obliged him to devote as many as twenty hours a week, sometimes more, encompassed, in addition to numerous philosophical subjects: pure mathematics, physics, mechanics, physical geography, anthropology, jurisprudence and pedagogy. All lecturers were required by the Prussian authorities to expound a particular text, and for his teaching of metaphysics Kant employed the *Metaphysica* (1739) of Alexander Baumgarten (1714–62), which exposited the Leibniz–Wolffian system. A humble assistant librarianship later provided Kant with his first stipendiary post.

Not until 1770, at the age of 46, did Kant receive a professorship in philosophy, still at Königsberg. Over the preceding years Kant had published a number of works, the majority on scientific-cum-metaphysical subjects, which had earned him a secure reputation within Germany as a powerful, independent thinker. The year of his professorial appointment saw also the publication of his *Inaugural Dissertation*, an ambitious and innovative work, but one that remained within the bounds of rationalism. Had Kant's life or career ended at this point, in 1770, it is probable that his name would now figure only in works on the history of rationalism and (for his cosmological theories) in the history of science.

The lengthy and arduous period that preceded his appointment at Königsberg had however allowed Kant to expand greatly his philosophical horizons. Some time in the 1750s Kant almost certainly made acquaintance with Hume's *Enquiry Concerning Human Understanding* (1748), the significance of which would later dawn on him; in 1762 Rousseau's *Émile* appeared and immediately inspired Kant; and in 1765 Kant studied intensively Leibniz's previously unpublished *New Essays on Human Understanding* (1705), which exposed him directly to the full force and sophistication of Leibniz's epistemology and metaphysics, unblunted by Wolff's mediation. All three encounters were to prove crucial for Kant's development. Kant would later say that it was a 'recollection' of Hume that had first interrupted his 'dogmatic slumber' and given his investigations into metaphysics 'a quite new direction' (*Proleg* 260); Rousseau was to provide the pattern for his moral philosophy, and Kant would pay him the tribute of having done for human nature what Newton had done for material nature, namely, revealed its underlying essence; and Leibniz was to be one of the two towering protagonists in the *Critique*, the other being Hume.

But a long gap was to follow the *Inaugural Dissertation* before Kant gave any further public sign of philosophical creativity. The evidence for Kant's crucial development over the 'silent decade' that ensued, during which he published next to nothing, derives mainly from his manuscripts and correspondence. These show Kant quickly coming to appreciate that the position he had taken up in the *Inaugural Dissertation* was flawed, and his growing awareness of the depth, importance and difficulty of the new metaphysical problem he had unearthed. Finally, in 1781, at the urgings of his friends, Kant at last published the *Critique of Pure Reason*. He was now in his fifty-seventh year. He had, he said, assembled the manuscript over the course of a few months 'as if in flight'.

The other texts composing Kant's philosophical system then followed rapidly. A second edition of the *Critique* appeared in 1787, incorporating great changes. Between the two editions of the *Critique*, Kant produced his *Prolegomena to any Future Metaphysics* (1783), a short book intended to render the ideas of the *Critique* more accessible, and the first of his works on ethics, the *Groundwork of the Metaphysics of Morals* (1785). Kant's moral theory was then recast in his second Critique, the *Critique of Practical Reason* (1788), wherein is also presented his account of the grounds of religious

11

belief. A third Critique, the *Critique of Judgement*, which contains Kant's aesthetic theory and a theory of teleology, and which he claimed concluded his Critical enterprise (*CJ* 170), appeared in 1790.

The trilogy of Critiques constitutes the core of Kant's philosophical system, but reference to several other works is required to grasp its full extent. These include *Metaphysical Foundations of Natural Science* (1786), a supplement to the *Critique*'s account of natural science; *Religion Within the Boundaries of Mere Reason* (1793), a fuller treatment of religion along the lines set out in the second Critique; a number of writings on political philosophy and the philosophy of history, including *Toward Perpetual Peace* (1795); and *The Metaphysics of Morals* (1797), the most comprehensive exposition of his moral system.

In the background to Kant's life were a set of great political and historical developments. The Prussia in which he lived was governed from 1740 to 1786 by Frederick II, the Great (1712–86), a remarkable ruler who shared the goals of *Aufklärung*, gave the state constitutional form, and promoted learning and religious tolerance. Also bearing the imprint of the Enlightenment was the creation in America, through the War of Independence (1755–83), of an independent, republican form of government; and the same historical vector seemed, initially, to be manifest in the French Revolution (1789). The march of progress did not, however, continue unimpeded throughout Kant's lifetime: Frederick II's liberalising measures were partially reversed by his successor, and Kant himself came up against the renewed forces of censorship when his book on religion was declared contrary to Christian teaching.

Kant died in 1804. By that time, the reception of his philosophy, though by no means exclusively favourable, had given sufficient indication of its permanent place in history. Over Kant's grave was mounted a plaque inscribed with his own words: 'Two things fill the mind with ever new and increasing admiration and reverence, the more often and more steadily one reflects on them: *the starry heavens above me and the moral law within me*' (*CPracR* 161).

There is little to give us insight into Kant's inner life. What we know of him as a man derives from the recollections of his friends and acquaintances, and the anecdotal material, much of it merely incidental, amassed by early biographers. The portrait that nevertheless emerges is profoundly impressive, and recalls Kant's own description of a true Pietist. Kant was austere and stoical, disinclined to intimacy and remained unmarried. But he was neither deficient in feeling nor unappreciative of society. Up until his last years, the well-defined pattern of his day incorporated an extended lunch-time gathering at which he would lead his guests, drawn from the cosmopolitan society of Königsberg, through lively conversation on worldly topics. Accounts of those who knew him communicate respectfulness, integrity and humanity. Herder, who in his youth attended Kant's lectures (though he later criticised his philosophy), wrote this of him:

> I have enjoyed the good fortune of knowing a philosopher, who was my teacher. . . . His open brow, built for thought, was the seat of undisturbed contentment and joy; there flowed from his lips a discourse rich in thought; jest and wit and humour were always at his command. . . . Nothing worth knowing was indifferent to him; no cabal, no sect, no prejudice, no desire for fame, could ever distract him in the slightest from broadening and illuminating the truth. He encouraged and gently impelled others to think for themselves; despotism was foreign to his nature. This man, whom I name with the utmost thankfulness and reverence, is Immanuel Kant; his image, to my delight, stands before me.

Kant's pre-Critical vacillation: the indispensable dreams of metaphysics

In contrast with the lack of incident in his life, Kant's philosophical development was characterised by constant and unforeseeable change.

Kant's original philosophical orientation may be safely described as rationalist, but his early, 'pre-Critical' writings, taken as a whole, do not express a unified philosophical outlook. Nor do they display cumulative progress towards one. The impression they give is rather of continual dissatisfaction and experimentation. The inconclusiveness of Kant's pre-Critical writings makes them, however, extremely illuminating from the point of view of the *Critique*, because they allow us to identify the concrete materials and forces out of which it was formed. For Kant did not of course find himself presented initially with the grand task of refounding the Enlightenment: what his philosophical environment confronted him with was a web of more circumscribed problems attached to the theories of particular writers, above all Newton, Leibniz and his successors Wolff and Baumgarten, Rousseau and (at a later date) Hume.

Kant never subscribed to the Leibniz–Wolffian philosophy without qualification, and he was from the outset well acquainted with Crusius' writings, which contained powerful criticisms of the rationalist equation of logic with epistemology. Nevertheless, his first metaphysical work (*A New Elucidation of the First Principles of Metaphysical Cognition*, or *Nova Dilucidatio*, 1755) embraced its fundamental approach: Kant endorsed the Leibniz–Wolffian conception of the world as a rational totality wholly determined by the principle of sufficient reason, of which he offered a new proof. At this stage Kant believed that the discrepancy of Leibniz–Wolffian metaphysics with Newtonian science, of which he was well aware and which he took very seriously, could be resolved. His own whole-hearted commitment to the Newtonian conception of nature as a mechanical system is clear in his *Universal Natural History and Theory of the Heavens* (1755), in which, by hypothesising the nebular origin of the solar system, Kant shows that, contrary to what Newton had supposed, God need not even be assumed for the relatively limited purpose of explaining the order of the solar system. Kant thereby pressed mechanistic explanation further than Newton himself had done. But for Kant it did not follow that Newtonian science provides a complete description of reality. Scientific explanation does not flourish at the expense of theology, Kant argues, because the unrestricted application of Newtonian principles is the best proof of the world's origin in a divine intellect. Also, Kant upheld the principle, characteristic of Leibnizian rationalism, that natural science is not self-sufficient but requires metaphysical support. Rationalist metaphysics was therefore necessary for knowledge of nature, in addition to being required for theology. As his early scientific-metaphysical writings show, Kant also pursued the task of harmonising Leibnizian philosophy with Newtonian science on more technical fronts. In *Thoughts on the True Estimation of Living Forces* (1747), he sought to show that a dispute between the Newtonian and rationalist conceptions of nature concerning the calculation of physical force could be resolved by distinguishing their spheres of application; and in *Physical Monadology* (1756) he proposed a conciliatory solution to another Leibnizian–Newtonian conflict, regarding the infinite divisibility of space.

Kant's conviction of the fundamental adequacy of Leibniz–Wolffianism did not endure, however, and the trajectory of his development in the 1760s, though by no means uniform, was away from rationalism. In *The Only Possible Argument in Support of a Demonstration of the Existence of God* (1763) Kant rejected whole swathes of Leibniz–Wolffian doctrine, attacking all of the traditional arguments in rational theology for God's existence. More importantly, the project of reconciling Leibnizian metaphysics with Newtonian science had led Kant to reflect on the question of the correct method for metaphysics, and thence to question the fundamental validity of the rationalist approach. The more fundamental question of philosophical method overtook and subsumed the Leibniz–Newton problem. In *Attempt to Introduce the Concept of Negative Magnitudes into Philosophy* (1763) Kant distinguished real and logical relations in a way that undermined the Leibniz–Wolffian claim to be able to grasp the world of experience, including the causality it exhibits, through pure reason. And in *Enquiry Concerning the Distinctness of the Principles of Natural Theology and Morality* ('*Prize Essay*') (1764), his doubts about rationalism took a positive turn: Kant outlined the methodological transformation of metaphysics that he considered was required. After exhibiting some deep differences between the respective methods of mathematics and metaphysics – mathematics, he says, constructs the objects with which it deals, which metaphysics does not; mathematical notions can consequently be readily given clear definitions, as those of metaphysics cannot – Kant drew the conclusion that the future of metaphysics lies in duplicating the Newtonian method in natural science. That is, metaphysics should set out from given concepts (such as freedom or time) as its primary data, seek out the (unprovable) propositions associated with them, and through analysis proceed *to* definitions of concepts, as its final product; rather than attempting to proceed *from* definitions, in imitation of a mathematical system, as Wolff had done. Although, Kant says, 'so far no metaphysics has ever been written' (First reflection, §4; *Ak* II, 283), metaphysics can in principle, by taking this non-rationalist Newtonian route, equal the certainty of mathematics.

The expectations raised by the *Enquiry* were not, however, fulfilled. At stake in the question of method, Kant saw, is the very possibility of metaphysical knowledge, for a sphere of enquiry that cannot validate its own methodology cannot validate its results. In the *Enquiry* Kant had denied the actuality of metaphysical knowledge but affirmed its possibility. But in his next work, *Dreams of a Spirit-Seer Elucidated By Dreams of Metaphysics* (1766), there was a dramatic change: Kant decided *against* the possibility of metaphysical knowledge. In place of a new method, he now suggested a new (and much more modest) goal for metaphysics.

Dreams of a Spirit-Seer is written on the curious pretext of justifying the purchase and time devoted to reading a lengthy but 'completely empty' work by the occultist Swedenborg. Kant takes this opportunity to suggest – extraordinarily, in view of his earlier writings – that metaphysics may be as much of a wild figment of the imagination as the visions of E. Swedenborg, the content of which resembles that of metaphysical systems all too closely: both characteristically postulate a world of spiritual beings distinct from, yet somehow attached to and capable of influencing the sensible world. Kant denies that we can make any such notion properly intelligible to ourselves. *Dreams* concludes accordingly that the task of metaphysics is restricted to investigating the *limits* of human reason. Kant thereby relinquished the aspiration to metaphysical knowledge expressed in the *Enquiry*.

What nevertheless sharply distinguishes the skepticism of *Dreams* from the anti-metaphysical position of Hume (or any positivist) is that Kant continues to regard metaphysical speculations as perfectly meaningful – they *may*, for all we know, obtain. Furthermore, Kant asserts a connection between the concepts of metaphysics and morality. What most gives reason to believe in the existence of a spirit world, Kant says, is moral consciousness: obligation and the motive of benevolence involve a feeling as of an alien will constraining us in a direction opposed to that of self-interest – so inviting the thought that we are subject to a law stemming from another, non-sensible world, in which we exist as a moral community. The resultant hypothesis is that we have a double existence: as members of the sensible world we are subject to Newtonian laws, and as members of the spiritual world to moral laws. In the same vein, Kant grants the legitimacy of a religious conception of the spirit world: a virtuous man, he says, will not be capable of supporting the thought that with death everything is at end, and will hope for an afterlife. As regards the question of how this hope can be supported, if metaphysical knowledge is impossible, Kant's solution in *Dreams* is that the faith intrinsic to morality is properly grounded on an individual's virtuous disposition – it does not require a metaphysical theory.

Dreams does not contain a settled view of metaphysics; its position is a transitional one. Kant's ambivalence towards metaphysics – betrayed in his confession in *Dreams* that he had 'fallen in love' with metaphysics but could boast of having received in return 'only a few favours' – comes out in a letter apropos *Dreams* written shortly after its publication (to Mendelssohn, 8 April 1766):

> As to my expressed opinion of the value of metaphysics in general, perhaps here and again my words were not sufficiently careful and qualified. But I cannot conceal my repugnance, and even a certain hatred, toward the inflated arrogance of whole volumes full of what are passed off nowadays as insights; for I am fully convinced that the path that has been selected is completely wrong, that the methods now in vogue must infinitely increase the amount of folly and error in the world, and that even the total extermination of all these chimerical insights would be less harmful than the dream science itself, with its confounded contagion.

To which, however, Kant adds immediately:

> I am far from regarding metaphysics itself, objectively considered, to be trivial or dispensable; in fact I have been convinced for some time now that I understand its nature and its proper place in human knowledge and that the true and lasting welfare of the human race depends upon it.

The outstanding question which these remarks raise is of course what makes the difference between contagious, 'chimerical' metaphysics, and salutary, 'objectively considered' metaphysics. At the period to which *Dreams* belongs Kant had no contentful answer to this question, and indeed he did not do so until his Critical period. What *Dreams* does establish, however, is the crucial influence which the claims of morality had begun to exercise on Kant's philosophical development: it is through its connection with morality that metaphysics is bound up with the interests of humanity and thereby rendered, as he affirms, indispensable. Decisive in bringing Kant to this view were his reflections on Rousseau. Kant was deeply sympathetic to Rousseau's idea that reason is abused when put in the service of the vain pursuit of theoretical knowledge, and only properly employed when used to further the essential aims of humanity – a doctrine directly reflected in Kant's claim in *Dreams* that religion does not presuppose metaphysical proofs. But *Dreams* shows Kant at the same time coming to realise that Rousseau's own conception of the source of morality could not be made good without further, systematic philosophical elaboration. Specifically, Kant was coming to see that, for reasons brought to light by Rousseau, moral consciousness refers beyond the sensible world – that the Newtonian image of the world, taken on its own, contradicts the reality of the moral order. Metaphysics is therefore required either positively – to establish the existence of the non-Newtonian reality to which morality refers – or at least negatively – to undermine philosophical doctrines that dispute the moral agent's right to entertain the possibility of such a world. Thus at the very moment when Kant's confidence in metaphysics had collapsed, he had begun to formulate a new account of the role of metaphysics in morality that accords it a higher importance than ever.

In view of the thoroughly skeptical tone of *Dreams*, it is astonishing that Kant should be found claiming four years later in his *Inaugural Dissertation* (*On the Form and Principles of the Sensible and Intelligible World*) (1770) that our reason allows us to represent 'things *as they are*' as opposed to 'things *as they appear*'. What makes it possible to once again accept the rationalist doctrine that reason has access to Reality, Kant believes, is the new analysis of cognition that the *Dissertation* contains. Kant now divides cognition into two powers, sensibility and intellect. They function as independent sources of cognition, and have quite different objects: sensibility represents the world of sensible objects in space and time, these being nothing but subjective 'forms of sensibility' (a new doctrine of Kant's); intellect represents non-sensible, 'intelligible' objects. At a stroke the Leibniz–Newton opposition is dissolved, since on Kant's new account rationalist metaphysics is not about the same world that Newtonian science is about; to set them in competition with one another is simply to confuse their respective spheres of jurisdiction. Though Kant now rejects the rationalist view of sense perception as an inferior (confused) species of intellectual cognition, and furthermore emphasises that the bulk of what has hitherto passed for metaphysics rests on a confusion of sensory with intellectual cognition (which it is now, he says, one of the principal tasks of metaphysics to guard against), he holds that our intellect allows us to grasp at least God's existence – thereby reaffirming the fundamental rationalist conviction that ideas which originate in pure intellect have truth.

In 1770 Kant was confident that the *Dissertation* would be his final position. In this he was mistaken, for the *Dissertation* suffered from a fatal weakness, resulting from the sharpness of its separation of sensibility and intellect. If it is not the world of experience that provides the intellect with the objects of which its ideas are true, what reason is there for thinking that there *are* any such objects? And if the ideas of the intellect are quite independent of the sensible world, how can intellectual principles such as the law of cause and effect – which is a presupposition of Newtonian science and as such must surely be accorded objectivity – have valid application to the spatio-temporal world? The *Dissertation*'s reconciliation of science and metaphysics is therefore achieved at disastrous cost, and made ultimately pointless: intellectual concepts (such as substance, cause, existence, necessity) are left in limbo, without genuine, guaranteed application to any objects whatsoever. Kant's recognition of this grave difficulty – his first sighting of what is known as the Critical problem – is expressed in an important letter of 1772 (to Marcus Herz, 21 February), and his 'recollection' of Hume no doubt occurred shortly afterwards, providing further confirmation that the reborn rationalism of the *Dissertation*, however guarded, would not do. In a note written in the 1770s Kant declares: 'the value of my previous metaphysical writings has been completely destroyed' (*Ak* XVIII, 42; Reflexion 4964). The *Dissertation* had been, therefore, only another dream of metaphysical knowledge.

The contrast of *Dreams* with the *Dissertation* illustrates dramatically the systematically fluctuating attitude towards metaphysics exhibited in Kant's pre-Critical writings. His researches over that period, for all that they had revealed to him regarding the errors and illusions of metaphysics, left him with no positive conclusions worth the name, aside from his new doctrine of space and time. From the later perspective of Kant's Critical philosophy, it is possible to see how the positions of *Dreams* and the *Dissertation* are not as far apart as they seem – the *Critique* is at one level an attempt to square the anti-metaphysical thrust of *Dreams* with the *Dissertation*'s claim for the validity of purely intellectual ideas – and how his rigorous questioning of metaphysics had led him to the brink of a new kind of philosophical knowledge. But in the early 1770s that perspective had not yet been forged. The puzzle of metaphysics remained in pieces. Newton remained in conflict with Leibniz; morality, under Kant's new conception of it, and the religious faith that he in Rousseauian and Pietistic fashion associated with morality, remained unreconciled with Newton and without an adequate philosophical foundation; to which was then added the problem of Hume, whose skepticism, which shadowed the objection that had sunk the metaphysics of the *Dissertation*, contradicted the claims of Newton as much as those of morality and religion.

Is metaphysics possible? (The Preface)

The conflict of Newtonian science with Leibnizian metaphysics, of rationalist dogmatism with skeptical empiricism, of the scientific world-view with morality and religion – these, which caused the Enlightenment to falter and gave direction to Kant's pre-Critical endeavours, are instances of metaphysics in conflict with itself, and lie immediately behind Kant's description of metaphysics as a 'battleground'. Kant acknowledges that historical experience invites us to draw the skeptical inference that metaphysics is impossible, or to become simply indifferent to metaphysical questions. But according to Kant skepticism and indifference regarding metaphysics are not genuine options.

What, in the first place, rules out indifference is that metaphysics exists, as Kant puts it, 'if not as science, yet still as natural disposition': human reason is driven on 'by an inward need', and not by mere 'idle desire', to pose metaphysical questions (B21–2). The remedy that indifferentism proposes for our intellectual disquiet is consequently a practical impossibility – human reason is philosophically troubled and can be brought to rest only through more philosophy.

What makes skepticism about metaphysics unsustainable is that metaphysics cannot be repudiated in isolation from cognition in general. Metaphysical enquiry employs the same cognitive power as is employed in commonsense and scientific judgements about the world of experience: the very same principles of reasoning as are employed in empirical judgements about tables and atoms, are employed, in a purified form, in metaphysical judgements about God and the soul. The principles of metaphysics 'seem so unobjectionable that even ordinary consciousness readily accepts them' (Aviii); metaphysics simply pushes them further, in search of complete explanation (the 'unconditioned', as Kant calls it, Bxx). The 'perplexity' into which reason falls when it engages in metaphysical speculation is thus 'not due to any fault of its own', for it merely 'begins with principles which it has no option save to employ in the course of experience and which this experience at the same time abundantly justifies it in using' (Avii). If one and the same faculty of reason is employed in empirical and metaphysical judgement, and the empirical employment of reason is legitimate, then so should be its metaphysical employment; and if metaphysics results in contradictions, then reason as a whole contradicts itself. To allow the contradictions of metaphysics to stand is therefore to allow reason to perform a *reductio ad absurdum* upon itself; and to repudiate metaphysics is to repudiate cognition as a rational phenomenon.

Hume, whose view of the interdependence of metaphysics and cognition in general Kant shares, described himself as having followed just such a path and reached that very conclusion. He concludes the first volume of the *Treatise* by saying:

> The *intense* view of these manifold contradictions and imperfections in human reason has so wrought upon me. . . . that I am ready to reject all belief and reasoning. . . . Most fortunately it happens, that since reason is incapable of dispelling these clouds, Nature herself suffices to that purpose, and cures me of this philosophical malady and delirium.

Setting aside the paradox intimated by Hume's conclusion – viz. that reason can provide grounds for judging itself groundless – Kant has a different sort of reason for not allowing himself to collapse into the rescuing arms of Nature. If Kant is right that the moral welfare of humanity is at stake in metaphysics, then we are not *allowed* to repudiate metaphysics. The problem constituted by metaphysics must be solved otherwise than by its rejection. In some sense, in some form, metaphysics must be possible.

So when Kant formulates the task of solving the problem of metaphysics by saying that the *Critique* is intended to answer the question: is metaphysics possible (as science, i.e. as more than natural disposition)? (B22), this needs to be understood correctly. In one sense of metaphysics – knowledge of God and the soul, as promised by the Leibniz–Wolffian system – the possibility of metaphysics is something that has yet to be decided in the *Critique*. But in another sense – of metaphysics in so far as it is required for the rationality of cognition and for morality – its possibility is for Kant, unlike Hume, not open to doubt: the question is not whether, but *how* metaphysics is possible. (Kant's usage of the term metaphysics is, as a result, and understandably, ambiguous: he is uncertain whether it is better to say that Critical philosophy brings metaphysics to an end, or that it shows in what new form metaphysics is possible.)

Since what has to be decided is a question of legitimacy rather than of fact, it cannot be answered empirically, and since the question concerns the possibility of metaphysics, its answer cannot itself consist in a metaphysical claim or stand upon any metaphysical presuppositions. Because the problem of metaphysics is ultimately a matter of reason's relation to itself, the route to its solution, Kant argues, must also be reflexive. That is, reason must examine itself. To do this is to forebear from seeking knowledge of reality and instead to make cognition itself an object of philosophical enquiry. Accordingly, Kant calls for reason 'to undertake anew the most difficult of all its tasks, namely, that of self-knowledge, and to institute a tribunal which will assure to reason its lawful claims'. This tribunal, intended to replace the irrationality of a battlefield with the rationality of a court of law, is 'no other than the *critique of pure reason*' (Axi).

This strange-sounding phrase, which supplies the title of Kant's work, has a complex sense. 'Critique' does not for Kant imply a negative evaluation of its object: it means simply a critical enquiry, the results of which may equally be positive (Bxxv–xxvi). 'Pure', a technical term of Kant's, means not containing anything derived from sense experience. 'Reason' is also used here in a technical sense, to refer to conceptual elements in cognition which we bring to experience and which are not derived from it – in Kant's language, 'a priori' conceptual elements. (This is Kant's broader use of the term 'reason'; he also has a narrower use, indicated below.) So a critique of pure reason is a critical enquiry into our capacity to know anything by employing our reason in isolation, i.e. without conjoining reason with sense experience; more specifically, it enquires into our capacity to know things lying beyond the bounds of sense experience, such as God and the soul (Axii). Judgement is passed formally on our capacity to cognise such objects in the second half of the *Critique*, after Kant has supplied a detailed account of the conditions under which knowledge in general is possible.

It may seem puzzling that Kant should give his enquiry this particular slant, apparently building into the very statement of his philosophical task the highly disputable, anti-empiricist assumption that there *are* a priori elements in cognition. It will be seen that, far from going undefended, this claim is supported by a battery of arguments: Kant will spend much time showing that cognition is possible only if it has an a priori basis. The provisional justification for Kant's assumption is that, unless there are such elements, then it is a foregone conclusion that metaphysical knowledge of things lying beyond experience is impossible.

Looking ahead, Kant gives firm indications in the Preface of the results that the tribunal will reach, and of the means by which the problem of metaphysics will be solved (Bxix–xxi, Bxxvi–xxx).

The verdict will be, simply, that reason *is* competent to know things lying *within* the bounds of experience, but *not* to know anything lying *outside* them. Kant's corresponding strategy for solving the problem of metaphysics is to find a ground on which to distinguish between legitimate and illegitimate employments of reason, and to make a principled distinction between different kinds of metaphysics. This ground is supplied by experience: reason is legitimate when applied to the materials provided by experience; it comes into conflict with itself and becomes illegitimate at the point where it parts company from experience. The limits of knowledge therefore coincide with the limits of experience: what can be known is what can be experienced, and what cannot be experienced cannot be known. Thus in the *Critique* Kant will offer a defence, against Hume, of the metaphysics that is necessary to hold together the framework of experience, the principles presupposed by commonsense empirical judgement that we have 'no option save to employ', such as that every event has a cause; but he will not similarly vindicate the employment of reason in metaphysical speculation outside the bounds of experience, to determine the existence of God, for example, and to that extent, he stands in agreement with Hume. The metaphysics that Kant attacks, characteristic of rationalism, is speculative or *transcendent* (transcending experience), and that which he defends is immanent (internal to experience), or the *metaphysics of experience*. Metaphysics of experience is possible, transcendent metaphysics impossible.

By means of its self-examination, reason is simultaneously released from its contradictions and protected in its empirical employment: the ambitions of transcendent metaphysics are curbed, but (Humean) skepticism is defeated, and we are let off the see-saw of dogmatism and skepticism. The positive and negative results of the critique are solidly interdependent: the reasons why the employment of reason within experience is legitimate are precisely the reasons why its employment outside experience is conflict-engendering and illegitimate. The price to be paid for the security of empirical knowledge is the frustration of our desire for transcendent metaphysical knowledge. This cognitive bargain is, Kant maintains, something over which we have no choice: the problem of metaphysics must be solved;

its solution requires the Copernican revolution; and the implications thereof for metaphysics are those just described.

The final part of Kant's strategy, to be discussed much later, consists in showing that the Copernican revolution provides morality with all of the metaphysical support that it needs, and, therefore, a complete solution to the problem of metaphysics.

The structure of the *Critique*

A glance at the contents pages of the *Critique* reveals a complex, thickly layered and far from transparent organisation, the arcane titles of the sections giving little idea of their contents. The baroque architecture of Kant's text is bound up with his philosophical system, but the most important points about the work's structure can be grasped without going into much detail, as illustrated below.

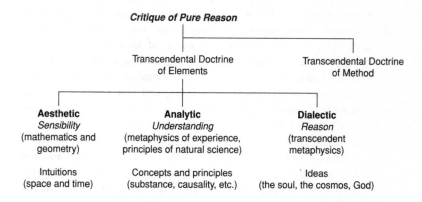

The three main divisions are the 'Transcendental Aesthetic', 'Transcendental Analytic', and 'Transcendental Dialectic'. Each corresponds to a different cognitive power or faculty, and a different area of presumptive knowledge.

The Aesthetic is concerned with what Kant in the *Dissertation* called the power of sensibility, and with mathematics, inclusive of geometry. It also covers certain fundamental pre-scientific propositions about space and time, e.g. regarding their number of dimensions.

The Analytic is concerned with the power of understanding, and with the metaphysics of experience and natural science.

The Dialectic is concerned with the power of reason (here used in a narrower sense than in the title of the *Critique*), and with transcendent metaphysics, which divides into three bodies of doctrine: the metaphysics of the soul (rational psychology), of the world as a whole (rational cosmology) and of God (rational theology).

Together the Aesthetic, Analytic and Dialectic fall under the heading 'Transcendental Doctrine of Elements' because each deals with a different 'element' (constituent) of cognition: the Aesthetic with what Kant calls intuitions, the Analytic with concepts and their associated principles, and the Dialectic with what Kant calls ideas (a species of concept). What we ordinarily refer to as the intellect is therefore split by Kant into two separate powers, understanding and reason.

The other – much shorter – official division of the work, the 'Transcendental Doctrine of Method', supplements the epistemological and metaphysical argument of the *Critique* with reflections on its methodology. It also includes a section called 'The Canon of Pure Reason', which contains important pointers to the rest of Kant's Critical system.

The organisation of the *Critique* can be grasped more clearly in the light of the conclusions that Kant comes to in the work. The real division is between, on the one hand, the Aesthetic and Analytic, which are jointly concerned with knowable objects, and on the other, the Dialectic, which is concerned with (concepts of) objects that cannot be known. The Aesthetic and Analytic are positive: they seek to prove that we can have knowledge of those things which we can experience. The Aesthetic deals with the sensible, specifically the spatio-temporal aspect of knowable objects, the Analytic with their conceptual aspect, including the concepts of substance and causality. Jointly they vindicate one kind of metaphysics – the metaphysics of experience. The Dialectic is negative: it seeks to prove that we cannot have knowledge of anything at all outside experience. It denies legitimacy to the other kind of metaphysics – transcendent metaphysics.

Chapter 2

The possibility of objects

After a brief summary of the Copernican revolution in the Preface, where it is advanced as the general solution to the problem of metaphysics, Kant leaves it to the reader to extrapolate the exact nature of his philosophical revolution from the specific doctrines that follow in the *Critique*. Understanding the arguments of the *Critique* is however made considerably easier by having in advance a fuller idea of the Copernican revolution than can be gleaned from the Preface. Accordingly, this chapter attempts to set out the line of thought underlying Kant's Copernicanism, in terms that as far as possible avoid the technicalities of his philosophy.

The Critical problem: Kant's letter to Herz

The place to start is with the letter referred to earlier in which Kant acknowledges the failure of the *Dissertation*, and first states the Critical problem. Kant is talking about a work that he had previously planned with the projected title, 'The limits of sense and reason':

As I thought through the theoretical part, considering its whole scope and the reciprocal relations of all its parts, I noticed that I still lacked something essential, something that in my long metaphysical studies I, as well as others, had failed to pay attention to and that, in fact, constitutes the key to the whole secret of hitherto obscure metaphysics. I asked myself: What is the ground of the relation of that in us which we call 'representation' to the object? If a representation is only a way in which the subject is affected by the object, then it is easy to see how the representation is in conformity with this object, namely, as an effect in accord with its cause, and it is easy to see how this modification of our mind can represent something, that is, have an object. Thus the passive or sensuous representations have an understandable relationship to objects, and the principles that are derived from the nature of our soul have an understandable validity for all things insofar as those things are supposed to be objects of the senses. In the same way, if that in us which we call 'representation' were active with regard to the object, that is, if the object itself were created by the representation (as when divine cognitions are conceived as the archetypes of all things), the conformity of these representations to their objects could be understood. Thus the possibility of both an *intellectus archetypi* (on whose intuitions the things themselves would be grounded) and an *intellectus ectypi* (which would derive the data for its logical procedure from the sensuous intuitions of things) is at least intelligible. However, our understanding, through its representations, is not the cause of the object (save in the case of moral ends), nor is the object the cause of the intellectual representations in the mind (*in sensu reali*). Therefore the pure concepts of the understanding must not be abstracted from sense perceptions, nor must they express the receptions of representations through the senses; but though they must have their origin in the nature of the soul, they are neither caused by the object nor bring the object itself into being. In my dissertation I was content to explain the nature of intellectual representations in a merely negative way, namely, to state that they were not modifications of the soul brought about by the object. However, I silently passed over the further question of how a representation that refers to an object without being in any way affected by it can be possible. I had said: The sensuous representations present things as they appear, the intellectual presentations present them as they are. But by what means are these things given to us, if not by the way in which they affect us? And if such intellectual representations depend on our inner activity, whence comes the agreement they are supposed to have with objects – how do they agree with these objects, since the agreement has not been reached with the aid of experience? . . .

Plato assumed a previous intuition of divinity as the primary source of the pure concepts of the understanding and of first principles. Malebranche believed in a still-continuing perennial intuition of this primary being. Various moralists have accepted precisely this view with respect to basic moral laws. Crusius believed in certain implanted rules for the purpose of forming judgements and ready-made concepts that God implanted in the human soul just as they had to be in order to harmonize with things. Of these systems, one may call the former [Plato and Malebranche] *influxum hyperphysicum* and the latter [Crusius; Kant might also have referred to Leibniz] *harmonium praestabilitam intellectualem*. But the *deus ex machina* is the greatest absurdity one could hit upon in the determination of the origin and validity of our knowledge. It has – besides its deceptive circle in the conclusion concerning our cognitions – also this additional disadvantage: it encourages all sorts of wild notions and every pious and speculative brainstorm.

(Letter to Herz, 21 February 1772)

Representation (*Vorstellung*) is Kant's generic term for a constituent or element of cognition, similar in scope to 'idea' in the writings of the rationalists and empiricists: anything subjective that can play a role in composing a judgement or knowledge claim counts as a representation for Kant (its sense is thus philosophical, not psychological). It is in general possible to understand how a representation can relate to its object, Kant claims, if it either causes its object, or is caused by its object. Consequently there is no problem in understanding how sensory representations can relate to objects, since the mind is straightforwardly passive with respect to the objects of the senses, which (we naturally suppose) produce representations of themselves in us. But it is not readily intelligible how intellectual representations – 'the pure concepts of the understanding', which the *Dissertation* had claimed can alone represent 'things *as they are*' – can relate to objects, for they are not produced through our being affected by objects (Kant assumes that empiricist accounts of concept-formation are false), and nor do they produce their objects (to suppose which would be to confuse the human intellect with the creative intellect of God). Hence the problem. Previous solutions to it, Kant points out, are evidently defective.

In the letter, Kant nevertheless goes on to claim that he possesses the solution to the problem, and says that he will publish 'within three months' a work bearing the title 'Critique of Pure Reason'. In fact the Critical problem of the ground of the relation of representation and object preoccupied Kant for the best part of a decade, and in the course of attempting to solve it, his view of it changed in two important respects: he ceased to think that a causal relation running from the object to the subject suffices to make it intelligible that the subject is able to represent objects; and, as a result, he came to think that the problem of agreement with objects is not restricted to intellectual representations but rather extends to all of our representations. The Critical problem which motivates the Copernican revolution in the *Critique* is thus a broader and deeper version of the problem identified in the letter to Herz. Furthermore, Kant discovered that the Critical problem does not admit of a solution under the rationalist assumption that he still upheld in the letter to Herz: there is, the *Critique* tells us, an answer to the question of how pure intellectual representations can apply to things '*as they appear*', but not to the question of how they may be applied to things '*as they are*'.

Interpretations of Kant: analytic and idealist

This is the appropriate point at which to introduce an important distinction between two different ways of reading Kant's strategy in the *Critique*. These may be called the analytic and idealist interpretations. Both are found in present-day English-language commentary. The following quotations give an idea of each:

It is possible to imagine kinds of world very different from the world as we know it. It is possible to describe types of experience very different from the experience we actually have. But not any purported and grammatically permissible description of a possible kind of experience would be a truly intelligible description. There are limits to what we can conceive of, or make intelligible to ourselves, as a possible general structure of experience. The investigation of these limits, the investigation of the set of ideas which forms the limiting framework of all our thought about the world and experience of the world, is, evidently, an important and interesting philosophical undertaking. No philosopher has made a more strenuous attempt on it than Kant.

(P. F. Strawson)

Such an account [of the constitution of the world] requires reference to the operations of the mind, without which the world in question would not be disclosed to us and could not possibly adopt its shape. In this way Kant explained nature and the world of nature by means of rules that guide the synthetic activities we must exert on what is given to us in sensation.

But the source from which a world originates is equally dependent on that world. Initially it might seem that the principle by which we are capable of accounting for a world remains independent of what it accounts for. Closer investigation, however, discovers that, unless it executes the activities from which a world originates, the principle itself would be incomprehensible. This kind of investigation is distinctive to the method of Kant's epistemology that he calls 'transcendental': it can be shown that the unity of self-consciousness could not even be conceived unless that very unity functions as the point of departure for constituting a world of objects. With this, we can understand not only the origin of this world but also why this world is natural and indispensable to us and why our knowledge claims about it are justified.

(Dieter Henrich)

The analytic interpretation, represented by Strawson, has its name because it identifies the task of Kantian philosophy as that of analysing the implications of our conception of experience. It seeks to find in Kant, or reconstruct from materials supplied by him, what are known as transcendental arguments. These attempt to demonstrate that experience necessarily has certain features, ones which accord with commonsense realism. To take a central example of Strawson's, the *Critique* may be held to contain an argument to the effect that we could not conceive ourselves as subjects of experience if we did not have experience of a world of spatio-temporal particulars existing independently of our experiences. The chief point of uncovering the structure of experience, on the analytic interpretation, is that it allows skepticism to be refuted. The analytic line of interpretation thus construes Kant as employing a novel means, transcendental argumentation, in pursuit of the traditional epistemological goal of justifying our knowledge claims, and holds that what is of value in Kant's philosophy has to do with transcendental arguments, everything in it that comes under the heading of the Copernican revolution falling by the wayside.

The idealist line of interpretation, represented by the quotation from Henrich, agrees of course that Kant meant to provide a justification of our knowledge claims, but holds that he rightly intended this to follow from a more fundamental investigation into how the subject constitutes the world. This primary investigation of Kant's, on the idealist view, proceeds at a different level from traditional epistemology. The idealist interpretation agrees that Kant's enquiry is directed to uncovering the structure of experience but understands this notion differently. On the analytic interpretation, the structure of experience ultimately reduces to the structure of *what* is experienced: to say that experience has structure is just to say that it is necessarily *of* certain kinds of things (such as objective spatio-temporal particulars). On the idealist interpretation, experience *itself*, the activity of experiencing, has an inherent structure, which it bestows on its objects.

Transcendental investigation shows that the operations of the mind give shape to the world, as Henrich puts it.

The two lines of interpretation thus disagree about the kind of philosophical explanation to be looked for in Kant. The analytic interpretation regards statements about the conceptual presuppositions of experience as self-sufficient, and the Critical problem as solved once the structure of experience has been specified. It grounds all claims about the structure of experience on an appeal to the impossibility of our forming any other conception of experience. The structure of experience, it holds, is nothing more than the necessary window onto the world, and cannot be said to give shape to it: that experience has a structure is ultimately just a matter of our having such and such concepts and being unable to conceive any alternative to them, and the attempt to invest it with metaphysical significance over and above the completely minimal sense of being necessary for experience it regards as gratuitous and erroneous.

The idealist interpretation, by contrast, sees the need for further explanation of the structure of experience, and it refers this structure to the operations of our mind. Why it takes this view, and why it considers that Kant was right to claim that the solution of the Critical problem requires the Copernican revolution, is explained in what follows.

The problem of reality

The deepest issue with which Kant is preoccupied, on the idealist interpretation, is that of the possibility of objects. To approach the special sense in which Kant regards the possibility of objects as standing in need of explanation, it is necessary to consider Kant's view of what may be called the problem of reality. This problem is a generalised version of the Critical problem identified in the letter to Herz.

There is, we naturally suppose, a real world. The proposition that there is such a thing as reality is one that can scarcely allows itself to be doubted. We suppose, furthermore, that reality is known or in principle knowable to us, if only in part. Reality is then naturally conceived as that which fundamentally explains how objects of experience and thought are possible for us.

Now in order for reality or any part of it to become known to us, some sort of condition must obtain whereby it becomes an *object* for us. As it may also be put, something must bring it about that the objects composing reality *appear* to us. But the question is: what makes reality into an object for us? Its being an object for us is not established by its simple existence. And whatever allows reality to be an object for us cannot be merely postulated or taken for granted as a primitive fact – it stands in need of philosophical explanation, if anything does.

Whatever it is that allows reality to become an object for us is naturally and perhaps inevitably conceived as some sort of fundamental connecting relation between reality and ourselves. The question is then what this relation consists in. It cannot consist simply in reality's impressing itself on our minds, for in order for this to result in knowledge of reality, there would have to be something about us which made us appropriately receptive to it: our minds would have to be capable of transforming the impress of reality into a representation of it. That is, we would have to be already immanently related to reality. Nor does it help to reverse the story and conceive our contact with reality as the result of our own activity, since in order for our minds to reach out and read off the features of reality, we would have to know how to locate and read it – and again this condition could not be fulfilled unless reality were already an immanent object for us.

The prospect of circularity or an infinite regress looms. It seems that, if objects are originally independent from the subject, as the natural conception requires them to be, then any description of the relation which connects us with reality will either presuppose what needs to be explained, or require the postulation of a further, more primitive connecting relation in a series without end. No attempt to break the circle, or block the regress, by appealing to some third term independent of us and reality (e.g. God), or by supposing that our capacity to represent reality somehow follows from our inclusion in it, can succeed. To do so would be to appeal to what Kant calls a 'preformation system' (B167), a transcendent state of affairs whereby the agreement of our representations with reality is guaranteed prior to our forming them. But we have reason to accept such a hypothesis only if we have a true representation of the system itself (a true idea of God or our place in reality), to assume which is again to presuppose that, the possibility of which needs to be explained. Hence the futility of invoking a '*deus ex machina*', as Kant puts it in the letter to Herz. A dilemma then arises: either it must be admitted that we cannot account for our relation to reality, which makes all assertions regarding the nature of reality and our relation to it dogmatic; or the idea that we stand in a knowledgeable relation to reality must be renounced, which is to embrace skepticism. (A third but scarcely more attractive option is to identify reality with the contents of our own minds, i.e. solipsism.)

The problem is rooted in what we are naturally disposed to think. On the story told by pre-philosophical common sense (what Kant calls 'our common understanding'), there is first of all a set of objects composing a world, into which the subject is then introduced as a further item; when the subject's eyes are opened and its cognitive functions are in working order, the world floods in and knowledge of the world results. Common sense itself is unable to say how the presuppositions of this story are fulfilled. The epistemologies of pre-Kantian philosophy provide many different attempts to show how they may be fulfilled, and thereby account for our presumed knowledge of reality, but because they all remain within the terms of the story told by common sense, the result, on Kant's view, is always the same: they all reduce on examination to the bare, non-explanatory claim that we represent real things because they affect us and because we have an immanent capacity to represent them.

It is easily seen how these remarks apply to rationalism and empiricism. For the rationalist, our representation of the world results from the intellect being struck by the rational order inhering in the world; for the empiricist, it is generated by the array of sensory data that results from the impinging of things on our senses. The form of explanation is however in both cases the same, in so far as both epistemologies take for granted the possibility of reality's becoming an object for us: they do this at the point at which they assume that we have innate ideas or ideas manifest to the light of our reason, the veracity and harmony of which with real things is assured; or, that we are fitted to form sensible ideas, and concepts from those ideas, in such a way as to map the qualities of real things; or, that the order that we discover in our ideas replicates the order of ideas in God's mind; and so on. The fundamental objection to making assumptions of this kind is not, for Kant, that it leaves room for skepticism – although that is true – but that it signifies a collapse of philosophical explanation at the crucial point. The only reason for believing that there is a pre-ordained harmony between reality and our representations, or for accepting any other fundamental epistemological principle intended to guarantee that reality is knowable, is the belief that we represent reality: the principles of rationalist and empiricist epistemology lend no support to this assumption, but merely re-express our natural confidence in it; the assertion that pre-ordained harmony or whatever gives us the capacity to represent reality does not make any philosophical advance over the mere assertion that we are capable of representing reality. The upshot is that our conviction of the reality of the objects of our representation is displayed as groundless: we are left unable to say anything about the status of those objects and why we ascribe any degree of reality to them. Hence the continual vacillations of pre-Critical philosophy between skeptical admission that no philosophical account of reality and our relation to it can be given, and dogmatic assertion regarding the nature of reality and our relation to it. For these reasons, it may be held that pre-Kantian epistemology does not so much attempt to solve as fail to recognise the problem of reality.

The problem of reality does not rest on any special assumptions regarding the necessary conditions of knowledge or the nature of cognition. The argument is not, for example, that human cognition inevitably puts its stamp on objects in such a way as to make it impossible for reality to survive its filtration through our medium of representation. What it presupposes is only that we have the bare distinction between a real thing and an object of representation, and that neither concept implies the other. The essential point is that, just as we lack any positive reason for believing that our representations do not match reality, that reality is *not* open to being represented by us, so we also lack any reason for believing that it *is* open to being represented by us – that reality is what our representations are of. The two assertions are equally groundless. The underlying problem is that, although there is nothing contradictory in the idea of there *being* a fundamental connecting relation that allows reality to become an object for us, in order for us to *represent* this relation, as would be required for philosophical knowledge of our relation to reality, we would need to stand outside our capacity for representation, which we cannot do.

That the assumption of a match between our representations and reality is natural and compelling, and even that there may be something unintelligible about the idea of there not being any such relation, is agreed by Kant. The question is whether we can have any rational insight into this fact, if it is one. What the foregoing suggests is that in order for the assumption of a connection between subject and object to be validated, it is necessary for philosophical reflection to depart from the realist story told by common sense. The fact that common sense is unable to conceive any alternative to the assumption that reality is known to us, other than skepticism, is thus beside the point; what it means is just that the most that we can be asked to do, in advance of seeing what a philosophical alternative to realism would look like, is to suspend our instinctive commitment to realism.

Nor, it will be seen, does Kant ultimately have any quarrel with the realist form of explanation as such. That it is legitimate to refer at some point in the explanation of our knowledge to the fact that things simply are so and so – the pattern of explanation shown most clearly in the case of simple perceptual knowledge – is accepted by Kant: in so far as we remain within the orbit of common sense, it is correct to say that it is because the objects which we perceive really exist, that we have the representations of them that we do. What Kant rejects is realism at the level of philosophical explanation: the possibility of there being objects for us, things that we can have experiences of and thoughts about, sets a problem which the concept of reality does nothing to help to solve.

Kant's Copernican revolution

This sketch of the problem of reality gives an idea of Kant's motive for reconceiving objects as conforming to our mode of cognition: on Kant's view, to conceive the objects that we cognise as independent from us – the presupposition of 'transcendental realism', in Kant's terminology, to be explained later – is to render the relation of the subject to its objects unintelligible. If, therefore, there is an alternative to realism that can explain how objects are possible for us whilst upholding everything that common sense affirms against the skeptic, there will be every reason for regarding the problem of reality as warranting the abandonment of realism. This alternative, Kant argues, consists in the radical change of methodology which he introduces under the title of a Copernican revolution in philosophy, and constitutes the correct response to the problem of reality.

Pre-Copernican philosophical systems, according to Kant, set out by assuming a domain of objects which are conceived as having being, and a constitution of their own – a class of real things. In this sense, previous philosophical systems are one and all realist. (This generalisation includes, strange though it may sound, idealism of George Berkeley's (1685–1753) sort, because the 'real things' in question may be mental. Hume too is included.) To proceed in this way is to help oneself to the notion of reality, and also to presuppose *ab initio* that we are in possession of a concept of object which has reference independently of the conditions under which we may cognise objects. In Kant's terminology, pre-Copernican, realist philosophy begins by ascribing reference to 'the concept of an object in general'. Having put this concept into play, it then considers how we may take ourselves to stand in relations of knowledge to (at least some) members of the class of real things. Showing this to be so is the task of epistemology, the cost of its failure being skepticism. It is a consequence of this way of proceeding that the concept of an object is fundamentally independent of any epistemological conditions: an object is simply an individual that has being and a constitution, and any epistemic relations that it may have to subjects are to that extent inessential to it. Objects in the same sense are thus in question whether they are known or unknown, knowable or unknowable; whether an object is known or knowable depends upon the experiential history and cognitive capacities of subjects, and has nothing to do, essentially, with what it is to be an object.

The alternative is to begin by making an absolute separation between the supposition that there is such a thing as reality, and the conception of objects which we are capable of cognising. The idea of a thing as it is constituted in itself, a fully real thing, is allowed to stand, but, because it cannot help to solve the Critical problem, denied any role in accounting for the possibility of objects for us. In this way, the concept of an object in general is not pre-assumed to have reference, and a class of real things is not posited at the outset. Instead, philosophical concern focuses on the task of explicating the concept of an *object-for-us*, that is, defining the class of knowable objects. Epistemological conditions, the possibility of being known, are thereby incorporated into the concept of an object in so far as we can suppose it to have reference; that the concept of an object has reference, and that its object is a possible object for us, Kant will try to show, rest upon one and the same set of conditions. What pre-Copernican philosophy treats as two distinct matters – objecthood and knowability – are thus treated as one.

The distinction of epistemology and metaphysics: the 'transcendental turn'

It is a consequence of this transformation in the concept of an object that Copernican philosophy revises the relation between metaphysics (or ontology) and epistemology, and in a sense blurs the boundary between them. In pre-Copernican philosophy, there is a clear conceptual division between the question of metaphysics/ontology (what is the constitution of reality?) and the question of epistemology (how do we attain knowledge of reality?). These two sets of concerns are bound to be intermixed in any worthwhile philosophical system, but they remain from the pre-Copernican point of view separable in principle, due to the detachability of knowability from objecthood to which pre-Copernican philosophy is committed. Kant's transcendental question concerning the possibility of objects – as expressed in the letter to Herz: 'What is the ground of the relation of that in us which we call "representation" to the object?' – differs from either of the traditional questions, precisely because the philosophical enquiry to which it leads is intended to undo their distinctness. The traditional metaphysical/ontological question is suspended by Kant – fully real things are not objects that we can intelligibly seek knowledge of – and the sense of the epistemological question revised accordingly. The transcendental question concerning the conditions under which objects are possible for us is therefore not equivalent to a question about the conditions of being, or to a question about the conditions under which objects can be known, and cannot be resolved back into either of them (or their conjunction).

The Copernican revolution is often identified with an 'epistemological turn' in philosophy, meaning that it considers all metaphysical questions from an epistemological, justificatory angle (it replaces 'the question of fact (*quid facti*)' with 'the question of right (*quid juris*)', as Kant puts it (A84–5/B116–17)). This formula points to something important and genuinely present in Kant's project, but it fails to capture the sense in which it is also intended to change the very framework within which epistemological questions are understood. It also obscures the important point that, because Kant's transcendental question differs from the traditional question of epistemology, it follows that, for Kant, *even if* epistemology could demonstrate that our cognitive relation to objects is immune to all of the familiar forms of skeptical doubt, it would still not supply what is most fundamentally needed philosophically, because it would still not have dealt with the question of what makes it possible for a real thing to become an object for us. It is, in fact, Kant's view that pre-Critical epistemologies are debarred from providing the kind of skeptic-proof justification for knowledge claims to which Descartes aspired, and that only transcendental philosophy can rectify this situation; but the motive for transcendental philosophy lies in a demand for philosophical explanation which is independent from Descartes' quest for certainty. In truth the epistemological turn is only one aspect of Kant's more wide-reaching *transcendental* turn.

Idealism

It is evident that the subtle but far-reaching adjustment to the concept of an object described above, which lies at the base of the Copernican solution to the Critical problem, implies straightforwardly a rejection of realism. If we now return to the original Copernican claim that objects should be reconceived as conforming to our mode of cognition, the positive commitment of Copernicanism to an idealist conception of objects emerges. To suppose that objects must conform to us is to reverse the customary direction of explanation of knowledge. In the realist scheme, the arrow of explanation runs from the object to the subject: if a subject S knows an object O, then the explanation for S's representing O lies ultimately in O's being the way it is; had O not existed or been otherwise, S would not have represented O or would have represented O differently. Kant reverses the arrow: the deepest, most abstract and encompassing explanation of representation lies in how S is. The constitution of objects is thus determined at the most fundamental level by the subject. And it is a corollary of this pattern of explanation that the subject is *active* in knowing objects. In order for the Copernican claim that objects must be regarded as conforming to our mode of cognition to be made good, the subject must be thought of as *making it the case* that objects conform to its mode of cognition, and this it can do only if it carries over its own constitution to the side of the object, i.e. in some sense actively produces the object. (Otherwise the story will be incomplete: a gap will remain between the subject's having such and such a constitution, and its object's being such as to conform to it.) As Henrich puts it, the principle by which the world is accounted for is 'incomprehensible' unless it 'executes the activities' from which the world originates.

The general approach of Copernican philosophy in answering the question of how objects are possible for us, is therefore to say that, in a recondite philosophical sense, the subject *constitutes* its objects. It maintains, furthermore, that these subject-constituted objects compose the only kind of reality to which we have access: reality in the stronger sense of a realm of objects constituted independently of the subject may be admitted as something that we can (perhaps, must) conceive, but knowledge of it is held to be impossible. On this approach, skepticism is refuted by showing that, although claims to knowledge of real things in the strong sense must, as the skeptic says, be rejected as dogmatic and groundless, reality in the weaker sense is something that we can know precisely because we constitute it. Knowledge claims are thus defended on the basis that reason can have insight into 'that which it produces after a plan of its own' (Bxiii).

41

By drawing the analogy with Copernicus (Bxvi, Bxxii[n]), Kant does not mean therefore that transcendental philosophy demotes man from a position of centrality in the cosmos, in the way that Copernicus' discovery may have been felt as doing; in fact it has precisely the opposite – humanistic – implication that we stand at the centre of the natural world. Kant means by the comparison that his philosophy, like Copernicus' heliocentrism, explains what appears to be a wholly objective phenomenon in subjective terms: just as Copernicus explains the *apparent* movement of the sun in terms of the movement of the observer on the earth, Kant explains our knowledge of *apparently* independently constituted objects in terms of our mode of cognition. In both a phenomenon which had been regarded previously as having independent reality is redescribed as an appearance, dependent on the subject. In that respect both Kant and Copernicus break with common sense.

Kant's Copernican strategy immediately raises a question. If the subject constitutes its objects, how much of the object is the subject responsible for? How, indeed, can Kant's Copernicanism avoid collapsing objects in their entirety into the mind that experiences them, as in Berkeley's *esse* is *percipi*?

Kant has a clear and deep answer to this question, which provides him with a principled reason for claiming that his idealism is prima facie distinct from Berkeley's. Since, for Kant, the philosophical motivation for regarding objects as subject-dependent derives from the problem of reality, and not from the kind of considerations that move Berkeley, there is reason for regarding objects as subject-dependent *only* to the extent that they are conceived in terms of the conditions under which objects for us are possible at all, i.e. only with respect to those of their features by virtue of which they conform to the structure of experience; we are justified in regarding as subject-dependent only whatever in objects pertains to the possibility of their being objects for us at all. The writ of idealism runs no further. Crucially, it therefore does not extend to the existence of objects: 'representation in itself does not produce its object in so far as *existence* is concerned' (A92/B125). And in the *Prolegomena* Kant says that his Critical idealism, unlike Berkeley's idealism, is not after all a 'genuine' idealism, because it concerns not the existence of things but only the properties that we predicate of objects by virtue of which we can know them (289, 293–4).

To say that the subject constitutes its objects is therefore not to say that objects are *created* by our representations. The causing of objects by representations is in fact a form of knowledge that can be ascribed only to God. For us, the relation of representation to its object involves a complex mix of passivity and activity, and because our representations are neither simple effects nor simple causes of their objects, it is necessary to explain how object and representation can agree: not being related in the way that causes and effects correspond to one another, their relation needs to be specified, a task that occupies the first half of the *Critique*. The conformity of objects with our knowledge is not therefore assured at a single stroke by the Copernican hypothesis: the problem confronting realism of saying how representations relate to their objects reappears in transcendental philosophy, but with the difference, it is Kant's contention, that it can now be provided with a satisfactory solution.

In the light of all this, Kant's assumption that there are a priori elements in cognition, and the *Critique*'s exclusive concentration on them, is readily intelligible: the a priori element in cognition as a whole is the object-enabling structure of experience, the set of conditions that makes objects possible for us, and the a priori features of objects are those by virtue of which objects conform to that structure. Once this a priori structure is in place, knowledge becomes an a posteriori affair: objects may be regarded as independent from the subject and the realist model of explanation applied, i.e. our representations explained by objects rather than vice versa. Kant thus *accepts* realism (a subject S represents O because of how O is) at the level of common sense. This, it will be seen, is what Kant's conception of what he calls 'empirical reality', by means of which he seeks to harmonise his Copernicanism with the realism of common sense, amounts to: the empirically real features of objects are those which they have over and above (and conditionally upon) their a priori features, and on the basis of which the realist form of explanation has legitimate application. Philosophical realism may be regarded as confusing these two levels, the philosophical transcendental, and the pre-philosophical empirical: the realist projects the form of explanation which we employ at the pre-philosophical level onto the level of philosophical explanation, without considering what makes empirical reality possible in the first place.

The concept of a Copernican revolution just described is filled out in Kant's doctrine of transcendental idealism. This says, in the briefest summary, that the object of our knowledge is 'to be taken *in a twofold sense*, namely as appearance [*Erscheinung*] and as thing in itself [*Ding an sich selbst*]' (Bxxvii), and that objects are known to us only in the first sense, as appearance (Bxx, Bxxvi). Here there is a transition, from the bare Copernican precept that objects are to be considered as conforming to our mode of cognition, which is a strictly *methodological*, metaphysically neutral claim about the basis on which philosophical enquiry should proceed, to a non-neutral, substantive metaphysical, idealist claim about what the objects of our cognition *are*. The methodological and substantive claims are connected at a very basic level, because in so far as an object is conceived as an appearance, it is conceived as something which can be considered as necessarily (by its nature) conforming to our mode of cognition; in so far as it is conceived as a thing in itself (as 'real *per se*', Bxx), it is conceived as something which cannot be considered as necessarily (by its nature) conforming to our mode of cognition, but rather as something to which our mode of cognition must conform. The Copernican method commits us to the former, transcendental idealist, conception of objects.

It is a further thesis of Kant's – which surfaces, as we saw in the previous chapter, in the Preface (Bxvii-xx), and is defended in the first half of the *Critique* – that our mode of knowledge is sensible, and thus that objects are possible for us only when given in sense experience. From this it follows that appearances, objects that conform to our mode of cognition, are *exclusively objects of sense experience*. The distinction between appearances and things in themselves thus corresponds to the earlier distinction between the two different kinds of metaphysics: the metaphysics of experience has application to and provides us with knowledge of a reality composed of appearances; transcendent metaphysics attempts to gain knowledge of a reality composed of things in themselves.

'Transcendental'

The philosophical method which runs alongside transcendental idealism bears no resemblance to the rationalist's inspection of clear and distinct ideas or application of the principle of sufficient reason, or to the empiricist's anatomy of sense experience (Locke's *Essay* is a mere 'physiology' of human understanding, according to Kant, Aix). It consists in the identification of what Kant calls 'conditions of possibility', or transcendental conditions. These are variously said by Kant to be conditions of 'experience', of 'possible experience', of 'objects of experience', of 'appearances', of 'knowledge of objects', and so on. These conditions must be fulfilled before the subject can be epistemically related to an object. Kant attempts to show that they include the central tenets of common sense metaphysics, such as that there are substances that persist throughout change and that every event has a cause. The arguments that identify these conditions are called by Kant transcendental proofs. Each identifies a different respect in which objects must conform to our mode of cognition and so legitimates a different component of the metaphysics of experience. A transcendental proof has the peculiarity that it converts a possibility into a necessity: by saying under what conditions experience of objects is possible, transcendental proofs show those conditions to be necessary for us to the extent that we are to have experience of objects at all.

It is by now quite clear why Kant should call his philosophy an idealism, and it is called 'Critical' because it is premised on a prior examination – critique – of our cognitive powers. (Pre-Critical philosophy, omitting this task, fails to ground its claims properly, so that even where its conclusions are correct, it asserts them merely dogmatically.) Kant's characterisation of his Critical idealism as 'transcendental' requires further comment. No simple definition can capture the complex sense which this term acquires in the course of the *Critique*, but its core meaning is again bound up with the Copernican revolution. Kant says in the Introduction: 'I entitle *transcendental* all knowledge which is occupied not so much with objects as with the mode of our knowledge of objects in so far as this mode of knowledge is to be possible a priori' (A11–12/B25).

And in the *Prolegomena*: 'the word "transcendental" ... does not signify something passing beyond all experience but something that indeed precedes it a priori, but that is intended simply to make cognition of experience possible' (373n). Transcendental is thus not to be confused with transcendent, which does precisely mean 'passing beyond all experience' (the distinction is drawn explicitly at A295–6/B352–3). Transcendental enquiry is therefore enquiry into the cognitive constitution of the subject to which objects must conform; its product, transcendental knowledge, is at one remove from objects, and concerns only what makes objects, and a priori knowledge of them, possible.

The contrast of analytic and idealist interpretations of Kant should now make more sense. The analytic interpretation seeks to extract from the *Critique* an account of our most basic conceptual presuppositions, with a view to refuting the skeptic directly. The idealist interpretation by contrast regards the *Critique* as attempting to answer a kind of question not formulated in pre-Critical philosophy, and transcendental enquiry into the possibility of objects as subsuming the task of justifying our knowledge claims. Whereas on the analytic interpretation the *Critique* provides new answers to traditional philosophical questions, on the idealist interpretation it reconceives the framework within which philosophical questions are raised and answered. On the idealist view, what is missing from the analytic interpretation is an account of how the structure of experience relates to reality. Reality must share the structure of experience, if our experience is to be experience of reality. The structure of experience is however not a set of logical truths. Nor, being necessary for experience, can it itself be grounded on experience. Merely to appeal to what is contained in our concept of experience in a sense leaves everything open, for what is to say that anything answers to that concept? That the parts of the structure of experience are mutually supporting, and that we are unable to see how our most basic concepts could be discarded, is not enough. For these reasons, on the idealist interpretation, the question of what secures an object for our conceptual scheme as a whole – Kant's Critical problem, once again – warrants the Copernican conception of the subject as shaping the world.

Proving the doctrine

Kant's description of the Copernican revolution as a 'hypothesis', with which we may 'make trial', may give the impression that the *Critique* is ultimately founded on a naked choice of methodology, and that as a result transcendental idealism is just a proposal about how objects may be conceived, rather than a doctrine about what they really are. If transcendental idealism did rest on a methodological decision alone, then Kant's project would be hollow in an important sense, for there would be nothing to show that considering objects *qua* conforming to our mode of cognition has the significance that Kant claims for it. At most Kant would have shown transcendental idealism to be a coherent alternative to other, realist positions, which would remain in themselves untouched. Furthermore, the skeptic could then point out, with justification, that the fact that we *can* tell a story about objects which, if true, would entitle us to claim knowledge of objects, does not mean that the story *is* true and that we *are* entitled to claim knowledge of objects: that the Copernican hypothesis instructs us to proceed *as if* objects are knowable does not show them to *be* so.

A purely methodological Copernicanism would therefore be in its own way every bit as dogmatic as the metaphysics that Kant rejects. It is consequently important that this is not how Kant's argument actually runs. Kant does not intend to merely assume the truth of transcendental idealism at the outset and trace its consequences. Recognising that something positive must be done to establish his metaphysic, Kant describes it as the 'main purpose' of the *Critique*, not merely to articulate, but to *prove* the doctrine of transcendental idealism (Bxxii). Two attempted proofs are presented: an 'apodictic' proof in the Transcendental Aesthetic and Transcendental Analytic, concerned with space and time and the concepts of the understanding (Bxxii[n]); and an 'indirect' proof in the Antinomy of Pure Reason, according to which the assumption that the objects of knowledge are things in themselves leads unavoidably to contradictions (Bxx).

Kant's success in attempting to prove transcendental idealism is highly disputed. For this reason it is crucial to appreciate the difference made by the problem of reality. If the problem goes as deep as Kant believes, then the injunction to consider objects as things inherently conformable to our mode of cognition is grounded on the impossibility of making cognition intelligible on the basis of the only alternative, viz. considering them as things in themselves; Kant may justly deny that his Copernican methodology is arbitrary. And, with the problem of reality located in the background to the *Critique*, Kant does not have to accept the entire burden of proof in his argument with the philosophical realist: realism ceases to count as the default position. This is the point of Kant's statement in the Preface that the history of metaphysics gives us reason to 'make trial' with Copernicanism: though realism has the strength of the incumbent – its hold on our thinking *de facto* is beyond question – its authority *de jure* need not be accepted in philosophical contexts. So although the *Critique* cannot begin by assuming that the objects of our knowledge are mere appearances, it can proceed on the basis that no appeal is to be made to the independent reality of things in order to explain the possibility of objects for us: realism can be legitimately suspended without being assumed to be false. In this respect Kant's procedure is genuinely experimental: it asks us to begin by bracketing our natural realist convictions and to entertain an unfamiliar hypothesis, the content of which cannot be properly grasped, let alone evaluated, in advance of its systematic development. In this way Kant accommodates the difficulty, noted earlier, that at the outset we can have no clear notion of what it is to abandon realism without abandoning our natural conviction of the reality of the world, and it is left open to him to show that Copernicanism costs us nothing in terms of this conviction.

This point concerning where the burden of proof lies is, it will be seen, particularly important with regard to the first of the two proofs of transcendental idealism in the *Critique*. It also turns out to make a difference to the understanding and evaluation of Kant's more specific arguments in the *Critique*, concerning concepts like substance and cause. If Kant is regarded as at each point having to defeat a presumption in favour of realism, then his arguments are largely unpersuasive and indeed hard to follow. If on the other hand Kant's arguments are interpreted against the background assumption that there is pressure to account for objects in some non-realist set of terms, they regain force and intelligibility.

In conclusion, it will help to recapitulate, and indicate the interrelations of, the various descriptions that have been given so far of Kant's philosophical project and the motivation of the *Critique*.

The tensions within the Enlightenment that Kant grappled with in his pre-Critical writings led him to question the possibility of metaphysics, and in the Preface Kant describes the *Critique* as having the job of deciding if it is possible for us to have metaphysical knowledge. Bound up with the problem of metaphysics is a complex set of concerns. The failed metaphysics of the *Dissertation*, Kant's last attempt at rationalist realism, had led him to formulate the Critical problem, first stated in the letter to Herz, and his view of this problem changed over the course of the silent decade, as he came to see that the difficulty of relating intellectual representations to things '*as they are*' is insuperable, and that no account can be given of our relation to reality conceived as subject-independent (in other words, that the problem of reality has no solution). The new task of transcendental philosophy, which replaces ontology and epistemology as traditionally conceived, is to account for the relation of representation and object independently of realism, i.e. to explain how objects are possible at all for us without assuming their independently constituted reality.

The fate of metaphysics therefore hangs on the solution to the problem of transcendental philosophy. Since in metaphysical speculation reason attempts to grasp objects lying beyond experience, what needs to be determined in order for it to be decided if metaphysics in this (transcendent) sense is possible, is the conditions under which objects in general are possible for us. The self-examination of reason which Kant says is required in response to the conflicts of metaphysics thus coincides with the transcendental task of explaining how objects are possible. Both require an investigation into the nature and scope of human cognition.

The Copernican revolution is Kant's answer to the question of how objects are possible and his solution to the problem of metaphysics. The transcendental enquiry which follows from the Copernican hypothesis tells us, in the form of transcendental proofs, how we must constitute objects in order that experience be possible, and so provides us with a priori knowledge of objects. But it does so only on the condition that the objects in question are identified with appearances rather than things in themselves, i.e. on the condition of transcendental idealism. This yields the first verdict of the *Critique*, that metaphysics is possible in the (immanent) sense of the metaphysics of experience. All pre-Critical philosophy, Kant maintains, has assumed that the objects of our knowledge are things in themselves, and he claims to be able to show both that knowledge of things in themselves is impossible, and that it is this assumption which gives rise to the contradictions of metaphysics. This yields the second verdict, that transcendent metaphysics is impossible: 'we can know a priori of things only what we ourselves put into them' (Bxviii).

Chapter 3

How are synthetic
a priori judgements
possible?
(The Introduction)

Kant's logical formulation of the problem of metaphysics

In the Introduction, Kant claims to have discovered a new distinction between kinds of judgement, and a new class of judgements which neither rationalism nor empiricism can account for. The distinction is between what Kant calls 'analytic' and 'synthetic' judgements, and the judgements which are problematic for rationalism and empiricism are 'synthetic a priori' judgements. The task of the *Critique* is restated as that of finding an answer to the question of how synthetic a priori judgements are possible (B19). Kant attaches such importance to this problem that he says that the unhappy state of metaphysics is due entirely to the fact that it has never previously been considered (B19). (In his later writings Kant formulates the fundamental problems of ethics and aesthetics too in terms of synthetic a priority.) The Introduction contains, therefore, Kant's opening move against rationalism and empiricism. It is designed to clarify significantly the problem of metaphysics and even advance the case for its possibility.

Kant's target

Kant's specific target is a view of the sources of knowledge which is shared by Leibniz and Hume. For all their massive disagreements, both Leibniz and Hume regard our knowledge as divided into two fundamental types – necessary and a priori knowledge, and contingent and a posteriori knowledge – and each type as accounted for in a single way, their accounts of which are fundamentally similar. Leibniz divides all our knowledge into what he calls truths of reason and truths of fact: truths of reason are necessary, and necessary truths are held to be true by virtue of logical principles (they can be analysed into statements of identity or statements the opposite of which implies a contradiction): truths of fact are contingent and known through experience. Metaphysical knowledge falls of course on the side of truths of reason, along with mathematics and geometry; it is regarded as derivable from logical principles. In parallel fashion, Hume divides knowledge into what he calls relations of ideas and matters of fact: relations of ideas are necessary and 'discoverable by the mere operation of thought without dependence on what is anywhere existent in the universe', and again include mathematics and geometry; matters of fact are contingent and distinguished by the conceivability of their contradictory (for any matter of fact 'x is F' we can conceive 'x is not F'). Hume's critique of causation, and general repudiation of metaphysics, is based on this division: there is, he argues, no room for knowledge of causation construed as necessitation because causal relations are not relations of ideas (the contradictory of any causal judgement is always conceivable) and yet cannot derive from experience (there is no 'impression' of necessity). Leibniz and Hume thus agree in bifurcating human knowledge, while disagreeing about its scope.

A priori knowledge

Kant's argument against this well-entrenched position is preceded by a discussion of the a priori, which shows him accepting the connection affirmed by Leibniz and Hume between necessity and independence from experience. Kant first makes a concession to empiricism: he affirms that all our knowledge 'begins with' experience in the 'order of time', asking what else could awaken our cognitive faculties (A1, B1). But from this, he observes, it does not follow that all of our knowledge 'arises out of' (i.e. is derived from or grounded on) experience, for it is possible that the onset of experience merely precipitates knowledge claims which are not derived from or justified by experience – that is, a priori as opposed to empirical knowledge (Kant's preferred term of contrast for a priori is 'empirical' rather than a posteriori). To determine whether we have a priori knowledge, Kant proposes two criteria: a judgement is a priori if it is necessary, or if it has what he calls 'strict universality' (B3–4). A judgement has strict universality if no exception is possible to what it predicates of its objects, i.e. if it is necessarily true of its objects. (The criteria are therefore logically equivalent.) Generalisations which we reach through induction may have 'comparative' or 'relative' universality, but not strict universality. Kant makes necessity criterial for a priority because he holds that experience can teach us 'that a thing is so and so, but not that it cannot be otherwise' (B3, A1), a point which he does not trouble to defend, since it is accepted by Leibniz and rammed home forcibly in Hume's critique of causation. (To challenge it would be to assume that we can experience as given the difference between things merely being so and so, and their having to be so and so.)

Now there are, Kant indicates, signs that these criteria are met, or at least that we suppose ourselves to have a priori knowledge: mathematical judgements are deemed necessary, and the principle of causality, that every event must have a cause, if true, has strict universality (B4–5). Kant also gives – shifting the discussion from whole judgements to their elements, and looking ahead to a line of argument pursued later, in the Aesthetic – examples of concepts which are a priori: the concept of body, he claims, contains the a priori concepts of extension and substance; these remain when a body's empirical features (colour, hardness, weight, impenetrability) are removed (B5–6). Further, there is a field in which we aspire to knowledge that is by definition a priori, namely transcendent metaphysics, which employs the non-empirical concepts of God, freedom and immortality (A2–3/B6–7).

The analytic/synthetic distinction

The new distinction among knowledge claims introduced by Kant – analytic/synthetic – is independent from these older distinctions of necessary/contingent and a priori/a posteriori (A6–7/B10–11, *Proleg* 266–7). A judgement is analytic if the predicate is '(covertly) contained in' and 'thought in' the concept of the subject. The connection of subject and predicate is thereby 'thought through identity'. An analytic judgement merely displays a constituent of the concept of the subject and is true by virtue of the principle of contradiction: 'a triangle has three sides' is analytic because the concept of three-sidedness is contained in that of triangularity and its negation is contradictory ('a triangle does not have three sides' says: something that is three-sided is not three-sided). Similarly with 'all bodies are extended': the concept of extension is contained in that of body (B11–12). The form of all analytic judgements is therefore 'that which satisfies concept A (where A = B + C) satisfies concept B'. Analytic judgements do not extend our knowledge, Kant says, but merely 'explicate' our concepts.

A judgement is synthetic if the predicate that it connects with the concept of the subject is not contained or 'thought' in it. The connection of subject and predicate is 'thought without identity', and the judgement must be true by virtue of something other than the principle of contradiction: it rests on a 'synthesis', a bringing into connection of elements not previously joined. 'All bodies are heavy [have weight]', for example, is synthetic, because the concept of weight is not contained in that of body and is added to it through experience (B11–12). The form of all synthetic judgements is therefore 'that which satisfies concept A (where A = B + C) satisfies concept D'. For this very reason, synthetic judgements add to the content of cognition and *extend* our knowledge, as analytic judgements cannot.

Kant says that the principle of contradiction is the 'highest principle of all analytic judgements' and that it explains how they are possible (A150–3/B189–93). Analytic judgements are the only ones whose truth can be determined with the aid of this principle: with respect to all other, i.e. synthetic, judgements, its role is restricted to establishing only that they are either contradictory, and so cannot be true, or not contradictory, and so may be true. The truth of a synthetic judgement presupposes a third element – 'something else (X)' – in addition to subject and predicate, showing them to be connected (A8). In the case of empirical judgements, all of which must of course be synthetic since they are contingent, this 'X' is straightforwardly 'the complete experience of the object' (in judging a particular cat to be black, the 'X' is simply the cat-perceived-as-black). As Kant explains it, I find in experience the subject and predicate concepts of my judge-ment combined 'contingently, as parts of a whole' (B12).

The term 'synthetic' as applied to judgements has, therefore, the double sense of connecting a predicate with a concept in which it is not contained, and of presupposing a corresponding act of synthesis or putting together on the part of the subject (transcendental synthesis, in Kant's language, the concept of which will be treated at length in the Transcendental Deduction). The two senses are connected because only an act of synthesis can make a non-analytic judgement possible.

Synthetic a priori knowledge: mathematics, geometry and metaphysics

It may now be asked how Kant's new distinction relates to the old distinction between necessary and a priori, and contingent and empir-ical knowledge. In the perspective of Leibniz and Hume, one would expect all necessary and a priori judgements to be analytic, and all contingent and empirical judgements to be synthetic. Any other result would be unaccountable.

But the expectations of Leibniz and Hume are not, Kant shows, fulfilled: all contingent and empirical judgements are indeed synthetic, but not all necessary and a priori judgements are analytic. Metaphysical judgements, whilst being a priori, are synthetic (A9–10/B13–14). There are, Kant agrees, some propositions found in metaphysical writing, like 'God is a perfect being', which are merely analytic. But those that really interest us are intended to extend our knowledge, to tell us something new, and so must be synthetic. Consider 'every event has a cause'. Because it is necessary, it must be a priori. But it is not analytic, for the concept of the predicate is not contained in the concept of the subject: the concept of an event (something happening) does not contain that of being an effect. That is why the judgement is informative, and that makes it synthetic. Metaphysical judgements are therefore a priori and synthetic. Which means that they cannot be derived from either logic (since they are synthetic) or experience (since they are a priori).

To say that metaphysics is synthetic a priori is to say that Leibniz is wrong about the source of metaphysical knowledge, but it is not yet to say what that source is – nor even to show that it exists. On the contrary, thus far Kant may seem to have merely led us back, via a new route, to Hume's conclusion that metaphysical knowledge is impossible, for as yet we have no idea how metaphysical judgements, given their synthetic a priority, may be possible; the 'X' on which their synthesis rests, if it exists, is unknown to us (A9/B13). As Kant acknowledges readily, there is a genuine puzzle surrounding metaphysical judgements. If they are a priori, how is it possible for them to extend our knowledge? Any extension of knowledge would seem to require experience. It is of course Hume's argument that for just this reason metaphysics cannot extend our knowledge. The anomalousness of metaphysical judgements, relative to the assumption that all knowledge derives either from logic or experience, is something that Hume may be held to have recognised obliquely: it is in effect what is signified by his claim that causation is neither a relation of ideas nor a matter of fact. And Kant allows that we might well follow Hume in repudiating metaphysics, were it not that there are other sorts of synthetic a priori judgements which not even Hume repudiated. These are mathematical and geometrical judgements (B14–18).

That mathematical judgements are necessary and a priori is obvious, but that they are synthetic is not. This claim of Kant's (B14–17; *Proleg* 268–9) contradicts Leibniz's view that mathematical judgements are true by virtue of the principle of contradiction and so analytic by Kant's criterion. Leibniz supposes that '7 + 5 = 12' is true in the same way that 'a triangle has three sides' is true, i.e. that its truth can be established by means of purely logical principles. Kant argues, however, that the concept of 'the sum of 7 and 5' does not contain the concept of 'the number 12'. It does contain the concept of *a* number which is the union of 7 and 5, but it does not tell us *which* number that is; in order to determine which number it is, 'intuition' (a concept which will be explained in the Aesthetic) is required. The principle of contradiction can show that '7 + 5 does not = 12' is contradictory only if we add in further premises, such as '7 + 5 = 4 + 8' and '4 + 8 = 12': premises which are themselves not logical but mathematical. (In the *Critique* Kant does not spell this out, but he makes it clear in *Proleg* 268, and more fully in a letter, to Johann Schultz, 25 November 1788.) Synthesis is required, therefore, to make the connection between the subject, 'sum of 7 and 5', and the predicate, '12'. (This is more easily seen, Kant observes, with large numbers.) So Leibniz is wrong to suppose that mathematics can be derived from logical principles.

The same synthetic status is assigned by Kant to geometrical judgements. 'A straight line is the shortest distance between two points' is synthetic because the concept of straightness does not contain any information regarding the relative lengths of different lines joining two points. Again synthesis is required, to bridge the gap between 'straight line' and 'shortest distance between two points'. Similarly with our knowledge that space has three dimensions and no more (*Proleg* 284–5). (Kant also declares that the principles of Newtonian physics – e.g. the laws of conservation of mass, and of equality of action and reaction – are synthetic a priori, B17–18. This however looks forward to the Analytic, rather than serving the purposes of his present argument.)

It follows that, if mathematics and geometry are to be possible, we must reject Leibniz and Hume's view of the sources of knowledge. And metaphysics is now in with a chance. There is still no guarantee that metaphysics is possible, but Kant has shown that metaphysical judgements cannot be rejected for Hume's reason, that is, simply on the grounds that they do not derive from either logic or experience: mathematics and geometry, which Hume did not doubt, show that it is possible for us to have knowledge which is necessary but not logically necessary, so there is reason for thinking that metaphysical knowledge, which lays claim to the same status, may equally be possible. The 'X' which is responsible for the synthesis of a metaphysical judgement is so far unknown to us, and it must be of a philosophically unfamiliar kind, since it is supplied by neither logic nor experience, but we may nevertheless attempt to discover it. Kant supposes that if Hume had seen mathematical and geometrical judgements in the correct light (i.e. not relegated them to mere relations of ideas), he would have recognised the need to investigate the possibility of synthetic a priori judgement in general and thus to seek out the grounds of judgements such as the principle of causality (B19–20, *Proleg* 272).

The Introduction thus undermines Leibniz's claim that knowledge of reality is derivable from logical principles, and opens the door to demonstrating, against Hume, the possibility of metaphysics. In the light of Kant's new distinction, it would seem that Leibniz implicitly assimilated metaphysics to analytic judgements, and that Hume, though he more perspicaciously arrived at the edges of the problem of synthetic a priori judgement, did not contribute to its solution, because he failed to grasp its full generality.

Synthetic apriority: objections and replies

Because Kant sets such store by the notion of synthetic a priori judgement, and because it has been much criticised, it is important to determine the degree to which the overall argument of the *Critique* depends on the claims of the Introduction.

Mathematics and geometry: Kant's assumptions

One set of issues is raised by Kant's treatment of mathematics and geometry. Kant's claim that mathematics is synthetic is defensible, and it accords with some later schools of thought about mathematics. The claim that geometry is a priori, however, has been rendered hard to defend by subsequent developments in the subject: geometry is now divided into pure geometry, which consists of formal systems based on axioms for which truth is not claimed, and which are consequently not synthetic, and applied geometry, a branch of physics, the truth of which is determined empirically, and which is therefore not a priori.

The question is, then, what difference is made to the claims of the Introduction if Kant's claims about either mathematics or geometry are rejected. This raises a broader and important issue concerning the interpretation of Kant's argument in the *Critique*. If Kant is in the

Introduction assuming that mathematics and geometry are not open to repudiation, this might suggest that their truth is premised in this context and thus in the *Critique* as a whole. The text permits (though it does not compel) this reading: for example, Kant says that the sciences of mathematics and geometry, in contrast with that of metaphysics, 'actually exist' (B20). Correspondingly, there is a view according to which Kant intends to work back in the *Critique* from the mathematical and perhaps also natural sciences, the validity of which he is assuming, to their necessary presuppositions, and thence to show how one may advance from these to metaphysical conclusions. On this reading, Kant means to render the metaphysics of experience epistemologically dependent on mathematics and geometry, if not natural science as well.

There is, however, a clear statement in the *Critique of Practical Reason* (52–4) that Kant does not regard the truths of geometry and mathematics as beyond skeptical doubt and so cannot be operating this strategy. There he says that Hume only failed to extend skeptical doubt to mathematical and geometrical truths because he mistakenly regarded their propositions as analytic, and that once it is realised that they are synthetic, it becomes possible to doubt their alleged necessity, and indeed that empiricism demands such skepticism. Furthermore, Kant goes on to describe himself as having followed in the *Critique* the strategy of first disposing of the empiricism witnessed in Hume's critique of causation, and then overthrowing 'its inevitable consequence, skepticism, first, in natural science and, then, in mathematics' (53). (Less overt statements of the point, regarding mathematics, can be found in the *Critique* itself at A149/B188–9, A160/B199.)

The *Critique* is intended, therefore, to secure rather than assume the truth of geometry and mathematics. Kant's justification of the metaphysics of experience should be regarded as autonomous: it belongs to the same project as that which adds to the defence of mathematics and geometry, but it does not draw on their epistemological prestige, and the *Critique* is not undermined by any defects in Kant's account of mathematics or geometry (or natural science). This interpretation is substantiated by the discussion of methodology which we find in the *Prolegomena* (274–6). Kant says that he is proceeding in this expository work on the basis that mathematics, geometry and even natural science are objectively valid, because he is following a different methodology from the *Critique*, one that is 'analytical' or regressive, rather than 'synthetical' or progressive. Analytical enquiry rests 'upon something already known as trustworthy, from which we can set out with confidence and ascend to sources as yet unknown, the discovery of which' will 'explain to us what we already knew'. The synthetical method, which he follows in the *Critique*, is based on no data 'except reason itself'.

The force of Kant's appeal to mathematics and geometry in the Introduction is restricted, therefore, to alerting us to the 'universality' of the problem of the synthetic a priori (B20), and creating an onus in favour of the presumption that synthetic a priori judgements are possible. If the appeal is defeated, then Kant loses his claim to have advanced the case for the possibility of metaphysics in the Introduction, but he may still claim to have clarified the problem set by metaphysics, and the central line of argument in the *Critique* will remain untouched.

Conceptual containment

A different line of criticism concerns the analytic/synthetic distinction itself: specifically, what it is for one concept to 'contain' another, and how this relation is to be determined. If the metaphor of containment is unpacked in terms of 'belonging to the definition of', then it may seem that Kant's account presupposes a naive view of the possibility of determinate definitions of concepts. Arguably, there is no such thing as *the* definition of a term: all definitions are to a degree stipulative and nominal. If containment is understood instead in terms of our 'thinking' the predicate either in or outside the concept of the subject, as Kant puts it, then the test of analyticity/syntheticity may seem to become merely introspective or phenomenological. This would open Kant to the charge of psychologism (of reducing the norms of logic to matters of psychological fact). It would also make it possible for a judgement to be analytic for one person but synthetic for another, and for a concept to be contained in another but inspection fail to reveal it. Again the analytic/synthetic distinction becomes variable and arbitrary.

Kant does not in fact hold a naive view of definition: he maintains that 'mathematics is the only science that has definitions' (A727–30/B755–8), and that analytic judgements provide the materials for the construction of definitions rather than presuppose them. In defence of Kant's notion of containment, it may be said that although the edges of concepts are usually blurred, there must be identifiable core elements in concepts – criteria of identity for concepts – or it will follow that we cannot know the content of our concepts, and perhaps even that there are no such things. (This, in a sense, may be what Quine and others who have attacked the analytic/synthetic distinction, and the associated intensional conception of meaning, wish to maintain. Their position assumes, however, an underlying metaphysical picture so remote from Kant's that it may be held to one side in the present context.) Kant's view of concepts is subjectivist but not psychological in any empirical sense, and in the course of the *Critique* it becomes clearer, as the theory of cognition surrounding Kant's notion of containment emerges, that Kant is not committed to psychologism but rather opposed to it. The only point that Kant need make at this stage is that any account of concepts must make reference to what we believe they contain, and that these beliefs must be substantially correct. His account of the analytic/synthetic distinction strictly presupposes no more than that.

Two versions of the distinction

On a different tack, it has been argued that Kant arrives at the concept of synthetic a priori judgement only because he confuses two different versions of the analytic/synthetic distinction. Allegedly, Kant's account of analyticity is ambiguous, because it advances two criteria which are not equivalent: a judgement is said to be analytic if (1) its truth can be determined by the principle of contradiction – in modern parlance, on the basis of purely conceptual considerations or the meanings of the terms involved; (2) it is self-evidently true rather than such as to extend our knowledge. These need not yield the same result, because a judgement could be true for conceptual reasons without being self-evidently true: much philosophical labour might be needed to show the conceptual connection between the subject and

61

the predicate. So-called synthetic a priori judgements would then be analytic by Kant's first criterion, because they would be true for concep-tual reasons. They are, it is claimed, better described as 'non-obvious analytic judgements'.

Kant's distinction as epistemological

It is not clear that this charge of confusion can be made to stick, or that the proposed reconception of synthetic a priori judgement has great significance, for it does not answer the question as to *how* conceptual considerations can in general support the judgements that Kant calls synthetic a priori, or provide genuine extensions of our knowledge a priori. In any case, what has by this point become clear is that the primary force of Kant's characterisation of certain judge-ments as synthetic a priori is not logical in any ordinary sense but rather *epistemological*, i.e. concerned with the grounds or justification of judgements. This accords with Kant's statement in the *Prolegomena* (266) that the analytic/synthetic distinction concerns the 'content', not the 'logical form' of judgements. If so, the notion of synthetic a priority needs to be understood in terms of the conception of transcendental philosophy described in the previous chapter. In this light, synthetic a priori judgements are those that define the structure of experience, this structure being manifest in, and identifiable through, our acceptance of certain judgements as non-logically necessary; to say how synthetic a priori judgements are possible is to account for the structure of experience. This explains why synthetic a priority should be anomalous for empiricism and rationalism, since these philosophical traditions either fail to recognise that experience must have a structure (empiricism) or falsely suppose it to derive from logical principles (rationalism).

Pursuing this line, the problem of synthetic a priori judgement can be re-expressed in terms of the problem of the possibility of objects. The difference between analytic and synthetic judgements is that the former are true by virtue of the relation of concepts to one another, whereas synthetic judgements are true by virtue of their relation to something 'X' outside the circle of concepts. With regard to *empirical* synthetic judgements, i.e. at a level where the possibility of objects is already assumed, there is no difficulty in understanding how this extra-conceptual relation is possible: X is the object as given in experience. But with regard to synthetic *a priori* judgements, i.e. at a level where the possibility of objects is not assumed, it has yet to be understood how judgements can relate to objects, since this relation cannot arise out of either experience or the formal logical features of judgements. To solve the problem of synthetic a priori judgement is, therefore, to explain the relation of judgement to its object, a relation that logical principles cannot account for, and that empirical judgements presuppose. Kant articulates precisely this view of the problem of synthetic a priori judgement at A154–8/B193–7, where its solution is identified with the task of what he calls transcendental logic, which deals with the relation of thought to objects. The analytic/synthetic distinction is therefore logical in Kant's sense of transcendental logic, and not in that of formal – what Kant calls 'general' – logic.

This way of understanding synthetic a priority reduces the force of many of the objections described above, though it is also to concede something to Kant's critics, who have assumed, with some justification, that Kant means in the Introduction to stake the motivation of the transcendental enterprise on the existence of a purely logical problem.

The anti-rationalist and anti-empiricist strategy initiated in the Introduction is expanded on in the *Critique* in the following way. Kant will side with empiricism in rejecting the rationalist claim that knowledge can be derived from concepts alone: concepts, he will claim, suffice only for analytic judgements and so do not provide for truths about objects. But he will also, agreeing with rationalism, reject the empiricist claim that knowledge of objects can be derived from experience of the unconceptualised kind that empiricism presupposes: Kant will seek to show that 'experience is itself a species of knowledge that involves understanding' (Bxvii). On Kant's view, neither concepts nor sensory experience are individually sufficient for knowledge: they are jointly necessary (and sufficient) for knowledge; sense experience is needed to provide the content of knowledge and concepts give it its form. In this picture the judgements that Kant calls synthetic a priori hold centre stage because, as will be seen, they determine the manner in which sensory experience and concepts are conjoined.

Chapter 4

The sensible conditions of objects (The Aesthetic)

The Transcendental Aesthetic is concerned with sensibility, and thus with objects in so far as they are sensed (the Greek root 'aesthesis' denotes the capacity for sense perception). Its focus, however, is principally on space and time, regarding which its first central claim is that space and time provide the sensible *form* of experience, and on that account play a fundamental role in making objects possible. This sets space and time apart from other elements in sense experience. Kant formulates this claim in thoroughly technical terms: space and time are said to be 'pure a priori intuitions' 'forms of intuition' and 'forms of appearance'. The second central claim of the Aesthetic is that space and time are not features of absolute reality but only 'forms of sensibility', elements of our subjective cognitive constitution, and that everything that has spatial or temporal properties – all the objects of our experience – are mere appearances as opposed to things in themselves. This, the first of Kant's two promised proofs of transcendental idealism, will be discussed in the next chapter.

Kant's analysis of cognition

The Aesthetic's discussion of space and time is prefaced by Kant's analysis of cognition, which introduces an unfamiliar philosophical terminology (§1: A19–22/B33–6; see also A15–16/B29–30, A50–2/B74–6).

Intuitions and concepts

Kant holds that if we clear our minds of the doctrines of rationalism and empiricism, and try to say how in the most general terms our cognitive powers are composed and relate to objects, we find that the deepest distinction to be drawn is between, on the one hand, an object's being *given* to us, and, on the other, its being *thought* about. Intuitions are those representations by means of which objects are given to us, and concepts those by means of which we think about objects. The cognitive power in us that enables objects to be given, Kant calls sensibility, and the power that enables objects to be thought he calls understanding.

Intuitions relate to objects immediately: an intuition 'is that through which it [an object] is in immediate relation to us' (A19/B33). The German for intuition, *Anschauung*, means 'looking at' (without any connotations of special insight), and Kant's technical use of the term incorporates the sense of an object's phenomenological presence to the subject (*Proleg* 282). Concepts, by contrast, when they relate to objects, do so mediately, 'by means of a feature which several things may have in common' (A320/B377). Having a concept does not therefore imply a relation to an object: once an object is given, it can be thought about, but what allows it to be given in the first place is something other than an act of thought; concepts must 'relate ultimately to intuitions' (A19/B33) if they are to have objects. The distinction of intuition and concept thus corresponds to the distinction between the particular and the general. Intuitions are 'singular representations' (B136n): an intuition is a representation of one particular, individual thing, 'a single object' (A32/B47). Kant regards this feature of intuition as of a piece with the immediacy of its relation to the object. A concept by contrast is inherently general: necessarily a concept can apply to more than one particular, since to apply a concept to an object is to say that it belongs to a kind of which there are or could be other instances.

The kind of intuition that we possess is sensible as opposed to intellectual (the concept of intellectual intuition will be considered later). Sensibility is the cognitive power that gives rise to intuitions, and it is a capacity of 'receptivity': the subject forms its sensible representations passively, through being 'affected' (A50–1/B74–5). The faculty of understanding, which produces concepts and applies them to objects, is by contrast active and 'spontaneous', meaning that it is not caused to do what it does. Subjects such as ourselves need to be affected in order for objects to be given to us, and the mark of affection is sensation. Sensation, and being affected, is an entirely contingent, a posteriori matter: there is no necessity to our having any sensation. Having agreed with empiricism that sensation is a posteriori and originates through the subject's being somehow impinged upon from the outside, Kant will say nothing more about sensation itself other than that it composes a 'manifold' (multiplicity). In contrast with Locke's meticulous typology of sensible ideas, everything that Kant will go on to say about sense experience has to do with what the mind makes of its manifold of sensation.

The concepts of intuition and sensibility are by intention extremely abstract. As will be seen, the concept of sensibility abstracts from the particular sense modalities of sight, hearing, touch and so on that we humans actually possess. The concept of intuition is distinct from that of perception, which for Kant presupposes concepts as well as intuitions, as well as being more abstract than that of sensibility, which is just the particular form that intuition takes in subjects such as ourselves.

Epistemological implications

Kant extracts a crucial implication from his division of our cognitive powers into the two heterogeneous and mutually irreducible functions of intuiting and thinking. Intuitions on their own do not amount to any sort of cognition of the objects that they merely give; intuition does not comprise knowledge by acquaintance of anything at all (not even of 'inner' sensory objects). As the Analytic will make clear, strictly an intuition can only be said to relate to an object at all under the condition that it is brought under a concept: if I remove 'all thought' from experience, 'no knowledge of any object remains', because 'through mere intuition nothing at all is thought' and 'affection of sensibility' alone 'does not amount to a relation of such representation to any object' (A253/B309). And concepts on their own lack objects. It follows that knowledge of an object requires the conjunction of an intuition and a concept. An intuition is needed in order that there should be an object to which a concept may be applied. And a concept is needed to provide intuition with a relation to an object: conceptualisation transforms the primitive object-directedness which intuitions possess intrinsically into a genuine relation of representation. The mutual dependence of intuitions and concepts is an absolutely fundamental proposition of Kant's epistemology:

> Without sensibility no object would be given to us, without understanding no object would be thought. Thoughts without content are empty, intuitions without concepts are blind. It is, therefore, just as necessary to make our concepts sensible, that is, to add the object to them in intuition, as to make our intuitions intelligible, that is, to bring them under concepts. These two powers or capacities cannot exchange their functions. The understanding can intuit nothing, the senses can think nothing. Only through their union can knowledge arise.
>
> (A51/B75)

Kant's claim that irreducibly different representations perform the functions of giving and thinking objects weighs against rationalist and empiricist accounts of knowledge. These Kant charges with falsely assimilating intuitions and concepts to one another, each in a different direction: rationalism, by reducing the difference between sensory and intellectual representations, which is in fact a difference of 'origin and content', to the merely 'logical' difference between confused and clear ideas, mistakes sensory representations for intellectual ones; whilst empiricism, by seeking to derive the material of thought from sensory data, makes the opposite mistake (A43–4/B60–2, A271/B327).

Intellectual intuition

Since Kant's analysis of cognition is not by any means philosophically neutral, it might be asked if it is not open to the rationalist or empiricist to simply reject it. Kant may appear at the beginning of the Aesthetic to lay down an epistemological theory on a purely terminological basis, but an argument supporting his analysis can be located. It turns on a contrast between the type of our mode of cognition and another logically possible type. We should consider what it would be for there to be no such distinction as that which Kant makes between intuitions and concepts. According to Kant, we can form some idea of a subject whose mode of cognition is not divided in the way that ours is. This would be a subject for whom the act of thinking, and being presented with an object, were one and the same event; the same representations in the subject would perform both functions. Such a subject would possess what Kant calls *intellectual intuition* (or, equivalently, an intuitive intellect or intuitive understanding) (B68, B71, A252), so called because in such a subject the same faculty that thinks objects would also intuit them. Now it is evident that we do not have intellectual intuition. For a subject with intellectual intuition, there would be no room for sense experience, since to merely think of an object would be to be presented with it; nor would it be necessary to apply concepts to objects, since each given object would be grasped immediately in its full individuality; nor for such a subject would there be any distinction between the actual and the possible, since this distinction disappears if objects become actual merely by virtue of being thought of (*CJ* 401–3, 406–7). Kant observes that in intellectual intuition the distinction between knowing an object and creating it would also vanish. The only subject to which we can meaningfully attach the notion of intellectual intuition, Kant suggests, is God (B72).

Our intuition is by contrast sensible, or, as it may also be put, our understanding is discursive (A230). For us, the functions of intuiting and thinking are not collapsed into one another: to think of something is not to grasp it immediately in the way that perception grasps its object; our thoughts can grasp objects only by bringing them under concepts; we can know things only by thinking of what they are like (our knowledge assumes judgemental form); the actual remains distinct from the possible. Contemplating the notion of intellectual intuition throws into relief and serves to reveal the structure of our own mode of cognition, which rationalism and empiricism fail to grasp.

The basic structure of our cognition is to be regarded from the viewpoint of transcendental enquiry as an ultimately contingent matter and not susceptible to further explanation. To underline the point, Kant states that we may suppose sensibility and understanding to stem from a common root, but that, if this is so, it is unknowable (A15/B29). Also, he affirms that forms of sensible intuition other than our human sort are logically possible (A27/B43, B72): human intuition, Kant is just about to argue, is defined by its spatio-temporality, but we can form the idea of a way of sensing that employs something else in place of space and time; although we can form no contentful or definite idea of what this could be, there can be no justification for declaring non-human kinds of sensible intuition impossible.

The sensible form of experience: space and time

We come now to Kant's claim that a unique and privileged status must be accorded to space and time. In the background to his discussion are two other philosophical views of space and time: Newton's 'absolutist' view, and Leibniz's 'relational' (reductionist) view. Kant refers to these respectively as the view that space and time are 'real existences', and that they are 'only determinations or relations of things' (A23/B37). The opposition between them was the major topic of dispute in the Leibniz–Clarke correspondence.

Briefly, Newton's view is of space as an absolutely real, self-subsistent 'container' which would exist even if no physical objects were contained within it. To which extent, space is akin to a substance, since it exists self-sufficiently. The same holds for time. The opposite, Leibnizian view is of space as a logical construction out of relations between objects: to say that objects are in space is to say that they stand in certain relations to one another; statements about space can be reduced to statements about objects and their interaction. Another way of expressing the difference between them is to say that, on Newton's view, there are such things as spatial points and temporal instants, which are ontologically irreducible and exist independently of the objects that coincide with them; and that for Leibniz there are no such entities. The difference shows up with respect to the kinds of possibilities that each view is able to countenance. It follows from the absolutist view that the universe could shift its position in space (begin to drift in one direction), and could have been created at a different time from that at which it actually came into existence; the relationalist must deny the intelligibility of these suppositions. The absolutist grants the plain possibility of empty space and empty time; the relationalist can understand these possibilities, if at all, only conditionally, in terms of possibilities of relations between objects.

Kant's own view of space and time he expresses by saying that they are a priori intuitions. To say that they are a priori is to say that they do not derive from experience. And to say that they are intuitions is to say that our awareness of them is immediate and non-conceptual, and that each of space and time is in some sense a 'single object'. Kant's view differs from those of Newton and Leibniz, for it entails (contra Leibniz) that space and time are irreducible, and also (contra Newton) that they are not real in an absolute sense. The irreducibility of space and time is what is at issue in this chapter, and their non-absolute reality in the next.

Kant's arguments that space and time satisfy the description of a priori intuitions are given in their respective Metaphysical Expositions (discussed in the following section). But the discussion in the opening pages of the Aesthetic also contains a number of points designed to make room for the notion of a priori intuition in a preliminary way, and which indicate how Kant's view of space and time fits into the general transcendental theory of experience.

Pure intuition

The notion that there is something a priori in intuition contradicts our natural conception of sense experience as an entirely a posteriori affair; it is, common sense supposes, up to experience alone to decide what to present us with. But Kant has a number of reasons for holding that intuition must contain an a priori element. In the first place, the existence of a priori intuition is suggested by the concept of synthetic a priori judgement. Synthetic judgements are made true by objects not concepts, and intuitions are the representations whereby objects are given; a priori judgements require a priori grounds; thus synthetic a priori judgement is possible if there is a priori intuition on which it may be grounded.

The existence of a priori intuition is furthermore implied by an analysis that Kant gives of appearances into 'matter' and 'form'. 'Appearance' is defined as 'undetermined object of an empirical intuition' (A20/B34), so in the present context appearances may be understood simply as objects of experience *qua* sensed (the contrast with things in themselves playing no role for the moment). Thus a table as given to me in sense experience counts as an appearance. The matter of an appearance is that in it which corresponds to sensation, for which reason it is necessarily given to us a posteriori (since sensation is a posteriori). But an appearance is not simply a manifold of sensations: it presupposes that sensations are in some way ordered, i.e. have form. Kant's striking idea is that experience cannot be 'all content': however minimal and atomised it may be, it must have form, because a subject can only be cognitively conscious of its experience *as* something if it is organised in some way. Experience that had no form would be a mere buzzing confusion, and a subject of such experience would be cognitively unconscious of it; form is the unifying structure that allows the content of experience to show itself as such. The form of appearance, whatever it may be, consists in a structure of relations, and according to Kant it must be supplied a priori by our power of intuition, because whatever gives order to sensation cannot itself consist in or derive from sensation – sensation cannot either bring with it or give rise to the form that it has in our apprehension of it. This form must also be intuitive rather than conceptual, since it concerns the shape that sensation has in so far as it provides a content for thought. The form of appearance is thus located between sensation and thought: like sensation, it is prior to the application of any concept, but like thought, it does not arise out of sensation. (The line of argument sketched here will be more fully explained and defended in the Transcendental Deduction.)

If intuition contains formal, a priori elements, then it follows that we have a kind of intuition that is independent of sensation, of our minds being affected. Kant calls this 'pure intuition', pure being defined as 'not containing anything belonging to sensation' (A20–2/B34–6). The contrast is with empirical intuition, which contains sensation and the objects of which are appearances. Pure intuition and the form of appearances are, Kant says, the proper topic of the Aesthetic, whose task it is to analyse the form of experience by isolating sensibility from understanding, and then separating off from it everything that belongs to sensation. Our pure intuition of space is exemplified, Kant claims, by the representations of figure and extension contained in the representation of body (A20–1/B35, discussed earlier in the Introduction at B5–6), and our other pure intuition is time (A22/B36).

The doctrine of pure intuition of space allows Kant to make a claim about geometry (B40–1). The Aesthetic contains three distinguishable claims about geometry, and the first of these is that pure intuition of space allows it to be explained how the synthetic a priori judgements of geometry are possible. In all cases of synthetic a priori judgement, we need to discover a 'something X' synthesising subject and predicate, and we know that this X cannot be experience because the judgement is a priori. Our pure intuition of space is fitted to play the role of the non-empirical 'X' synthesising subject and predicate in geometrical judgements: geometry may be regarded as knowledge derived from pure intuition of space. This accords with the fact that the necessity of geometric truths can be grasped simply on the basis of mental constructions of lines, triangles and so on, i.e. by representing space empty of appearances, without our minds being affected in any way. Not only does pure intuition of space permit space to be studied independently of physical objects: it also makes possible synthetic a priori knowledge of the spatial properties of outer objects, since appearances in space must of course conform to the laws of geometry.

Pure intuition of time, according to Kant, also gives rise to a body of synthetic a priori knowledge. Included are 'apodictic principles' such as that time has only one dimension and that 'different times are not simultaneous but successive' (A31/B47), and also certain judgements concerning 'alteration' or change in general and 'motion' or change of place. Here Kant has in mind such rudimentary metaphysical judgements as that a thing may have different properties at different times (something which mere analysis of the concept of a thing does not show to be possible), and, more substantially, 'the general doctrine of motion' comprised by Newtonian mechanics (A32/B48–9), the position of which in Kant's treatment of time is symmetrical with that of geometry in his treatment of space. In the *Prolegomena* (283) Kant also relates arithmetic to pure intuition of time, his claim being that the concept of number presupposes 'the successive addition of units in time' (see also A142–3/B182).

Inner and outer sense

On the basis that space and time constitute the form of sense experience, Kant elaborates his theory by describing space as the 'form of outer sense' and time as the 'form of inner sense' (A22–3/B37). By a sense, Kant means a mode of intuiting objects, a way in which objects of a certain sort are made available to a subject in intuition. Outer sense is then the way in which outer objects, i.e. objects distinct from ourselves, are made available to us in intuition; to say that space is the form of outer sense means that the way in which we become aware of things as distinct from ourselves is by representing them as being in space. Inner sense is the way in which inner objects, i.e. our mental states, are made available to us in intuition, and the corresponding claim is that the way in which we become aware of our mental states is by representing them as being in time. Kant adds that things could not be otherwise, in that time 'cannot be outwardly intuited' and space cannot be 'intuited as something in us' (A23/B37): their roles could not be reversed and nor, for us, could anything except space and time play the roles of outer and inner sense.

That time 'cannot be outwardly intuited' does not mean that external objects are in space but not in time. It means, in the first place, that time cannot be outwardly intuited without being inwardly intuited: if our mental states were not in time, we could not experience outer objects as being in time. Kant's further implication – and this is a further matter, which pertains to the transcendental idealist implications of his account to be considered later – is that outer objects are in time because, and only because, they are represented by our mental states, which are in time: the temporality of outer objects derives from that of our mental states.

Space and time as a priori intuitions: Kant's arguments

The thesis that space and time are a priori intuitions thus coheres with the principles of transcendental philosophy, but Kant also argues explicitly in its support. It is easiest to attend in the first instance to Kant's account of space, which his treatment of time mirrors for the greater part. Six arguments in all concerning the a priori and intuitive character of space may be found in Kant's writings, four of which are given as a set in the Metaphysical Exposition of Space (§2 of the Aesthetic). The first and second of these are designed to show that space is a priori, the third and fourth that it is an intuition.

The Metaphysical Exposition of Space, first and second arguments: space as a priori

The first argument is that the representation of space must be a priori, and 'not an empirical representation which has been derived from outer experiences', because it is presupposed for outer experience as such: 'outer experience is possible only through that representation [of space]' (A23/B38). (Again, 'outer' does not mean external in a spatial sense – which would reduce the claim that outer objects must be represented in space to a tautology – but rather distinct from myself.) My sensations cannot 'be referred to something outside me', i.e. distinct from me, unless I presuppose the representation of space. Nor, Kant adds, can my sensations be represented 'as outside and alongside one another' without the representation of space, meaning that space is also presupposed for determining the numerical distinctness of outer objects from one another.

Kant's statement of the argument is compressed, and it is not immediately obvious what form it is intended to take. It cannot rest on the bald premise that in order for experience to represent objects as F, the representation F must be a priori, since that would have the absurd consequence that even the representation of colour must be a priori; and, in any case, Kant is not arguing that space is presupposed for experience of objects as spatial but for experience of objects as outer, i.e. distinct from oneself (as well as from one another). Kant's argument must rather be the following. If the representation of space were not a priori, then it would be empirical; but if it were formed empirically, then it would be obtained from experience of outer objects. But this is impossible, since outer experience is impossible without the representation of space. So the representation of space must be a priori. In sum, because the representation of space is invoked in the very act of representing a world of outer objects, it cannot be based on experience of outer objects.

The second argument says that although we can think space empty of objects, it is impossible to represent the absence of space. Space 'must therefore be regarded as the condition of the possibility of appearances, and not as a determination dependent on them' (A24/B38–9). From which it follows that space is a necessary and therefore again an a priori representation.

The point of the second argument is to rule out a possibility which the first leaves open, namely that although outer objects cannot be represented without space being represented, the reverse is also true, i.e. space cannot be represented without a world of outer objects being represented (as Leibniz's view implies). If the representations of space and an outer world were mutually necessary, then the representation of space would not be prior to the representation of an outer world, which would imply that space is after all an empirical representation.

The second argument is accordingly designed to secure the a priority of space by establishing that the representation of outer objects is not necessary for that of space, and it does this by indicating a difference in the behaviour of the two representations. We can represent the absence of outer objects by representing space empty of objects: empty space is conceivable, whether or not we could have cognition of it (something which Kant in fact denies, for independent reasons). But we cannot in the same objective sense represent the absence of space, for in order to do so it would be necessary to represent an outer world from which space was missing, and this is something which, the first argument has indicated, we are unable to do. The representation of space can survive the subtraction of all outer objects but not vice versa. Kant's argument has therefore nothing to do with the merely subjective, psychological impossibility of ridding ourselves of the idea of space.

Jointly the two arguments establish an asymmetrical relation of dependence between the representation of space and that of a world of outer objects: the former is presupposed for the latter, but the reverse is not the case. And Kant regards this as sufficient to show that our representation of space is a priori in the sense of not being derived from experience. The truth that Kant's arguments ultimately rest on – that we cannot represent a non-spatial outer world – cannot be dismissed as reflecting a merely contingent limitation of our imagination, for we cannot begin to explain how *our* representational powers could be otherwise; it would mean nothing to describe the necessity that it expresses as merely psychological. It is to be noted that the kind of necessity that Kant is claiming for the representation of space, though not psychological, is not logical either: his claim is that space is necessary in the specific sense of being a transcendental presupposition (of experience of outer objects).

The Metaphysical Exposition of Space, third and fourth arguments: space as an intuition

The third and fourth arguments of the Metaphysical Exposition are designed to show that the representation of space fulfils the criteria for an intuition and not those for a concept. By describing the representation of space as an intuition, Kant does not mean to deny that we have a concept of space in general and concepts of spaces – evidently we do have the concepts 'a space', 'a space measuring 1 m^3', and so on, which can be applied generally, i.e. to an indefinite number of spatial regions; and we also have the concept 'in space', which can be applied to an indefinite number of objects. Kant's claim is rather that intuition of space *underlies* all of our spatial concepts (A25/B39).

The third argument claims that 'we can represent to ourselves only one space', i.e. that space is unitary, singular and unique (A24–5/B39). Kant gives two connected reasons for thinking this, both having to do with the relation of space to its parts: first, to talk about 'diverse spaces' is to talk about different 'parts of one and the same unique space'; second, these parts 'cannot precede the one all-embracing space' and 'can be thought only as *in* it'.

The parts of space – particular spaces such as 'the space between here and the wall' – are not related to space – the dimension of Space – in the way that instances of a concept are related to that concept (instances of the concept of a tree are not similarly 'parts of Tree'). Particular spaces are, as Kant puts it, arrived at through 'limitations' of the all-embracing space: we can identify them only by so to speak slicing them out of Space (see also A169–79/B211). What makes something an instance of space is nothing but its relation to Space (it is defined by the limits beyond which it does not extend), and what distinguishes different instances of space from one another is nothing but their relations to one another in Space. Since their relation to Space is the only feature which bestows identity on particular spaces, Space is what makes particular spaces possible. Similarly, awareness of Space must precede awareness of particular spaces. Awareness of Space is furthermore necessarily not mediated by any feature which Space could have in common with other things.

It follows that the representation of space is an intuition: it presents an individual object – Space, the whole which precedes its parts – immediately, i.e. independently of any other representation. Conceptual representations of individual objects, by contrast, are necessarily mediated by other, logically independent representations; for example, the representation 'the totality of A's' employs the mediating representation 'A'.

It has been objected to Kant that experience of non-unitary space is perfectly imaginable, as testified by fictions like *The Lion, the Witch and the Wardrobe*, in which subjects travel back and forth between spatially discrete worlds. It is true that thought-experimentation can come up with descriptions of sets of experiences which we may be led to think of as comprising experience of 'a world containing two spaces' or 'two spatial worlds', but whatever is to be made of such speculation, it is not to the point in the present context. To the extent that fictions make the notion of non-unitary space intelligible, they do so on the basis of inference and conceptual extrapolation, whilst presupposing our ordinary intuitive grasp of space, in which it is given to us as unitary. Because they do not show that we are able to imagine non-unitary space being given to us in the relevant sense, they do not give reason for thinking that space could fail to be experienced as unitary in the sense of 'experience of space' relevant to Kant's argument.

The fourth argument says that space is 'represented as an infinite *given* magnitude' (A25/B39–40), and that this is to be explained by its being an intuition.

Kant does not mean that we perceive space as an infinite whole, which we obviously do not, but that space is given to us, first, as unbounded (we cannot represent the end or 'edge' of space; behind any space, more space lies); and second, as infinitely divisible (the product of dividing any spatial volume always allows of further possible division; division does not terminate with the discovery of 'granules' of space). It is because space is given as infinite in these two senses that we represent it as having an infinite number of parts. Carrying over from the third argument the conclusion that space is unitary, it follows that the possibility of an infinite number of parts of space is secondary to, and derivative from, the infinity of Space itself. Now a concept cannot be infinite in the same sense: the concept of tree has an infinite number of possible instances, but this is not because there is something represented by it, to be called 'Tree', which is itself infinite in the sense of having an infinite number of parts; as Kant puts it, the infinite parts of space are contained *within* it, whereas the infinite possible instances of a concept fall *under* it. A concept that did resemble Space in containing an infinite number of parts, as distinct from having an infinite number of possible instances, would be one with an infinitely rich content, and could not be grasped by a finite mind. Therefore space cannot be a concept.

The fourth argument thus protects the conclusion of the third by showing that the existence of infinitely many instances of space does not (as might be thought) make the representation of space a concept; on the contrary, this fact is explained by its being an intuition.

Incongruent counterparts

A fifth argument, known as the argument from incongruent counterparts, provides a more graphic demonstration of the intuitive character of space. The argument occurs not in the *Critique* but in the *Inaugural Dissertation* (403) and *Prolegomena* (285–6). Suppose (modifying Kant's own examples) the world to contain only two gloves, left and right, and that these gloves share all of their properties apart from their left- and right-handedness. They are counterparts. Now we are to consider what the difference of left- and right-handedness, the respect in which they are incongruent, consists in. It cannot be relational, for the world as described contains nothing apart from the two gloves, and they differ in relation to one another only in the very respect that we are trying to analyse. The respect in which they differ is one of orientation. And this difference is not relational but 'internal' to the gloves. The spatial properties of objects are therefore intrinsic, irreducible and underived. This is sufficient to refute Leibniz's view that spatial relations are constructed conceptually from non-spatial relations between objects, and it also, Kant holds, shows space to be an intuition, because the internal difference between the gloves, their incongruity, 'cannot be described discursively or reduced to intellectual marks' (*Dissertation* 403) and 'cannot be made intelligible by any concept' (*Proleg* 286): to explain what a difference of orientation consists in, one is ultimately obliged to simply *point* to it.

The argument from geometry

The sixth and final argument to be mentioned is the argument from geometry (included in the Metaphysical Exposition in the first edition at A24, and in the second edition renamed the Transcendental Exposition of Space, at B40–1). Geometry here makes its second appearance. Earlier Kant was seen to argue that if space is a pure intuition then the synthetic a priority of geometry can be explained. Now all that Kant need do, in order to turn this into an argument for the conclusion that space is an a priori intuition, is to add that *only* if space is a pure and therefore a priori intuition can the truth of geometry be explained. This is easily done. Geometrical judgements cannot be based on concepts, since they are not analytic, and they cannot be a posteriori, since they are necessary. So unless they are based on intuition, furthermore on intuition that is a priori, their synthetic a priori truth is unaccountable. The argument from geometry serves therefore the double function of showing that space is a priori and that it is an intuition.

Evaluating Kant's arguments

To dispute Kant's claim for the intuitivity of space would be to assume the burden of explaining why, despite the unique manner in which space is given to us and the several deep respects in which the representation of space differs from concepts, it is nevertheless better thought of as a concept than an intuition; which would in effect mean taking issue with Kant's original criteria for distinguishing intuitions from concepts. The success of Kant's arguments for the a priority of space is however less straightforward. It may be held that the first and second arguments of the Metaphysical Exposition show that space plays a special, indispensable role for us, and that there is a difficulty, perhaps insuperable, for Leibniz's view of space as a construction, since this implies that outer objects have priority over space; but that Kant's arguments do not establish the priority of the representation of space over that of outer objects and hence its a priority. For, it can be argued, it may be that the outer world is indissolubly bound up with space in such a way that it cannot be experienced without being represented as spatial, just as Kant claims, but that the world and its spatiality are given to us a posteriori at a single stroke: the fact that it is impossible to experience the world without representing it as spatial does not entail that the representation of space is a priori in the sense of not being derived from experience, for there is no contradiction in supposing that experience may present one with that without which experience would not be possible. Nor is there any obvious contradiction in supposing that the representation of space, once formed empirically, may enjoy the sort of independence from the representation of a world of outer objects indicated in Kant's second argument. It is thus, arguably, left open by the Metaphysical Exposition that space and outer objects are, as Strawson puts it, 'contemporaneous', that neither is prior to the other; and Kant may consequently be charged with sliding illicitly from one sense of a priori, 'presupposed for experience', to another, its earlier sense of 'not arising out of experience' (a tendency for Kant to run together the two meanings of the term may seem to be visible at A23–4/B38–9 and A30–1/B46). In the view of some who regard the arguments of the Metaphysical Exposition as, for these reasons, unsuccessful, the burden of argument for the a priority of space in the Aesthetic shifts to the argument from geometry. This has, however, the effect of leading Kant into serious difficulties on account of the altered historical fortunes of Euclidean geometry; the apparently close association of Kant's theory of space with his theory of geometry has indeed led some to claim that the Aesthetic as a whole collapses with the discovery that Euclidean geometry is not true of physical space, and that geometry is therefore not synthetic a priori.

The underlying difficulty is that, for as long as it assumed that space is to be understood as being in the first instance a characteristic of things, the considerations adduced in the Metaphysical Exposition cannot be persuasive, for it will inevitably seem that supposing space to be a priori in Kant's sense makes it mysterious in a way that it is not if we simply suppose that our idea of space somehow derives from how the world is. The arguments of the Metaphysical Exposition regain their force, however, when they are restored to their proper and intended Copernican context.

It may be granted that a direct inference from the necessity of the representation of space for that of outer objects, to its not being derived from experience, would be invalid. But this is just a consequence of the fact that the issue of the *origin* of our representations is logically distinct from that of the *relations of presupposition* between them. The question is why Kant moves from the latter to the former: what justifies Kant's going from the necessity of space for the representation of outer objects to its a priority, his implicit principle of inference that if a representation R is necessary for empirical representation then R is a priori. Kant's justification can be grasped if we return to the problem of reality and consider what view of the origin of the representation of space is coherent in the light of its being presupposed for the representation of outer objects.

The representation of space cannot derive from antecedent experience of the world, because there cannot be any experience of the world without its being already represented as spatial. The suggestion that the representations of space and the outer world arise contemporaneously is however not satisfactory either. The contemporaneity of spatial and outer representation cannot be a sheer coincidence, if our representation of the outer world as spatial is to count as knowledge. It would not be a coincidence, of course, if the contemporaneity of spatial and outer representation were grounded in and appropriately reflected reality. In order for this to be upheld, what would need to be claimed is not just that we represent outer objects spatially because outer reality is spatial, but also that if outer reality were not spatial, then we could and would represent outer objects in whatever other, non-spatial mode was required. That is, it would need to be claimed that whatever sensible form outer reality had possessed, we would have been able to represent it. Otherwise our mode of representation will lack the non-accidental agreement with reality required for knowledge. To suppose that spatial and outer representation are contemporaneous is, therefore, to suppose that our capacity for representation is such that we are able to determine what mode of representation is appropriate to reality in the very act of representing it. Though not contradictory, this supposition is evidently unable to answer the question of how outer objects are possible for us. It simply assumes that they are. The contemporaneity view thus runs headlong into the problem of reality.

No option remains, then, but Kant's view of the representation of space as neither posterior to nor contemporaneous with outer representation, but prior to it – a view which makes it no accident that the outer world is represented spatially, and allows us to claim knowledge of spatial reality, by making spatiality constitutive for us of outer-ness. This notion will become clearer in the next chapter in connection with the doctrine of transcendental idealism.

On this reading, the arguments of the Metaphysical Exposition need to be understood in the broader context of the issues discussed in chapter 2: they refer implicitly to the fundamental question of how representation of an outer world is possible at all, and it is Kant's implicit premise that there must be *some* representation that makes representation of outer objects possible, and which, for that reason, is not derived from experience. As it may also be put, Kant is assuming that something or other must constitute (the form of) outer sense, and that whatever does so cannot be derived from the objects of outer sense (similarly for inner sense and its objects). The two senses of a priori, 'presupposed for experience' and 'not arising out of experience', are therefore quite properly connected.

Kant's arguments about time are largely structural replicas of his arguments about space, with appropriate adjustments made to accommodate the fact that, whereas only outer objects are represented as spatial, all objects of intuition are represented as temporal. Thus Kant argues in the Metaphysical Exposition of Time (§4 of the Aesthetic) that the representation of time is presupposed for the representation of objects as either coexistent or successive, that time can be represented as 'void of appearances', that different times are parts of one and the same time, and that time is infinite in the sense of being given as unlimited. Taking the place of geometry in the argument for the intuitive a priority of time are the principles concerning time, alteration and motion referred to earlier (A31/B47). The critical remarks above concerning space apply, *mutatis mutandis*, to Kant's claim that time is an a priori intuition.

Space and time in the Analytic

The Aesthetic is not by any means Kant's last word on space and time, which figure prominently throughout the *Critique* and Kant's account of which is amplified in the Analytic. Kant's theory of space and time requires supplementation because it is so far incomplete in a fundamental respect. The Aesthetic has described space and time as intuitions, and this is not, according to Kant's theory of cognition, sufficient to account for knowledge of space and time (see A77/B102, B137–8). Thus it does not explain how we can cognise determinate regions of space and stretches of time. In the Transcendental Deduction (B160–1) Kant explains that when space and time are considered as objects of cognition rather than mere forms of sense experience – as 'formal intuitions' rather than 'forms of intuition' – the unity of space and time, which is merely assumed in the Aesthetic (legitimately, given that its task is confined to isolating pure intuition), requires a ground which sensibility cannot itself supply, and which presupposes the complex conceptual machinery described in the Analytic. This ground is supplied by conceptually driven cognitive operations (syntheses) unifying the manifolds of space and time. These establish 'limitations' of all-embracing space and time, by means of which particular spaces and times become possible.

The complexification of the theory of space and time in the Analytic may superficially give the appearance of inconsistency with the Aesthetic. The notion that cognition of space and time presupposes synthesis of a manifold may seem to imply that the wholes of space and time are not, after all, prior to their parts. Also, in the Analytic Kant denies that space and time are in any sense objects of perception, and that they have any sort of existence apart from the empirically intuited spatio-temporal relations of appearances (for which reason empty space and time are uncognisable). The form of experience is thus, on Kant's account, inseparable from its content, just as the content of experience is inseparable from its form: only particular, determinate, object-occupied regions of space and temporal durations are cognisable, and Space and Time themselves are objects for us only in the attenuated sense that they are given as unperceived backgrounds implicated in all empirical intuition by virtue of its form. Connectedly, it is Kant's doctrine that determination of the spaces and times occupied by objects presupposes certain relations (such as causality) among objects, which is suggestive of a relational, reductive theory of space and time of the sort rejected in the Aesthetic.

Consequently, in view of these apparent discrepancies, it is crucial to bear in mind that the Analytic is concerned with the conditions of empirical knowledge and not with space and time *qua* merely intuited: Kant's (consistent) position is that space and time do precede their parts and are irreducible to relations among appearances, but that the indeterminate spatiality and temporality of pure intuition is rendered determinate through being subjected to conceptual synthesis, which necessarily begins with the spatial and temporal positions of appearances. Once again, intuition is required to stand under conceptual conditions in order to make its distinctive, non-conceptual contribution to cognition.

Chapter 5

Transcendental
idealism

Thus far in the Aesthetic Kant has been seen to argue that space and time, unlike anything else in intuition, are presupposed for experience of objects, and so not derived from experience.

As noted in the previous chapter, Kant makes a further and even stronger claim about space and time in the Aesthetic. Right at the beginning of the Aesthetic, he asks:

> What, then, are space and time? Are they real existences? Are they only determinations or relations of things, yet such as would belong to things even if they were not intuited? Or are space and time such that they belong only to the form of intuition, and therefore to the subjective constitution of our mind, apart from which they could not be ascribed to anything whatsoever?
>
> (A23/B37–8)

Of the three views described here, the first is that of Newton, the second that of Leibniz and the third is Kant's own. Newton and Leibniz are opposed on the issue of the substantiality versus reducibility of space and time, but they agree in affirming the *reality* of space and time: for Newton, space and time are themselves 'real existences', and for Leibniz they at least 'belong to things' even when those things are not intuited. Both therefore maintain that space and time are contained in the world independently of the subject's awareness, and that we have representations of space and time because we have knowledge of reality. That is what Kant denies.

Kant's denial appears at first blush to contradict common sense, which thinks of the size and shape of objects, and their position in space and in time, as objective features that inhere in them independently of our experience, in contrast with their colour, smell, taste and so on, which are accepted to be in some sense subjective – in line with Locke's distinction of primary and secondary qualities. In fact, Kant has no quarrel with this picture, so long as it is understood at the level of common sense. The sense in which Kant holds spatial and temporal features to be subjective is very different from, and much more complex than that in which secondary qualities are subjective, and it is intended to be consistent with everything that common sense maintains about the empirical world. Kant formulates it by saying that space and time, and objects with spatial and temporal properties, are *transcendentally ideal*. The first two sections of this chapter aim to explain what Kant means by this claim, and those that follow consider his defence of it.

The doctrine of transcendental idealism

As we saw in chapter 2, the basis of the doctrine of transcendental idealism is the distinction of appearance and thing in itself. When this distinction is introduced in the Preface, it is explained in terms of the Copernican reversal of the relation of the object to our mode of cognition: a thing considered as necessarily conforming to our mode of cognition is an appearance (transcendentally ideal), and a thing to which our cognition must conform is a thing in itself (transcendentally real).

The Aesthetic reworks the distinction of appearance and thing in itself in terms of Kant's theory of sensibility. It now expresses the more definite contrast between things as apprehended through the lens of human sensibility, and things as they may be conceived apart therefrom (A26–7/B42–3). Objects given in human sensibility are appearances (transcendentally ideal), objects considered apart from it are things in themselves (transcendentally real). Now human sensibility, Kant has argued, is distinguished by spatio-temporality: all objects of our intuition are either temporal (inner objects) or spatial and temporal (outer objects). (Henceforth 'spatio-temporal' will be used for convenience to cover both cases.) All spatio-temporal objects are therefore appearances (transcendentally ideal), and since they are the only objects given to us, all objects for us are appearances (transcendentally ideal).

The relation between the two versions of the distinction is straightforward: we move from the broader one in the Preface to the narrower one in the Aesthetic, as soon as it is said that our mode of cognition is constituted by spatio-temporal intuition. The Copernican sense of 'appearance' thus converges on its sense as 'object of empirical intuition', the definition given at A20/B34 in the Aesthetic.

Transcendental ideality and empirical reality: the empirical/transcendental distinction

To explicate transcendental idealism further, it is necessary to introduce Kant's notion of empirical reality, which is an essential component of the doctrine. That the objects of our cognition are transcendentally ideal provides, according to Kant, the basis for the further claim that they are at the same time *empirically real* (A27–8/B43–4, A35–6/B52–3, A42–3/B59–60). Earlier the term empirical was used to contrast with a priori. In this context it contrasts with transcendental. The empirical/transcendental distinction originates with Kant, and is best grasped in terms of different standpoints from which things may be considered in philosophical reflection. Unlike the distinction of objects into sensible and non-sensible (immanent and transcendent), with which it should not be confused, the primary force of the empirical/transcendental distinction is not to distinguish objects into different kinds; the same object may be considered in both empirical and transcendental respects. (Kant will be found talking later of the 'transcendental object' as opposed to empirical objects, but such talk is based on the distinction of transcendental and empirical modes of consideration of objects.)

To consider things in empirical respects is to consider them, as Kant puts it, 'from the human standpoint' (A26/B42), and thus as appearances. The term empirical retains here its original connection with sensation, since the human standpoint is one of being related to objects through sensation. To say that space and time and spatio-temporal objects are empirically real is to say that they are real when considered from the human standpoint. The contrast is with *empirically ideal* objects – 'sense data', mental images, hallucinations and other purely phenomenal entities. The empirical reality of space and time is guaranteed by the fact that they are the forms of human intuition and necessary for us to have any experience of objects at all. The empirical reality of appearances is guaranteed by the fact that space and time are the forms of human sensibility and that appearances are consequently necessarily spatio-temporal: if all objects of human experience must be spatio-temporal, then spatio-temporal objects must indeed be considered real – from our standpoint.

To consider things in transcendental respects is to consider them from the standpoint of enquiry into the conditions under which objects are possible for us (in line with Kant's definitions of 'transcendental', pp. 45–6). The transcendental standpoint differs from the human standpoint in that it considers things *in relation to* our mode of cognition, without considering them merely as they appear to us *through* our mode of cognition, as does common sense. The transcendental standpoint allows the dependence of objects on our mode of cognition to be determined. In order for a thing to be real when considered from the transcendental standpoint, it would need to have its constitution – the constitution that we represent as belonging to it – independently of the human standpoint, and thus without regard to human sensibility. In that case, it would be transcendentally real, a thing in itself. If, on the contrary, the constitution of a thing depends in the relevant way upon human sensibility, or upon any other limitation of the human standpoint, then the thing is transcendentally ideal, an appearance.

The 'relevant way' is one that concerns the bare possibility of objects – transcendental dependence, as opposed to the kind of dependence exhibited by things like rainbows, which are mere appearances when considered empirically (see A45–6/B62–3).

Thus, in order to know things in themselves, it would be necessary to represent things as they are 'by whatever subject intuited or whether they be intuited or not' (A27/B43) – that is, either (1) as they would be given in intuition to any possible subject, or (2) as they are independently from any intuition and thus knowledge of them whatsoever. The objects of our experience would be things in themselves, therefore, if space and time were not merely 'special conditions' of our sensibility but 'conditions of the possibility of things' in general (A27/B43), and we would have reason to think of space and time as 'conditions of the possibility of things' *if* they were known either (1) to be the forms of any possible intuition, or (2) to belong to the independent constitution of things. But Kant maintains that we cannot know this. Therefore:

> What objects may be in themselves, and apart from all this receptivity of our sensibility, remains completely unknown to us. We know nothing but our mode of perceiving them – a mode which is peculiar to us. . . . Even if we could bring our intuition to the highest degree of clearness, we should not thereby come any nearer to the constitution of objects in themselves.
>
> (A42–3/B59–60)

Again, the restriction of our knowledge asserted here cannot be properly understood independently of the way in which it makes room for the notion of empirical reality. Though space and time and the spatio-temporal form of objects are not features of absolute reality, they do enjoy a conditional reality, which derives from the fact that they are necessary for the constitution of any objects of experience whatsoever for us. Though subjective from the transcendental standpoint, they meet in full the conditions of objectivity from the human standpoint. Hence Kant's claim that nothing is taken away from common sense by describing the objects of its knowledge claims as mere appearances: 'This ideality of space and time leaves, however, the certainty of empirical knowledge unaffected, for we are equally sure of it, whether these forms necessarily inhere in things in themselves or only in our intuition of them' (A39/B56). The ocular ('lens') analogy for human sensibility is consequently misleading, in so far as it suggests, first, that some other medium could take the place of human sensibility in giving the same objects, and second, that human sensibility to some degree misrepresents ('colours') objects. On Kant's account, the objects of our spatio-temporal intuition could not be given in any other mode, because they could not exist without our forms of sensibility: 'if the subject . . . be removed, the whole constitution and all the relations of objects in space and time, nay space and time themselves, would vanish' (A42/B59). The constitutive function of human sensibility means that no sense attaches to the notion that sensibility distorts what it presents.

The reality of things when considered from the human standpoint, and their ideality when considered transcendentally, are therefore intimately related: the reason why objects of experience are transcendentally ideal (they cannot be accorded reality independently of the structure of experience) provides the basis of their empirical reality (they are constituted by the structure of experience). Transcendental ideality and empirical reality are correlates.

Some clarifications

Before moving on to draw some comparisons of transcendental idealism with other philosophical positions, a number of points need to be clarified.

First, it is to be emphasised that the transcendental standpoint does not lie outside the human standpoint in the sense of being independent from the latter – in which case it would coincide with the standpoint that transcendent metaphysics seeks to occupy, the non-perspectival standpoint of God. It is, according to Kant, impossible for us to occupy such a standpoint, but there is no need to do so in order to engage in transcendental reflection. Although we cannot step outside the human standpoint, we can move to its edge; using in our reflection only resources available from within it, we can attempt to say something *about* that standpoint, rather than about the world which it presents us with. The transcendental standpoint is thus positioned at the boundary of human knowledge.

Second, the unknowability of things in themselves is not merely a matter of definition or methodology. Although the sense of Kant's claim that things in themselves are unknowable depends, of course, upon the meaning that he has given to the term 'thing in itself', the unknowability of things in themselves does not follow directly from their original Copernican definition. Nor does it follow from the mere concept of the transcendental standpoint that the objects of our cognition are not things in themselves. The definition of things in themselves and concept of transcendental reflection leave it open that we can know things in themselves, for we could have such knowledge *if* we could assume either (1) that objects appear to us as they must be given to any subject, or (2) that human sensibility represents objects as they are constituted anyway. This is important because, if transcendental idealism had simply defined the reality which it says we cannot know as consisting of objects in so far as we cannot know them, it would obviously lack significance. In fact, it is a result achieved on the basis of a metaphysical theory of sensibility, whence its philosophical interest.

Third, it is worth noting that Kant's term a priori has accumulated several different senses in the course of the discussion. It originally meant 'not arising out of experience', and then came to mean also 'presupposed for experience'. It has now incorporated a third sense: 'belonging only to the subjective, transcendental, object-enabling constitution of our mind'. Standardly, when Kant uses the term, he intends it to carry all three senses, which, according to transcendental idealism, are bound up with one another. (The fact that a priori is in Kant such a heavily loaded term makes it of course all the more important, for the purpose of understanding and evaluating his arguments, to separate out the various senses.)

Fourth, included in Kant's claims regarding what cannot be known as a thing in itself is the self: I know myself only through inner sense, thus necessarily in time, and so only as I appear (A37–8/B54–5, B67–9). The non-spatiality of the self and its representations – the fact that they are subject to one form of intuition rather than two – distinguishes them from outer objects, but it does not make them any the less transcendentally ideal. To know myself as a thing in itself, I would need to intuit myself without sensibility, and so would require intellectual intuition.

Kant's ontological claim that the distinction of appearance and thing in itself applies to the self as much as it does to outer objects is connected closely with his opposition to the epistemological view, of Descartes and many others, that the reality of the self is immediately evident in a way in which that of outer objects is not: for Kant, just as the self and outer objects are equally appearances, so our epistemological relation to both is 'the same' (A38/B55). (Kant's argument for the epistemological parity of the outer and the inner will be seen in the next chapter, and the special difficulties involved in his claim that the self is transcendentally ideal will be reviewed in chapter 8.)

Fifth, there is a complication to be added to the picture given of empirical reality. Purely phenomenal entities such as mental images, it was said, are empirically ideal; and yet they are given in time, a form of sensibility, on which account they qualify as empirical real (see A35/B52). So long as Kant agrees that there are or could be purely phenomenal entities, and that empirical ideality and empirical reality are exclusive, this yields an inconsistency.

The situation can be clarified by observing that the notion of empirical ideality figures in Kant's account in two ways. On the one hand, empirical ideality refers to a particular conception of the status of empirical objects *in general*, viz. the conception of 'empirical idealism', which reduces the empirical world as such to mere seeming, in opposition to Kant's own empirical realism (see A361, A491/B519). On the other hand, empirical ideality refers to the status of a *specific sub-class* of empirical objects, namely purely phenomenal objects such as mental images, hallucinations and sensations, and public objects of the same sort, such as mirages and rainbows. The two senses are connected because, Kant believes, to reject empirical realism is to put empirical objects in general on a par with mental images. But they also need to be distinguished. This allows it to be said that purely phenomenal objects such as mental images, though empirically ideal in the second sense, none the less belong to an empirically real, unified spatio-temporal world. As it may be put, they are empirically ideal contents of an empirically real world.

This means that Kant's view of purely phenomenal objects is not quite the same as that of a classical empiricist, for whom the reality of a purely phenomenal object consists in nothing but its bare presence to an individual sensing mind. For Kant, even the most fleeting sensation is essentially temporal, and time has empirical reality. In this sense Kant accords purely phenomenal objects greater reality than does empiricism: he agrees that their *esse* is their *percipi* but has a stronger conception of what the latter involves.

Finally, it is important to emphasise that everything said so far about empirical reality – especially the notion just emphasised, of the unity of the empirical world – looks ahead to the rest of Kant's theory of experience, in relation to which the present stage of enquiry is highly limited. Properly speaking, empirical reality cannot be accorded to objects independently of the conceptual conditions which all objects of cognition are required to satisfy, so that everything said by Kant in the Aesthetic about empirical reality is strictly a simplification; in the full picture, it is the meeting of the conceptual conditions laid down in the Analytic (under which the sensible conditions of the Aesthetic are subsumed) which confers empirical reality on spatio-temporal objects.

Transcendental idealism versus transcendental realism

In sum, transcendental idealism may be defined as the thesis that the objects of our cognition are mere appearances: they are empirically real but transcendentally ideal. To say that they are transcendentally ideal is to say that they do not have in themselves, i.e. independently of our mode of cognition, the constitution which we represent them as having; rather our mode of cognition determines this constitution. Transcendental idealism entails that things cannot be known as they are in themselves.

All other philosophical positions are united in supposing that the objects of our cognition are transcendentally real, i.e. that they have the constitution which we represent them as having independently of (without being determined to do so by) our mode of cognition, and so that things can in principle be known as they are in themselves. Kant calls this claim *transcendental realism*.

Transcendental idealism expresses the Copernican precept that objects are to be considered as necessarily conforming to our mode of cognition; transcendental realism is committed to the pre-Copernican conception of our mode of cognition as conforming to objects. Since all pre-Critical philosophies have presupposed, implicitly or explicitly, that things in themselves can be known, they are all so many different forms of transcendental realism. Kant's intention in the *Critique* is to show, by demonstrating their diametrically opposed implications for the central problems of philosophy, that the deepest distinction to be drawn between philosophical positions is that between transcendental idealism and transcendental realism in its various guises.

The distinctiveness of transcendental idealism

The differences of transcendental idealism from Hume's skeptical empiricism and Leibniz's 'dogmatic' rationalism are straightforward and need no comment, but it will help to now make clear how Kant's doctrine differs from certain other philosophical positions in closer vicinity.

First, transcendental idealism differs from Locke's realism: Kant maintains that objects conceived as substances and in terms of their primary qualities do not comprise independent reality, as Locke supposes. The level that Locke conceives as reality, and as knowable with some difficulty but in principle, is transformed by Kant into mere appearance, and independent reality itself is pushed back out of our grasp.

Second, transcendental idealism differs from Berkeley's idealism. Kant is emphatic that transcendental idealism does not degrade the external world to mere 'illusion', as he charges Berkeley with doing, since it does not say that bodies merely *seem* to be outside me, but that they really *are* outside me (B69). As already noted, by calling outer objects appearances Kant does not mean that external objects are appearances in the ordinary empirical sense in which a mirage or rainbow is a mere appearance. That space and time and spatio-temporal objects, despite not being the way things are in themselves, do not reduce to ideas in our minds, marks a deep difference from Berkeley, who does think that tables and chairs and the space they occupy share the purely phenomenal existence of mental images. Berkeley is, in Kant's terms, an empirical idealist. For Kant, space and time and spatio-temporal objects are not ideal in the empirical sense that applies to the sensible ideas associated with the secondary qualities of objects, pleasure and pain, and purely phenomenal items in general (A28/B45): the sense in which they are 'in the subject' rather than in the object is strictly transcendental (the transcendental sense of 'inside us' is carefully distinguished from the empirical at A373). The transcendental ideality of a representation such as space is marked by the fact that it yields a priori knowledge, which empirically ideal representations do not (A28–9, B44). This reflects its transcendental role, lacked by colour and other purely phenomenal qualities, which do not similarly make outer experience possible. This is why, as observed in chapter 2, Berkeley's idealism, unlike Kant's, extends to the existence of things. Kant's relation to Berkeley involves some complexities, however, and will be re-examined later.

Because Kant's position is not Berkeley's, it is possible for him to uphold Locke's distinction of primary and secondary qualities: describing the empirical realm as a whole as appearance is consistent with drawing a distinction within it between properties of objects that are dependent on the subject to different degrees or in different ways (B69–70). Kant agrees that primary qualities have greater (empirical) reality than secondary qualities (*Proleg* 289): the primary/secondary quality distinction may be 'merely empirical' (A45/B62), but it is none the less genuine. Kant consequently affirms that, in one sense, the senses represent 'objects *as they appear*' and the understanding objects '*as they are*' (A258/B313–14), corresponding to Locke's distinction between objects represented with and without their secondary qualities. But knowledge through the intellect of reality as opposed to appearance in this empirical, non-transcendental sense does not, of course, imply knowledge of things in themselves.

Locke's distinction of primary and secondary qualities may also serve, Kant suggests, as a partial analogy for the distinction of things in themselves and appearances: the grounds for Kant's description of empirical objects as appearances bear some analogy to Locke's widely accepted reasons for describing secondary qualities as subjective. The subject-dependence of Kantian appearances does not, any more than that of secondary qualities, entail illusoriness – it is no more an illusion that appearances exist than that things have colours (B70n, *Proleg* 289). The analogy also enables Kant to compare the mistaking of appearances for things in themselves to the mistaking of a secondary for a primary quality (B70n).

Third, transcendental idealism is distinct from skepticism. It agrees with skepticism in so far as both positions deny that absolute reality is known to us, but the transcendental idealist's reasons for saying this are not the skeptic's. Skepticism thrives on the bare conceptual *possibility* of the objects of our knowledge being things in themselves, which it says we lack justification for supposing to be fulfilled. It assumes knowledge of things in themselves to be a metaphysical possibility for us, whilst denying its epistemic actuality. Kant, however, does not merely cast doubt on but actually forecloses this possibility: his doctrine of the unknowability of things in themselves is not an expression of uncertainty regarding our epistemological capacities. For Kant it is not doubtful but *certain* that things in themselves cannot become objects for us: knowledge of things in themselves is for us a metaphysical impossibility. Thus the boundary of knowledge – the division between what can and cannot be known – is itself known very definitely. The anti-skeptical force of transcendental idealism – which differs from the sort of rebuttal of skepticism which we are trained to expect – will be discussed in the next chapter.

Several important questions about transcendental idealism remain. One is the exact nature of Kantian appearance: despite all that has been said regarding Kant's differences from Berkeley, it may seem left open that appearances are mental things, albeit of a complex sort. Another is the existence of things in themselves, regarding which Kant has so far expressed no commitment either way. Yet another concerns the relation of appearances to things in themselves: Kant would seem to have spoken of appearances and things in themselves ambiguously, both as two different sets of objects and as one set of objects considered in two different ways. These three questions will be taken up in chapter 8.

Kant's ontological denial

Transcendental idealism has been presented as a doctrine about the status of the objects of our cognition, and as saying about things in themselves simply that we can have no knowledge of them. There is, however, a further aspect to Kant's conception of the doctrine. The full strength of Kant's transcendental idealism is grasped only when it is appreciated that Kant maintains not just that we *cannot* know that things in themselves *are* spatio-temporal, but that we *can* know that they are *not* spatio-temporal. This claim was visible at the beginning of the chapter: it is implied directly by the passage from A23/B37–8 quoted above (p. 87), where Kant indicates that space and time belong *only* to the form of intuition and *could not* be ascribed to anything apart from the subjective constitution of our mind. (Kant makes the point entirely explicit again at A26–8/B42–4 and A30/B45.)

In other words, according to Kant, we can know that reality in an absolute, unqualified sense does not correspond to the spatio-temporal world that we experience. It would seem that Kant reasons as follows: because space and time cannot amount to anything more than forms of our sensibility – because things can be spatio-temporal only under the limitation of the human standpoint – it is impossible for space and time to also be the way that things are in themselves; because it is impossible for things in themselves to *be* spatio-temporal, we can *know* that they are *not*. (This point can stand whether or not things in themselves actually exist, a matter on which, as remarked, Kant remains silent in the Aesthetic; as it may be put, according to Kant we know that *if* things in themselves exist, then they are not spatio-temporal.)

This may seem puzzling: Kant tells us that things in themselves are unknowable, but also that we can know that they are not spatio-temporal. Do we not then have knowledge of things in themselves after all?

The appearance of contradiction is removed by drawing a distinction between contentless negative knowledge, and contentful positive knowledge. Kant's claim is that we cannot have contentful positive knowledge of things in themselves, since they cannot become objects for us; but we can have negative contentless knowledge of them, given the result that space and time are only forms of sensibility.

Though Kant's position is not contradictory, evidently it generates a question: is Kant entitled to the crucial claim that space and time are *only* forms of sensibility?

To attempt to decide this question we need to look at Kant's arguments for transcendental idealism, but before entering discussion of them, it is essential to be quite clear about what is required to answer the question and how matters stand in general with transcendental idealism.

Up until now, transcendental idealism has been equated with a thesis exclusively about the objects of our cognition. The stronger conception of transcendental idealism maintained by Kant includes an additional thesis, consisting of a negative ontological claim about objects outside the scope of our cognition. Corresponding to each version of transcendental idealism are, consequently, different argumentative requirements. To establish transcendental idealism in its weaker version, it will suffice for Kant to show that the epistemology of space and time – our knowledge of our representations of space and time – gives us reason to conclude only that they are forms of sensibility. If Kant can do this, then he will have shown that we cannot know things in themselves to be spatio-temporal. He will also have shown – assuming the principle that knowledge that p presupposes at least the possibility of knowing that one knows that p (which rests upon the idea that knowledge is something which it must be possible for a subject to take itself to have) – that even if things in themselves are spatio-temporal, then we have no knowledge of them, i.e. that things in themselves, whatever their constitution, are not objects of our knowledge.

This will not suffice, however, to show that things in themselves cannot *be* spatio-temporal. To establish the stronger version of transcendental idealism, further argument is required, and only if it can be provided will Kant's ontological denial go through. If not, then the most Kant is entitled to is agnosticism regarding the spatio-temporality of things in themselves, and only the weaker version of transcendental idealism will have been established.

Kant does not distinguish explicitly between the weaker and the stronger versions of transcendental idealism, but it is important to do so in considering his arguments for the doctrine. As will be suggested in the next section, the Aesthetic makes a powerful case for the weaker version of transcendental idealism. The section that follows will show the stronger version to be considerably more problematic.

The argument for transcendental idealism in the Aesthetic

Arguably some slight reason for regarding space and time as transcendentally ideal has already been given: we have, Kant pointed out, no reason to think that our form of sensibility is the only one, and can in some manner conceive of intellectual intuition. But nothing of transcendental idealism is yet proven, for it *may* be that reality is spatio-temporal and that our pure intuitions of space and time are what allow us to represent it.

The four salient arguments

Four arguments in the Aesthetic for the transcendental ideality of space and time jump to the eye. The first of these, and the one that has received most comment, is the argument from geometry (A46–9/B64–6). Geometry figures now in the argument of the Aesthetic for the third time. Kant argues that it shows space and outer objects to be transcendentally ideal. Geometry tells us not just what the spatial properties of the objects of our experience happen to be, but what they *must* be – seeing two straight lines enclose a space, for example, is not a possible experience for us. Now if the objects described by geometry were things in themselves, then they would have their geometrical properties not by virtue of our sensibility but by virtue of how they are independently of us, and Kant asks what, in that case, could explain how we can know that *necessarily* two straight lines cannot enclose a space: because necessities inhering in things in themselves cannot simply migrate into our minds, we can only come to know them through some sort of contact with things in themselves, i.e. through experience; but Kant, like Hume, holds that experience cannot provide us with knowledge of necessity. All that experience could entitle us to say, therefore, is that no pair of straight lines enclosing a space has yet been perceived, warranting a merely inductive judgement with comparative rather than strict universality, and leaving it open that one day a pair of straight lines will indeed be seen to enclose a space.

Since the truths of geometry would be contingent if they were truths about objects constituted independently of our mode of cognition (things in themselves), Kant infers that they must be truths about objects whose constitution derives from our mode of cognition (appearances). Their necessity can be accounted for on the basis that space is a subjective condition of intuition, because this, and this alone, is able to explain how we can know them a priori and thus as necessary. The objects of geometry – objects in space – must therefore be regarded as having no reality in abstraction from the subjective conditions of our intuition: they are transcendentally ideal.

According to a second argument, the result of regarding space and time as 'properties which, if they are to be possible at all, must be found in things in themselves', is to transform everything in our experience into 'mere *illusion*' (B70–1; see also *Proleg* 291). That is, if we take the transcendental realist view of space and time as absolutely real objects, then we are obliged to suppose that our cognitive powers are capable of knowing two infinite and yet non-substantial things, and this, Kant thinks, is an absurdity which will drive us to Berkeley's conclusion that the concepts of space and time really refer to what is given immediately in experience, namely mere seemings. Thus transcendental realism destroys empirical reality.

The third argument says that space and time consist in nothing but relations, and that things in themselves cannot be constitutionally merely relational, from which it follows that space and time, and spatio-temporal objects, cannot be things in themselves (B66–8).

The fourth argument has to do with theology (B71–2). Kant argues that if God is to be at least conceivable (whether or not God exists), then space and time must be regarded as transcendentally ideal; for if they were transcendentally real, they would be conditions of God's existence, which would make it impossible for God (whose intuition is non-sensible) to know himself, contradicting the concept of God as an omniscient being. Spatio-temporal reality needs to be conceived as transcendentally ideal in order for the concept of God to be coherent.

The second argument is conditional: it says that *if* we wish to avoid reducing empirical reality to mere seeming, then space and time must be regarded as transcendentally ideal. But it relies on the premise that it is absurd to credit ourselves with knowledge of infinite, non-substantial entities, a supposition about the limits of epistemic powers which is, though not implausible, certainly disputable, and not supported by Kant; so its strength remains uncertain.

The third and fourth arguments rest upon premises – that things in themselves cannot consist in relations, and that the concept of God is coherent – which are evidently contentious and which it would hardly be appropriate for Kant to attempt to defend at this point in the *Critique*; Kant himself seems to intend them as only confirmatory.

A problem with geometry

The view most commonly taken is that only the argument from geometry has a chance of succeeding. It is, however, quickly pointed out that, even if Kant is justified in claiming that transcendental realism is incompatible with the necessity of geometry, developments in geometry have undermined the argument's premises: as noted in chapter 4, modern physics shows that Euclidean geometry, though approximately true, is strictly false, the correct description of space being given by non-Euclidean geometries, and because it is therefore an empirical question what geometry best fits physical space, Kant is wrong to suppose that geometry is a priori and necessary – it is in fact a posteriori and contingent.

Before considering whether the Aesthetic has any other way of establishing transcendental idealism, it needs to be shown that transcendental idealism does not *imply* that space is necessarily Euclidean, a commitment which would obviously cause it great embarrassment. Transcendental idealism can be freed from any such implication by distinguishing two different concepts of space: the transcendental concept of space, and the concept of the space which comprises outer empirical reality. The former is the representation of space which Kant has argued to be an a priori intuition and tran-scendentally ideal, and it is indeterminate. The latter is determinate, and the properties of space in this sense, which is what geometry studies, can be known only a posteriori. Since spatial form *qua* indeterminate transcendental representation is all that a priori enquiry is concerned with, the Aesthetic cannot be committed to Euclidean geometry: all that may be upheld regarding geometry on the basis of the Aesthetic is that Euclidean (and any other) geometry presupposes space *qua* transcendental representation.

A different argument

Even if the Aesthetic's case for the transcendental ideality of space survives the falsification of Euclidean geometry, it nevertheless collapses if all of the weight falls on the argument from geometry, for the reason just seen: if Euclidean geometry is not necessarily true, then it cannot provide the premise of a sound argument for transcendental idealism, whatever the argument's validity. The question, then, is whether there is anything more to the case for transcendental idealism in the Aesthetic than the four salient arguments just discussed.

An argument for the doctrine, one which is independent of any assumptions about geometry, can be found in the Metaphysical Expositions of space and time. It is, reflection reveals, a short step from the a priority of space and time to their transcendental ideality. If space and time are a priori representations, they cannot be conceived as *also* giving us knowledge of the way that things are in themselves, because representations of things in themselves cannot be a priori. This follows from the concept of a thing in itself as a thing to which our mode of cognition must conform: for subjects such as ourselves, whose intuition is sensible, such conformity can only take place a posteriori, and for us all a posteriori representation is empirical. Thus Kant says that 'a determination or order inhering in things themselves . . . could not precede the objects as their condition, and be known and intuited a priori' (A33/B49), implying that if things in themselves were spatio-temporal, their spatio-temporality could not be known a priori; and that 'no determination . . . [of objects] can be intuited prior to the existence of the things to which they belong' (A26/B42), implying that in order to know that things in themselves were spatio-temporal, it would be necessary to intuit them, which would make space and time a posteriori representations.

The underlying argument for transcendental idealism in the Aesthetic, expressed in the most general terms, is therefore:

1 It must be explained how objects are possible for us.
2 Transcendental realism cannot explain how objects are possible for us.
3 The possibility of objects for us is explained by supposing that we have a priori representations that constitute objects.
4 The possibility of objects for us requires that they be conceived as transcendentally ideal.

A passage confirming this interpretation appears in the *Prolegomena* §14, where Kant makes it plain that he regards *any* kind of knowledge of things in themselves, not just knowledge of their necessary properties, as impossible for us:

> Should nature signify the existence of things in themselves, we could never cognize it either a priori or a posteriori. Not a priori, for how can we know what belongs to things in themselves, since this never can be done by the dissection of our concepts (in analytic judgements)? . . . A cognition of the nature of things in themselves a posteriori would be equally impossible. For if experience is to teach us laws to which the existence of things is subject, these laws, if they refer to things in themselves, would have to refer to them of necessity even outside our experience. But experience teaches us what exists and how it exists, but never that it must necessarily exist so and not otherwise. Experience therefore can never teach us the nature of things in themselves.

Things in themselves are things constituted independently of our experience, to which our cognition must conform, and to have knowledge of them is to have knowledge of their natures or constitutions. Knowledge of a thing in itself is thus knowledge of how a thing 'must necessarily exist', in the sense that it is knowledge of how the thing is independently of the possibility of its appearing to us; in contrast with knowledge of appearances, which has no implications for the constitution of anything outside our experience. Such knowledge cannot come through concepts alone, since analytic judgements, which are all that concepts alone suffice for, do not yield any knowledge of objects. And experience cannot give us knowledge of the constitution of a thing conceived as independent from our mode of cognition: it can give us knowledge of the constitution of a thing only if it is conceived as a Copernican object, i.e. within a transcendental framework that refers to our subjectivity to explain how the object can have a constitution represented by us. So if we are to claim knowledge of empirical objects, then these, being things whose constitutions we claim to know, cannot be things in themselves.

Kant's reason for making necessity the criterion of a priority is therefore, at the deepest level, that the necessity of some feature of objects signals a respect in which they conform to the structure of experience – since, without that feature, the object could not figure in the structure of experience and so would not be possible at all – and hence qualifies as an a priori feature. Necessity therefore entails being not derived from experience, not just for Hume's reason that necessity cannot be sensed, but because we know independently that there must be elements in our cognition of objects, reflected in features of the objects cognised, that are a priori, and that such elements will show up as necessary features of objects: necessity allows itself to be interpreted as a 'marker' of transcendental status. The connection between necessity and a priority is thus mediated by Kant's general conception of what is needed to solve the problem of reality.

This casts a new light on two other arguments examined earlier. First, we can now see the force of the 'illusion' argument for transcendental idealism. Kant can now be seen to be arguing that, if we do not take the view that space and time are the forms of outer and inner sense, and therefore a priori and transcendentally ideal, then we have no answer to the question of how representation of objects beyond the contents of our own minds is possible; in which case, Berkeley is justified in declaring that such representation is not possible and inferring that all that exists is mere seeming. The crux of the argument is, therefore, the general illegitimacy of supposing that objects can be given to us without some account of how this is possible. Second, the argument from geometry may now be regarded as a special application of Kant's general argument for transcendental idealism: geometry, for Kant, specifies the structure of our experience of outer objects determinately, in terms of their conformity to the laws of geometry rather than in terms of their mere indeterminate spatiality, and like any other element of the structure of experience, it must be grounded in the subject's cognitive constitution. Thus, had Kant's assumption of the necessary truth of Euclidean geometry been correct, the argument from geometry would have succeeded. The key to the success of the Aesthetic as a whole, however, lies not in any specific theory of geometry but in the short but pregnant paragraph which attempts to prove the a priority of space. This – when read against the background described in chapter 2 – allows Kant to defend simultaneously his inferences to the a priority and transcendental ideality of space.

Trendelenburg's alternative

There is a famous objection to Kant, often referred to as the 'neglected alternative', and associated historically with Adolf Trendelenburg, who wrote (in 1862):

> even if we concede the argument that space and time are demonstrated to be subjective conditions which, in us, precede perception and experience, there is still no word of proof to show that they cannot at the same time be objective forms.

According to Trendelenburg, Kant has been supposing that space and time are *either* forms of sensibility *or* real existences, but another alternative is that they are *both*: Kant does not rule this out, because even if he is right that space and time are subjective and a priori, still he has no grounds for saying that they cannot also be the way that things really are; his exclusion of this possibility is dogmatic and un-Critical.

Note that all that is at issue here is the mere conceptual *possibility* that space and time both belong to our subjective constitution and characterise things in themselves. Regarding the connection, if there is one, between these two facts, nothing is said. For this reason Trendelenburg's alternative is not equivalent to transcendental realism, since transcendental realism is the thesis that things can be *known* as they are in themselves, for which it is precisely necessary that the two facts be connected (the independent constitution of things must provide the *explanation* of our representing them as having that constitution).

Trendelenburg's alternative does not, therefore, contradict transcendental idealism, understood as a thesis exclusively about the objects of our cognition. What it does contradict is Kant's ontological denial, his claim that things in themselves cannot *be* spatio-temporal. If Trendelenburg's alternative is cogent, then, although Kant's arguments may show that space and time function as forms of sensibility, and that it is because they do so that the objects of experience are spatio-temporal, they do not show that space and time are forms of sensibility in a sense that *precludes* their also being forms of things in themselves. Trendelenburg's alternative thus highlights the difference between the weaker and the stronger versions of transcendental idealism, and provides us with an opportunity to consider how close Kant may get to establishing the latter. This is what is at stake in Trendelenburg's objection.

As said earlier, it is not sufficient for the purpose of Kant's ontological denial merely to show something about our representations of space and time: even if the epistemology of space and time leads us to conclude only that they are forms of sensibility, the residual, non-epistemic possibility that things in themselves are spatio-temporal remains. Now it should be clear that everything seen so far in the Aesthetic's argument for transcendental idealism which can be regarded as successful concerns our representations of space and time: the only arguments examined with logical bearing on Kant's ontological denial are the arguments from relations and from theology (p. 102), neither of which, it was suggested, can be judged successful. Is there, then, any way of advancing from the weaker version of transcendental idealism to the stronger?

The central issue is the intelligibility of the identity envisaged on Trendelenburg's alternative. Trendelenburg grants that space and time are subjective conditions. Now whether a subjective condition can also be an objective form depends on how 'subjective condition' is understood. If a subjective condition is just a presupposition for the representation of objects – a condition of no particular sort on how objects must be represented in order that they can be known – then there is no incoherence in identifying a subjective condition with an objective form. Subjective conditions in this indeterminate sense obviously do not preclude objective forms. Kant, however, takes 'subjective condition' to mean something more definite. He identifies subjective conditions with representations that constitute the form of their objects, and believes he has shown that space and time need to be conceived in this way, if they are admitted to be presuppositions of experience. Granted this sense of subjective condition, Kant may deny the coherence of supposing that something could be both a subjective condition and an objective form, on the grounds that a way in which objects are *brought to appear* could not also be a way in which they are *constituted in themselves*. The two statuses are completely heterogeneous. The one is a mode in which the subject makes objects possible for itself – a subjective function or 'sense', in Kant's terminology – and the other a way in which things are constituted independently of any subject. Kant may add that the only way in which space and time can be described as both subjective conditions and objective forms is the one which he himself affirms: namely on the condition that the 'objective form' of objects is understood as *derived* from the subject's form of representation, i.e. if the objects in question are conceived as transcendentally ideal; which is to conceive space and time as 'objective forms' of objects in an *empirical* sense.

This is not enough to vindicate Kant's ontological denial. Let it be granted that space and time *qua* forms of sensibility cannot be the very same thing as space and time *qua* forms of things in themselves. It still seems coherent to suppose that things in themselves may be 'isomorphic' and 'share a form' with appearances. And this shared form, it may be added, has at least a partial claim to the title 'spatio-temporal'. So all that has been shown is that things in themselves cannot be spatio-temporal in exactly the same (specific) sense as appearances; it has not been shown that there cannot be a (generic) sense in which both are spatio-temporal. We seem to have come full circle.

Kant considers the 'shared form' possibility explicitly in the *Prolegomena*. In response he appeals to the sensible character of space and time. He claims that the supposition that spatio-temporal appearances formally resemble non-spatio-temporal things in themselves is as lacking in meaning as the idea that 'the sensation of red has a similarity to the property of cinnabar which excites this sensation in me' (*Proleg* 290). In amplification of Kant's remark, the following might be said: Given that space and time are sensible intuitions, what can be 'like space' or 'like time' but space and time themselves? Other forms of sensibility, perhaps, but they are not what is in question here. Spatio-temporal form consists in relations such as adjacency and succession. If these are missing from things in themselves, nothing is left to constitute a resemblance. How, for example, could a relation that was non-temporal 'resemble' the relation of succession? The hypothesised resemblance is not a possibility that we can coherently formulate on the basis of our representation of time.

Kant's underlying point is that we cannot entertain comparisons of the forms of our sensibility with other, non-sensible forms, because we cannot stand outside our mode of cognition: we have no notion of what our sensibility is, except in terms of the world of objects of experience that it makes possible for us; we cannot objectify our intuitive cognitive powers in a way that transcends the conditions under which we can recognise them as ours. Our knowledge of space and time is perspectival knowledge from their own inside: we can know our sensibility 'completely, but always only under the conditions of space and time' (A43/B60). Since we cannot conceive our sensibility as having a constitution in itself, we can conceive space and time only as forms of sensibility: so it makes no sense for us to suppose that something non-sensible could be like space and time, nor that something could be left of space and time if our sensibility were subtracted.

Whatever its force, all this remains far from decisive. Everything that has just been said concerns what *we* can achieve cognitively with respect to space and time. But the question is whether this exhausts what *can* be achieved cognitively – e.g. by God – with respect to space and time. We can only know these to be the same if we can know from the inside of our representations of space and time that there is nothing more to be known about them, i.e. that they have no outside, no non-perspectival existence, no constitution in themselves. Can we know this?

Kant may argue that we can, on the grounds that space and time are intuitive representations. As such, he may say, their content is exhausted in the pre-conceptual relation that they establish between subject and object; so it makes no sense to suppose that they can be objectified in the way required by Trendelenburg.

This is the most that Kant can say. But it is still open to doubt that Kant has not again begged the question. The by now familiar objection returns: can we in fact know that the content of our intuitive representations is exhausted in the perspective that we have on them? It would seem that every attempt Kant may make to draw an ontological conclusion about things in themselves can be reduced to a conclusion about our representations, leaving Trendelenburg's alternative logically intact.

Though the discussion has not been brought to a conclusion – we cannot be sure one way or the other about the intelligibility of Trendelenburg's alternative – it does suggest that Kant's ontological denial is not provable. All the same, Kant's position looks better than it did at the outset. To the extent that the identity presupposed by Trendelenburg no longer seems straightforward, the logical gap between the weaker and the stronger versions of transcendental idealism is reduced; and because there is less of a deficit in Kant's argument than originally appeared, it is at least now intelligible that Kant should have regarded his proof of transcendental idealism from our representations of space and time as entailing his ontological denial.

Even if transcendental idealism is not provable in its stronger version, no loss attaches to the shortfall. As will be seen, nothing that is to come later, in either the *Critique* or the rest of Kant's Critical system, is affected by the failure to establish conclusively Kant's ontological denial. Transcendental idealism remains a philosophical position without parallel. It may even be argued that the weaker version is the more consistently Critical, since it makes the veil of ignorance separating us from things in themselves – our agnosticism – complete. And it is clear that Trendelenburg's alternative is without philosophical significance. From the point of view of our cognition, the hypothesised double status of space and time – which we cannot even be sure is a genuine possibility – can only be a bare coincidence: for us it is inconceivable that there should be any connection between the spatiotemporality of appearances and that of things in themselves.

The argument for transcendental idealism in the Antinomy

As noted earlier, Kant tells us in the Preface (Bxx) that he has a second, wholly independent proof of transcendental idealism to offer, in the Antinomy of Pure Reason. Kant himself put great weight on this proof: he reports in a letter (to Christian Garve, 21 September 1798) that the antinomies were what first awoke him from his 'dogmatic slumbers' and drove him to 'the critique of reason itself in order to end the scandal of reason's ostensible contradictions with itself'. This argument will be explained in detail in chapter 7, but it is worth saying here something about its place in Kant's overall case for transcendental idealism.

The Antinomy goes right back to the wars of reason which Kant referred to in launching the Critical enterprise. Kant's argument, very briefly, is that the contradictions of transcendent metaphysics are logically unavoidable from the standpoint of transcendental realism. The specific contradictions that he has in mind concern the spatiotemporality and other essential features of the empirical world. To take the first of the four that Kant examines: Kant argues that if we suppose space and time to characterise things in themselves, then we are committed to affirming *both* that the world is unlimited in space and time past *and* that it is limited in space and has a beginning in time. Now this is a *reductio ad absurdum*: whatever entails a contradiction must be false. By inferring the falsity of transcendental realism, we have a proof of transcendental idealism. Indeed, transcendental idealism in its stronger form would be proven, for the argument, if successful, would show that it is impossible for things in themselves to be characterised by space and time.

In order for the overall argument to succeed, Kant needs to show that the contradictions he alleges are genuinely inescapable on the assumption that the empirical world is a realm of things in themselves, and on this front he has been sharply criticised. The grounds for the widespread negative estimate of Kant's attempts to derive contradictions from transcendental realism will be described in chapter 7. Here it may be considered what may be said in Kant's favour on the assumption that he does, as is generally believed, fail to score a clean victory.

If transcendental realism is not shown strictly to entail any contradiction, then Kant fails to deliver it the *coup de grâce* he intends. Nevertheless, so long as the Antinomy remains convincing as a demonstration that there are at any rate systematic tensions in metaphysical speculation which can be traced back to the underlying assumption of transcendental realism, i.e. that a peculiarly symmetrical pattern of oppositions inhabits the transcendental realist's picture of the world, Kant will have created at least a presumption against it. And the Antinomy will have succeeded in showing that tensions are germane to transcendental realism, if it shows that they are not due to contingent errors in the history of philosophy, but products of the endeavour to know reality as it is in itself. If Kant can also show that whereas the transcendental realist must engage in *ad hoc* manoeuvring in order that these tensions should not turn into contradictions, i.e. has no unitary and independently motivated way of dealing with them, transcendental idealism straightforwardly releases us from them, then he may claim that transcendental idealism surpasses transcendental realism with regard to its power of solving philosophical problems. This is to place a burden on Kant's exposition of the implications of his doctrine, but it is certainly a challenge he believes it can meet.

Evidently there are limits to how far Kant can get by playing up the virtues of transcendental idealism in this way, since the transcendental realist will dispute the value of achieving putative solutions to philosophical problems at the cost of giving up all claims to knowledge of Reality, and may counter that all that the Antinomy shows is that there is something puzzling, perhaps inexplicably so, about our cognitive relation to the world. All the same, it is not nothing to show that the wars of reason are a non-accidental consequence of transcendental realism, and on that basis the Antinomy may be held to make an independent contribution to the case for transcendental idealism. For instance, someone who regards the case for transcendental idealism in the Aesthetic as significant but inconclusive – or who finds its specific arguments about space and time unpersuasive, but accepts that the problem of reality constitutes a deep objection to transcendental realism – might plausibly regard the Antinomy as tipping the balance in Kant's favour. In chapter 7 this view of the Antinomy will be defended.

Chapter 6

The conceptual conditions of objects (The Analytic)

The argument of the Analytic: questions of method

By the end of the Aesthetic, the sensible form of experience has been analysed, and transcendental idealism has been established, but a positive account of knowledge has yet to be given. To describe the conditions for objects to be sensed is not to show that objects can be *thought*; so although the Aesthetic provides an account of how objects are intuited, it does not establish their givenness in a *cognitive* sense. It is the job of the Analytic to show, through an account of the faculty of understanding, how objects of intuition, and space and time themselves, become objects of thought, and thus how empirical knowledge is possible.

The Analytic accordingly does for thought what the Aesthetic does for intuition: it uncovers the conceptual components of the structure of experience. Its task proves, however, much more complicated than that of the Aesthetic, for reasons that are already visible. In the first place, the Analytic cannot proceed by taking

115

for granted any given set of concepts in the way that the Aesthetic can help itself to the given spatio-temporal character of experience, since none is free from the suspicion cast by (Humean) skepticism. The Analytic must therefore *justify* concepts in a sense which does not apply to space and time. Furthermore, the Analytic needs to explain the connection between the conceptual and the sensible components of the structure of experience, a task of which there is no analogue in the Aesthetic, since intuition is not added onto any other, previously established level of cognition.

The composition of the Analytic in summary

The course of the Analytic may be summarised, and its principal sections identified, as follows. Before the 'Transcendental Analytic' proper begins, Kant explains his 'Idea of a Transcendental Logic'. This notion was referred to briefly in chapter 3. So far as the Analytic is concerned, transcendental logic is the theory of the conditions under which judgements can express truths about objects. The Analytic is then divided into an 'Analytic of Concepts' and 'Analytic of Principles'. (This, like many of Kant's textual distinctions, has an architectonic rationale, but does not help to display his argument.) In the first chapter of the Analytic of Concepts, entitled 'The Clue to the Discovery of all Pure Concepts of the Understanding', generally known as the metaphysical deduction, Kant argues that a particular set of (twelve) concepts is privileged. These 'pure concepts of the understanding' or 'categories' are a priori, employed in all judgement, and provide the basis for the formation of all other, empirical concepts. The question arises whether we can know these categories to have justified application to what we intuit. This is what 'The Deduction of the Pure Concepts of Understanding', or Transcendental Deduction, is meant to prove. Here Kant develops an account of self-consciousness – the 'transcendental unity of apperception' – as the fundamental condition of cognition. Self-consciousness presupposes, Kant argues, 'a priori synthesis' of the data of intuition in accordance with the categories, whereby their application to appearances is justified.

The Analytic of Principles follows. In its first, short chapter, 'The Schematism of the Pure Concepts of Understanding', Kant argues that the categories require modification – they need to be 'schematised' – in order for them to become applicable to objects of temporal intuition. The rest of the Analytic of Principles, 'The System of the Principles of Pure Understanding', is divided into four parts, which comprise about half the text of the Analytic: 'Axioms of Intuition', 'Anticipations of Perception', 'Analogies of Experience' and 'The Postulates of Empirical Thought in general'. Each argues for the necessity of a particular sub-set of the categories or, more precisely, of principles for their employment. The most important is the Analogies, where Kant argues, against Hume, that our experience must take the form of causally interacting substances. Buried away in the Postulates is a short but highly important section, inserted by Kant in the second edition, called the 'Refutation of Idealism'. This attempts to prove the incoherence of skepticism about the external world (the idealism referred to in the title is not, of course, transcendental idealism). Set apart from the main argument of the Analytic, the final chapter, 'The Ground of the Distinction of all Objects in general into Phenomena and Noumena', and the appendix to the Analytic, 'The Amphiboly of Concepts of Reflection', draw out the negative, restrictive implications of the preceding analysis of knowledge.

Difficulties posed by the Analytic

This summary, which sticks to Kant's descriptions of the tasks of individual sections, conceals a number of difficulties that arise in attempting to understand the Analytic. A basic difficulty concerns the distribution of its argument between the different sections of the text. There is much apparent overlap, and it is on many occasions desperately unclear whether earlier and later sections are related as successive steps in a single argument or as reworkings in different terms of previously established results. There is room for wondering whether the metaphysical deduction and Transcendental Deduction are both necessary (or really distinct), whether the Schematism is a genuinely essential part of the argument, and what the Refutation of Idealism is supposed to add to the Deduction and Analogies. The exact point in the Analytic at which the existence of the objective, commonsense empirical world is supposed to have been secured, is consequently a matter of dispute.

More deeply, the Analytic gives rise to puzzles concerning its philosophical method. First, a problem arises concerning the relation of the arguments in the Analytic to transcendental idealism. It is not unreasonable to think that the Analytic is meant to amount to a further proof of transcendental idealism, this time on the basis of concepts. Thus Kant may be regarded as arguing, in the first place, that principles such as that every event must have a cause are necessary truths so far as our experience is concerned, and then inferring the transcendental ideality of objects subject to such principles, on the grounds that necessities of experience are explicable only on the supposition that they derive from our mode of cognition.

The problem with this, as many commentators underline, is that Kant does not give reason for thinking that concepts are on a par with sensible forms with respect to subjectivity: on his own account, the fundamental concepts employed in empirical knowledge (the categories) are concepts of, as he puts it, 'objects in general', not specifically of objects for us. This makes it mysterious how the Analytic's demonstration that such and such concepts are necessary for experience could be held to show that the objects of experience are not in themselves characterised by those concepts. The theory of experience contained in the Analytic can, moreover, as Kant's analytic interpreters again emphasise, be made to seem quite independent of idealist metaphysics: all of Kant's proofs of necessities of experience, it is held, can simply be read as telling us about our conceptual scheme, and about what reality must be like in order for us to be able to experience it. If so, the *Critique* is not the unified work it is presented as, and we should conclude that Kant confuses two quite distinct epistemological strategies, transcendental idealism on the one hand, and metaphysically neutral transcendental argumentation on the other.

Second, there is a fundamental uncertainty concerning the direction in which the whole argument is meant to proceed. It is clear that the Analytic aims to vindicate the commonsense picture of an objective world composed of public external objects, characterised in terms of the concepts of substance and causality. It is, therefore, meant to bear on skepticism, specifically Hume's. What is not clear is whether knowledge of an objective empirical world is something the necessity of which Kant is trying to prove from scratch, or whether he is instead assuming provisionally the validity of ordinary empirical knowledge claims, and merely seeking to show through analysis what their presuppositions are, and that these are free from contradiction. Kant is well aware of this distinction: as we saw in chapter 3 (pp. 59–60), he calls the first sort of method (which starts from a priori principles and goes in the direction of a posteriori knowledge) 'synthetical' or progressive, and the second (which goes from bodies of a posteriori judgement to their a priori presuppositions) 'analytical' or regressive. But he does not tell us explicitly in which way the Analytic should be read. This is, however, a highly important matter, since each method yields a different strength of conclusion. The synthetical method entitles Kant to unconditional conclusions ('our experience *must* be causally ordered'), whereas the analytical method secures only conditionals ('*if* our criteria for objective empirical knowledge are to be fulfilled, then our experience must be causally ordered'). Reading the Analytic in the first, progressive way allows it to be claimed that Kant shows that we can and must have (e.g. causally ordered) experience and objective empirical knowledge; reading it in the second, regressive way would allow us to say only that Kant shows what is presupposed by our ordinary claims to objective empirical knowledge. To be noted in this connection is the frequent ambiguity in Kant's language in the Analytic between talk of showing such and such (e.g. causality) to be possible, and showing it to be necessary. Puzzlingly, Kant seems to view these results as equivalent.

A third difficulty, connected with the preceding one, arises in connection with Kant's claim that the Analytic establishes the necessity of the metaphysics of experience which it identifies. Kant's claim that causality, for example, is a necessity of experience implies that in some sense there could not be experience without causality, i.e. that a subject that did not represent its experience as causally ordered is an impossibility. The problem is that it is hard to see on what basis any such result could conceivably be established. Kant does not pretend that the concept of causality is contained in that of (a subject of) experience. And if the necessity of causally ordered experience is not conceptual, then it seems the most that Kant can do is show that employment of the concept of causality has some other, weaker sort of justification. Even if Kant can show this, it is hard to see how he can demonstrate uniqueness, i.e. how he can rule out other concepts having the same sort of justification, or our perhaps at some future time exchanging causality for some other concept. Kant's arguments, it seems, may establish sufficient conditions of experience, but necessary ones appear beyond its scope. This problem arises whether one reads the Analytic progressively or regressively.

Given these points of uncertainty regarding Kant's method, it is unsurprising that interpretations of the Analytic should conflict. On one view (Strawson's) Kant is attempting to prove the necessity of an objective empirical world from premises to which the skeptic himself is committed; Kant is interpreted as seeking to demonstrate that skepticism is self-refuting. At the other extreme, the Analytic may be interpreted much more modestly, as a theory merely designed to explain why our experience has the conceptual character that it seems to have: its starting point is phenomenological – the world as we find it – and the argument for its truth is that it accounts for the appearances. Each kind of interpretation has its problems. The former burdens Kant with demands which, critical commentary tends to suggest, cannot be met, whilst the latter can deliver only results which are apparently too weak for the anti-skeptical purposes of the *Critique*.

A way of reading the Analytic

In view of these difficulties, we might try viewing the Analytic in the following light. We may interpret it as, in the first instance and most importantly, premised on the truth of transcendental idealism. It is an account of how the world is (must be) constructed conceptually on the assumption that the fundamental conceptual features of the objects of our cognition derive from our mode of cognition, rather than being determined by how things are independently of our subjectivity. (That the Analytic is premised on transcendental idealism is signalled at Bxvii, A92–4/B124–7, A95–7, A111, A114, A128–30, B163–4, B166–8, A139/B178, A180–1/B223–4; see also *Proleg* §§ 26–30.) Kant's warrant for proceeding in this way goes back ultimately to the general case for making the Copernican experiment in philosophy, but it is supported also by the Aesthetic: if objects are transcendentally ideal *qua* their a priori sensible features, then it is hard to see how they could be transcendentally real *qua* their a priori conceptual features. This point will be strengthened in the Analytic, where Kant will argue that conceptual form is shaped by sensible form, and that the a priori sensible and conceptual features of objects are related as content and form, rather than comprising discrete sets of properties of objects; so they cannot be conceived as respectively ideal and real in the way that an object's primary and secondary qualities arguably may be. This inseparability of the sensible and the conceptual in the constitution of objects will allow transcendental ideality to flow from the Aesthetic into the Analytic.

This makes a difference to how Kant's arguments are understood, one which carries advantages. Kant's proof of the principle of causality, for example, can now be read as having to show, not that there is something wrong with the supposition that things in reality are not causally ordered, or that if they are then we cannot know this, but that the principle of causality performs some *transcendental function*, i.e. that it has the same sort of object-enabling status as the Aesthetic showed the forms of intuition to possess. Similarly for objectivity in general: Kant need only show that the conceptualisation of an objective order plays some transcendental role. On this reading, Kant does not need to rule out other, logically possible metaphysics of experience. The key to the Analytic, on this account, consists in the identification of a general transcendental function for concepts to perform, and the success of any given proof will depend upon its demonstrating a relation of fit between this function (or sub-specification of it), and a given component of the commonsense metaphysics of experience.

Nor, it should be added, need Kant's proofs engage with the issue of whether there are thinner, Humean descriptions of the contents of our experience, e.g. as a mere stream of sense impressions, in the light of which our beliefs about the empirical world lack justification. Kant has, as will be seen, an independent set of arguments against empiricism, so that empiricist challenges to his conclusions regarding necessities of experience are undercut in general, and need not be refuted individually. (It is, therefore, not quite right to say that the

Analytic merely assumes the truth of transcendental idealism, because, in attacking empiricism, it presents a new case against one of the two major forms of transcendental realism.)

In this light, there is no reason why Kant should not refer to a posteriori judgement – our stock of commonsense empirical beliefs – as grounds for his transcendental theory of experience. Our claims to empirical knowledge may be taken as supplying the basis for inferences as to which a priori concepts we employ in constituting experience. For example, given that we commonly believe the empirical world to be causally ordered – a belief that even Hume admits we hold – Kant may take this datum as an indication that the concept of causality is one that has transcendental status, and accordingly seek a transcendental role to explain its presence in our thought about experience. In this way, Kant may claim to have established simultaneously a possibility, and a necessity: if his argument succeeds, he will have shown how a posteriori causal judgements are possible – namely by virtue of our employment of the a priori concept of causality in constituting the objects of our experience – and the necessity of the concept of causality for experience.

This necessity will, again, not be conceptual: Kant's arguments do not allow him to claim that there is any contradiction in the concept of a subject whose objects of experience are not causally ordered. But he can claim to have established a necessity of a different sort, in so far as he succeeds in showing that the warrant for causal judgement is not contingent upon the content of experience. If causality is a concept that we use, not because our experience has a certain character, but because it makes objects of a certain (transcendentally specified) sort possible for us, then it has necessity *for us*; it is what *we* use to constitute an objective world, and so necessary relative to the human standpoint. The metaphysics of experience that the Analytic shows to be necessary are so, therefore, if its argument succeeds, in the same non-logical sense as space and time.

This interpretation helps to resolve the methodological difficulties described above. If transcendental idealism is integral to Kant's conception of the Analytic's mode of argument, this explains why it should seem not to be implied by Kant's transcendental proofs: if transcendental idealism is assumed in the argument for the necessities of experience, and in the very conception of the kind of necessity which they possess, then it does not need to be inferred from them. The *Critique* does not then disintegrate into two disjoint strategies, one idealist and one metaphysically neutral.

Interpreting the Analytic as an attempt to reconstruct empirical knowledge on a transcendental idealist basis also narrows the difference between the progressive and regressive readings of the Analytic, and allows it to be seen how Kant may in a sense be pursuing both strategies at the same time. Kant can be read progressively, as beginning with an account of the general transcendental function which conceptualisation performs, elaborating a theory of what particular concepts perform specific transcendental functions, and then joining his theory up with ordinary empirical knowledge. Or he may be read regressively, as starting from the fact that we commonsensically conceive the empirical world in such and such terms, and then inferring, on the basis of his assumption that the proper explanation of our fundamental conceptualisation of the world has Copernican grounds, what set of concepts we employ for this purpose, and what transcendental functions they serve. Either way, the product is a theory of experience which occupies a mediating position between the basic transcendental framework and common sense: it should make sense in the light of Kant's analysis of cognition and Copernican conception of philosophical explanation, and it should specify a conceptual form which corresponds to that which our experience actually exhibits.

On this account, Kant can be held to show the necessity of our basic concepts in the sense described above, but not their uniqueness. He can be held to show that causality, for example, is the concept which for us plays a certain transcendental role – a role which, being transcendental, something needs to play – and to that extent, that it is necessary. But he does not show that causality is unique in the sense that nothing else *could* play its role, and in that sense he does not establish its necessity. To the extent that it is limited in this way, the interpretation arguably does not match Kant's aspirations, because he does appear to believe that the metaphysics of experience detailed in the Analytic comprise a set of principles to which there is no alternative. (This is because he thinks that our basic concepts are fixed by the logical nature of judgement. However, it will be seen that this claim, which belongs to the metaphysical deduction, is dubious.)

Even if demonstrations of logical uniqueness are beyond its scope, the Analytic can be held to do all that is necessary to fulfil the objectives of transcendental philosophy, including the securing of ordinary empirical knowledge claims. As said, included in Kant's theory of experience is a set of arguments directed to undermining empiricism and therefore skepticism of Hume's sort; and, as will be explained at the end of the chapter, transcendental idealism provides a broad and deep strategy for defusing the threat of skepticism in general. If so, then it will suffice, to validate our claims to empirical knowledge, to show that they involve concepts with transcendental roles.

It should be noted that, in the context of transcendental realism, this would not be the case. If empirical knowledge is construed as knowledge of an independent reality, then a body of judgements cannot be validated merely by showing something (anything) about their function for the subject. Explaining how a certain type of judgement is possible, in the sense of identifying the subjective function of their conceptual presuppositions, and validating it, are necessarily distinct for transcendental realism, and the first is insufficient for the second (as skepticism serves to underline). In the context of transcendental realism, a proof of the principle of causality would need to establish conceptual connections in order to have significance – it would have to be shown, for example, that the concept of a subject of experience implies that of causally ordered experience.

In the context of transcendental idealism, this is not necessary, because a demonstration that a concept such as causality has transcendental backing is equivalent to a demonstration that judgements employing it are prima facie warranted. Put another way, a regressive analysis can legitimate knowledge claims in the context of transcendental idealism, but not in that of transcendental realism, and this is because it can reveal them to have transcendental grounds, as a transcendental realist analysis of conceptual presuppositions cannot. The Analytic is entitled to proceed on the basis that our ordinary empirical knowledge claims are valid, as per the regressive reading, without risk of incurring a charge of circularity: so long as the attempt to reconstruct empirical knowledge on a transcendental basis succeeds, the assumption of its validity will by the end have been legitimated – Kant's philosophical experiment will have confirmed his Copernican hypothesis.

It remains true that, on the account suggested, Kant will not have explained why causality, rather than some other logically possible concept, should be what for us occupies the particular transcendental role that it does. But it is true of Kant's account of space and time too that it does not explain why they, rather than some other logically possible forms of intuition, should be the forms of outer and inner sense, and so leaves their transcendental status as a brute fact; so it cannot be a serious embarrassment if the categories end up in the same position (Kant affirms as much at B145–6). The notion that causality might give way to some other concept is, in any case, as incoherent as the supposition that we might change our forms of intuition: it is inconceivable to us that our identity as subjects of experience should survive such a transformation.

What we should expect to find in the Analytic, then, is an account of the general transcendental function of conceptualisation, and an account of which particular concepts perform this function for us and how they do so. The first is contained in the Transcendental Deduction, the second in the Analytic of Principles. Before going on to the Deduction, the earlier sections of the Analytic, which put its task in sharp focus, need to be looked at.

The relation of thought to objects: the apriority of conceptual form (Idea of a Transcendental Logic)

Kant prefaces the Analytic with an account of what he calls transcendental logic ('Idea of a Transcendental Logic', A50–64/B74–88; also relevant are the introductory sections of the Analytic of Principles, A130–6/B169–75). Transcendental logic is concerned with the rules governing thought in so far as it relates to objects: in sum, it tries to say how thought about objects is possible. The contrast is with 'general logic', which considers only the relations of thoughts to one another (and is what we call logic). One part of transcendental logic (that which comprises the Analytic) is a 'logic of truth': it specifies the conditions under which thoughts have objects and judgements can be true. The other, subsidiary part (which comprises the Dialectic) is a 'logic of illusion': it specifies complementarily the conditions under which thoughts *fail* to have objects yet falsely seem to do so.

Since, for us, thought about objects requires intuition, and our intuition is sensible, it follows that transcendental logic is concerned with the relation of thought to objects as given in space and time: unlike general logic, it has 'lying before it a manifold of a priori sensibility, presented by transcendental aesthetic, as materials for the concepts of pure understanding' (A76–7/B102). Because, as already noted, the fact that we have intuitions does not explain how thought relates to objects, the task of developing a transcendental logic is genuinely distinct from anything belonging to the Aesthetic.

Involved in Kant's conception of transcendental logic are some further elements, which tie it closely to his transcendental idealism.

Kant regards transcendental logic as committed to the existence of a priori concepts, and to a conception of the relation of thought to objects as fundamentally a priori (A56–7/B80–1, A85/B117). In other words, the very notion of transcendental logic involves a rejection of empiricism. This needs some explaining: from the beginning of the Analytic Kant seems to assume, without making his reasons explicit, that there are a priori concepts. Plainly, this assumption may appear question-begging. Nor is it immediately obvious why, even if our fundamental concepts are a priori, it should follow that experience is not what establishes their relation to objects.

Kant's assumption that there are a priori concepts follows from transcendental idealism in conjunction with his analysis of cognition. If objects are to be explained in Copernican terms, then their conditions of possibility cannot be regarded as supplied by the received content of experience – experience of objects cannot supply its own conditions of possibility. And if these conditions must include whatever is necessary for objects to be thought, and the function of thought is irreducible to and not derived from that of sensing, then there must be a priori conceptual conditions. Transcendental conditions, rather than experience of independently existing objects, must be taken as constituting the fundamental relation of thought to objects: the subject must be regarded as contributing 'the pure thought of an object' (A55/B80). Kant accordingly describes transcendental logic as treating 'of the origin of the modes in which we know objects, in so far as the origin cannot be attributed to the objects' (A55–6/B80).

At the empirical level, we can speak of experience as establishing a relation of thought to object, but the empirical relation of thought to its object presupposes an a priori relation, by virtue of which the object is originally constituted. This is why Kant draws a sharp line between fundamental (a priori) and non-fundamental (empirical) concepts: the categories are those concepts by virtue of which objects of experience are originally constituted, and only on their basis can empirical concepts of objects be formed (by whatever process is involved in the distillation of concepts out of experience, a topic about which Kant – in contrast with Locke, for example – says little).

Synthetic unity

This argument may seem so abstract, and so bound up with Kant's choice of methodology, as not to cut much ice with the empiricist. Kant has, however, in the Transcendental Deduction, a further argument to the same conclusion, which meets empiricism on its own terms (B129–31). The argument is at once very simple and very powerful. It is continuous with the argument in the Aesthetic at A20/B34 regarding a priori intuitive form, discussed in chapter 4 (p. 72).

At the bottom line in the cognition of empirical objects, on any empiricist analysis at any rate, there must be something which we can describe as the apprehension of unity in experience: an array of red sensations must be *taken as* a red patch, a sequence of auditory sensations as a sound of a certain pitch and so on. Now the apprehension of this unity cannot, Kant emphasises, be the work of experience itself, in the empiricist's sense of experience as a received content ('the mode in which the subject is affected', B129). For, whatever order or form we suppose batches of sensory data to possess in themselves, it will have relevance for the process of cognition only if the subject apprehends it as such, and this *apprehending* of the form must be something over and above its merely *inhering* in the data. It is one thing for the data of experience to *have* an order of its own, and another for us to *represent* it. Even if the manifold were in itself ready-combined, there would still have to be an act of recognising its combination, which would amount to its re-combination. The hypothesised inherent combination is consequently redundant.

Now, if 'the combination (*conjunctio*) of a manifold can never come to us through the senses' (B129), and thus 'cannot be given through objects' (B130), then it must be a priori; and if it is something over and above the reception of some content, then it must be the work of understanding rather than sensibility. We are, then, entitled to claim that there must be at least one a priori concept, namely unity. Kant calls this – the most minimal form that we must discover in experience in order for it to have cognitive significance – '*synthetic* unity' (B130). It is called synthetic because it involves, on Kant's account, an act of combination, Kant's general term for which is synthesis.

It might be wondered if the empiricist cannot undercut Kant's argument simply by *identifying* the inherence of unity in sensory data with its apprehension. This brings out something extremely important and not yet considered in Kant's conception of cognition. If the empiricist's identification is made, then there is no difference between the mere *occurrence* of a group of sensations, and my *taking* myself to be aware of it; and if there is no more to the latter than the former, then the notion that *I* stand in a *relation* to my cognitions disappears. This aspect of our cognitive acts, whereby the 'I' positions itself in relation to them as their subject, Kant calls our *spontaneity*, and its status as a defining feature of our cognition is emphasised throughout the Transcendental Deduction ('it is owing to this spontaneity that I entitle myself an *intelligence*', B158n). If Kant is right, then any account of cognition which omits our spontaneity, such as Hume's, fails to concern itself with the proper, rational phenomenon which deserves that name. Hume's assimilation of judging to breathing, in Kant's terms, substitutes a natural event for a cognitive act. (It is thus no coincidence that Hume also countenances the paradoxical claim that the self does not exist.)

The problem of connecting the sensible and the conceptual

Kant's commitment to the apriority of conceptual form and correlative rejection of empiricism is, therefore, well founded. As a consequence of this commitment, however, transcendental logic faces a problem. The problem is due to the fact that the fundamental concepts necessary for experience are not derived from experience, and yet need to be applied to sensible objects. This creates a possibility which Kant needs to rule out: namely, that there should fail to be any fit between objects as sensed and a priori concepts, between the sensible and conceptual components of the structure of experience. If there were nothing in what is given in intuition that allowed a priori concepts to get a grip, then the objects of intuition would appear chaotic from the point of view of the intellect, or, at the very least, the application of concepts to them would be groundless and arbitrary. (Kant states the problem in these terms at the outset of the Transcendental Deduction, A89–91/B122–3, and restates it at B159–60.)

To show that objects can be thought *only if* there are a priori concepts is not, therefore, to show that objects *can* be thought. To rule out the possibility that our a priori concepts float free of intuition is, in Kant's terminology, to show them to have 'objective validity' or 'objective reality'. The need to complete this justificatory task is a further reflection of the disanalogy of the Analytic with the Aesthetic noted earlier: whereas sensible form (space and time) is bestowed upon something which is without form and itself sensible in nature (the manifold of sensation), what conceptual form is applied to already has a form and nature which is intrinsically non-conceptual. Nothing in our bare possession of a priori concepts guarantees, therefore, the thinkability of any objects.

It is to be noted that this problem of connecting up the sensible and the conceptual does not arise in remotely similar terms for transcendental realism. For the transcendental realist, no deep difficulty concerning the very possibility of objects for a subject is involved in the relation of the sensible and the conceptual: the object unites in itself its various, sensible and non-sensible properties. The only further question is whether sensible presentations of properties are reducible to conceptual specifications or vice versa, i.e. the choice between rationalism and empiricism.

It would be a mistake, however, to think that this is a point in favour of transcendental realism. In fact, in Kant's perspective, the contrary is true: transcendental realism avoids any deep difficulty concerning the relation *per se* of the sensible and the conceptual, only because it is wedded to an inadequate picture of concept application.

Just as transcendental realism ultimately takes for granted the possibility of there being objects for us, so it ultimately takes for granted the possibility of applying a concept to an object. The transcendental realist supposes that an object exists in such and such a way independently from our conceptual powers, and that we apply a concept to an object by recognising how it is and, concomitantly, some sort of fit between the object and a concept. Whilst this pattern of explanation is, in Kant's view, entirely appropriate at the empirical level, it is empty when reapplied at the transcendental level. At this level, the notion that we possess the capacity for recognising instances of particular concepts, and relations of fit between concepts and objects, means nothing more than that we possess the capacity to apply concepts with justification. The transcendental realist's commitment to explanation in terms of independently constituted objects hides from view the problem of concept application as such, and therewith the problem of relating the sensible and the conceptual.

The question raised by the problem of relating the sensible and the conceptual – which lies at the heart of the Analytic, though it is not formulated explicitly until the Transcendental Deduction – is therefore: how is the justified application of a priori concepts to objects possible? Properly understood, this question is quite different from superficially similar questions that may arise in the context of transcendental realism – e.g. whether I have any assurance that something corresponds to my clear and distinct ideas – where what is wanted is a ground for a belief concerning what lies in the world independently of the subject. Kant's question needs to be answered with reference to the structure and capacities of the subject, and could not be answered by any information about subject-independent reality.

The details of Kant's answer to the questions how the sensible and conceptual are related, and how the justified application of a priori concepts is possible, are given in the Transcendental Deduction. For the present, it may be noted in outline that transcendental idealism, just as it gives rise to the problem of connecting the sensible and the conceptual, at the same time supplies the key to its solution. Transcendental idealism disposes of the idea that the objects of experience have a constitution of their own, and hence of the possibility that they have a constitution discrepant with the cognitive needs of the subject. To justify the application of a priori concepts it suffices, therefore, to show that the subject has cognitive needs which can be fulfilled if its objects have a form determined by those concepts, and how objects can assume that conceptual form. This is what Kant's theory of apperception, synthesis, schematism and the analogies of experience, is meant to provide.

The elements of thought: the categories (The Clue to the Discovery of all Pure Concepts of the Understanding)

In 'The Clue to the Discovery of all Pure Concepts of the Understanding' (A66–83, B91–115), later referred to as the metaphysical deduction of the categories (B159), Kant attempts to say which concepts supply the conceptual conditions of human knowledge.

The metaphysical deduction is based on the supposition that the function of judgement provides a 'clue' to the pure concepts of the understanding. The rationale for this is simply that judgement is what the employment of concepts consists in. Kant accordingly starts with what he considers to be the basic forms of judgement, and then claims that a specific concept corresponds to each of them. The attempted move is thus from formal logic to concepts with content.

Kant begins by considering what is involved in conceptual activity or thought as such. The cognitive acts in which concepts are employed are judgements, and judgement employs, Kant says, 'functions of unity', meaning that in judgement one representation is brought into relation with another in such a way as to yield a unity (one with what we would call propositional form). Kant thinks – and this is because he takes Aristotle's logic to be definitive (Bviii) – that there are precisely twelve 'functions of unity in judgements' or forms of judgement. Each yields a different kind of unity. For example, the representations 'body' and 'divisibility' are unified in the categorical judgement 'this body is divisible' in a different way from that in which they are unified in the hypothetical judgement 'if something is a body, then it is divisible'. The forms of judgement are set out in the Table of Judgements (A70/B95), where they are divided into four groups (quantity, quality, relation, modality), each containing three 'moments'. Every judgement takes one moment from each group. Thus a judgement may be universal, affirmative, categorical and assertoric ('all crows are black'); or singular, negative, disjunctive and problematic ('that bird might be neither a crow nor a raven'); and so on.

To explain how the clue provided by the function of judgement may be followed up, Kant returns to the theme of transcendental logic (A76–80/B102–5).

The pure concepts of the understanding that we are trying to identify must have a relation to judgement, but they must also have content. The logical functions of judgement identified in the Table of Judgements are, however, purely formal (which is why they can do no more than provide a 'clue' to the pure concepts of the understanding). In order to identify the pure concepts of the understanding, it must therefore be considered how they get their content. Now their content, Kant argues, can derive only from their relation to (their role in organising) intuition – pure intuition, of course, since we are concerned with the understanding in exclusively a priori respects. This instructs us as to how the pure concepts of the understanding may be identified: it is necessary to identify concepts which *both* correspond to the logical functions of judgement *and* have the capacity for playing a role in organising intuition. As Kant puts it, we must look for concepts which give rise to unity in both judgements and intuitions (A79/B104–5).

The pure concepts of the understanding can now be identified, and Kant sets them out in the Table of Categories (A80/B106). They are: unity, plurality, totality (categories of quantity); reality, negation, limitation (categories of quality); inherence and subsistence, causality and dependence, reciprocity (categories of relation); im-/possibility, non-/existence, necessity/contingency (categories of modality). Kant takes himself to have extracted from each of the logically different kinds of judgement that we make, a corresponding concept which has a relation to objects given in intuition. So, to take the most salient examples, corresponding to the logical function of 'hypothetical' judgement (if p then q), there is the category of causality (if one event, then another); and corresponding to the function of 'categorical' judgement (x is F), the category of substance (that which subsists and in which F inheres). Similarly for the other categories. The categories are defined as 'concepts of an object in general, by means of which the intuition of an object is regarded as determined in respect of one of the logical functions of judgement' (B128). Kant renames the pure concepts of the understanding categories to mark the fact that they are now considered in relation to intuition; the choice of term echoes Aristotle's notion of a category as a concept which is not derived from any more general concept.

The shortcomings of the metaphysical deduction

Kant's intention in offering this derivation of the categories is not fully clear, and lends itself to different interpretations. The modest interpretation is that, at this point, Kant is taking the categories for granted, as the most basic concepts that we find we actually have, and merely showing of them that they correspond to forms of judgement, with a view to confirming their candidacy for the status of pure concepts of the understanding at a later date. The metaphysical deduction would then be akin to the Metaphysical Expositions in the Aesthetic, where Kant took space and time as given representations, rather than trying to provide them with any sort of derivation. On the ambitious interpretation, by contrast, Kant means to prove in the Clue that these categories and no others must be the pure concepts of the understanding, i.e. that they are necessary for any subject with a discursive intellect and that any other pure concepts that such a subject has will be formed from them ('pure derivative concepts' or '*predicables* of the pure understanding', in Kant's language, A81–2/B107–8).

Probably the latter is what Kant means (see B159). His critics, in any case, have standardly interpreted him in this way, and thereupon dismissed the Table of Categories as an arbitrary list (reapplying to Kant the very charge that he makes against Aristotle, A81/B107). Hegel, for instance, complains of the lack of a 'genuine *deduction*': 'Kant, it is well known, did not put himself to much trouble in discovering the categories.'

Up to a point, Kant can be defended. It is obvious that the mere concept of judgement (or of thought in accordance with the laws of logic) does not contain, even implicitly, any metaphysical concepts, and this can hardly be what Kant intends. Kant's derivation needs to be located in the context of transcendental logic: his claim is not that the categories are logically deducible from the forms of judgement, but that *if* one looks for concepts that satisfy the conditions of being both associated with concepts of formal logic and capable of playing a role in organising intuition, then one arrives at the twelve categories.

However, the Table of Judgements itself is not immune to criticism: Kant does not explain on what principle it is based, and its organisation is hardly self-evident (for instance, it is unclear why 'infinite' judgements are included under the heading of quality, alongside affirmative and negative judgements; a judgement's being infinite does not seem to be a matter of its logical form). And even if the general idea that metaphysical concepts might, under the special conditions of transcendental logic, be developed out of the forms of judgement is granted, and doubts about the Table of Judgements are set aside, Kant's specific derivations are by no means straightforward. It is, for example, unclear in what way the logical function of categorical judgement corresponds to the rich concept of substance. There are categorical judgements in mathematics ('the number 2 is even'), and these rest on intuition, according to Kant, but they do not import the concept of substance, if we assume (as we must) 'substance' to mean more than 'occupant of subject position in categorical judgement'. Employing a certain form of judgement does not, therefore, entail application of the corresponding category. Nor is the converse true: the concept of causality can be applied without a hypothetical judgement being made ('fire is a cause of smoke'). And aside from the weakness of the basic alignment of the categories with the forms of judgement, it is hard to see how Kant has demonstrated the uniqueness of the correspondences he claims. It would appear, for example, that Hume's concept of constant conjunction could do the same job of organising intuition in such a way as to permit hypothetical judgements, in place of Kant's stronger concept of causation. Kant does not, therefore, rule it out that someone dissatisfied with his list of categories could propose a different set of concepts with an equally good claim to identify a structure common to judgement and experience. Such difficulties tend to undermine the claim that specific ways of conceiving objects can be extrapolated from the function of judgement.

The shortcomings of the metaphysical deduction are not, however, ultimately crippling for Kant's argument, because the important work in vindicating the categories will be done later in the Analytic, when the necessity of each of the concepts that figures in the Table will be shown individually – Kant will go through the list one by one, instead of attempting to prove them *en bloc*. What is most important in the metaphysical deduction is the suggestion, which is pursued in the Transcendental Deduction, that if there were not a conceptual form shared by thought and intuition, neither would be possible. Even if this claim is not made good in the metaphysical deduction at a single stroke, it is defended in more painstaking fashion later. On the assumption that this later argument succeeds, the modest reading of the metaphysical deduction is all that Kant need lay claim to.

The question of what particular concepts provide the a priori conceptual conditions of objects can, therefore, be suspended for the time being. In the Transcendental Deduction which now follows, it may simply be assumed that there are some concepts, to be called the categories, the identity of which has still to be determined, which provide these conditions.

The preconditions and source of conceptual form: the subject–object relation (The Transcendental Deduction)

The Transcendental Deduction is the heart of the Analytic. Even by Kant's standards, it is one of the most original, abstract and taxing parts of the *Critique*. Certainly it is the most enigmatic; the text is of such complexity that it may reasonably be doubted that a single line of argument comprehending all its themes and theorems can be extracted from it. Kant recorded dissatisfaction with his exposition in the first edition and rewrote it entirely for the second (Bxxxviii, *Proleg* 381), but as with other major changes between editions, the B Deduction is far from being a mere clarification of its predecessor, and we are left with two contrasting versions of the Deduction whose relation raises many questions. This section begins with a summary of the Deduction, and then presents a selective reconstruction of its argument.

A synopsis of the text of the Deduction

In synopsis, the text of the Deduction is as follows. In the two sections preceding the division of first and second editions, Kant formulates the problem addressed in the Deduction (§13) and specifies the method appropriate to its solution (§14). The problem is the one described earlier: nothing in what has been said so far about the objects of empirical intuition justifies the application of a priori concepts to them; for all that has been said, objects may 'appear to us without their being under the necessity of being related to the functions of understanding' (A89/B122); appearances 'might very well be so constituted that the understanding should not find them to be in accordance with' its own conditions, the categories (A90/B123). (Kant means that this possibility remains in so far as we consider appearances solely in terms of their sensible conditions; his ultimate goal is to show that it is not a genuine metaphysical possibility.) The problem is therefore 'how *subjective conditions of thought*' – this being the only status which the metaphysical deduction has shown the categories to have – can also 'have *objective validity*' (A89/B122).

To demonstrate the objective validity of the categories requires a deduction which is transcendental, not empirical (A85–6/B117–18). The term 'deduction' is juridical in origin and means the legitimation of a disputed legal title or claim. A philosophical deduction is required whenever we seek to answer a question of rightfulness or justification, as opposed to a question of fact, a distinction which Kant regard as absolute in a way that Hume perhaps does not (A84–5/B116–17).

Kant says a number of things to emphasise the 'unavoidable necessity' (A88/B121) of a transcendental deduction of the categories. First, there are in common circulation a number of 'usurpatory' concepts, such as 'fate' and 'fortune', which lack justified application, and a demonstration is needed that the categories are not similarly arbitrary (as Hume in effect claims). Second, empiricism offers a merely 'physiological derivation' of concepts, an account of their 'occasioning causes', not the 'principle of their possibility' (A86–7/B118–19). (Rationalist, innatist justifications are rejected later, at B167–8.) Third, the deduction of the categories is independent from and cannot be like that of space and time, or geometry, since the categories have not been shown to be necessary for appearances to be given (A87–9/B119–22). Fourth, the metaphysical deduction is not sufficient for the deduction of the categories, because (*pace* rationalism) the mere possession of the categories does not incorporate any knowledge of objects (A88/B120, B288). It is therefore appropriate, Kant grants, that the categories should 'arouse suspicion' (A88/B120), as they did in Hume.

To illustrate the problem, Kant gives the example of causality (A90–1/B122–4). There is nothing in appearances, considered merely as objects of empirical intuition, to license judgements of necessary connection: all that regularities among appearances justify is the judgement that one appearance will succeed another, not that it will be caused by it. Hume's constant conjunction amounts to a merely physiological derivation of causality: it concerns the subjective conditions of the concept, not its objective validity.

In §14 Kant describes the general form of his solution (in the first edition this material extends to A95–7). First the problem of the Deduction is located in the context of transcendental idealism, where it is assumed that representations make objects possible, rather than vice versa (A92/B124–5). Now this idea can be used in justifying the categories. We have simply to ask if there is any respect in which concepts may be said to make objects possible, in the hope of identifying some that make objects *qua* thought possible, in the same way that space and time make objects *qua* sensed possible. What we are after is a conceptual condition that makes it 'possible to *know* anything *as an object*' (A92/B125). If so, the obvious candidate is the concept of an object itself. If the concept of an object in general – or rather the plurality of more specific concepts into which it is differentiated – is required for experience, then its application to objects of intuition must be justified. Kant says:

> Now all experience does indeed contain, in addition to the intuition of the senses through which something is given, a *concept* of an object as being thereby given, that is to say, as appearing. Concepts of objects in general thus underlie all empirical knowledge as its *a priori* conditions.

> (A93/B126)

A priori concepts are justified, therefore, if they are 'contained in the concept of possible experience [of objects]' (A95), i.e. if they are (in accordance with Kant's definitions at A11–12/B25 and A56/B80) *transcendental* conditions: 'If we can prove that by their means alone an object can be thought, this will be a sufficient deduction of them, and will justify their objective validity' (A96–7).

The a priori relation of concepts to objects postulated by transcendental logic would thus consist in their being contained in the concept of possible experience. Making explicit the link with the metaphysical deduction, Kant reminds us that the categories are intended to be 'concepts of an object in general, by means of which the intuition of an object is regarded as determined in respect of one of the logical functions of judgement' (B128). Moreover, assuming that the Deduction shows that objects can be thought *only if* the a priori concepts applied to them are ones through which experience becomes possible – that justification of the application of concepts to objects is otherwise 'contradictory and impossible' (A95) – it will follow that cognition of objects is restricted to appearances. That is, transcendental idealism will be reconfirmed in the Deduction.

If it is to be shown that the categories make objects of experience possible, then 'the a priori foundation of the possibility of experience' (A97) needs to be analysed: 'we must enquire what are the a priori conditions upon which the possibility of experience rests' (A95–6). In the A Deduction, this is begun in the preamble (A97), and in the B Deduction at its very outset (§15). At both points we find Kant giving the anti-empiricist argument cited earlier, to the effect that sense experience can serve cognition only if a non-empirical 'synthetic unity' is presupposed. The arguments that Kant then develops on the basis of this requirement of unity differ between the two editions.

The A Deduction is expressed in the language of cognitive powers and their operations. Kant sets out the argument twice, dividing the A Deduction into a 'preparatory' (A98–114) and a 'systematic' exposition (A115–30). These differ in their order of presentation but cover roughly the same territory. In both cognition is conceived as requiring a multi-layered set of synthetic operations attributed to different cognitive powers: receptivity of *sensibility*, combination of the data of sense by the *imagination* (a newly introduced, mediating faculty), and finally conceptual operations on the part of the *understanding*. With each upward shift of level, a new kind of unity is created, the higher levels presupposing the lower. Kant's primary concern is with unity across time, synthetic unification of the temporal manifold (the need for which is brought out in the example of counting given at A103). The highest unity, that of the understanding, is held to be sufficient for the unity of self-consciousness.

The preparatory exposition works its way up from sense to intellect, and distinguishes carefully the three stages of a priori transcendental cognitive operation: *synthesis of apprehension in intuition* attributed to sense (A98–100), *synthesis of reproduction* attributed to imagination (A100–2, running on to A104) and *synthesis of recognition in a concept* attributed to understanding (A104–10). In this last of these, Kant's key concepts of the transcendental object (A104–5, A108–10), and the transcendental unity of apperception (self-consciousness) (A106–8), are introduced and explained. The systematic exposition reverses this route: it begins with the claim that the transcendental unity of apperception provides the 'inner ground' of the connection of representations required for all cognition (A116–19), and moves on to consider the various synthetic operations which such unity presupposes (A119–25). Both expositions close with explicit statements to the effect that the categories have been justified and an explanation of why transcendental idealism is a concomitant of their justification (A110–15, A125–30).

The B Deduction differs most markedly through its contraction of the synthesis story, which is confined to a few passages (B151–2, B160; the a priori synthesis of imagination is renamed 'figurative', and that of understanding 'intellectual' at B151). The concept of synthesis itself remains vital, but Kant does not highlight the detailed operations of synthesising faculties. The A Deduction is in fact termed by Kant a 'subjective deduction' (Axvi–xvii), because it proceeds by asking what cognitive powers and operations a subject must have and perform, if it is to have experience of objects: it focuses on the 'subjective sources which form the a priori foundation of the possibility of experience' (A97). An 'objective deduction', by contrast, would spell out the transcendental conditions of experience without reference to the subject's cognitive powers. In principle the two ways of expressing the argument of the Deduction are only different formulations of a single account, 'two sides' (Axvi) of the same enquiry. Their position is not truly equal, however, for Kant regards the subjective deduction as strictly inessential (Axvii).

The B Deduction is an objective deduction. Here too there is a textual division into two halves, but it has a different basis: they comprise two steps in a single proof, rather than two expositions of the same material. The first half comprehends §§15–20. Having in §15 identified the need for synthetic unity, §16 immediately argues the need for transcendental unity of apperception, now identified as the requirement that it should be possible for the 'I think' to accompany all my representations. §17 argues that this synthetic requirement is a condition for any object to be thought. §§18–19 refine the argument. In §18 Kant introduces the notion of an 'objective', 'necessary' unity of self-consciousness and distinguishes it from its merely empirical, contingent unity. §19 connects this objective unity to (objectively valid) judgement, thereby reconfirming the identification of the conditions of self-consciousness with those of conceptualisation of objects. Thus in §20 Kant can claim that the manifold 'so far as it is given in a single empirical intuition' is subject to the categories.

§§21–6 comprise the second half of the B Deduction. Further work is needed, Kant explains in §21, because the argument of §§15–20 assumes that the intuitions to which the categories are applied possess unity: it does not show that the received content of intuition must allow this unity, and so does not remove the possibility that appearances might be so constituted that they would not accord with the categories. If Kant stopped at this point, therefore, he could claim to have analysed the conditions under which objects can be represented in thought by us, but not to have shown that the categories are more than subjective conditions of cognition, i.e. have objective validity. For this, he needs to show that the categories are required in order for there to *be* objects of intuition, rather than just for those objects to be *represented*.

This goal is achieved in §26 by means of an appeal to pure intuition: all sensory content is represented in space and time, the unity of which is necessary but depends on conceptual operations (as noted in the final section of chapter 4), in view of which the subjection of all experience to the categories is guaranteed – the categories must enter into intuition and thus be constitutive of anything presented in intuition.

In the intervening sections (§§22–5), Kant concentrates on emphasising that the categories gain their cognitive significance through their relation to spatio-temporal intuition, for which reason their validity is necessarily restricted to appearances, and introduces an account of how they are implicated in self-knowledge. The B Deduction, like its predecessor, ends with an account of why transcendental idealism is required for the justification of the categories (§27).

Interpretations of the Deduction

It is evident from this overview that the Deduction is not merely intricate, but contains a number of argumentative routes: at different points the concepts of an object, experience and its temporality, self-consciousness and judgement take centre stage, and the problem is to know which line of thought is taking the lead, and how the others are integrated with it.

The dominant line of interpretation finds in the Deduction a progressive, anti-skeptical argument, from the incontrovertible premise that we have experience or are self-conscious, to the strong conclusion that we have experience of an objective world. The minority view is that the Deduction is concerned with the conditions of empirical knowledge, not those of self-consciousness: its argument is regressive, and effective against empiricism but not skepticism.

A well-known example of the progressive reading is that of Strawson. Strawson reconstructs the Deduction in terms of an argument against what he calls the 'sense-datum hypothesis', which is the hypothesis that there could be a subject whose experience included only qualitative sensory items, and never objects capable of existing unperceived. Such a subject, according to Strawson, is impossible, because the contents of its experience do not allow it to draw a distinction between the items that it is said to recognise, and its recognition of those items: its awareness of objects is absorbed in the objects of its awareness, depriving it of the materials that are necessary to form, express or sustain the conceptual contrast of the 'I' with its states or experiences, as is necessary for self-consciousness. Experience must, therefore, include objects capable of existing unperceived.

Strawson's interpretation exemplifies the kind of strength and unity of argument which it would be desirable to find in the Deduction. However, holding aside some well-recognised problems which Strawson's argument faces, it is not a convincing candidate for modelling Kant's intentions in the Deduction. At best, what it shows is something about our concept of experience, viz. that it presupposes the concept of a physical object. In Kant's terms, such a conclusion expresses a merely analytic judgement, and as such cannot serve transcendental purposes: whatever it shows about our conceptual scheme, it does not establish the scheme's legitimacy. This limitation shows up when it is reflected that Strawson's argument has trouble answering the skeptic. That our concept of experience should presuppose our having the concept of a physical object does not entail that there is anything for the latter to be applied to, i.e. that there *are* physical objects; even if the belief that the concept of a physical object has application is unavoidable for us, it remains entirely open that this belief is false.

Generally, it would seem that any analytic interpretation of the Deduction will concern itself merely with what Kant calls subjective conditions of thought, and so fall short of establishing the objective validity of these. And in Kant's terms, such a result is worse than useless: merely to show 'that I am so constituted that I cannot think' otherwise 'is exactly what the sceptic most desires': it reduces all our cognition to 'nothing but sheer illusion' (B168).

This is one reason for interpreting the Deduction in terms of the general view of the Analytic suggested earlier. In this light, the Deduction should not be interpreted as seeking to extract a refutation of skepticism from the concept of experience or any other basic concept. Nor does it merely identify the presuppositions of empirical knowledge by showing that a posteriori, empirical knowledge claims rest on a priori conditions. Rather, it attempts to show that a priori concepts have justified application to objects, through showing that they perform a transcendental function, and on the basis that the objects to which they are applied are transcendentally ideal. The identity of these a priori concepts is not at issue in the Deduction. The Deduction is intended to vindicate (against Hume) objectivity in a general sense, not objectivity as determined by the specific concepts of substance and causality; so it does not aim to defend the external world against skepticism, a task which belongs to later sections of the *Critique*. Kant's concern in the Deduction is to reinterpret in Copernican terms the concept of an object for us – to show what objectivity must be, in order that our thoughts should have objects – as a necessary but not a sufficient condition for empirical knowledge claims. The Deduction thus contains Kant's response to Hume's skepticism regarding the employment of metaphysical concepts *in general*; later Kant will reply to Hume with respect to the particular metaphysical concepts of substance and causality.

A further proposal regarding the interpretation of the Deduction is that it should be viewed not as a linear proof, of either a progressive or regressive variety, but as a theory composed of several segments. This is not to deny that it contains arguments, and that its success depends on their soundness. What it means is that the Deduction should be measured in the terms appropriate to a theory: its several parts should cohere and explain one another, the whole should explain something not otherwise explicable and so on. This accords with the fact that we find in Kant's text a number of argumentative connections, all bearing on a single concern, but forming in all a web rather than a chain.

A theory of the subject–object relation

The Deduction attempts to provide a theory of, as it may be called, the subject–object relation. To see what this might mean, we should consider what is needed in transcendental philosophy for a complete account of cognition.

To pose any question at all concerning the conditions of cognition is to introduce, as it may be put, a factor of orientation or perspective. This is true whether epistemological questions are formulated in first-personal terms ('How do I know that p?') or as questions about what is ordinarily believed ('How may the knowledge claim that p be justified?'). In the former case, the philosophical enquirer takes up the perspective of a cogniser; in the latter, this perspective is allocated to human believers as such, sometimes under the title 'we'. Most certainly for Kant, if not for all philosophers since Descartes, it is constitutive of philosophical enquiry that its questions should be expressible in this form: an enquiry that does not satisfy this condition must instead be psychological, sociological, biological, etc.

Now the present significance of this familiar point is that when, in the Analytic, the conceptual conditions of objects are investigated, and the notion of a domain of objects for concept application is introduced, this domain is conceived as orientated towards, and lying in the perspective of a thinking subject. It must be so conceived, because a domain conceived as existing outside this perspective is for us a nothing. This condition, which must obtain in order for even the highly minimal notion of a domain of objects as candidates for cognition to make sense, is what is meant by the subject–object relation, and it is the ultimate ground of cognition, and most basic explanandum for transcendental philosophy. For purposes of philosophical analysis, three elements may be abstractly distinguished in it: the subject, the object and the relation which allows the object to be taken as such by the subject. What the Deduction supplies is a theory of how these elements may be conceived, in order that they should interlock intelligibly. This is the sense of the question Kant poses in the Herz letter: 'What is the ground of the relation of that in us which we call "representation" to the object?' Here 'representation' refers not to any particular (e.g. mental) kind of entity, but to the perspectival function which allows objects to be taken as such by subjects.

Kant's conception of the subject–object relation is completely original, and he is brought to it by his attempt to reinterpret human knowledge in Copernican terms. Pre-Copernican conceptions of the relation between knowing subject and object known regard them as existents constituted independently of our knowledge, and our knowledge of each as explicable in terms of their antecedently conceived constitutions. This realist model being ruled out for Kant, a properly transcendental explanation can proceed only by forswearing any assumptions about the constitution of subject and object. That is why it must make the very distinction of subject and object, and our grasp of this distinction, a primary object of philosophical elucidation. On such an approach, transcendental enquiry cannot start with the application of a particular concept to an object, be it the self or a thing distinct from it. It must instead press behind the case in which any concept is applied, and begin by describing the conditions which need to obtain in order for the categories to be brought into play at all, the *pre-categorial* structure of a possible domain of cognition.

The transcendental unity of apperception

The first element in this structure to be examined is the subject. Kant's account of the subject may be understood as attempting to steer a path between, on the one side, Descartes' *sum res cogitans* (the identification of the self with a substance), and on the other, Hume's avowed failure to discover any such thing as the subject over and above ideas (the reductionist or 'bundle' view of the self).

In the Aesthetic, Kant asserted that the self is known only as appearance: through inner sense I cognise myself in terms of temporal, empirical objects. As regards this empirical knowledge of the self, Kant's view recalls Hume: 'No fixed and abiding self can present itself in this flux of inner appearances' (A107); 'the empirical consciousness, which accompanies different representations, is in itself diverse and without relation to the identity of the subject' (A133). But contrary to Hume, Kant maintains that this cannot be the whole story. Precisely because the self is not, and cannot be given empirically, there must be a priori self-consciousness, *transcendental unity of apperception*, a 'pure original unchangeable consciousness' of self (A107). (The term apperception is borrowed from Leibniz, for whom it signifies perception of one's own states; Leibniz, however, conceives apperception in merely empirical terms.)

It is necessary, with regard to all representations which are to qualify as 'mine', that they be attributable to a single subject: something 'has *necessarily* to be represented as numerically identical' (A107) in the flux of inner appearances. In the B Deduction Kant expresses the requirement of transcendental apperception as follows:

It must be possible for the 'I think' to accompany all my representations; for otherwise something would be represented in me which could not be thought at all, and that is equivalent to saying that the representation would be impossible, or at least would be nothing to me.

(B131–2)

It is not that each of my representations must be actually accompanied by the reflection that it is mine, nor that I must be able to form a single thought comprehending all of my representations in one grand totality: Kant's claim is just that *each* of my representations must be such that it is *possible* for me to recognise it as mine in an act of reflection. For the satisfaction of this condition, the representation 'I', an invariant, a priori representation free from empirical content, is essential; 'otherwise I should have as many-coloured and diverse a self as I have representations of which I am conscious' (B134). Hence the requirement of *transcendental* unity of apperception, in addition to and as a condition of the *empirical* unities of apperception given in inner sense.

This necessity is at bottom one of transcendental method: the 'I think' (or more precisely, the necessity of the possibility of its accompanying my representations) expresses the condition that any domain of objects must be conceived in the perspective of a thinking subject. Transcendental apperception fixes the starting point for transcendental discourse. The reason why the 'I' seems absent and superfluous to Hume is that, in line with his transcendental realism, he conceives his bundles of ideas as a domain of things in themselves, outside any perspective. So conceived, it is true that bundles presuppose no 'I', but they also have no relation whatsoever to our cognition. To the extent that Hume's ideas are taken as a domain of objects for us, they must be conceived perspectivally and so must contain an 'I' implicitly. Hume has, as it were, employed his 'I' to create his bundles in thought, and then incoherently attempted to delete it. (Closely involved in Kant's disagreement with Hume, as intimated earlier, is the issue of spontaneity, our representation of our thoughts as products of our activity. In this light, Hume's bundles are again conceived incoherently: having introduced them under the description 'what is

THE CONCEPTUAL CONDITIONS OF OBJECTS

immediately given', Hume as it were suppresses the condition on their introduction, namely that *I take* them under that description. The concept of a bundle in abstraction from this condition is, however, as empty as the general thought of things in themselves.)

Assuming the unity of apperception to be the transcendental condition Kant says it is, there is then the question of what it is, or consists of. At one level, Kant's answer is clear: transcendental apperception consists in a merely *formal* unity that does not amount to knowledge of any object. The formal unity in question is just that unity of representations, whatever it may be, which makes it possible for me to reflectively attach the 'I think' to each of them. Transcendental apperception cannot, therefore, be identified with the cognition of anything that can be brought under the concept of substance – a *res cogitans* – for which an intellectual intuition of the self would be required.

However, matters are not quite so simple. In discussing apperception, Kant employs not only the concept of unity but also that of identity (e.g. A113: 'numerical identity is inseparable from it [self-consciousness], and is a priori certain'). The condition of apperception is that all representations be related to something that can *represent itself as identical* in relation to them. But this raises the question: *is* there something identical throughout and related to all the representations I call mine?

Kant's position can now seem very puzzling. On the one hand he appears to be telling us that it is necessary to employ the concept of a self existing over and above our representations and possessing numerical identity, and therefore justifying the status of 'I' as a referring expression. But the equivalence of the unity of apperception with a formal unity of representations seems to return us to a Humean ontology of the self, in which all that exists are representations and their relations (albeit inclusive of some that are a priori, if Kant is right). Thus Kant seems to be saying both that we must *take* the 'I' to have reference beyond representations, and that it *has* no such reference. This is a logically consistent position, but it entails that we are subject to a tortuous illusion concerning the self – viz., we need the fiction of a supra-Humean self in order to exist as mere Humean bundles.

Now Kant does believe (the Dialectic will reveal) that reason is subject to a necessary illusion regarding the self, but it is quite different from this one, and does not concern the understanding. In any case, here in the Analytic Kant is supposed to be validating the conceptual conditions of knowledge and defending a metaphysics of experience; so it would be bizarre if these turned out to include an illusion.

One way of squaring Kant's claims is to suppose that, contrary to what was said earlier, he does mean the 'I' to be understood as referring to a thing in itself. His position would then be that the self, *qua* the world of appearances, is just a unity of representations, but that, in transcendent terms, it is a thing in itself. This is an improvement, in so far as it avoids imputing an illusion of selfhood, but it cannot be right, for it conflicts with the original claim in the Aesthetic, reiterated in the Deduction at B157–9, that the self is *known only* as appearance, and also, more seriously, requires Kant to admit an intellectual intuition of the self and at least partially undoes transcendental idealism.

Kant is well aware of this issue, and attempts to clarify our situation regarding the 'I', most notably in §25 of the B Deduction, and at various points in the Paralogisms of the Dialectic, where, in direct confrontation with the Cartesian view of the self, he refines his account of apperception in order to accommodate Descartes' insight, which he has no wish to challenge, that the cogito expresses a truth (one which is not available to the Humean).

Transcendental apperception is consciousness of *thinking*. It is purely intellectual, not empirical consciousness – consciousness independent of intuition (B278), and thus not experience – and it provides the ground of our representation of ourselves as spontaneous. Further, apperception 'is something real' (B419): something 'real is given' in the 'I think', 'something which actually exists' (B423n). But of this, we have no concept: it cannot even be brought under the category of existence (B423n); self-consciousness gives us 'the feeling of an existence without the slightest concept' (*Proleg* 334n); 'we cannot even say that this [the representation "I"] is a concept' (A346/B404). So Kant allows that an intellectual consciousness of *something* existing is given with the 'I think'. Now, this 'something' is not to be identified with a thing in itself: in apperception 'I am conscious of myself, not as I appear, nor as I am in myself, but only that I am' (B157); 'consciousness of self is thus very far from being a knowledge of the self' (B158).

So Kant's position is that, though the unity of apperception guarantees the numerical identity of something, we cannot know what. The reference of the 'I' is undecidable, because our consciousness of the existing 'something' cannot be put together with the formal unity of apperception to yield knowledge of an 'I'-identical thing. It *may* be that the existing something given in apperception shares the identity of the thinking subject, and if so, then the 'I' is a thing in itself, though still it is not something that I have knowledge of, for which a determinate concept would be required. But it may also be that the something whose existence I have intellectual consciousness of in apperception has nothing to do with the identity of anything individuable through apperception: the 'something' underlying apperception may be without 'I'-mirroring features. If this is the case, then all that is determined through apperception is the identity of something that, unlike a thing in itself, exists solely within the sphere of representation, its numerical identity fixed by the formal unity of representations – something which we can conceive only as the thinking subject which is a condition of possibility of experience. (At some points, this seems to be the sense of Kant's concept of the 'transcendental subject': A346/B404, A355, B427, A478–9n/B506–7n. At A492/B520 and A545/B573, however, this entity seems to be a thing in itself, suggesting either that Kant failed to decide the meaning of this concept, or that it must be other than the subject of apperception.)

Whereas in other philosophical frameworks, notably rationalism, it would follow plainly from the necessity of the representation 'I', that I do exist as an identical object, for Kant it does not: my having to represent myself as identical is neutral as regards the existence of any object corresponding to that representation. Fundamentally, this is because necessities of representation in general are not equivalent to judgements about the real existence of objects. Kant is not, therefore, however it may appear, ambiguous between a Humean and Cartesian ontology of the self: his transcendental framework precludes a commitment to either. Kant's account of apperception drives a wedge between the position of Hume, for whom the 'I' does not refer to anything, and that of Descartes, for whom it refers to something that has determinable reality beyond its role in representation. For Kant, 'I' refers to something over and above my representations, but we cannot know if it is to the subject of representation or a thing in itself.

As emerged in the earlier synopsis of the Deduction, transcendental apperception provides one of the routes by which Kant pursues the goal of legitimating the categories. This part of the argument will be filled in later, when the interdependence of the two terms of the subject–object relation is described. For the present, anticipating this step, two points may be noted. First, although the principle of the necessary unity of apperception – that all my representations must belong to one self-consciousness – is, Kant says, an analytic truth (B135, B138), it 'reveals the necessity of a synthesis' (B135): 'the *analytic* unity of apperception is possible only under the presupposition of a certain *synthetic* unity' (B133). That is, the identity of the 'I' cannot, in transcendental philosophy, be taken as a given cognition, and, like all unities, must be based on synthesis of representations.

Second, Kant elaborates, in §19 of the B Deduction, an account of how transcendental apperception is related to judgement. To judge that something is so, e.g. that the body is heavy, there must be a connection in the subject between the representations 'body' and 'heavy', one which is not merely associative and empirical, but in some manner necessary: otherwise the two representations will not be 'combined *in the object*' (B142), and no judgement will be made. Judgement presupposes, therefore, a necessary unity of consciousness. Now the only possible source of this necessity (given that, for Kant, it cannot migrate into consciousness from the object) is what Kant calls in §18 of the B Deduction 'objective' unity of consciousness, unity which has an a priori basis, in contrast with the merely subjective unities comprised by Humean bundlings of associated ideas. This means that judgement is possible only if the unity of apperception requires that representations be synthesised according to certain a priori principles. Hence Kant's claim that the transcendental unity of apperception is an 'objective condition' of all knowledge: it is 'not merely a condition that I myself require', but a 'condition under which every object must stand in order *to become an object for me*' (B138). (In the Paralogisms, A352, Kant observes a more direct dependence of judgement on transcendental apperception. In order to think 'A is B', e.g. 'all bodies are divisible', the thinker must be able to represent the subject which has representation A as identical with the subject which has representation B. Otherwise the parts of thought would be as scattered as they are when they belong to different people: when you think 'A', and I think 'B', neither of us thinks 'A is B', and no judgement is made between us.)

The transcendental object

The second element in the pre-categorial structure of experience to be explicated is the side of the object, the fundamental notion that our representations are *of* things. Experience of objects is possible only through the *concept* of an object. That experience is of objects is something which the Aesthetic alone, restricted as it is to the contribution of sensibility, does not show to be possible. Now it is clear that the concept of an object must have a peculiar status. It cannot, we have seen Kant argue, derive from experience, for which reason it could not be due to the independent existence of any objects. But nor, if it is to play its role in constituting the pre-categorial structure of experience, can it have the status of a category, and Kant omits it from the Table of Categories.

Kant begins by asking what is meant by 'object of representation' (A104). He answers that we represent objects as 'corresponding to, and consequently also distinct from' our representations, and that this distinctness allows the object to be viewed as that which 'prevents our mode of knowledge from being haphazard or arbitrary': it 'determines' our representations 'a priori in some fashion'. The distinctness from representations in question here is not the strong distinctness of an object's independent existence in space, but mere judgemental distinctness, and the corresponding notion of object is not that of something external to the mind, let alone a substance, but simply the correlate of a judgement, that to which a concept is applied, a judgemental object.

It is important to see that, because the sense of object in play at this point is so weak, Kant does not beg any questions against the Humean or solipsist. The Humean, it might be supposed, could object to Kant's analysis of 'object of representation' that the primary objects of thought need not be distinct from representations, because they may themselves *be* representations. However, this is not something that Kant is deciding yet. The relevant point at this early stage in the Analytic is that even the solipsist, in making judgements about his own mental states, erects a world of objects (subjective objects, as they might be called) and thereby articulates the rudimentary distinction of subject and object. Whether our primary judgemental objects can *ultimately* be regarded as exclusively subjective states, or whether they must include empirically real, outer objects, is another matter, to be determined later (it is, as will be seen, partly decided once the Deduction has run its course, and fully settled in the Analytic of Principles).

Assuming, then, that Kant is right in thinking that a step in the direction of objectivity, of some degree, must be taken, the question is what makes it possible for our experience to be directed to objects, bearing in mind that for Kant a realist answer is of course ruled out ('outside our knowledge we have nothing which we could set over against this knowledge as corresponding to it', A104). We achieve this, Kant says, by employing the concept of the 'transcendental object'. This is the mere concept of an object 'thought only as something in general $= x$' (A104), a concept which 'throughout all our knowledge is always one and the same' (A109). The transcendental object is thus different from the concept of appearance. Its role is to provide a point to which the elements of the manifold of intuition may be referred, allowing appearances to be determined as thinkable objects of intuition. In order to play this role, it is essential that the transcendental object should not 'itself be intuited by us' (A109): if it were intuited, it would be another element in the manifold, and would need to be referred in turn to something else not contained therein. The transcendental object must, therefore, be excluded from the manifold of intuition if an infinite regress is to be avoided – which is why its concept cannot be any richer than that of an 'x' which 'is nothing to us', and of which all that can be said is that it 'has to be distinct from our representations' (A105). The concept is therefore quite obviously non-empirical (A109). The transcendental object thus adds another plank to Kant's refutation of empiricism.

The transcendental object cannot fulfil its role as providing a reference point distinct from representations by virtue of its content, because it has none. All it can amount to, then, is a function of unity: all it can refer to is 'that unity which must be met with in any manifold of knowledge which stands in relation to an object' (A109). It can give unity to the manifold of intuition by determining the synthesis of its elements. Hence the transcendental object maps directly onto the concept of synthetic unity with which Kant attacks empiricism. What it adds is a connection with objectivity: the transcendental object is what confers 'objective reality' on our representations (A109). (Objective reality and objective validity are Kant's frequently used terms for objectivity. Usually, though not invariably, the former is used with reference to concepts and the latter with reference to judgements and principles: a concept has objective reality if it has an object, and a judgement or principle has objective validity if its predicate is necessarily true of all objects within its domain, i.e. if it has strict universality.)

The envisaged role of the concept of transcendental object in the construction of experience is clear: by unifying our representations, it allows intuition to yield objects of thought; it interposes a distance between representations and objects, and at the same time guarantees the agreement of objects with our representations. What makes the concept puzzling, and a source of controversy, are the many further things that Kant says about it. At later points in the *Critique*, the transcendental object is described as unknown to us (A191/B236, A250–1, A366, A372, A565/B593), as the underlying ground or cause of inner and outer appearance (A277/B333, A379–80, A288/B344, A358, A372, A391, A393, A494–5/B522–3, A538/B566), and tentatively associated with the non-empirical entities that Kant calls noumena (A288/B344, A358, A545/B573, A564/B592, A565/B593). These statements strongly suggest an identification of the transcendental object with the thing in itself, a thing that is transcendentally real. Now this is something one might be inclined to accept anyway, on the grounds that it provides the only possible answer to the question of the transcendental object's identity: it might be argued that the transcendental object needs to be a *transcendent* object, since it is called upon to supply a non-subjective, outer reference for representations, and in Kant's scheme the only thing that is in a position to play this role, i.e. provide a term of contrast for subjectivity, is the thing in itself.

This interpretation has been defended, but it is obvious what difficulties it (like the parallel interpretation of apperception) creates. If this is Kant's position, his transcendental idealism disintegrates, for it implies that we *do* know things in themselves after all: the spatio-temporal etc. features of empirical objects become genuine, albeit relational attributes of things in themselves, and Kant is committed to affirming that the thing in itself is *given* to us as the object distinct from our representations. Our relation to things in themselves would then be very much like our relation to substratum on the traditional model, and Kant would merely have added to Locke a Berkeleyan claim about the subjectivity of primary qualities. His account of objects of representation would have become, contrary to the intention he avows at A104, transcendentally realist, and his position as vulnerable to skepticism as Locke's.

The problem, then, is to find an interpretation of the concept of transcendental object that avoids identifying it with the thing in itself, yet makes sense of Kant's further statements about it. One that meets these conditions is the following.

The concept of the transcendental object as 'a something $= x$' contains no reference to a constitution, but any existing object, cognised or not, must of course have a constitution, i.e. exist in such and such a way. The concept of the transcendental object therefore stands in need of concretisation or realisation – 'determination', in Kant's language (the transcendental object is 'a completely indeterminate thought', 'determinable' through the categories and manifold of appearances, A250–3). Properly speaking, then, the transcendental object itself, as opposed to its actual and possible realisations, cannot be an object of knowledge at all. Now, though the concept of the transcendental object *as we finite subjects with sensibility realise it* amounts to no more than a necessary unity of representations, the concept itself admits of a possible alternative, ontologically stronger realisation, viz. as a thing in itself. So realised, the concept of the transcendental object would contain no reference to representations or their unity.

The concepts of thing in itself and transcendental object should therefore not be confused. They are the same in respect of both being completely blank, and the transcendental object is the sole representation by means of which we can think of things in themselves; but it is the transcendental object, not the thing in itself, which is the source of the unity of objects, and each is unknowable for quite different reasons: the thing in itself is unknowable because it has a constitution inaccessible to our mode of cognition, the transcendental object because it is, as the concept of an object prior to any constitution, not an entity at all.

To this there is a complication, which brings the two concepts together, and helps to explain Kant's statements that the transcendental object is unknown to us, underlies appearance, etc. Our employment of the concept of the transcendental object carries with it, as said, the thought of things in themselves in a non-assertoric, neutral mode, i.e. without any affirmation of their existence. The existence of things in themselves as the ground of appearance is, however, affirmed by Kant in a separate context, for reasons unrelated to the question of how objectivity arises from our representations (discussed in chapter 8). The transcendental object does, therefore, have its ontological superior realisation. And this means that the concept of the transcendental object ultimately has two uses, in one of which it contrasts with the thing in itself, and in the other of which they are identified. What is important in the present context is that Kant's later statements regarding the transcendental object should not mislead us into thinking that the Deduction's account of objectivity is staked on the existence of transcendent objects: the thesis that things in themselves exist *qua* ground of appearances is not part of the theory of experience articulated in the Analytic.

The question of the identity of the transcendental object should, therefore, be answered in the following terms: 'Although to the question, what is the constitution of a transcendental object, no answer can be given stating *what it is*, we can yet reply that the *question* itself is *nothing*, because there is no given object [corresponding] to it'; 'A question as to the constitution of that something which cannot be thought through any determinate predicate ... is entirely null and void' (A479n/B507n). That is, no further question of identity remains once it has been explained how the concept functions in the constitution of experience, and that its ontologically superior realisation is necessarily inaccessible to us.

If this is right, then Kant's account of objectivity is purely immanent: it does not presuppose an epistemic relation to anything outside the sphere of our representations, and it avoids appeal to anything transcendent in accounting for objects of representation. Saying this raises the question whether Kant is not, like phenomenalism, seeking to *reduce* objectivity to a logical construction out of subjective materials (representations). Reasons for resisting this interpretation will be given in chapter 8, but for the moment it may be noted that the concept of transcendental object does not lend it support.

While it is true that, according to Kant, we can represent objects in our experience only by *taking* necessary unities of representations *as* representings of objects, it does not follow that for Kant the concept of an object as such reduces to that of a necessary unity of representations. On the contrary, the whole point of talking, as Kant does, of 'a something = x', in addition to talking of necessary unities of experience, is to mark this distinction. Kant says that an object is 'that in the concept of which the manifold of a given intuition is *united*' (B137), not that an object *is*, or that the concept of an object is that of, a unified manifold. To make this identification would be to conflate the concept of object with the function it has in synthesis, and objects themselves with the means by which we realise them in representation.

If this is right, then Kant does not reduce objectivity to a logical construction out of subjectivity. Nor is he eliminating the relation of correspondence between object and representation in favour of relations of coherence among representations: his analysis is instead a non-reductive one, according to which the two relations simply imply one another.

The concept of the transcendental object may consequently be regarded as expressing the irreducibility of the concept of an object, as well as its a priority – just as the 'I' of apperception expresses the irreducibility of subjectivity and is not to be reduced to relations between representations. The transcendental object should not, therefore, be identified with the immanent contents of our experience any more than with something transcendent; exactly paralleling the transcendental unity of apperception, it sits on the borderline between the inside and outside of experience (as must any pre-categorial condition of experience).

Subject and object as making one another possible

The pre-categorial conditions of experience on the sides of subject and object having been spelled out, their connection – the subject–object relation, the third element in the pre-categorial structure of experience – may now be accounted for. This is best grasped by considering that Kant's account of subject and object raises a question. Granted that the transcendental unity of apperception and the transcendental object are necessary for experience, what makes *them* possible? So far Kant's account of the grounds of each is merely negative: neither, he has argued, is empirical. Kant's master stroke in the Deduction is to propose that each explains the other.

First, the subject makes the object possible. The relation of representation to object is, Kant says, constituted by the necessary unity of representations, and this unity is in turn identical with the necessary unity of consciousness (A109). This means, in the first place, that the conditions under which self-consciousness is possible are the same as those under which representations can be taken to have objects: 'the unity which the object makes necessary can be nothing else than the formal unity of consciousness' (A105); objects of experience 'must stand under the conditions of the necessary unity of apperception' (A110). But it also means, Kant is clear, that the unity of objects *derives* from the unity of consciousness, that the latter is the *ground* of the former: 'it is the unity of consciousness that alone constitutes the relation of representations to an object' (B137). The unity of the subject is, therefore, reproduced on the side of the object, a priori synthesis being the means by which this takes place. The production of synthetic unity is thus revealed to be identical with cognition of objects: 'when we have thus produced synthetic unity in the manifold of intuition . . . we are in a position to say that we know the object' (A105).

Second, the object makes the subject possible, again through a priori synthesis. Because I cannot become aware of my identity directly, by intuiting a single continuing thing, consciousness of self-identity can be achieved only through awareness of myself as the source of the synthetic unity of objects: 'the mind could never think its identity in the manifold of its representations . . . if it did not have before its eyes the identity of the act, whereby it subordinates all synthesis of apprehension . . . to a transcendental unity, thereby rendering possible their interconnection' (A108); 'apperception can demonstrate a priori its complete and necessary identity' only in 'synthesis according to concepts' (A112); the relation of representations to the identity of the subject comes about 'only in so far as I *conjoin* one representation with another, and am conscious of the synthesis of them. Only in so far, therefore, as I can unite a manifold of given representations in *one consciousness*, is it possible for me to represent to myself the identity *of the consciousness in* [i.e. throughout] *these representations*' (B133).

The argument here can be reconstructed as follows. What needs to be explained, primordially, is how we can prise ourselves as subjects apart from our representations to achieve self-consciousness. The distinction of one's identical self from one's manifold of representations cannot be a given fact, any more than can the combination of the manifold of intuition (i.e. the argument of §15 of the B Deduction applies to it too). The distinction of self and representation, if not given, must be made, and the question is what allows us to make it. Now if we were pure receptivity, appearances would, as Kant puts it, 'crowd in upon the soul', and yet 'be such as would never allow of experience', because 'all relation of knowledge to objects would fall away' (A111). A subject merged into its representations would be unable to think of itself as having representations, and for that reason, though it might be said to have consciousness of some sort, could not be self-conscious. What allows us to make the distinction is, Kant proposes, a priori conceptual activity. This is the only thing that could do the job: self-consciousness is consciousness of spontaneity (myself as perceiv*ing*, remember*ing*, etc.), so it must involve representation of oneself in terms of activity, and this activity needs to be conceptual, or it would not make the 'I' thinkable, and it must be based on a priori conditions, or it would be empirical and, therefore, mere receptivity.

We must, furthermore, have consciousness of our a priori synthesis of objects, if it is to play a transcendental role. The consciousness of a priori synthesis that Kant postulates is of course not of any introspectable sort: it consists, not in awareness of myself as doing such and such, which awareness could only be empirical, but in intellectual awareness of the results of synthesis *as* products of my activity. The existence of this consciousness is testified to by our representation of ourselves as spontaneous, which is a condition of our representing ourselves as thinkers of thoughts and makers of judgements. Kant's argument, in sum, is that consciousness of a priori synthesis explains transcendental apperception, and that nothing else can be conceived to do so, and since this synthesis implies the representation of synthetic unities, self-consciousness presupposes consciousness of objects; unless we took our representations as having a reference beyond themselves to objects, consciousness of self-identity would not be possible.

By showing the dependence of transcendental apperception on a priori synthesis, the Deduction establishes the necessity of there being objects corresponding to and distinct from our representations, i.e. of use of the concept of transcendental object. The Deduction has, in consequence, made progress against the Humean position that the primary objects of our thought are exclusively subjective (representations): if self-consciousness is possible only in the way Kant describes, then its objects cannot be represented as 'I'. This is not to say that they must be empirically real, outer objects: the distinctness from the self of the objects described in the Deduction is not yet of any determinate kind, and the Analytic of Principles is needed to add these further determinations. But it does mean that the Humean position is incoherent, because Hume requires me to represent as subjective something that I must contrast with myself in order to be self-conscious. Whatever the ultimate status of the primary objects of our thought, the Deduction has eliminated any ground for the claim that they are of necessity to be regarded as 'mine'.

Subject and object thus make one another possible: neither creates the other, but neither could be represented without the other. That a representation is mine is not, the Deduction shows, a brute or given fact: the thinking of my representations involves a world of objects, the unity of which is grounded on apperception. The process whereby subject and object are articulated as distinct yet interdependent items supplies the pre-categorial condition of the possibility of objects.

The result is a picture of self and nature as mirroring one another, and a reconception of self-consciousness. If Descartes may be credited with having discovered the significance of subjectivity for philosophical thought, Kant's achievement is to have transformed the Cartesian approach by suggesting that self-consciousness be viewed, not as a relation in which a pre-existent object of a special kind becomes known to itself, but as the encompassing ground of the world of objects. Descartes sought to bring out the distinguishing features of subjectivity by isolating it from the world of objects, yet continued to regard it as a content of that world. Kant, by contrast, conceives self-consciousness as something not included in the world of objects.

The legitimation of the categories

Finally, Kant's theory of the subject–object relation realises the epistemological goal of the Deduction, the legitimation of the categories: a priori synthesis, on which the subject–object relation turns, is, Kant claims, necessarily synthesis in accordance with rules derived from the categories.

Kant does not spell out the rationale for this transition, but it does not present much difficulty. There are several ways in which Kant may justify the identification of the conditions of apperception with synthesis according to the categories. One rests on familiar Kantian doctrines: synthesis is an act, and activity is a feature of the understanding, not of sensibility; the understanding is the source of a priori concepts, the categories; so a priori synthesis must be synthesis according to the categories. Another is a simple extension of the argument given above for the dependence of self-consciousness on objects: transcendental apperception is possible only if there is a priori conceptual synthesis (for the reasons given above), and this is possible only if there are a priori concepts, i.e. categories. (This second argument provides, therefore, a new ground for Kant's claim that there are a priori concepts.) And a third argument: the transcendental object is the concept of a 'something in general', and the categories are concepts of objects in general, so synthesis dictated by the transcendental object is necessarily in accordance with the categories.

Not included in the Deduction itself, but belonging to it as a kind of coda, is a later section called 'The Highest Principle of all Synthetic Judgements' (A154–8/B193–7). Here Kant explains how the problem of synthetic a priori judgement in general is solved in the Deduction. In synthetic judgement, Kant reminds us, 'we must advance beyond a given concept in order to compare it synthetically with another', for which 'a third something is necessary, as that wherein alone the synthesis of two concepts can be achieved' (A155/B194). The problem is to understand how this is possible in the case of synthetic judgements that are a priori.

The Deduction has shown that all representations, and hence all objects of experience, stand under transcendental conditions, and the possibility of synthetic a priori judgements derives from these. The 'highest principle of all synthetical judgements', inclusive of those which are a priori, 'is this: every object stands under the necessary conditions of synthetic unity of the manifold of intuition in a possible experience' (A158/B197). The third something in the case of synthetic a priori judgements is provided, therefore, by the conditions of possible experience, included in which are pure intuition and the unity of apperception. It follows that the categories cannot be employed outside possible experience (Kant challenges the transcendent metaphysician, who would seek to do so, to say what other 'third something' their would-be synthetic judgements could be based on, A258–9/B314–15).

By the end of the Deduction, the basic problem of the Analytic has been solved. The task was to show that a priori concepts function as transcendental conditions. In order to do this, a transcendental function for conceptuality needed to be discovered, and the transcendental unity of apperception has supplied this: it is what necessitates that there be objects, and that they have a priori conceptual form (as such it is the 'highest principle in the whole sphere of human knowledge', B135). We still have objectivity in only a weak sense – a realm of objects qualifying as 'not-I' and providing for truth as distinct from mere seeming; of states of affairs without any ontological determination, comprising simply 'what is the case' – but, as said earlier, the reality of nature is not Kant's target in the Deduction.

The more specific problem for the Analytic, expressed in the worry that appearances might be chaotic, was to say how there can be any connection at all between the sensible and the conceptual. Although transcendental idealism rules out one way in which appearances might be unjudgeable – it entails that they cannot be so by virtue of their independent constitution – there remained the task of securing for objects a positively subject-agreeing constitution: it is one thing to show that appearances cannot have a constitution discrepant with the conceptual powers of the subject, and another to show that their sensible constitution must conform to our conceptual powers. The question is how one and the same object can figure in relation to both sensibility and understanding – why are there not (as Kant had ventured in his *Inaugural Dissertation*) two worlds of objects, one for each faculty?

The theory of a priori synthesis, which entails that appearances are intrinsically fitted to receive the categories, provides Kant's solution: it shows that the given is conceptually constituted. The Deduction shows that the empiricist idea of two stages in cognition or levels of consciousness – a level of experiential data given independently of thought, and a level of thought directed at that data – is incoherent. The job of getting consciousness to transcend itself towards the world, on Kant's account, is already performed at the level of the given, which is such that thought based immediately on it is necessarily directed at *objects* presented in it, not at mere 'experiential data' from which objects might be extrapolated by means of subsequent intellectual operations. The given presents itself as providing the grounds for judgements about objects, and it could not have this property, the Deduction shows, if it did not have conceptual form. What is given is so to speak as good as thought. As a result no gap appears for the subject between objects' being given, and concepts' having application: the internal tie between experience and concepts precludes the possibility that concept application rests fundamentally on inference. It is not, therefore, that the given is abolished, but that it is shown to include objectivity. The Deduction has, then, worked out the idea advanced in the metaphysical deduction, that there must be a structure common to thought and intuition: the 'same function that gives unity to the various representations *in a judgement* also gives unity to the mere synthesis of various representations *in an intuition*' (B104–5).

Further issues

In conclusion, some of the many further issues associated with the Deduction should be mentioned. First, a puzzle is created by the passages which correspond to the Deduction in the *Prolegomena* (§§ 17–20, 21a). There Kant argues for the justification of the categories in terms of a distinction between 'judgements of perception' and 'judgements of experience', the latter being objective and presupposing the categories, the former subjective and grounded on merely empirical unities of consciousness. Prima facie this conflicts directly with the teaching of the *Critique* that judgement is altogether impossible without the categories, in which terms the concept of a judgement of perception is contradictory. One way of harmonising the texts is to suppose that in the *Prolegomena* – consistently with its aim of recasting Critical philosophy in a more assimilable form – Kant is admitting the (empiricist's) notion of a judgement of perception merely for the sake of argument, in order to then explain its insufficiency for empirical knowledge.

A second issue concerns the Deduction's conclusion that experience presupposes categorial concepts. Kant might be interpreted as claiming either that there cannot *be* experiences independently of the categories, or only that experience presupposes the categories in so far as it is to provide a basis for judgement, or function representationally for a subject. Kant says that perceptions not subordinated to the categories 'would be without an object, merely a blind play of representations, less even than a dream' (A112), and that an appearance without necessary connection to the understanding would be unaccompanied by consciousness and so 'would be nothing to us', indeed 'nothing at all' (A120; see also B131–2). These remarks suggest the first interpretation.

Taking Kant in this way has led to an objection. Our experience includes dreams, hallucinations and other presentations of which we are conscious but which lack objects. Equally, some of our mental connections are triggered by mere association, independently of any a priori rule of ordering. Presumably, on Kant's account, such experience amounts to 'a blind play of representations' and fails to conform to the categories. On this basis it has been argued that the mere fact of such 'extra-categorial' experience refutes the Deduction's conclusion that experience presupposes the categories.

However, it is easily seen that dreams and suchlike are not extra-categorial in a sense inconsistent with the Deduction. First, while it is true that dreams etc. are not *fully* determined by the categories, they are not without connection to the understanding: to dream or hallucinate is necessarily to have experience expressible in judgemental form; the intentional objects of dream or hallucination are dependent on the categories. Second, we can and do conceptualise dreams and other imaginary experiences as representations of objects, namely ourselves: they are modifications of our minds, in Kant's terms, objects of inner sense. Dreams and suchlike can, therefore, be accommodated by Kant as dependent cases of experience: they are possible by virtue of their subordinate place in a system of fully categorially ordered experience; they could not comprise the whole of the experience of a rational self-conscious subject, but can comprise part of it.

It is none the less important to remember that, as the alternative interpretation of Kant's position reminds us, Kant's goal is a transcendental theory of human cognition, not a theory of the human mind *qua* empirical phenomenon. It follows from the Deduction's anti-empiricism that cognition cannot be built on or out of states with a purely sensory character, mental states whose content is non-conceptual, but not, arguably, that such states cannot figure at some level of empirical consideration. If so, it is left open by the Deduction that such states may occur in non-rational subjects such as infants and animals, and perhaps also in rational self-conscious subjects. But if they do, then it is not as elements of cognition: they do not belong to the 'given' in the objectivity-including sense discussed earlier, and whether they may even be described as states of consciousness remains a moot point.

A third issue, with broad implications for reading Kant and a controversial history in Kant commentary, is his so-called 'transcendental psychology' (not Kant's own term). By this is meant everything that Kant says about the structure and operations of the subject, above all his theory of synthesis and distinction of faculties. Transcendental psychology is frequently rejected as a superfluous and, because of its allegedly speculative character, damaging addition to transcendental philosophy. The simplification of the synthesis story in the B Deduction, and its discarding of the apparatus of a 'subjective deduction', may seem to support this view.

The animus against transcendental psychology is standardly bound up with a rejection of Kant's idealism, and this is appropriate, because it is an integral component of transcendental idealism. If the Analytic is to show not merely *that* objects must receive conceptual form, but also *how* they may do so, then it is essential that Kant should offer some account of how the subject realises this end. As such, transcendental psychology is not mere speculation: Kant does not merely venture hypotheses about the inner workings of an unknown transcendental mind, because his claims about the structure and activities of the subject are direct extrapolations from descriptions of how objects must be conditioned in order for experience to be possible. Transcendental philosophy specifies subjectivity in terms of the a priori functions that it must perform, but it does not say anything about their 'underlying mechanism'.

The specific conceptual form of human experience: causally interacting substances (The Schematism, The Analogies, The Refutation of Idealism)

With the Deduction in place, the method and overarching claims of the Analytic are established. In the Analytic of Principles which then follows – more precisely, in the System of the Principles of Pure Understanding, which composes the bulk of the Analytic of Principles – Kant identifies principles for the employment of the twelve categories, and defends them as necessary for experience, thereby vindicating the Table of Categories on the basis of its individual concepts. The System of the Principles contains a quantity of complex discussion, but the central arguments are more clearly stated than in the Deduction.

In the preamble to the System of Principles, Kant defines an a priori principle as a judgement which provides the ground of other judgements, but is not itself deduced from any other, more universal judgement (A148/B188). The proof of a principle must consequently be transcendental (A148–9/B188). Also he distinguishes mathematical and dynamical principles of understanding (A160–1/B199–200). The former, the Axioms and Anticipations, are concerned with 'the mere *intuition* of an appearance in general'. The latter, the Analogies and Postulates, provide conditions of 'the existence of the objects of a possible empirical intuition': they are rules for connecting and unifying empirical intuition, whereby it becomes cognition or experience (Kant uses 'experience' – *Erfahrung* – as equivalent to empirical knowledge, B218). The force of the distinction is that mathematical principles are necessary but not sufficient for objectivity, which requires also dynamical principles.

As noted earlier, the section which is crucial for the *Critique*'s legitimation of the metaphysics of experience is the Analogies of Experience (supplemented by the Refutation of Idealism). Here Kant argues that the objectivity which the Deduction has shown to be necessary must, for subjects of spatio-temporal intuition, assume a particular form, namely that of a world of causally interacting substances – against Hume's contention that we lack rational grounds for employing the concepts of body and necessary connection, and that our causal judgements reduce to assertions of mere constant conjunction. Because the Axioms and Anticipations make a relatively slight (and uncontentious) contribution to Kant's objectivity argument, and the Postulates are somewhat dissociated from it, these chapters are held over for consideration in a later section.

The Schematism

Before looking at the Analogies, it is essential to grasp the main point that Kant makes in the Schematism, the short but extremely dense chapter which precedes the System of Principles. Here Kant returns to the question of how the sensible and the conceptual are related.

The new context for considering this question is provided by the concept of judgement, *qua* activity: in the introductory sections of the Analytic of Principles (A130–6/B169–75), Kant explains that judgement is 'the faculty of subsuming under rules' (A132/B171), for which reason the Analytic of Principles may be described as a 'canon' or 'doctrine', i.e. set of instructions, for judgement (A132/B171).

The Deduction has shown that the categories must be applied to objects given in intuition. This requirement, Kant now argues, leaves behind it a problem. Whenever an object is subsumed under a concept, i.e. judged, the representation of the object must be, Kant says, '*homogeneous* with the concept' (A137/B176). Initially, this may sound peculiarly empiricist – it recalls resemblance theories of ideas – but what Kant means by homogeneity is something quite different, which precisely cuts across the barrier between the sensible and non-sensible. In order for a concept to get a grip on an object given in intuition, there must be something in the concept which is *capable* of being represented in intuition – concepts must be such that it is *possible* for intuitions to conform to them. And the problem is that the categories, as they stand, are too abstract for this condition to be met: they are 'quite heterogeneous' from sensible intuition (A137/B176).

The category of causality illustrates the point. All it contains is the highly abstract idea of a relation of ground to consequent, of one thing's being the case because something else is the case. Now it is clear that, so far in the transcendental theory of experience, we have no idea of what it would be for our experience to exhibit 'becauseness': it is not yet intelligible that this purely intellectual relation should be sensibly intuited, or contained in appearance. It is consequently not enough for the Deduction to have told us that the sensible and the conceptual must be connected, and that the connection is effected in a priori synthesis, for we have as yet no notion of what the sensible instantiation of a pure concept could amount to. Concepts must, therefore, be brought somehow closer to intuition, if objects of intuition are to be able to assume conceptual form.

The solution, Kant suggests, is to assume 'some third thing', which is homogeneous with both the categories and intuition or appearance (A138/B177). This 'mediating representation' must be in one respect intellectual, and in another sensible. Kant calls it a *schema* (plural, schemata). Schemata are, Kant says, produced by imagination (A140/B179, A142/B181), the mediating faculty introduced in the Deduction. Schematism is the process by which schemata are generated and conjoined with concepts. We may consequently speak of schematised and unschematised versions of concepts, i.e. concepts considered respectively in relation to, and apart from their schemata.

Schemata differ emphatically from mere images (A140–1/B179–80): Kant characterises them as methods or procedures, in opposition to the empiricist tendency to model concept application in pictorial terms. Schemata are, on Kant's account, presupposed for the generation of images, and it is they, not images, which facilitate the subsumption of objects under concepts. Echoing Berkeley's criticism of Locke's theory of abstract ideas, Kant says that no image of a triangle, for example, 'could ever be adequate to the concept of a triangle in general', the schema of which 'can exist nowhere but in thought'; similarly for the concept 'dog' (A141/B180). Again, the series of dots '. . . . .' may serve as an image of the number five (A140/B179), but its doing so presupposes a method for representing images in conformity with concepts of magnitude, viz. the schema of number ('the successive addition of homogeneous units', A142/B182). Thus on Kant's account, concept application in general, inclusive of empirical concepts, rests on schemata.

The schemata with importance for the Analytic's theory of experience, and in need of specification here, are those associated with the categories, the *transcendental schemata* (A138/B177). A transcendental schema, Kant proposes, consists in a 'transcendental determination of time' (A139/B178), i.e. way of conceptualising time. Kant's claim, then, is that the categories gain application through being equated with, or realised in, thoughts about time, or time as thought in certain ways.

It cannot be pretended that this idea is easily grasped, and it may at first seem quite arbitrary, because on Kant's own account, there is nothing intrinsic to time *qua* form of intuition to suggest an imminent connection with the categories. But Kant is not claiming that time has incipient conceptual meaning: he is instead, once again, reasoning in terms of transcendental functions, and arrives at his conclusion by elimination (A138–40/B177–9, A145–6/B185). Transcendental schematism requires a mediating representation which has a sensible aspect, and is a priori rather than empirical; and within the confines of his transcendental theory of experience, only pure intuition fits this description. Since something must provide the meeting point between pure concepts and empirical intuition, and nothing else could do so, pure intuition must do so. And the reason why it should be time specifically which provides the key to transcendental schematism, is that time is the most general unifying condition of intuitions and concepts: all sensible objects are intuited in time, and all conceptual activity stands under the condition of self-consciousness, the objects of which are temporal. Subjects with non-temporal forms of sensibility would, therefore, schematise the categories differently, and could not comprehend the categories as schematised by us.

On this basis, Kant specifies twelve transcendental schemata, one for each category (A142–5/B182–4). To take the two that matter most for the Analogies: the pure logical concept of substance, a something which can be thought only as subject, becomes when schematised 'permanence of the real in time' (A143/B183). And the pure logical concept of causality, a relation of ground to consequent, becomes the concept of 'the real upon which, whenever posited, something else always follows', 'the succession of the manifold, in so far as that succession is subject to a rule' (A144/B184).

The role of time, brought to the fore in the present context of connecting the sensible and the conceptual, assumes further importance in the Analogies, where Kant attempts to derive strong metaphysical commitments from it. For this reason, it is possible to regard the Schematism as offering a fresh start in the transcendental theory of experience: some commentators read the chapter as re-executing, in a more promising fashion, the task Kant set himself in the Clue, of identifying a privileged set of a priori concepts which supply the conceptual conditions of experience, a metaphysics of experience. This has the arguable advantage of making the unsatisfactory metaphysical deduction redundant: the categories are then connected with the concept of judgement just in so far as bringing objects under the categories is a case of judging, and their purported intimate relation to the logical forms of judgement drops away. It also has the effect, however, that the notion of an *un*schematised category

THE CONCEPTUAL CONDITIONS OF OBJECTS

disappears, or becomes a dubious abstraction from the conditions of empirical knowledge – a result which clashes, in ways that will be seen later, with other, essential elements in Kant's philosophy, which require the categories to have meaning independently of schematism.

Whatever is made of this approach, it should be noted how Kant's proposal for connecting the sensible and the conceptual, though superficially straightforward, is at another level extremely perplexing. Is a transcendental schema a *thought* about time, or is it *time* as thought in a certain way? Our ways of referring to transcendental schemata inevitably assimilate them, it would seem, to one side or the other of the concept/intuition divide. Moreover, it appears necessary to do exactly this, if we are to answer the question of what they are, or say anything contentful about them. The cost of the assimilation, however, in either direction, is to make them apparently unfit for their designated mediating role: if they are either concepts with a special relation to intuition, or intuitions as formed conceptually, then they seem to presuppose the very possibility of connecting the sensible and the conceptual which transcendental schematism is invoked to explain.

Kant may declare that transcendental schemata are irreducibly sensible-*and*-intellectual, and that this is how the question of their identity should be answered. If so, Kant's original division of our representations into intuitions and concepts is not exhaustive, for there is a third class, about which we can say very little, other than that it is dependent on and somehow derivative from the others. We can specify it in terms of the transcendental role to which the problem of relating concepts and intuitions gives rise, but the manner of its derivation, and the nature of schemata, we cannot specify. Note, it is not just that we can say relatively less about schemata than we can about intuitions and concepts, and that we cannot identify their ultimate source; we are equally ignorant of the grounds of our faculties of sensibility and understanding. Transcendental schemata remain in a *special* sense hard to grasp, because they are required to combine in themselves two kinds of property, or representational functions, the seeming immiscibility of which is precisely what made us introduce them in the first place. That this is nevertheless Kant's own view of the matter is, plausibly, what is suggested by his statement that schematism is 'an art concealed in the depths of the human soul, whose real modes of activity nature is hardly likely ever to allow us to discover' (A141/B180–1).

It is, no doubt, consistent to claim that the transcendental theory of experience forces us to assume just this, but it marks a singular point in the theory's development, because it means that we have come to a limit of transcendental explanation, in a sense not previously encountered. The obscurity attaching to the doctrine of schematism is the price which Kant ultimately pays for escaping from rationalism and empiricism, and rejecting the transcendental realist model of concept application.

The Analogies of Experience

The Schematism having shown what sort of content the categories must have if they are to play a role in constituting objects of experience, and how they can acquire it, the Analogies proceed to show that the schematised categories of substance and causality perform a transcendental function. This function is tied specifically to the circumstance that we are subjects immersed in time. Our temporality gives rise, in the context of the transcendental theory of experience, to a problem concerning temporal judgement, namely: how is it possible for us to represent objects as being in time, in a sense which transcends the temporality of our representations? Substance and causality, Kant argues, provide the answer. Substance is dealt with in the first analogy, and causality in the second; the third analogy assembles their results, and puts space into the picture. The three analogies correspond to the relational categories (subsistence, causality, community) and modes of time (duration, succession, simultaneity, A177/B219, A215/B262). (Kant also associates the analogies with fundamental propositions in Newtonian physics – see Part Two of the *Prolegomena* – but he is not attempting to prove these here.)

If a realm of objects is to be represented, then it must be possible to draw a distinction between the subjective and the objective aspects of our representations, i.e. between the aspect of our representations which refers to us their subjects, and the aspect which can be taken to refer to a world of objects. Now the very first thing that is needed here, Kant argues, is a distinction between the temporal order of our representations, and the temporal order of objects: if we are to think of objects as distinct from our representations, then we need to be able to think of them as existing in time, as a matter over and above the inner flow of our representations. In other words, we need to be able to form the idea of an *objective time-order*, in which objects exist with determinate temporal locations, as distinct from the merely subjective time-order in which our representations succeed one another.

That something additional to what has already been supplied in the Analytic's theory of experience is genuinely necessary for this condition to be met, can be appreciated by recalling Kant's doctrine of inner sense. In the Aesthetic Kant told us that time 'cannot be outwardly intuited' (A23/B37), meaning that it cannot be intuited as outer without first being intuited as inner: time is given primordially as the dimension in which our representations exist. Something is needed, then, simply to make it *thinkable* that objects, as opposed to our representations, are in time. If I am to think, 'the sound of thunder occurred after the flash of lightning', then I need to be able to think more than just that a certain succession of representations occurred. If not, all that I will be able to judge is that I, the subject, was first in one mode and then in another.

A crucial element in the construction of Kant's problem concerning temporal judgement of objects is his further premise, stated repeatedly in the analogies, that time 'cannot itself be perceived' (B219, B225, A183/B226). If time could be perceived, then we would have knowledge of the moments of time in the same sense as we have knowledge of tables and chairs: time would comprise a fixed and determinate, self-subsistent framework, known independently of the events that occur in it, and there would be no problem in distinguishing an objective from a subjective time-order – the objective time-order would be given to us directly. It would comprise a kind of ruler lying visibly behind events, and against which we could locate them. But we do not have such knowledge of time, because it is a form of sensibility, not a thing in itself. Kant says: 'time is not viewed as that wherein experience immediately determines position for every existence. Such determination is impossible, inasmuch as absolute time is not an object of perception with which appearances could be confronted' (A215/B262).

The first analogy

The first analogy aims to establish the principle of permanence of substance: 'In all change of appearances substance is permanent' (B224). The formulation in the first edition is clearer: 'All appearances contain the permanent (substance) as the object itself, and the transitory as its mere determination, that is, as a way the object exists' (A182). The argument, in brief, is that in order to think of appearances as being in time, I need something fixed and unchanging, and since I do not perceive time itself, I need to conceive of something permanent in appearances, which is as much as to say that I need to employ the concept of substance.

Set out in detail, the argument goes as follows. All appearances stand, the Aesthetic shows, in relations of coexistence and succession in time. Now the time in which appearances are thought must *itself* remain the same: 'change does not affect time itself, but only appearances in time' (A183/B226). Kant does not mean that time itself persists throughout time, which would be confused, and nor is he denying that time passes, which would be absurd. What he means is that time is unitary, all changes taking place in one and the same time, and that time is the itself unchanging framework to which all change is referred (it cannot be true at one moment that A preceded B, and true at a later moment that A followed B; the temporal locations of events cannot themselves change).

Now, because time cannot itself be perceived, something must be found, *in the realm of appearances*, to play the role of an unchanging 'substratum which represents time in general' (B225), an 'abiding correlate of all existence of appearances' which 'expresses time in general' (A183/B226). This something, representing or expressing time, cannot be subjective, i.e. its role cannot be played by our '*apprehension* of the manifold', because there is nothing permanent in that: the manifold of inner sense is 'always successive, and is therefore always changing' (A182/B225). It must, therefore, be objective, which means that there must be a permanent in appearances, something persisting throughout change. And this, by the definition of the category, is *substance*. The permanence required of substance is, Kant says, incompatible with its coming into existence *ex nihilo*, or ceasing to exist, i.e. absolute permanence (A185–6/B228–9, A188/B231).

Kant reformulates the conclusion (B232–3) by saying that '*all change* [Wechsel] *(succession) of appearances is merely alteration* [Veränderung]', meaning that whenever appearances change, this must be regarded as consisting in changes occurring *in* substances. This reformulation is straightforward: if the concept of substance is to do any work, then it must mean that experience is of things that endure throughout change – things that are different ways at different times – and this means regarding changes in one's experience as representing changes in substances.

Kant's legitimation of the concept of substance, unlike that of earlier philosophers, avoids establishing the existence of substance dogmatically, as rationalists do when they argue to the reality of substance on the basis of a mere concept (A184–5/B227–8). And it does not have the usual and unwelcome upshot that substance is unknowable: nothing remains to be known about substance, because it is nothing more than the 'mode in which we represent to ourselves the existence of things in the [field of] appearance' (A186/B229). Where Locke wrestled with the concept of an unknowable substratum to which no sensible idea corresponds (paving the way for Hume's skeptical empiricism), Kant's account makes the question of what substance itself is disappear: *qua* form of experience, it has no mysterious inner nature.

The second analogy

The second analogy is less straightforward. It aims to establish the principle of causality: 'all alterations take place in conformity with the law of connection of cause and effect' (B232), i.e. every event must have a cause. This principle is rejected by Hume, on the grounds (as Kant would express them) that no representation of necessity is given in intuition, and that the objective validity of the causal principle cannot be derived from merely analytic considerations. Hence, for Kant, its synthetic a priori status, and the possibility of its receiving a transcendental proof, i.e. justification through being shown to be a necessary condition of experience.

The argument, briefly stated, is that experience of objective change, i.e. of the world as changing, as opposed to merely oneself or one's representations changing, is necessary for experience of an objective time-order, and that the distinction between change occurring in our representations, and change occurring in an objective world, can be made only by employing the concept of causality.

In detail, the argument is this. The first analogy shows that all change must be regarded as change in substances. The next question is how change can be referred to substances rather than to the subject. The concept of substance alone is not sufficient for this. What is also necessary is that we be able to think of the relation of succession in appearances as objective, i.e. as a succession in the objects themselves, independent from the succession occurring in the subject's representations. Unless I am able to think that objective successions, as opposed to merely subjective successions, take place, we have, Kant says, only a subjective 'play of representations, relating to no object' (B239).

Now, in order to be thought as objective, the relation of succession must be, Kant says, 'determined', meaning that it must be *necessary* and *irreversible* (A198–9/B243–4). To explain this point, Kant contrasts two cases, one in which my experience changes whilst the object remains the same, and another in which my experience changes because the object itself is changing. The first is that of viewing a house by moving round it, and the second that of watching a ship move downstream (A190–3/B235–8). In both there is a subjective succession: my experience changes, different representations coming one after the other. But in the first case, the change is just in experience, the house itself remaining unchanged, and my experiences could just as well – as regards their objective content – have occurred in the reverse order: I could have walked round the house clockwise instead of anti-clockwise. In the case of the ship, where my experience changes because the object itself is changing, it is not the case that my experiences could just as well have occurred in the reverse order: if they had, my experience would have been of something different, a ship moving upstream instead of downstream. So in the case of the ship, unlike that of the house, there is an *objective* succession, corresponding to my subjective succession, and what makes the difference, according to Kant, is that in the case of the ship I organise my experience according to a rule which makes the order in which I experience things necessary and irreversible. And the concept of a necessary and irreversible succession is, Kant says, the concept of a causal relation: the relation of cause and effect is both necessary and irreversible. The principle of causality is justified, therefore, on the grounds that only an a priori rule, by virtue of which one appearance can be regarded as *necessitating* another, allows us to refer change to objects, as required for an objective time-order. Again, no further question concerning the nature of causality can arise.

The third analogy

The third analogy extends the second analogy's claim that causality is required for objectivity. Its principle is that of coexistence: 'All substances, in so far as they can be perceived to coexist in space, are in thoroughgoing reciprocity' (B256). Whereas the second analogy was concerned with causality in the form of relations between events, the third is concerned with causality in the form of causal interaction between substances. This is why Kant uses the example of a ship in the second analogy: it exemplifies causality in so far as the ship's state at one moment is causally dependent on its state at the immediately preceding moment. The third analogy deals with the case where one event causes another in a different substance, as in the billiard ball scenario.

If time is to be determined as unitary, as required for an objective time-order, then it must be determinable that two things 'exist in one and the same time' (A211/B258); otherwise each object has, in effect, its own time stream (A213–14/B260–1). The third analogy argues that things can be determined as coexistent only through being determined as capable of causal interaction in space. Again it is the unperceivability of time, and the successiveness of our apprehension, which creates the initial problem: I cannot know through bare intuition that the moon and the earth are things which coexist, because all that intuition yields is a succession of moon- and earth-representations.

Objects can be determined as having the same location in time only when I can view the order of my representations as *reversible* (A211/B258). This allows me to take my representations as identifying an order of existence of objects which is not itself temporal. And what allows me to conceive objects as related to one another in a way to which the temporality of my representations is indifferent, Kant holds, is the concept of 'influence', whereby 'each substance reciprocally contains the ground of the determinations in the other' (B258).

Evaluating the Analogies

Expressed in broad terms, the idea underlying the analogies is that experience must, on two counts, form a unity: it must conform to the unity of apperception, and in order to do this, it must conform to the unity of time (A177–8/B220). Because 'connection is not the work of mere sense and intuition' (B233), it must be the work of the intellect, i.e. determined conceptually, and substances and causality are, the analogies show, fitted to this purpose on account of their capacity to make temporal relations determinate. Kant thus states the general principle of the analogies as: 'Experience is possible only through the representation of a necessary connection of perceptions' (B218). (This claim is made earlier, in the Deduction at A112–14, where Kant talks of a 'transcendental affinity' of appearances as being required for the numerical identity of apperception, but without any reference to the unity of time.) The upshot is that we inhabit a world of a particular type, one in which all objective empirical facts have a particular form, and all appearances collectively compose '*one* nature' (A216/B263). The unity of nature established by Kant is consequently very different from that of either Leibniz or Hume: it is internal to experience, and constitutive of the existence of appearances, rather than being transcendent (Leibniz's monadology) or merely subjective (Hume's mental propensity to associate).

Kant is generally acclaimed as having articulated something extremely important about objectivity in the Analogies, but standardly criticised as having inflated his conclusions. What Kant shows, it is alleged, is that, in order to make objective judgements, we need some way of organising our experience which goes beyond what is sensorily given, but this condition does not demand as much as Kant claims: it will do if we suppose substances possessing relative permanence, instead of the absolute permanent inferred in the first analogy; and in the second analogy, the weaker idea of some degree of regularity in our experience will serve in place of necessary connection between events. Consequently Kant does not rule out Humean constant conjunction as an analysis of causality.

This line of criticism might be justified, if Kant were asking either how the world must be in itself, or what assumptions a subject that is already in a position to take itself as making judgements about an objective world could at a minimum use to hold onto this conception of itself. But both of these questions are at variance with the terms of reference of the analogies: Kant is not seeking to establish something about a pre-formed world which might in itself be one way or another; nor is he considering the point of view of a subject that can already take itself to be in contact with objectivity. The analogies address the question – which is, in transcendental terms, much more fundamental, and which cannot be formulated independently of the theory of experience already set forth in the Analytic – of what a priori concepts can satisfy the conditions of having a double relation to the forms of judgement and forms of intuition, and of serving a constitutive role in acts of synthesis, whereby a domain of objects distinct from representations can become thinkable and be given. Kant's question concerns the initial conceptual form of the given, not inferences about reality that may be made on the basis of it.

The concepts of relative permanence and constant conjunction are not appropriate to this transcendental function. Relative permanence is not fit to play the role of expressing 'time in general' and thereby making an objective time-order thinkable: there could only be reason for conceiving things with the complex qualification 'relatively permanent' in the context of some particular theory, i.e. once an objective world has already been constituted and the unity of time determined. And constant conjunction does not itself specify an a priori conceptual form that intuition can take: it merely imposes a constraint on the content of experience. Kant's claims about absolute permanence and necessary connection are thus not metaphysically ambitious – they appear to be so only in an empiricist light. They are consequences of the rudimentary, all-or-nothing situation of the subject under consideration.

Kant may agree with his critics, therefore, that the analogies' account of the conditions of possibility of objectivity does not bear on the questions they have in mind, and point out that this is irrelevant to what he is arguing. To challenge the conclusions of the analogies, it would need to be shown either that they fail to cohere with the transcendental theory of experience, or that something else in this theory besides substance and causality could play the same role.

There remain, it should be added, some issues of interpretation surrounding the Analogies which the text does not clearly settle. The second analogy seeks to prove not merely the necessity of singular causal relations between events, but also that events must fall under causal laws. If so, a question arises concerning our knowledge of the particular causal laws under which events fall: must we know the relevant law in order to make a causal judgement, in which case laws of nature fall within the scope of the second analogy – or is it necessary only that we should suppose there to be such a law? Though the first interpretation is perhaps more natural, it is plausible that Kant ascribes the task of discovering the laws of nature to the faculty of reason (the role of reason in upgrading empirical knowledge is explained in the following chapter).

A similar uncertainty surrounds the conclusion of the first analogy, which says nothing about how substance is individuated for the purposes of our cognition. The natural supposition here is that the analogy is meant to prove a plurality of substances, corresponding to common sense's ontology of medium-sized physical objects. Kant's view is however, most probably, that the permanent is to be identified with the matter composing nature as a whole (see A185/B228), the substantiality of individual appearances being derivative and presupposing additional factors (A189/B232).

The Refutation of Idealism

The final section to be considered is the Refutation of Idealism. Here Kant aims to prove that we have experience of *outer objects* – objects distinct from us in space – and thus to refute skepticism about the external world, the continued existence of which Kant describes as a 'scandal to philosophy and to human reason in general' (Bxxxix).

In the brief prefatory note to the Refutation (B274–5), Kant analyses the different species of idealism. Idealism of a non-transcendental kind is referred to as 'material idealism'; Kant might equally have called it 'empirical idealism' (he employs this term at A369, though there with a particular form of it in mind). Transcendental idealism by contrast is a 'critical idealism' or 'formal idealism' (B519n, *Proleg* 294, 375), because it affirms that, while the sensible and conceptual form of appearances derives from the subject, the matter (that which corresponds to sensation) does not. Empirical idealism does affirm that the matter of appearance is supplied by the subject, so it is an idealism regarding the existence of objects, unlike transcendental idealism (*Proleg* 289). Kant's objective in the Refutation is to refute material or empirical idealism, and to defend empirical realism. The rationale for locating the Refutation in the Postulates is that it deals with the conditions under which objects are actual, a modal concept.

Material or empirical idealism divides into two sorts (B274–5). First, the 'dogmatic' idealism of Berkeley, which holds the existence of an external world to be 'false and impossible'. It is dogmatic because it claims that we can *know* there to be no external world. (Kant also describes Berkeley's philosophy as 'mystical and visionary idealism', *Proleg* 293, presumably with its quasi-platonistic elements in mind; see *Proleg* 374.) Second, the 'problematic' idealism ('skeptical idealism', A377) of Descartes, which asserts the existence of an external world to be possible but 'doubtful and indemonstrable', on the grounds that any claim to knowledge of the external world involves a dubious (problematic) inference from inner states to outer objects (see A367–8).

Kant groups Berkeley and Descartes together as material or empirical idealists on two counts: first because both assume that the immediate and primary objects of knowledge are exclusively subjective, private, mental entities, rather than empirically real objects, whereby they accept that knowledge of objects in space rests on inference from knowledge of inner states; and second, because neither, according to Kant, succeeds in defending commonsense belief in empirical reality. Berkeley may intend his idealist analysis of empirical knowledge as a defence of common sense against skepticism, but the upshot of Berkeley's account, for Kant as for most, is to reduce things in space to 'merely imaginary entities'. And though Descartes may intend skeptical doubt as only a methodological tool, on Kant's view he fails to escape from solipsism: if only inner objects are known immediately, there is no inferential route to the external world. Kant's reasons (given at A367–8) are the familiar ones that come up in criticism of representative theories of perception such as Locke's. (Kant ignores Descartes' appeal to God as guarantor of our knowledge claims; it is of course, in Kant's terms, wholly illegitimate.)

Kant directs the Refutation against problematic idealism alone, saying that the ground of Berkeley's idealism 'has already been undermined by us in the Aesthetic' (B274). It remains only to refute problematic idealism – i.e. to show 'that we have *experience* [*Erfahrung*], and not merely imagination, of outer things'. In order to do this, it is necessary, Kant says, to prove that 'even our inner experience, which for Descartes is indubitable, is possible only on the assumption of outer experience' (B275).

The argument is stated in one short paragraph (B275–6, amplified in the long footnote in the Preface, Bxxxix–xli[n]). It begins with the assumption (to which Kant supposes even the skeptic will agree) that 'I am conscious of my own existence as determined in time' (B275; I have '*empirical consciousness of my existence*', Bxl). That is: I take myself to make true judgements about objective changes in my experience, I locate my mental history in an objective time-order. This is stronger than the assumption of the Deduction, that I have transcendental self-consciousness, which is mere consciousness of myself as thinking: empirical self-consciousness presupposes inner sense and a corresponding empirical manifold (the distinction between empirical and transcendental apperception is made at A107 and B132–3). And it differs from the Analogies, because it concerns temporal judgement of my representations rather than of objects.

Now such awareness, like all determination of time, 'presupposes something permanent in perception' (B275). This is just the lesson of the first analogy. And since all that I intuit inwardly is the succession of my representations, in Humean fashion, this permanent cannot be something inside me (it 'cannot be an intuition in me', Bxxxix[n]). Even if there were something intuitable in me that remained constant throughout my experience (e.g. a 'feeling of self-ness'), it would be a *permanent representation*, not a *representation of a permanent* – an intuition that abides, not a thing that remains the same throughout change. Emphasising this distinction, Kant points out that permanent representation is no more necessary than it is sufficient for the representation of a permanent: representations may themselves be transitory yet refer to something permanent (Bxli).

With Descartes' *res cogitans* thus eliminated as a candidate for the permanent, Kant infers that it is possible 'only through a *thing* outside me and not through the mere *representation* of a thing outside me' (B275); and if the permanent must be outside me, then it must be spatial, because space is the form of outer sense. (Also relevant to Kant's exclusion of a purely temporal permanent is his doctrine that, because time itself cannot be perceived, we can make temporal judgements only through presupposing space: 'we are unable to perceive any determination of time save through change in outer relations', B277. This idea is better explained later in the Postulates, where Kant says that we cannot even think of time without representing it as a line, i.e. on the analogy with space; see B291–3.)

So, Kant concludes, empirical consciousness of my existence 'is at the same time an immediate consciousness of the existence of other things outside me' (B276). That is, not only must there *be* things outside me, but I must have *consciousness* of them, and this consciousness must be immediate, since I would otherwise have to infer the time-order of outer objects (as the Cartesian assumes, B276), which would require me to identify the time-order of my representations prior to that of their objects – this being, the first analogy has shown, impossible.

From this it does not follow that 'every intuitive representation of outer things' is veridical (B278), only that 'the proposition that there is such a thing as outer experience' is 'always presupposed' (Bxli). How we make the distinction between veridical and non-veridical perception is another matter; Kant refers to the rule that '[w]*hatever is connected with a perception according to empirical laws, is actual*', the criterion of coherence, coherence determined by a priori rules (A376; see also Bxli, B279, A492/B520–1, *Proleg* 290–1, 337).

The upshot is that inner and outer experience are necessarily correlated: they are 'bound up in the way of identity' (Bxl). If so, the crucial Cartesian assumption that subjective states can be known independently from the external world, that self-consciousness is prior to knowledge of objects, is undermined: Kant has shown that Cartesian 'indubitable certainty' attaches in the first instance not to empirical self-consciousness, as Descartes supposed, but to transcendental self-consciousness, and that knowledge of inner experience (empirical self-consciousness) is a further matter, which presupposes outer experience. The 'game played by [material or empirical] idealism has been turned against itself' (B276): the Refutation has shown that the move from a subjective to an objective view of one's own existence – a move which the skeptic must make if he is to refer to *facts* of inner experience as grounds for skeptical doubt – compels the move from inner to outer objects. It tells us why there must be an external world, and explains why its existence should be self-evident in the way we take it to be.

The Refutation and the Fourth Paralogism

The argument in the Refutation is relatively easy to grasp, but its presence in the *Critique* creates a puzzle, and its interpretation is highly controversial.

It is not initially obvious why the Refutation should be needed, in view of the Deduction and Analogies, and so how its argument maps onto theirs. Though it returns to the Analytic's themes of self-consciousness and temporality, it does not simply recapitulate earlier material. But if the Refutation does add something genuinely new, then the question arises whether this is strictly necessary for Kant's defence of objectivity. If it is, then it would seem to follow that the Deduction and Analogies, despite their apparently doing all that is needed in Kant's terms to refute the skeptic, must be in his eyes inadequate in some respect.

A consideration, which some think helps to resolve the puzzle, is that the Refutation was inserted only in the second edition, and it coincided with the elimination of a long section in the Dialectic of the first edition called the Fourth Paralogism (A366–80), in which Kant had argued against Cartesian skepticism on the following basis (see also *Proleg* 336–7). Since, according to transcendental idealism, external objects are 'outside' us only in an empirical sense – in a transcendental sense they are inside us, since space belongs to our sensibility – they 'are mere appearances, and therefore are nothing but a species of my representations' (A370). The sub-class of my representations which comprises outer objects is distinguished by being given in outer as well as inner sense (A371). Because my representations are known immediately in inner sense (in Descartes' terms, I have incorrigible knowledge of my cogitations), it follows that my knowledge of external objects must be on a par with my knowledge of my own mental states. Inner and outer objects differ in the kind of representations that they are, but my access to them is the same in each case: the existence of outer objects 'is proved in the same manner as the existence of myself as a thinking being' (A370), for it stands 'upon the immediate witness of my self-consciousness', and 'immediate perception' of them counts as 'sufficient proof of their reality' (A371).

The trouble with this argument, Kant discovered, is that it allows itself to be read as a statement of Berkeleyan idealism: it echoes Berkeley's claim that skepticism evaporates as soon as it is realised that there is nothing more to being an empirical object than being a certain sort of idea in the mind. So what Kant may appear to have advanced in the Fourth Paralogism is not an argument against empirical idealism, but an argument against Descartes' form of empirical idealism from the standpoint of Berkeley's form of empirical idealism – a Berkeleyan refutation of Descartes. That the Fourth Paralogism, and hence transcendental idealism in general, could be so construed was brought home to Kant by a hostile review of the *Critique* that appeared in the year after its publication, in which Kant's position on empirical reality was described as Berkeleyan. Kant vehemently repudiated this suggestion (as can be seen from the Appendix to the *Prolegomena*, 372–80). It is thus reasonable to suppose that Kant meant in the second edition to reassign the anti-skeptical task of the Fourth Paralogism to the Refutation, thinking that it would discourage the false assimilation of transcendental to merely empirical idealism.

On one view, the substitution of the Refutation for the Fourth Paralogism in the second edition marks a new, and extremely important development in Kant's philosophy. On this account, the outer objects which the Refutation argues to be presupposed for empirical self-consciousness may rightfully be regarded as things in themselves. In support of this view, it may be observed that there is in the Refutation no appeal to the transcendental ideality of outer objects.

Some analytic interpreters of Kant claim accordingly that the Refutation is the culmination of the Analytic, in which the true epistemological insight contained in Kant's theory of experience is freed from its idealist trappings. On this view, the Refutation is a proof of realism in opposition to the Berkeleyan metaphysics which Kant had espoused in the first edition: its introduction is tantamount to an admission that transcendental idealism is not distinct from Berkeley's idealism. In the Refutation Kant therefore breaks, unconsciously or not, with transcendental idealism.

Whether this interpretation of the Refutation is justified depends obviously on what overall estimate is put on transcendental idealism: if the doctrine really is as unsatisfactory, or as close to Berkeley's idealism, as its critics allege, then there will be good reason for regarding Kant as having in the Refutation forced himself beyond it. In chapter 8 some of the relevant issues will be discussed. The narrower question, to be considered here, is whether there is a plausible reading of the Refutation which makes it consistent with earlier sections of the Analytic (without merely recapitulating them) and with transcendental idealism.

To see what this might be, we should return to the argument itself. The crucial point is that at which Kant says that there must be 'a *thing* outside me' not 'the mere *representation* of a thing outside me'. What is striking about this step in the argument is the suggestion that reflection on the necessities of representation can lead outside the circle of representations; hence its powerful attraction for realists. It is plain, however, that this inference cannot go through without some further assumption. 'X exists' can be inferred from 'X is a necessity of representation' in only one of two ways: either on the basis of some general theory about the real, extra-representational conditions of representation, which has that implication; or alternatively, on the basis that X is a kind of thing the existence of which is tied to (a function of) necessities of representation. Without one or other of these assumptions, the Refutation would be committed to the claim that something can exist in its own right simply because we need it to so exist – it would be attempting something genuinely magical.

Now it ought to be obvious that transcendental philosophy is flatly opposed to the first assumption: Kant's Copernicanism is founded on the denial that we can have knowledge of what needs be the case independently of our representations in order for representation of objects to be possible, so we cannot construct the general theory which the inference would require. Clearly the second alternative is Kant's: the existence of X can be inferred from the necessity of our representing X, because X is something whose very existence is a function of such necessities (crudely: it exists because we make it, and we make it because we need it). If so, transcendental idealism is built into the Refutation, and the outer things which it establishes are appearances.

Confirming this interpretation, it may be observed that, without transcendental idealism, the Refutation has little force against the skeptic. What needs to be shown is that we have 'experience', not mere 'imagination' of outer things. The problem for any transcendental realist reading of the Refutation is that, since real things can only play justificatory roles in cognition via their representations, a representation will, it seems, always do just as well as a real thing. Thus, faced with the claim that X is a necessity of representation, the skeptic can agree that it is necessary that we have the representation of X, and deny that this representation can be known to have an object. What the transcendental realist needs, of course, is to demonstrate that the necessity of X is not merely representational, but of a kind that pertains to extra-representational things. But, first, as noted earlier, Kant's transcendental method does not have the resources to yield any such conclusion; and second, it is highly doubtful that any such putative demonstration could meet the skeptic's standards of proof. It is safe to say, therefore, that an argument based on requirements of representation, like the Refutation, can lead to conclusions about objects only if 'object of representation' is understood in the sense of the Deduction.

If the argument of the Refutation is understood in these terms, the following account of its place in the *Critique* suggests itself. The Refutation plays a double role, one internal to Kant's theory of experience, the other external. In its internal respect, the Refutation is a straightforward extension of the Deduction and Analogies, to which it might have been appended. It makes a number of important additions to the earlier argument: the permanent required by the first analogy is specifically determined as material (B277–8); the dependence of empirical self-consciousness on outer experience is established; and outer experience, hitherto taken for granted in the Analytic, for which reason its reality remained dubitable, is demonstrated to be necessary.

In its external capacity, the Refutation does something different. Again it is not independent of transcendental idealism – as we have seen, it cannot be so construed – and so presupposes something alien to the skeptic's outlook. Nevertheless, it addresses the empirical idealist with a powerful challenge, namely to explain the basis on which he makes the judgements about his own mental history which he claims as prior to all others. If the empirical idealist refuses the challenge – by claiming that empirical self-consciousness is an absolute given – then he becomes dogmatic; but if he accepts it, then he is faced with the arguments of the Analytic. And in the course of all this, transcendental idealism is advertised as a means of defending empirical realism.

In this light, the Refutation is continuous with the Fourth Paralogism (as Kant implies at Bxl[n]): it adds something important and missing from the latter, namely a demonstration that outer intuition is necessary, but both make essential use of transcendental idealism in replying to the skeptic. The general nature of this reply is discussed further in the following section, and in chapter 8 it will be argued that transcendental idealism as it figures in the Fourth Paralogism should not be interpreted as Berkeleyan.

It may be wondered why Kant does not direct the Refutation against Berkeley, as well as the problematic idealist. The reason, it would seem, is that Kant wishes to insist on the sufficiency of the

Aesthetic for this purpose: he considers that Berkeley denies reality to space solely because he deems it an impossibility, so that all grounds for Berkeley's idealism disappear as soon as it is understood that space need not be transcendentally real in order to be empirically real (B69–70). Kant is right that it would not be appropriate to aim the Refutation at Berkeley: it fails to engage Berkeley on his own terms, because it assumes the intelligibility of the concept of an outer object in a sense which Berkeley would deny. (A further reason would be that Berkeley's accounts of time and judgement are so etiolated that it is not even clear that Kant should allow that he has a right to the claim of empirical self-knowledge which supplies the Refutation's premise.)

Transcendental arguments, transcendental idealism and Kant's reply to the skeptic

It is worth now considering in a little more detail a set of closely related and controversial general issues surrounding the Analytic: the concept of a transcendental argument, mentioned briefly in chapter 2, and its relation to transcendental idealism; whether the Analytic can be held to advance the case for transcendental idealism; and how Kant deals with skepticism.

Transcendental arguments

The term transcendental argument, in modern philosophical vocabulary, refers not specifically to those arguments actually given by Kant, but to a type of argumentation putatively inaugurated in the *Critique*. A transcendental argument is distinguished by the status and use made of its chief premise. This consists in a claim, typically expressed in the first person, which is logically contingent, uninferred, and advanced without further grounding, but the denial of which would yield some absurdity. Examples are: I have experience; my experience is temporal; I am self-conscious; I think; I make judgements. Conceptual connections are then teased out to show that the premise can be true only if a certain other proposition, of a controversial and more philosophically interesting character, such as the principle of causality, is also true. Transcendental arguments thus generate conclusions which are strictly conditional – e.g. if I am to have experience, then causality must obtain – but where the consequent inherits (if the argument is successful) the incontrovertibility of the argument's premise. The target proposition is thereby rendered immune to skepticism, since in order to challenge it the skeptic would need to doubt something that cannot be doubted intelligibly, e.g. that he has experience. Transcendental arguments, it may then be claimed, show something about reality: the knowledge that we can have experience only if its objects have causal form, together with the given fact of experience, allows us to know that reality is indeed causal.

Reasons have already been given for denying that transcendental arguments so conceived, despite their obvious proximity to the method of the Analytic, especially the Refutation of Idealism, should be attributed to Kant. Quite apart from the fact that it fractures the *Critique* by dissociating Kant's epistemology from his metaphysics, transcendental arguments repose on purely conceptual connections: their conclusions are analytic rather than synthetic a priori, so that, in Kant's terms, they identify mere 'subjective conditions of thought' rather than demonstrating objective validity. As a consequence, transcendental arguments are not effective against skepticism, at least not on terms acceptable to Kant. The essence of this point was explained in the earlier discussion of what happens to the Refutation of Idealism if transcendental idealism is stripped from it. Faced with a transcendental argument purporting to show the necessity of the principle of causality, for example, the skeptic is free to raise the question why we should suppose that the argument shows anything at all about *how things are*, rather than just something about *how we must think*, i.e. a merely psychological necessity. Transcendental arguments can be defended here by appealing to verificationism ('the notion of a reality that we cannot think about is meaningless') or naturalism ('nature ensures the agreement of our thought with reality'), but neither mode of defence is acceptable to Kant.

Kant, aware that purely conceptual connections will not serve his ends, makes it clear that his arguments are to be taken idealistically, and have force only on that understanding. In addition to the many places where the metaphysics of experience is said to have objective validity solely with respect to appearances, Kant affirms, in his most explicit discussion of the method of transcendental proof (A782–94/B810–22), that it turns on the concept of possible experience, and that this is to be understood in the following way: 'The proof proceeds by showing that experience itself, and therefore also the object of experience, would be impossible without a connection of this [synthetic a priori] kind' (A783/B811; see also A216–17/B263–4, A736–7/B764–5). This crucial identification of the conditions of *experience* with those of its *objects* is made also in the Analytic: 'The a priori conditions of a possible experience in general are at the same time conditions of the possibility of objects of experience' (A111); 'the conditions of the *possibility of experience* in general are likewise *conditions of the possibility of the objects of experience*, and . . . for this reason they have objective validity in a synthetic a priori judgement' (B197). On the analytic interpretation, which reduces conditions of possibility to epistemological conditions, these statements come out as either tautologous or confused; the notion of a condition of *cognition* that is also a condition of an *object* makes sense only on an idealist basis. Kant does not, therefore, think of transcendental proofs as in any way distinct from the implementation of the Copernican revolution and the strategy of applying transcendental idealism to metaphysical problems.

Transcendental idealism and the Analytic

This allows Kant to be read as pursuing a unitary method in the Analytic, but a new issue now arises. If transcendental idealism is not superfluous to the Analytic, it may be asked whether the Analytic actually advances the case for the doctrine. The natural expectation would be to find in the Analytic an argument for transcendental idealism parallel to that of the Aesthetic, based on the substitution of conceptual for sensible conditions of objects. The Preface suggests as much: at Bxxii[n] Kant says that transcendental idealism will be proved 'from the elementary concepts of the understanding' as well as from space and time. In that case, Kant would possess two independent arguments for the doctrine, the content of which would furthermore be enlarged, since objects would then be transcendentally ideal with respect to their conceptual as well as their sensible form, i.e. transcendentally ideal *qua* thought or conceptualised, as well as being transcendentally ideal *qua* sensed or intuited. The difficulty, noted earlier, is that the Analytic deals with concepts of objects in general, not just with concepts of humanly accessible objects: Kant does not declare the categories to be a peculiarity of the human mode of cognition in the same manner as our forms of intuition. This makes it hard to see why conformity to concepts should be considered to reduce an object to mere appearance, even if conceptual form is, as the anti-empiricist argument of the Deduction is intended to show, a priori.

This issue has importance for the broader interpretation of Kant: if the Analytic's account of the conceptual conditions of cognition does not of itself entail transcendental ideality, this makes it more reasonable to seek to detach Kant's transcendental argumentation from his metaphysics, as per the analytic interpretation. It would of course remain entirely possible to read the Analytic according to the idealist interpretation, but it could not be claimed that the nature of the conceptual conditions of human knowledge compels an idealist understanding of them.

Now there is one clear sense in which Kant can claim that the Analytic extends transcendental ideality to conceptuality, namely by virtue of the Schematism: a priori conceptualisation of objects involves temporalising the categories, and temporality is a subjective form, so conformity to the schematised categories entails transcendental ideality. (The same point can be made with reference to apperception: the application of concepts to objects is ultimately determined by the principle of the unity of consciousness in the temporal manifold of representations; so objects *qua* thought have invested in them the form of time as expressed in the unity of consciousness.) Still, this does not make transcendental idealism a properly conceptual idealism, because it remains the case that transcendental ideality stems ultimately from the sensible conditions which mediate the application of concepts to objects, not from concepts as such. Schematism only recycles at the conceptual level the sensible idealism of the Aesthetic.

Yet Kant himself certainly believes that the connection of conceptual conditions with transcendental ideality amounts to more than this, because he says, before any mention of schematism has been made, that the Deduction entails transcendental idealism: it shows that 'nature is not a thing in itself but is merely an aggregate of appearances' (A114), that 'the order and regularity in the appearances, that we entitle *nature*, we ourselves introduce' (A125), that the understanding is the 'lawgiver of nature' (A126), and that categories 'are concepts which prescribe laws a priori to appearances, and therefore to nature' (B163), laws which 'do not exist in the appearances but only relatively to' the subject's understanding (B164).

Although there is nothing inherent in the categories, prior to schematism, which precludes their application to things in themselves, Kant does have grounds for regarding conceptuality as a source of ideality. As observed earlier, the Deduction's account of concept application is pitted against transcendental realism. On Kant's theory of a priori synthesis, the fitting of concepts to objects involves the generation of intuitions in accordance with rules associated with concepts, such that conceptual form is internal to intuition. According to transcendental realism, by contrast, conceptual form inheres in objects independently of intuition. For this reason, transcendental realism cannot avail itself of the Deduction's defence of the objective validity of concepts. Nor, as Kant spells out at A128–30 and B166–8, has it any other account of objective validity to offer. Kant's argument is therefore: if the application of concepts to objects is to be justified at all, then it must be on the basis that objects have conceptual form by virtue of the subject's activity, and not by virtue of how the object is constituted subject-independently; the recognition of fit between concept and object which the transcendental realist presupposes must be eliminated in favour of the subject's conceptual constitution of the object. 'It is only when we have thus produced synthetic unity in the manifold of intuition that we are in a position to say that we know the object' (A105; recalling the statement in the Preface that 'reason has insight only into that which it produces after a plan of its own', Bxiii). Expressed more broadly, the argument of the Deduction is that, if subject and object are not connected internally, then it is unintelligible that they should be connected at all; and an internal connection presupposes a theory of a priori synthesis, which entails the transcendental ideality of conceptual form.

Transcendental idealism thus has an appropriately different basis in the Analytic, where it turns on subjective activity, from the Aesthetic, where it hinges on the subject's mode of receiving data. It should also be pointed out that the Analytic achieves a formally weaker result than the Aesthetic. The latter sought to show, contra Trendelenburg, that our forms of pure intuition *could not* also be objective forms. The Analytic does not even seek to show the same of the pure concepts of the understanding. This is, however, of no importance, because, as noted in chapter 5, the merely logical possibility described by Trendelenburg is idle: if our application of concepts to objects somehow corresponds to the features of transcendentally real things, this is, as far as we are concerned, a mere (and miraculous) coincidence.

The Aesthetic and Analytic therefore stand in different relations to the doctrine of transcendental idealism. Both presuppose, of course, Kant's methodological Copernicanism, but whereas the Aesthetic tries to argue from scratch to the conclusion that our forms of intuition constitute an independent source of transcendental ideality, the Analytic does not attempt the same for the categories; instead it tries to work out what it would be for objects to be transcendentally ideal with respect to their conceptual form. In the course of executing this task, it shows how the transcendental ideality of sensible form established in the Aesthetic carries over, via schematism, to conceptual form. To the extent that the Analytic's account of conceptual form has the strengths identified above, it can be held to advance the case for transcendental idealism.

Kant's reply to the skeptic

Finally, there is the question of skepticism. On the analytic interpretation, as said previously, the Analytic is a set of transcendental arguments showing skepticism to be self-refuting on the basis of purely conceptual considerations. The difficulty with this, as has been seen, lies in showing that these arguments establish more than psychological necessities.

But without the analytic interpretation, it is not immediately obvious that the Analytic can truly dislodge the skeptic. Even if the

Deduction does refute empiricism and therefore skepticism in its Humean form, there remains the challenge of non-empiricist skepticism, such as Descartes'. And if the Analytic's defence of the commonsense metaphysics of experience depends on transcendental idealism, as maintained in this chapter, then it is unclear why the skeptic should accept its conclusions: the skeptic may, as noted in chapter 2 (p. 47), agree that we could credit ourselves with knowledge *if* we regarded objects as mere appearances, and decline the invitation to do so. It is not clear that Kant has any way of forcing the skeptic to think in the terms of transcendental philosophy, and the Refutation will leave the skeptic unmoved, if he rejects the notion that knowledge presupposes transcendental conditions; it is one thing to put pressure on the skeptic to explain how the judgements he regards as basic are possible, and another to show the base of skepticism to be incoherent. It may seem, then, that the argument which extends through the Analytic, though it may show the possibility of objectivity, fails to show its necessity on terms that will impress the skeptic.

On the idealist interpretation, the *Critique* as a whole constitutes an adequate response to skepticism, but it is subtle, and not designed to meet the skeptic head-on. The key, as Kant emphasises in the Fourth Paralogism, is transcendental idealism. Certainly Kant does not expect the fact that transcendental idealism allows a story to be told in the light of which our ordinary knowledge claims come out as justified, to function in isolation as a reason to repudiate skepticism. Kant's strategy is instead to undermine the framework that provides skepticism with its motivation, namely transcendental realism. In Kant's terms, skeptical doubt is appropriate to claims to knowledge of things in themselves, but not to claims to knowledge of ontologically inferior objects conceived as having a necessary relation to human cognition. In pre-Critical philosophy, in which empirical and transcendental reality are not distinguished, claims to knowledge of empirically real objects do need to satisfy the conditions for knowledge of things in themselves, and as a response to this position, the skeptic's claim that the conditions for knowledge are not fulfilled is justified, because there is a mismatch between the aspiration to knowledge of transcendentally real objects, and the limitations of finite, sensible subjects. Skepticism is thus an accurate statement of the problem of reality: it displays the gaps in transcendental realist explanations of knowledge. Transcendental idealism, Kant may claim accordingly, acknowledges and incorporates the truth in skepticism, namely that things in themselves are inaccessible to us. On the idealist interpretation, therefore, Kant does not refute skepticism so much as overtake it: the skeptical challenge is defused by showing that it depends upon a conception of the nature of human knowledge which is mistaken, and that what is true in it is preserved in the account of empirical knowledge which transcendental idealism provides. The net effect of Kant's diagnosis of skepticism and provision of an alternative account of knowledge is to rob skepticism of its power to make our knowledge claims seem doubtful. Kant sets up no logical or semantic barrier to the formulation of skeptical possibilities, but he removes the motivation for thinking that satisfaction of our ordinary criteria should be rejected as insufficient for knowledge, because the Analytic has shown that we have an a priori warrant for taking the deliverances of experience at face value. Skeptical possibilities such as Descartes' dream doubt are silenced by the Analytic's account of the necessity of our representing an objective world.

The skeptic might try to restore meaning to skeptical doubt by protesting that Kant's Copernican revolution, in reforming our philosophical conception of knowledge, loses sight of what knowledge really involves. What Kant calls empirical reality, the skeptic may say, is something too ontologically weak to do justice to our ordinary knowledge claims. An interpretation of Kant according to which this is so, and Kant's anti-skeptical strategy fundamentally no more convincing than Berkeley's, is discussed in the next chapter. If, as will be suggested, this interpretation should be rejected, then the skeptic will need to show that the very concept of knowledge requires what is known to be independent of the knowing of it in every sense but the merely logical. If this were so, then even Kant's non-empirical, transcendental dependence of objects on the subject would be incompatible with knowledge, and transcendental idealism would itself amount to a conversion of skeptical doubt into metaphysical doctrine. But it is hard to see how this could be shown without simply begging the question against Kant. (As noted in chapter 2, p. 37, Kant grants that our pre-philosophical conception of empirical knowledge is unqualifiedly realistic; see e.g. A389. This concession is, however, of no use to the skeptic, whose own arguments provide the strongest reason for saying that common sense ought to accept the revision of its self-understanding proposed by Kant, rather than stand by its instinctual tendency to transcendental realism.)

To the extent that transcendental idealism allows skepticism to be overcome, it gains a tactical advantage over transcendental realism, and the Analytic may be held to strengthen the case for the doctrine in a further respect.

Measurement and modality (The Axioms of Intuition, The Anticipations of Perception, The Postulates of Empirical Thought)

The three sections of the Analytic of Principles not yet discussed are the Axioms of Intuition, Anticipations of Perception, and Postulates of Empirical Thought. They are important for completing Kant's theory of experience, but marginal to his defence of objectivity. The Axioms and Anticipations describe a rudimentary conceptual condition which intuitions must meet if empirical knowledge is to be developed from them. The Postulates – really a reflection on the transcendental theory of experience, rather than a further component of it – explains how modal concepts should be understood in the light of the Analytic.

The Axioms and Anticipations

As said earlier, the Axioms and Anticipations are concerned with 'mathematical' principles of pure understanding (not to be confused with principles *of* mathematics). These are a priori conceptual conditions for the generation of intuitions: they tell us what rules empirical intuition must conform to, and thus what conceptual conditions are constitutive of appearances, independently of the unification of appearances, governed by 'dynamical' principles, which comprises empirical knowledge.

The Axioms are concerned with appearances in quantitative respects, the Anticipations in qualitative. Their respective principles are: 'All intuitions are extensive magnitudes' (B202), and: 'In all appearances, the real that is an object of sensation has intensive magnitude, that is, a degree' (B207). Their force is to justify us in employing numerical concepts in empirical judgement (A178–9/B221, *Proleg* § 24); what they require of intuition is simply that it be such that mathematics is applicable to all possible appearances.

Their proofs and treatment need not be nearly so complex as those of the Analogies. The principle of the Axioms follows from the fact that appearances are intuited as aggregates – manifolds of homogeneous parts – in space and time, and that their representation as wholes presupposes conceptual synthesis (B202–3; A142–3/B182 in the Schematism fills in the argument). The importance of this principle is that through it alone mathematics and geometry possess objective validity, which is thereby restricted to appearances (A165–6/B206–7).

In the Anticipations Kant indicates that, although the specific quality of any sensation can only be known a posteriori, there is one (and only one) respect in which we can know something a priori about it: viz. we know in advance that any sensation we apprehend (e.g. heat) will allow itself to be represented as having a determinate degree greater than zero on a continuous scale. Degree of sensation serves us as a resource in empirical judgement: we make judgements about the real corresponding to sensation (e.g. of the temperature of bodies), on the basis of the degree to which we find ourselves affected.

The Postulates

In the Postulates Kant analyses the three categories of modality: possibility, actuality and necessity. Kant is concerned with these categories as schematised, i.e. with modal concepts in their application to objects; he is not, therefore, offering an account of logical possibility and necessity. His general claim is that modal characterisations of objects do not 'in the least enlarge the concept to which they are attached as predicates' – rather they 'express the relation of the concept to the faculty of knowledge' (A219/B266; A233–5/B286–7). That is, to say that something is possible, actual or necessary, is not to say anything about the object itself, but to say something about how it is cognised by the subject. Something is possible if it 'agrees with the formal conditions of experience', i.e. intuition and concepts, actual if it 'is bound up with the material conditions of experience', i.e. sensation, and necessary if it is connected with something actual in accordance with 'universal conditions of experience', i.e. the law of causality (A218/B265–6). Thus an object is possible in so far as it is consistent with the system of experience, actual in so far as we are related to it through sensation and necessary in so far as it connected by laws of nature to what is actual. From these definitions, and other claims of the Analytic, it follows that the three modal concepts are coextensive: everything that is an object for us is possible, actual and necessary (A230–2/B282–4).

This account of modality has important implications for rationalism. Leibniz holds that pure thought, independently of experience, is able to determine what is possible and what is necessary. For Kant, by contrast, the concepts of possibility and necessity, in so far as their employment is not merely logical, relate exclusively to the world of experience (A219/B266–7). Consequently 'the possibility of things' cannot be established from 'concepts taken in and by themselves' (A223/B270–1). Kant also expresses the point by distinguishing 'logical' from 'transcendental' (or 'real') possibility: 'the logical possibility of the *concept*', i.e. that it is not contradictory, does not entail 'the transcendental possibility of *things*', i.e. that an object corresponds to the concept (A244/B302). Leibniz, in Kant's view, fails to grasp this distinction, and its corollary that the 'possibility of a thing can never be proved merely from the fact that its concept is not self-contradictory' but requires intuition (B308).

Transcendent objects: the concept of noumenon (The Ground of the Distinction of all Objects in general into Phenomena and Noumena)

The Analytic's account of the conditions under which our thoughts can be known to have objects raises a question: what is to be said about thoughts that fail to meet those conditions, thoughts of objects that we cannot intuit? The Dialectic contains Kant's detailed theory of the content and origin of our thoughts about specific transcendent objects, but in the penultimate chapter of the Analytic, 'The Ground of the Distinction of all Objects in general into Phenomena and

Noumena', Kant prepares the way by spelling out in general terms the implications of the Analytic regarding transcendent objects. At the same time Kant completes two other tasks: he engages explicitly with rationalism, fundamentally Leibniz, whose particular doctrines are to be scrutinised in the final chapter of the Analytic; and he makes clear his position on the hitherto unaddressed topic of things in themselves. Kant's broad intention is to sharpen our appreciation of what is involved in any attempt to think beyond the limits demarcated in the Analytic: before leaving the 'island' of empirical knowledge we should, Kant says, cast a glance at the map of the 'land of truth' we are about to leave, and ask both 'by what title we possess even this domain', and whether we can 'be satisfied with what it contains' (A235–6/B294–5). The chapter on noumena thus provides a bridge from the Analytic to the Dialectic.

The scope of the categories

Kant begins by spelling out at some length (A235–48/B294–305) how the Analytic has confirmed the thesis, of which notice was given in the Preface of the *Critique*, that cognition of transcendent objects is impossible and our knowledge limited to the realm of experience. The conditions of employment of the categories are such that they 'can *never* admit of *transcendental* but *always* only of *empirical* employment' (A246/B303) – the 'transcendental' employment of a concept being 'its application to *things in general and in themselves*', i.e. transcendent, and empirical employment being 'its application *merely to appearances*', i.e. immanent (A238–9/B298). Because they cannot be employed transcendentally, i.e. in their unschematised forms, the categories are therefore 'not of themselves adequate to the knowledge of things in themselves' (A287/B343).

What one might have expected Kant to then say is that the traditional division (made sharply by Plato and Leibniz) of objects into two classes, those that can be grasped by sense perception and those that can be grasped by the intellect, must be replaced with a unitary and exhaustive conception of all objects as necessarily both sensible and intelligible. That is, one might have expected Kant to declare the very notion of a transcendent object incoherent. Had Kant's view been that the categories are *by virtue of their intrinsic nature* restricted in the scope of their application to objects of experience, he would have had no choice but to draw this conclusion (since under that condition any employment of the categories independently from experience would be nonsensical).

But this is not Kant's view of the scope of the categories. Again, on Kant's account, the categories are forms of thought or judgement, and concepts of objects *in general* (A88/B120, A241–2, A247/B304, A248/B305, A290/B346–7) – not merely concepts and forms of judgement of *empirical* objects. Thus, as Kant says in a footnote to the Deduction, '*for thought* the categories are not limited by the conditions of our sensible intuition, but have an unlimited field. It is only the *knowledge* of that which we think, the determining of the object, that requires intuition' (B167n; the distinction of thinking and knowing is made earlier at B146). Transcendent objects are therefore thinkable. (That Kant is entitled to this view is however disputed, and the issue will be reconsidered in chapter 8.)

The distinction of noumena and phenomena

What Kant accordingly does next is reaffirm, with modification and on properly Critical grounds, the traditional distinction of sensory and intellectual objects. He does this by introducing a concept new to the *Critique*: that of *noumenon* (plural, noumena). A noumenon is an object *exclusively of understanding*: an object given to a subject but only to its intellect or understanding, i.e. not given by sensibility. This is not a contradiction, since (the Aesthetic affirmed) we can form the idea of a form of intuition that is non-sensible (intellectual intuition, the mode of cognition of God). A noumenon is thus something which 'can be given as such to an intuition, although not to one that is sensible' (A248–9; B306). Lacking all sensible features, it is a purely *intelligible* entity (intelligible being Kant's term of contrast for sensible), a thing of a purely intellectual nature, the constitution of which can be grasped wholly through the intellect. It follows that a subject with a discursive intellect, such as ourselves, could cognise a noumenon only if it could employ the categories independently of sensibility.

Now the concept of an object exclusively of understanding is of course closely related to that of a thing in itself, in so far as a thing in itself is also a thing considered apart from human sensibility. Thus noumena, if represented, are 'represented *as they are*', not '*as they appear*' (A249–50), and the concepts of noumenon and thing in itself, if they refer, refer to the same things (this is made clear at e.g. B306, B310). They are, however, not the same concept. The thing in itself is a bare ontological concept; it is the concept of an object as it is constituted in itself, without reference to our (or any other subject's) knowledge of it. (A thing in itself is thus a thing considered even apart from the categories; though that is not to say that it is a thing considered as non-categorial – as necessarily, intrinsically non-conformable to the categories – in the same way that it is non-spatial and non-temporal.) Noumenon by contrast is an epistemological concept, the concept of an object of a certain mode of cognition, namely intellectual intuition. In moving from the concept of the thing in itself to that of noumenon we thus reconceive transcendent reality as determined for cognition – as individuated and characterised in ways that allow of being known. The concept of noumenon thus provides a way of taking up the question of what would be required for things in themselves to become objects of knowledge. It also encapsulates what is presupposed by Leibniz's epistemology and metaphysics, since Leibnizian monads clearly satisfy the definition of noumena.

The contrast is of noumenon with *phenomenon* (plural, phenomena). Phenomena are objects of sensible intuition, sensible entities, and coextensive with appearances. Virtually all that Kant says about phenomena is that they are appearances 'so far as they are thought as objects according to the unity of the categories' (A248). All that the concept of phenomenon adds to that of appearance, therefore, is the idea of subsumption under the categories (appearance, recall, was defined as the *un*determined object of empirical intuition, A20/B34); but since in the Analytic Kant has most frequently used appearance in just this sense, the two terms are in most contexts interchangeable. Phenomena have, therefore, already been accounted for in the *Critique*. The outstanding question is what use may be made of the concept of noumenon.

Negative and positive senses of noumenon

The passages in which Kant gives his answer to this question (A248–53, B305–9, A253–6/B309–12) are somewhat labyrinthine, and complicated by differences of terminology and emphasis between the two editions. The upshot, however, is reasonably clear. It is logically possible for noumena to exist, since the concept is not contradictory (A254/B310). The concept of something non-empirical is furthermore forced on us by the recognition that empirical objects are mere appearances: the concept of appearance implies a contrast between 'the mode in which we intuit' things, and 'the nature that belongs to them in themselves', and so a contrast between appearances and 'other possible things', things in themselves (B306). The very concept of appearance points to that of noumenon: because appearance 'can be nothing by itself', 'something which is not in itself appearance must correspond to it' (A251); 'if the senses represent to us something, merely *as it appears*, this something must also in itself be a thing, and an object of a non-sensible intuition' (A249). Unless 'we are to move constantly in a circle' – of defining appearance as of something, and this something merely as that which appears – 'the word appearance must be recognised as already indicating a relation to something' which 'must be something in itself' (A251–2). In this way, we cannot be 'satisfied' with the Analytic's 'land of truth', and must postulate noumena in addition. For these reasons, then, and not the very different considerations that influenced Leibniz, Kant endorses the division of 'the world into a world of the senses and a world of the understanding' (A249).

Though all of this is true, what must at all costs be appreciated, Kant stresses, is that we cannot in any manner attain knowledge of noumena. The impossibility of our employing the categories transcendentally precludes our determining them as objects for us. And even though we have the concept of intellectual intuition, a concept which is not contradictory, we of course have no knowledge or contentful idea of such a faculty (B308). What is more, we have no right to assume that it is even possible in a real, extra-logical sense. Since the idea of intellectual intuition is just as empty for us as that of a thing in itself, we get no closer to things in themselves by thinking of them as objects of intellectual intuition.

This warning is needed because, according to Kant, we are prey to the illusion, which he considers enormously powerful, that the categories can be employed transcendentally, i.e. to know and not merely think things beyond the senses. Its source may be identified in several, complementary ways. Most straightforwardly, the fact that the categories do not arise out of sensibility makes it seems as if they ought to allow us to get hold of objects directly, without sensible mediation (B305). Kant made this observation earlier in the Schematism, where he said that we are tempted to think that by removing the condition of sensibility we may apply the categories to things 'as they are', as opposed to things 'only as they appear' (A147/B186). The illusion is related to a fundamental asymmetry between intellect and sensibility: whereas intuition without thought leaves no relation of representation to object, thought without intuition leaves 'the form of thought' or categories, which 'extend further' than intuition in the sense that they 'think objects in general, without regard to the special mode (the sensibility) in which they may be given' (A253–4/B309). This leads us to suppose that the categories determine, as opposed to merely think, 'a greater sphere of objects' than sensibility (A254/B309). The error may also be traced back to the consideration that 'apperception, and with it thought, precedes all possible determinate ordering of representations' (A289/B345). The Dialectic will analyse further this propensity of ours.

The overall situation may be clarified, Kant continues, by distinguishing two senses of the concept of noumenon: the *negative*, indeterminate concept of a thing in so far as it is *not* an object of sensible intuition, and the *positive*, determinate concept of a thing in so far as it is an object of *non-sensible* (thus intellectual) intuition (B307). In the first edition, at A250–3, this distinction is expressed in terms of a distinction between the concepts of transcendental object and noumenon. The remarks earlier in this chapter on the concept of the transcendental object (pp. 153–4) explain why Kant should have revised his terminology.

The negative sense of noumenon is that of 'the entirely *indeterminate* concept of an intelligible entity', 'a something in general outside our sensibility', and so converges on the concept of a thing in itself. The positive sense is that of the '*determinate* concept of an entity that allows of being known in a certain manner' (B307). The two senses thus identify different epistemological aspects of noumena: respectively, their unknowability for us, and their knowability for a species of subject other than ourselves. The concept of noumenon in the positive sense, because it incorporates the concept of intellectual intuition, cannot be identified with that of thing in itself, and because we cannot assume the existence of that mode of cognition, knowledge of the existence of noumena in the positive sense cannot be derived from knowledge of their existence in the negative sense: noumena in the positive sense, if they exist, will be the same things as noumena in the negative sense and things in themselves, but the existence of noumena in the negative sense does not entail – it is necessary but not sufficient for – their existence in the positive sense.

Kant affirms that his 'doctrine of sensibility' gives us grounds for employing (in transcendental reflection) the concept of noumenon in the negative sense (B307). The doctrine of transcendental idealism requires us to be able to say that objects that are not objects of sensible intuition are for that reason not possible objects for us: without the concept of noumenon in the negative sense, we would be unable to explain the concept of appearance, or assert that our knowledge has limits, and consequently unable 'to prevent sensible intuition from being extended to things in themselves' (A254/B310). Because it is in this way 'bound up with the limitations of sensibility', the concept is 'no arbitrary invention' (A255/B311). The concept of noumenon in the positive sense, however, we have no such grounds for employing (see A286–8/B342–4 in the Amphiboly): there is no need to refer to objects of intellectual intuition in order to explain Kant's doctrine of sensibility. By virtue of its negative sense, noumenon is a '*limiting concept*' (A255/B310–11). By virtue of its positive sense, the concept is 'problematic', meaning that is a concept forced on us by our reason (and hence not arbitrary), and yet the 'representation of a thing of which we can say neither that it is possible nor that it is impossible' (A286–7/B343; see also A254–5/B310). Since the possibility of non-sensible intuition can be neither proved nor disproved, the existence of noumena *qua* objects of intellectual intuition must remain an 'open question' (A252).

In the light of this distinction, the illusion of transcendent knowledge can be described as a slide, natural but illicit, from the negative to the positive sense of noumenon: we pass from the mere 'representation of an *object in itself*' to the supposition that we are 'able to form *concepts* of such objects' (B306–7). Rationalism is throughout an attempt to know reality as a world of noumena, and so presupposes application of the concept of noumenon in the positive sense (as did the position Kant himself had held in the days of his *Dissertation*).

Things in themselves exist

A final question needs to be addressed. Throughout the discussion Kant has emphasised the indispensability of the *concept* of the thing in itself or noumenon. Now, does Kant however think that we also need to assume the *existence* of things in themselves? Or is it only the concept that we cannot do without, so that we should remain neutral about (or may even deny) the existence of things in themselves?

If Kant's remarks quoted above (p. 202) on the need to assume something in itself corresponding to appearance do not quite settle the issue, the following statement does so: 'Doubtless, indeed, there are intelligible entities corresponding to the sensible entities' (B308–9). This is not an isolated statement. At numerous places in the *Critique* Kant is equally explicit: 'knowledge has to do only with appearances, and must leave the thing in itself as indeed real *per se*, but as not known by us' (Bxx); 'though we cannot *know* these objects as things in themselves, we must yet be in a position to at least *think* them as things in themselves; otherwise we should be landed in the absurd conclusion that there can be appearance without anything that appears' (Bxxvi); 'The non-sensible cause of these representations is completely unknown to us' (B522); 'If, in connection with a transcendental theology, we ask, *first*, whether there is anything distinct from the world, which contains the ground of the order of the world and of its connection in accordance with universal laws, the answer is that there *undoubtedly* is. For the world is a sum of appearances; and there must therefore be some transcendental ground of the appearances, that is, a ground which is thinkable only by the pure understanding' (B723–4). (For further confirmation, see *Proleg* 314–15, 318, 351, 354–5.)

Kant's affirmation of the existence of things in themselves has caused much perplexity and occasioned many objections. The problem, in brief, is that while it is clear that the *concept* of the thing in itself is needed for Kant to articulate the Copernican revolution and the doctrines of the Aesthetic and Analytic, it is not clear how Kant can consistently allow it to have an *object*, or why he should consider its having an object a matter of knowledge for us. On the contrary, it may seem that for Kant reference to things in themselves drops out of a correct account of human knowledge, and that any affirmation of their existence should be deemed dogmatic and un-Critical. The issue will be discussed further in chapter 8.

Kant's critique of Leibniz's method (The Amphiboly)

The purpose of the appendix to the Analytic, The Amphiboly of Concepts of Reflection, is to provide a systematic critique of Leibniz's metaphysics, again as a prelude to the Dialectic. The work of undermining Leibniz's methodology began in the Postulates with Kant's anti-rationalist analysis of modality. The point of the Amphiboly is again not to refute Leibniz by discovering any inconsistency in his position, but to weaken it by showing how in the light of the conclusions of the Aesthetic and Analytic, the correctness of which Kant here assumes, Leibniz's claim to be able to grasp the underlying reality of the world of experience by purely intellectual means must be regarded as reposing on a comprehensible but definite confusion.

To this end, Kant introduces a new panoply of notions. According to Kant we have at our disposal a distinctive set of concepts not yet treated in the *Critique*, called by him 'concepts of reflection' (A270/B326): identity/difference, agreement/opposition, inner/outer, and matter/form (A261/B317). Unlike the categories, these concepts have no synthetic function in experience. Their role is rather to facilitate comparisons between concepts: we employ them in judging that such and such concepts are the same or different, compatible or incompatible, etc. The activity of making such judgements Kant calls 'logical reflection' (A262/B318). Now it is, Kant contends, on the application of logical reflection to metaphysical issues that the Leibnizian edifice is erected: Leibniz 'compared all things with each other by means of concepts alone' (A270/B326). To take a crucial instance, Leibniz's monadic ontology presupposes an identification of numerical differences between things, with differences between concepts, whence he derives the principle that a plurality of things requires intrinsic rather than relational differences between things (A263/B319, A265/B321).

Kant's objection to this method in metaphysics is simply that logical reflection, because it takes into account only the form of concepts, and form alone is insufficient to provide for objects, is incompetent to determine the nature of things. Consequently, to seek to employ logical reflection to determine the nature of things is to confuse real with logical relations. Specifically, it is to treat all concepts as if they were intellectual and a fortiori all objects as if they were noumenal (A264/B320). What is needed, in fact, to determine the nature of things is not logical but *transcendental* reflection (A261/B317), in which we consider to which cognitive faculty – sensibility or understanding – a given representation belongs, and thereby decide whether the status of its object is that of appearance or thing in itself (A269/B325). This matter is crucial, for while it is true of things considered in themselves and so as objects of understanding that logical reflection suffices to determine their nature, the same is not true of appearances: the fundamental mode of differentiation of outer appearances is spatial, which means that their numerical difference is intuitive rather than conceptual, and relational rather than intrinsic; and appearances in general, whose being is purely relational, differ numerically without differing in themselves (A263–6/B319–22; Leibniz's principles are criticised in detail at A272–8/B328–34).

Fundamentally, Leibniz fails to see the need in metaphysics for transcendental as opposed to merely general logic, and the involvement of extra-logical elements in the constitution of objects. Consequently his metaphysics has application to noumenal reality, if it exists, but not to any reality that may be given to us. At root, Leibniz's '*intellectual system of the world*' is based on a 'transcendental amphiboly, that is, a confounding of an object of pure understanding with appearance' (A270/B326). (Locke's philosophy is amphibolous too, but in the opposite direction: whereas Leibniz '*intellectualised* appearances', Locke '*sensualised* all concepts of the understanding', A271/B327.)

Chapter 7

Unknowable objects (The Dialectic)

Beyond the land of truth

The Analytic has defined the 'land of truth' (A235/B294): it has told us under what conditions we can rightfully claim that our thoughts have objects, and that our judgements are capable of truth. These conditions are those of possible experience, and the Analytic implies that they are necessary as well as sufficient for knowledge. It follows that the limits of knowledge coincide with the limits of experience, and that the claims of transcendent metaphysics are unfounded.

Only the first half of the Critical enterprise is yet complete, however: in the Dialectic Kant goes on to provide a detailed critique of transcendent metaphysics. Whereas, in the Analytic, Kant argues against the empiricist's conception of experience in support of the rationalist's claim that pure reason is necessary for knowledge, in the Dialectic he turns against the rationalist's conception of the

scope of reason, in support of the empiricist's claim that objects must be experienced in order to be known. The target of the Dialectic is for the greater part Leibnizian philosophy.

There are a number of reasons why this further enterprise is necessary. The most obvious is that an examination of transcendent metaphysics is required for a conclusive solution to the problem of metaphysics and the full defence of his theory of knowledge.

At a superficial level, Kant could simply allow his verdict against transcendent metaphysics to rest on the results of the Analytic – as he may seem to do in for example the chapter on noumena, where he declares it already proven that the presumptions of 'Ontology' must give way to a 'mere Analytic of pure understanding' (A247/B303). But it would be inadvisable for him to maintain this line. Kant's relation to transcendent metaphysics is much more complex than that of other of its critics, such as Hume. Kant does not reject claims about non-empirical objects, however cognitively defective, as literally meaningless: his theory of the a priori origin of the categories commits him to affirming that thought about non-empirical objects is possible, and that the scope of our thought exceeds that of our knowledge. Kant's objection to transcendent knowledge turns entirely on the gap between thought and knowledge. He is therefore required to tread a line between granting reason the authority that rationalism claims for it, and endorsing Hume's demand that volumes of metaphysics be consigned to the flames. Kant has so far provided a principled basis for distinguishing between two forms of metaphysical claim, the immanent and the transcendent (namely possible experience, as the 'X' making the synthetic a priori judgements of metaphysics possible), and he has shown that transcendent metaphysics cannot share the grounds of the metaphysics of experience, but it needs to be confirmed that there is no other way in which they might be grounded.

It should be added that, as far as the balance of argument with rationalism is concerned, Kant is open to an objection. He has argued that, because knowledge requires experience, transcendent metaphysics cannot yield knowledge. But his opponents may reverse this reasoning, arguing that, on the contrary, since the questions that transcendent metaphysics addresses must have and deserve to be given answers, Kant's account of the conditions of knowledge should be rejected.

To the extent that the verdict against transcendent metaphysics appears unsafe, it threatens to rebound on his theory of knowledge. The Dialectic has, therefore, at a minimum, the job of vindicating the conclusions of the Analytic. The claims of transcendent metaphysics need to be confronted in all their specificity and deflated subtly, rather than dismissed *en bloc*. Ideally, Kant's critique of transcendent metaphysics would at no point rely on his theory of knowledge; his verdict would then have a double derivation. If this is too much to expect, Kant may still minimise the dependence, and to the extent that he does so, his position will be strengthened.

There are other reasons why Critical philosophy is obliged to investigate transcendent thought. Kant's avowed ambition is to achieve a comprehensive settlement in philosophy, and a permanent state of equilibrium for human reason. This provides a further reason for not bluntly repudiating transcendent metaphysics in positivistic or Humean fashion: to do so would perpetuate the wars of reason which it is Kant's aim to conclude. Now, the Analytic has remedied our situation in two important respects: it has protected empirical knowledge against skepticism, and (if the Dialectic can confirm its anti-metaphysical implications) taken us off the see-saw of dogmatism and skepticism, by showing that our ignorance of transcendent reality is a matter fixed by our cognitive constitutions. It has not, however, cured us of our propensity to speculate about transcendent reality. We are, Kant himself affirms, constitutionally disposed not merely to wonder what lies beyond experience, but also to believe certain things about transcendent reality. The dogmatic philosophers who have sought to describe reality have not selected their topics at random, nor are their doctrines arbitrary fabrications. Rather they give voice to convictions that are natural to human beings (above all, according to Kant: that there is a God, that our wills are free and that we have immortal souls, A337n/B395n, A466/B494). This requires explanation.

What also requires explanation, and resolution, is the fact that the transcendent claims which reason finds it natural to make fail to meet with its own abiding agreement. Reason repeatedly involves itself in conflicts regarding the finitude or infinitude of the world, the relation of mind to matter, the existence of God, freedom and the soul, and so on. Even though these disputes cannot be regarded by Kant as competing claims to knowledge, they cannot be left unconcluded, for to do so would leave reason opaque to itself; the paradoxical conclusion that reason is itself incoherent would continue to flicker on the horizon. For Kant, therefore, in contrast with positivism, transcendent metaphysics, despite the emptiness of its claims to knowledge, is as much of an intrinsically worthy object of philosophical investigation as the possibility of knowledge itself: critical philosophy must explain why transcendent speculation takes the particular forms that it does, and why we are disposed to form certain beliefs concerning transcendent reality, and it must resolve the conflicts that result therefrom.

It should, moreover, do all of this in a way that, as far as possible, increases our cognitive harmony. The Analytic's conclusion regarding the limits of our knowledge directly frustrates our desire for metaphysical knowledge, and our dissatisfaction on this count needs to be mitigated. The Dialectic will do something here, by showing that transcendent ideas are not futile but have importance for natural science. But our interest in transcendent reality is only really fulfilled, Kant believes, in the perspective of moral consciousness. Morality falls outside the *Critique*, but the Dialectic supplies some of the necessary materials for the construction of Kant's ethical theory, and so provides an essential bridge from Kant's theoretical to his practical philosophy. To that extent the Dialectic is also quietly concerned with the conflict of reason instantiated in the opposition of science to morality and religion.

Knowledge of the bounds of knowledge

There is one more way in which transcendent thought creates a task for Critical philosophy. As Kant explains (at A758–62/B786–90, and more clearly in the Conclusion of the *Prolegomena*), the limits of knowledge themselves comprise, in the Critical perspective, a further topic of philosophical investigation.

To have shown, as Kant has done in the Aesthetic and Analytic, that the objects of our knowledge are conditioned by the human standpoint, is one result of Critical philosophy, which allows us to speak of the limits of knowledge in a negative sense. But transcendental idealism entails that we must represent our knowledge as having also limits in a *positive* sense, or what Kant calls *bounds* (*Proleg* 352): we must picture the land of truth not merely as it appears to us from the inside, as having such and such a character and extent, but as adjoining a space which must remain for us a void: 'our reason, as it were, sees in its surroundings a space for the cognition of things in themselves, though we can never have determinate concepts of them and are limited to appearances only' (*Proleg* 352). That this space exists is something we can know, without knowing whether or not anything occupies it, simply because we know the land of truth to be constituted by us: it is a space *for* things in themselves, and it exists over and above our concept of it. This is what makes the bounds of knowledge real – like the surface of an extended object – in a sense in which mere limits are not. Transcendental realism, inclusive of positivism, has no use for the concept of a bound to knowledge, which it pictures as having – like God's knowledge – no inside and outside, and thus as not characterisable in spatial metaphors.

Now the bounds of knowledge can, Kant holds, be known determinately, which is to say, we can know *where* they lie. To map them, we need, first, to contemplate experience as a whole, and, second, to represent the bounds of knowledge in terms independent from experience, that is, in terms of concepts of transcendent objects. Understanding is of no use here, but our reason can, the Dialectic will show, do both, because it can form concepts of totalities of experience and of objects beyond experience. (The former are no less transcendent than the latter: wholes of possible experience are not themselves objects of possible experience.) These concepts lead us to 'the spot where the occupied space (viz. experience) touches the void' (*Proleg* 354), whereby we gain 'positive cognition' of something 'objective' (*Proleg* 361). It is possible for us to cognise the bounds of knowledge, even though they are not empirical, and even though we cannot grasp them from their other side, because they belong to experience as its 'highest ground' (*Proleg* 361). (It follows that the limits of knowledge fractionally exceed the limits of experience: we have knowledge of where experience stops, and this is not itself a matter of experience.) As Kant puts it, Hume's principle, 'not to carry the use of reason dogmatically beyond the field of all possible experience', needs to be matched by another: 'not to consider the field of experience as one which bounds itself in the eyes of our reason' (*Proleg* 360).

In this context, the true value of transcendent metaphysics for (theoretical) philosophy can be seen. Transcendent metaphysics has already, unbeknownst to itself, undertaken the task of marking the bounds of knowledge. If it were not for its endeavours, unsuccessful as they are from the point of view of knowledge, the bounds of knowledge would never have become visible: the bounds of experience are not themselves objects of possible experience, and experience does not, as Kant puts it, bound itself (all it can do is lead us from one empirical object to another). Retracing the steps of transcendent metaphysics, and mapping its transgressions, is therefore the proper way of achieving positive cognition of the bounds of knowledge.

In so doing, Kant continues to follow the groundplan of Critical philosophy, which tells us that questions about transcendent objects are to be turned around, so that instead of being regarded as questions about supposed objects, they are instead regarded as questions about the subject's cognitive constitution. The problems of transcendent metaphysics are to be reconceived as lying, so to speak, entirely in us. The Dialectic comprises, therefore, a further dimension of Kant's Copernican revolution, the reflexive shift of reason's turning back on itself: just as, in the Analytic, questions about the objects of our knowledge are answered through being referred to our mode of cognition, similarly with questions about unknowable objects in the Dialectic. (This approach does not, as will be seen, pre-judge their reality: a Copernican account of unknowable objects no more entails their non-existence, than a Copernican account of knowable objects entails their illusoriness.)

The Dialectic is, therefore, an integral part of the Critical enterprise, not merely a lengthy appendix to the *Critique*. Even though knowledge extends no further than experience, there is more to be said than is said in the Aesthetic and Analytic.

Transcendental illusion: reason's ideas of the unconditioned

Kant's account of how in general we come to suppose knowledge of objects beyond experience to be possible – and, indeed, how we can so much as form concepts of such objects – is contained in his theory of transcendental illusion (A293–8/B349–55), behind which lies his account of reason as a faculty with an agenda quite distinct from that of the understanding (A298–309/B355–66).

The preconditions of transcendental illusion

Illusion that is transcendental – or as Kant also calls it dialectical – is what results when principles not meant for use outside experience are employed as if they were. As Kant also puts it, principles which are properly subjective are misidentified as objective (A296–7/B353, *Proleg* 328). Because transcendental illusion rests on a specific kind of mistake, regarding the conditions under which objects can be given to us, it is quite distinct from the familiar species of illusion encountered outside the context of transcendental philosophy (empirical illusion, the result of sensory deception, and logical illusion, due to inattentive application of rules of inference) (A295/B351–2, A296–7/B353).

The seeds of transcendental illusion, and some of its preconditions, are identified earlier in the *Critique*. In the Introduction Kant proposes that the confident flight of transcendent metaphysics beyond the bounds of experience is fostered by a false analogy with the case of mathematics (A4–5/B8; see also A724–7/B752–5). It is false because, Kant says, mathematics is based on intuition, as metaphysics is not (Kant spells out the crucial difference between philosophical and mathematical methods of handling concepts at A726–7/B754–5).

Also playing a role is the erroneous assimilation of all metaphysical judgements to that small portion of the subject which does consist in analytic judgements and so is secure on logical ground (B23). These Kant describes in the *Prolegomena* as judgements merely 'belonging to metaphysics', as opposed to 'metaphysical judgements properly so called' (273). The absence of constraint by anything external to concepts, resulting from the failure to appreciate the consequences of the fact that genuine metaphysical judgements are synthetic, gives rise to the deceptive freedom enjoyed by metaphysical speculation.

In the Schematism Kant adds that we are tempted to think that by lifting the 'restricting condition' of sensibility – incorporated in the condition that the application of the categories be mediated by schemata – we can employ the categories transcendentally, i.e. to things not merely as they appear but '*as they are*' (A146–7/B186). Because we look on sensibility as a kind of filter clouding the vision of our intellect, we suppose that the unschematised categories, bypassing sensibility, get hold of objects as they really are; as if transcendental employment were analogous to empirical contexts where we speak of a thing as known as it really is, rather than as it appears, when it is known by the intellect rather than the senses.

Again, in the chapter on noumena Kant describes the illusion that the categories may be employed transcendentally – that noumena in the positive sense are knowable – as induced by their non-empirical origin, and their asymmetry with the forms of intuition (B305–6, A253–4/B309, *Proleg* § 33). It is thus natural, given that the pure concepts of the understanding do not arise from experience, and that they are concepts of objects in general, that we should suppose them to be applicable to things outside all experience.

The Dialectic adds further layers to the analysis of transcendental illusion. To date Kant has shown why it is easy for us to suppose that our desire for transcendent knowledge can be fulfilled, but not what motivates that desire. Only in the Dialectic is it explained why we take up the invitation to make judgements about things in themselves which the pure concepts of the understanding extend to us.

The faculty of reason

Kant's explanation turns on his conception of reason as a power distinct from the understanding (A298–309/B355–66). Whereas earlier in the *Critique* the term reason is used to mean simply the intellectual faculty as a whole, and so to include the understanding, the two are now sharply differentiated. In the Dialectic reason refers to an independent conceptual faculty whose primary function is to engage in reasoning of a special type, namely 'mediate' or syllogistic inference (A299/B355, A303–4/B360–1). Syllogistic reasoning is concerned with the general conditions under which one piece of knowledge follows from another; as when 'all men are mortal' provides the condition under which the mortality of a particular man, Socrates, may be inferred from Socrates' being a man. This narrow task of deducing conclusions from given premises Kant calls reason's 'descending' function.

In addition, Kant accords to reason the further, and much more interesting function of 'ascending' from given conditioned objects to the conditions from which they derive (A330–2/B386–9). Reason thus assumes its own cognitive motivation: it has to *discover the conditions* under which objects are as they are, and our judgements are true. Now reason can properly fulfil this task only if it can be brought to a conclusion, which it cannot if the regress of conditions is without end. Consequently, reason must refer ultimately to the *totality of the conditions* for conditioned objects, which is the same as to say that it must refer to an *unconditioned* totality (A307/B364, A322/B379), since a totality of conditions cannot itself rest on any condition (A417n/B445n). For all intents and purposes, reason's search for the unconditioned may be identified with the demand that explanation should be pressed to its limits: as it may be put, reason is concerned with discovering ultimate explanations for things – that which needs no explanation or explains itself – in contrast with the circumscribed, conditional explanations associated with the understanding's employment of concepts to the end of constituting objects.

Reason thus transforms itself from a purely formal, merely logical faculty, into a 'transcendental' faculty intended for a 'real use' (A299/B355–6). It produces concepts of its own, distinct from those of the understanding, concepts of unconditioned totalities or absolute unities (A324–6/B380–2). Kant calls these 'transcendental ideas' or ideas of reason (A311/B368, A320/B377, A327/B383; Kant uses the term *Idee* here, rather than *Begriff*). To form these ideas is to move from considering experiences singly, in the course of which we remain within the domain of experience, to considering experience as a whole, the 'collective unity' or 'absolute totality of all possible experiences' (*Proleg* 328). It means, therefore, quitting the empirical domain, since absolute totality cannot be given in experience.

The ideas of reason, like the concepts of the understanding, are not arbitrary but form a system (A333–8/B390–6). Kant's identification of the system of transcendental ideas does for reason what the metaphysical deduction of the categories does for the understanding. For each fundamental respect in which empirical objects are conditioned (each constituent of cognition) reason forms a different concept of an unconditioned totality. The transcendental ideas are accordingly the concepts of: (1) totality of the subjective conditions of all representations in general, or the absolute unity of the '*thinking subject*'; (2) totality of the temporal, causal and other series which provide the conditions of appearances, or the absolute unity of the '*series of conditions of appearance*'; and (3) totality of the conditions under which objects in general can be thought, or the absolute unity of the '*condition of all objects of thought in general*' (A334/B391). Because the different respects in which objects are conditioned correspond to different respects in which they are synthesised, the ideas of reason can also be regarded as ideas of complete syntheses (A322–3/B379–80).

Kant in fact introduces the ideas in a way which ties them closely to reason's logical function, such that each of them corresponds to a different species of syllogism and (relational) category (A321–3/B377–80). The artificiality and dubiousness of this architectonically motivated derivation is often remarked. What is important, however, is that the ideas should capture the most basic respects in which the world and our knowledge of it invite metaphysical explanation, and this they clearly do: the first and second ideas concern the subject and objects of knowledge respectively, and the third their unity.

Accompanying these ideas is a principle unique to reason, which Kant presents in its most general form as follows: 'if *the conditioned is given, the entire sum of conditions, and consequently the absolutely unconditioned* (through which alone the conditioned has been possible) *is also given*' (A409/B436; stated earlier at A307–8/B364 and A308/B365). This principle, an elaborate version of the principle of sufficient reason, is not analytic but synthetic (A308/B364), since it asserts real existences rather than mere logical relations between concepts, and it is transcendent (A308/B365), since it blatantly transgresses the limits of experience. Transcendent metaphysics regards it as an objectively valid principle on a par with the transcendental principles of the understanding, and interprets it to mean that we can assume the unconditioned to exist and to be in principle knowable. Kant, however, will be seen to argue that it should be understood as 'only a logical precept', instructing us, in the face of any given conditioned object, to 'advance towards completeness by an ascent to ever higher conditions' (A309/B365). That is, it tells us not that we can assume the unconditioned to exist, but what we must do, viz. always seek out further conditions.

Kant's conception of reason therefore differs radically from that of the rationalists, for whom reason has its own given stock of innate ideas which put it directly in touch with a set of objects independent from those given by the senses. For Kant, reason relates immediately not to objects but to judgements supplied by the understanding (A302/B359, A306–7/B363, A643–4/B671–2). It does not generate concepts out of itself but creates its concepts by converting the pure concepts of the understanding (A320/B377). Its autonomy consists in employing the concepts of the understanding in a way that goes beyond the understanding's exclusive concern with possible experience: whereas the concepts of the understanding are injected directly into our experience before we have any material for making inferences, the concepts of reason are ones that we form only after a world of appearances has been constituted and inference-making has begun (A310/B366–7).

If Kant's negative verdict on transcendent metaphysics is correct, then the transcendental ideas are concepts with a peculiar status. It is necessary that we should *have* them: they can be provided with a subjective deduction, since it can be demonstrated that they derive a priori from our mode of cognition. But they cannot receive an objective deduction, i.e. be demonstrated to have application to objects (A336/B393). We cannot, therefore, know that anything corresponds to our concepts of unconditioned totalities. Nor, however, can we know that nothing corresponds to them (except, it will be seen, in the special case where they imply a contradiction). Like the concept of noumenon, they are problematic. Reason therefore only half-fulfils its task: it tells us what kinds of objects need to be given *if* we are to grasp the complete conditions for appearances, but it does not enable those objects to actually *be* given.

Having established that reason is impelled to form ideas of the unconditioned lacking objective reality, Kant defines what he calls dialectical inference as reasoning whose conclusion asserts the objective reality of one or other of the ideas of reason (A338–40/B396–8). The term dialectic refers in Kant's usage to the 'logic of illusion', by which he means both the pseudo-reasoning in which transcendental illusion consists, and the corresponding philosophical study which exposes it as invalid (in which sense dialectic is the second branch of transcendental logic). The products of dialectical inference are the familiar central concepts of transcendent metaphysics: the three transcendental ideas provide the ideas of (1) the self as a subject which is never itself a predicate; (2) the sum-total of appearances, and (3) a being of beings. Or, more colloquially, the ideas of the soul, the world and God. These ideas are elaborated in three corresponding bodies of doctrine, which Kant calls rational psychology, cosmology and theology. Each attempts to determine objects for the transcendental ideas by means of (transcendental employment of) the categories. The main sections of the Dialectic follow this organisation, the Paralogisms, Antinomy and Ideal of Pure Reason exploring in turn the dialectical inferences of reason in each sphere. In each case (excepting, again, the case where reason's ideas are found to be contradictory), Kant's claim is that although the object in question is perfectly conceivable – one can coherently think *of* it – any kind of knowledge claim, even of the object's mere existence, is impossible. Transcendent metaphysics is thereby shown to rest on a transformation of what are legitimate concepts of unconditioned totalities, into illegitimate concepts of real and knowable objects.

Kant insists that transcendental critique is limited in what it can hope to achieve. Because of how our cognitive powers are fixed, we cannot help but project images of certain objects into the void beyond experience. Since transcendental illusion is a necessary conceptual hallucination, it 'does not cease even after it has been detected' (A297/B353). The most the Dialectic can do is expose the illusion and 'take precautions that we be not deceived by it' (A297/B354); the formation of the illusion cannot be prevented, only its effects controlled. Even this, however, can never be final: transcendental illusion will continually 'entrap' reason and its aberrations will 'ever and again' call for correction (A298/B355). (Kant draws a comparison with the appearance of greater size that the moon has when it is close to the horizon: the astronomer continues to perceive it as bigger, even though he knows this to be an illusion, A297/B354.)

Reason as regulative (The Appendix to the Dialectic)

The notion that the ideas of reason are concepts which it is right for us to have, but which there is no scope for employing in judgements, suggests a kind of futility in reason. Kant's response is to find another role for its ideas. Even though reason cannot grasp any objects by means of them, Kant holds that they play a necessary role in guiding those judgements that can and do grasp objects, viz. the judgements of the understanding. The legitimate use of reason is, according to Kant, regulative, as opposed to constitutive: employment of concepts to *constitute objects* is the exclusive prerogative of the understanding, but reason is entitled to employ its ideas in order to direct or *regulate the understanding* (A509/B537, A644/B672).

Kant devotes much space in the Dialectic to the regulative role of reason (within each of its three main divisions, and then in the first half of the Appendix, 'The Regulative Employment of the Ideas of Pure Reason'). His account again grows out of his original characterisation of reason as a formal, logical faculty. Because reason is concerned with the general conditions for particular pieces of knowledge, it can show a multiplicity of objects to derive from one and the same condition, thereby introducing unity into knowledge (A302/B359, A305/B362). The unity that the understanding gives appearances – the unity of a spatio-temporally and causally unified field of experience – is what is necessary for the unity of apperception, and no more: it is not sufficient for *knowledge itself* to form a unity. This requires our judgements to be inferentially interconnected. Giving unity to knowledge is the job of reason: just as the understanding works on the manifold of sensibility, so reason, which has the understanding as its immediate object, works on the understanding's manifold of judgements to create the unity of a system (A305–6/B362).

In concrete terms, what this amounts to is that reason provides the understanding with certain rules or methodological imperatives, called by Kant 'maxims' (A666/B694). These serve to unify, simplify and systematise the understanding, and direct it to its greatest extent, with a view to arriving at 'a whole of knowledge' (A645/B673). This whole is conceived by reason as containing a priori the conditions for each of its parts, so that the parts derive from the whole rather than the whole being a mere sum of the parts. By demanding this higher unity, reason leads us from the knowledge of indefinitely many individual states of affairs supplied by the understanding, to knowledge of Nature as a determinate whole. If this goal could be realised, our knowledge would be transformed from a 'mere contingent aggregate' into a 'system connected according to necessary laws' (A645/B673): the 'varied and manifold' knowledge of the understanding would be reduced to the 'smallest number of principles (universal conditions)' (A305/B361), and shown to be connected according to 'a single principle' (A648/B676).

This unity is, of course, only a '*projected*' unity (A647/B675), a mere ideal, but it has significance for how we approach the empirical world. Kant gives the following illustrations: under pressure from reason, we will search for fundamental (chemical) elements and powers in nature (A646/B674, A648–9/B676–7), employ concepts of ideal entities not to be found in nature (e.g. pure earth, water and air, A646/B674), develop hypotheses advancing universal laws of nature (A646–7/B674–5) and classify the organic and inorganic natural worlds into genera and species (A653–7/B681–5). The operative maxims are the three principles of 'genera', 'specification' and 'affinity', instructing us to seek out respectively 'homogeneity', 'variety' and 'continuity' among natural forms (A651–64/B679–92).

The regulative employment of reason amounts, therefore, to the elaboration and expansion of empirical knowledge through the construction of scientific theories with hypothetico-deductive form. The topic is consequently crucial for the understanding of Kant's theory of science. (Kant reworks it completely in his *Critique of Judgement*, where he attends particularly to teleological judgements of the kind found in biological science.) Regulative reason may also be regarded (depending on what view one takes of the strength of the conclusion reached in the Second Analogy) as essential for our knowledge of causal laws, as opposed to mere singular causal sequences, and as providing Kant's justification of induction against Hume (this is clear in the *Critique of Judgement*). In which case, it is responsible for a vast and indispensable part of common-sense empirical knowledge, as well as fully-fledged natural science.

The regulative role of reason, though a 'real' rather than merely logical use of the faculty, is thus a far cry from metaphysical speculation. In regulative employment reason is given its due by being allowed to set up unconditioned totality as a target for the understanding: the formation of a system of empirical knowledge takes the place of cognition of transcendent objects, and the transcendental ideas are shown not to be inherently faulty. (Kant notes that they are in themselves, i.e. apart from the use that may be made of them, neither immanent nor transcendent, A643/B671.) Reason's concern with unconditioned totality is thus vindicated, without its being assumed that the unconditioned exists ('is given') except in the form of a task; in this 'amended' form reason's principle that 'if the conditioned is given etc.' has validity (A508/B536).

The specific, research-guiding regulative principles that derive from reason may thus be accorded objective validity (A663/B691) and even objective reality (A665–6/B693–4): though they do not determine anything *in* the objects of experience, they do determine something *about* them, namely the procedure which the understanding should employ in gaining knowledge of them. The error of transcendent metaphysics may consequently be redescribed as that of mistaking a regulative for a constitutive principle (A644/B672): in dialectical inference, principles whose proper role it is to regulate the understanding are mistaken for principles whose role it is to constitute objects.

A deduction of the ideas of the soul and God

To exercise its regulative function, reason needs its original transcendental ideas of unconditioned totality, and not the dialectically transformed, hypostatised versions of these concepts found in transcendent metaphysical doctrine. Despite this, and rather surprisingly,

Kant adds an account of how our ideas of the soul and God may receive a transcendental deduction in the context of reason's regulative employment (in 'The Final Purpose of the Natural Dialectic of Human Reason', the second half of the Appendix, A669–682/B697–710).

The deduction is highly oblique. According to Kant, to say that we should proceed in empirical enquiry on the basis of a conception of appearances as capable of forming a systematic unity, is the same as to say that we should proceed *as if* the appearances of the self were appearances of an indivisible soul, and *as if* nature were the product of an intelligent being. And, he argues, to regard appearances in this 'as if' mode is to regard the ideas of reason as having *in*direct reference: they may be taken to refer to transcendent objects *via* objects that we can experience, namely appearances, in so far as appearances are regarded as having transcendent grounds. We are, however, entitled to do this only on the strict condition that the transcendent objects are conceived in *analogical* terms, as 'analoga of real things, not as in themselves real things' (A674/B702). We may, for instance, think of God's relation to the world of appearance on the analogy with causal relations between appearances. The object of an idea of reason is, Kant says, 'posited only in the idea and not in itself' (A674/B702). In more recent parlance, it has the status of a purely intentional object.

This reconceptualisation of the empirical world gives it new depth, but it does not extend our knowledge, since our ideas of transcendent objects, being analogical, remain wholly indeterminate. It is not, therefore, an inference from nature to the existence of some new object outside it, but simply another way of expressing reason's demand for systematicity in empirical knowledge.

Granting a legitimate regulative role to the ideas of reason, and discovering a slim sense in which the ideas of transcendent metaphysics may be ascribed objective reality, provides a kind of sublimation of the intellectual forces that give rise to transcendental illusion. But the true destiny of the ideas of reason awaits, as said earlier, the context of practical reason, where they do more than order our thought about the empirical world: in the context of morality, the ideas of reason are allowed to become constitutive of objects in a way that is impossible when we are reasoning theoretically.

The dialectical inferences of transcendent metaphysics (The Paralogisms, The Antinomy, The Ideal of Pure Reason)

The Paralogisms I

The first form that transcendental illusion takes is illusion about the self (The Paralogisms of Pure Reason). Rational psychology, the clearest exponent of which is Descartes, is a branch of transcendent metaphysics which claims to be able to know that the self is an in-divisible and immaterial *substance*, an incorruptible and immortal *soul* (A345/B403). In Kant's terms, rational psychology claims knowledge of the self as a thing in itself (B409–10).

Rational psychology, as distinct from empirical psychology, must base itself solely on apperception: the 'I think' (cogito) supplies its 'sole text' (A343/B401), on which all of its doctrines are to be grounded. Since the 'I think' is a non-empirical representation, rational psychology amounts to an attempt to answer the question, 'What is the constitution of a thing which thinks?' (A398), on an a priori basis. Kant divides it into four claims and corresponding (dialectical) inferences, which Kant calls paralogisms, a paralogism being simply an invalid syllogism (A341/B399). (The Paralogisms is the only chapter of the Dialectic that Kant rewrote in its entirety for the second edition. The earlier version is fuller and has a more architectonic form, with separate sections for each syllogism; the later version seems to allow that the claims of rational psychology blur into one another to some degree.)

In the first instance, the rational psychologist reasons as follows (which abstracts from the different versions given at A348, B407 and B410–11):

1　That which is the subject of judgement and cannot be predi-cated of anything else is substance.
2　I as a thinking being am always the subject of my thoughts.
3　Therefore I am a substance (in which my thoughts inhere).

The argument is at first glance compelling. Kant explains, however, why it is not valid (A349–51, B410–13). Expressed formally, the error of the rational psychologist consists in an equivocation over 'subject', a confusion of the logical sense of the term with its extra-logical, object-involving sense. Kant agrees that 'I' is always something of which things are predicated, and can never itself be predicated of anything. So it is true that the 'I' must always be regarded as the subject of thought. But, according to Kant, this is properly understood as a statement about the logical role of the *representation* 'I': it tells us that the 'I' must occupy subject-position in any judgement. So what is true is only that the 'I' must be regarded as subject in what Kant calls the *logical* sense of 'subject'. And from this nothing follows about the 'I' being a subject in the non-logical or *real* sense of subject as an underlying substratum. (As Kant showed in the Deduction, nothing at all follows about the nature of the 'I' as an object from the necessity of the purely formal 'I think'.)

The wedge that Kant inserts between the logical and real senses of subject, whereby the rational psychologist's inference is invalidated, depends on his account of the conditions of application of the concept of substance, and more generally of the conditions under which objects can be given, which according to Kant the rational psychologist fails to grasp (A349–50, A399–400, B407, B412–13). The point of the concept of the substance, the First Analogy showed, is to provide us with experience of something permanent. But there is nothing permanent in experience of the self: all that is given in inner sense is a succession of appearances subject to requirements of unity. The rational psychologist accepts that the permanence of the self is not given in intuition, since he regards it, not as an empirical datum, but as something that needs to be inferred by pure reason from the non-empirical representation 'I'. (The rational psychologist reasons: 'I' is a subject and *therefore* a substance, and *therefore* something that has permanence.) What however is needed for the concept of substance to have application, is for it to be employed in synthesis of the manifold of intuition. This is what legitimate application of the concept of substance consists in. The rational psychologist's conclusion would be justified, therefore, if and only if the concept of substance were employed in synthesising the 'I'. But all that is involved in synthesising the self is the 'I think', transcendental apperception. And transcendental apperception is a condition *for* application of the concept of substance along with the other categories, not conditional *upon* it.

The rational psychologist's basic mistake thus consists in a misreading of the major premise. Correctly understood, what (1) says is that when an object O corresponds to a representation R, and R is a logical subject, O is a substance. The inference that it licenses is conditional on an object's *already* being given: it says is that *if* an object O is given, and its representation is a logical subject, then O is a substance. The major premise, correctly understood, does not say anything about the conditions under which objects can be assumed to be given; all that it tells us about knowing objects to be substances stands under the condition that the objects in question are independently given. It cannot, therefore, license an inference *from* representations *to* objects, as the rational psychologist supposes and requires.

In the second edition's text of the Paralogisms, Kant reformulates his criticism (B416–20). Rational psychology is charged with a confusion of analytic with synthetic judgements: the rational psychologist tries to get from an analytic proposition (the 'I' that thinks must be regarded always as subject) to a synthetic proposition (I as an object am a substance). And this inference is invalid, because a synthetic judgement cannot follow from analytic judgements alone. (The Paralogisms contains in fact several, complementary statements of what goes wrong in rational psychology: at B411n–12n Kant describes it as resting on an equivocation over 'thought', corresponding to that over 'subject'; and at A402–3 he suggests viewing all four paralogisms as exemplifying a common pattern of invalid argument, in which categories are employed transcendentally in the major premises, but empirically in the minor premises and conclusions.)

The inference just discussed, the first paralogism, is the cornerstone of rational psychology, which collapses without it (B410, B413). But in order to make his case fully secure, Kant shows how the same dialectical pattern is repeated in the other inferences that comprise the Cartesian doctrine of the soul.

The fact that thought essentially involves unity leads the rational psychologist to claim that the self is not just a substance, but a *simple* (indivisible) substance. This is the second paralogism (A351–2, B407). Of this inference Kant says (A352–6, A400–1, B408) that whilst it is true that the thinking 'I' cannot be composite – if the different parts of my thought were distributed between different parts of me, they would not make up a whole thought – it does not follow that the 'I' possesses the unity of an indivisible object: the unity of *thought* does not imply the unity of the *thinker*, except in the tautologous (analytic) sense that a being that thinks must not be composite in a way that is inconsistent with the unity of thought. The unity of the 'I' is again merely *logical*. All that 'I am simple' really means is that the representation 'I' does not contain any trace of a manifold, which is just a consequence of the fact that the representation 'I' has no content of any sort. This is what plays tricks on us: because the 'I' is completely empty, we suppose that it must denote a simple object. In fact, what it means to say that the 'I' is simple is just that 'I have really nothing more to say of it than merely that it is something' (A400).

The same sort of mistaking of features of apperception for features of substances leads the rational psychologist to the further claim that the 'I' refers to a *person*, a substance that has consciousness of its identity throughout time and change; this being the third paralogism (A361–2, B408). The rational psychologist infers the personality of the 'I' from the fact that I am conscious of my identity throughout the time that I am conscious of anything at all. Again, Kant contends (A362–6, B408–9) that the inference involves a confusion of logical with non-logical uses of concepts, here the concept of identity. To make the point clear Kant employs an analogy (A363n–64n). If a number of billiard balls are placed in a line, the first to be struck will communicate its motion to its successor and so on down the line. Similarly, for all that we know, in the case of the 'I' it is perfectly possible for each of a series of successive, numerically distinct substances to communicate its representations and consciousness to the next. Unity of consciousness across time is fully compatible with changes in the identity of underlying substance, and there is no legitimate inference from the unity of apperception to that of a permanent thing across time.

A final mistake is made by rational psychology – the fourth paralogism (B409) – when it converts the truth that I distinguish my own existence as a thinker from that of other things outside me, including my body, into the claim that my *existence* is *independent* of that of my body (Descartes' argument for dualism). Kant's criticism is on the by now familiar pattern: the fact that things outside me in space are ones that I think of as distinct from myself is an *analytic* matter; it is a further, *synthetic* matter that I might exist without them. (The first edition's version of the fourth paralogism, A366–9, discussed in chapter 6, p. 184, is different. There Kant argues that the rational psychologist is committed to a view of self-knowledge as privileged over knowledge of outer objects – the former being immediate, the latter mediate – which makes skepticism about outer objects unavoidable; the epistemic proximity of the self affirmed in rational psychology pushes other objects out of our reach. Since this topic really belongs to the epistemology of outer objects rather than the metaphysics of the self, in the second edition Kant quite properly substitutes a more appropriate Cartesian doctrine as the fourth paralogism. He nevertheless reasserts rational psychology's solipsistic implications in the second edition, at B417–18.)

In sum, rational psychology is pervaded by a misconstrual of the original datum, 'I think' (which is, to repeat, all it has to go on). All of the knowledge that can in fact be derived from the cogito is contained in the following propositions: '1. I think, 2. as subject, 3. as simple subject, 4. as identical subject in every state of my thought' (B419). These follow from the cogito analytically, and they fall far short of the claims of rational psychology, since they tell me nothing about my constitution as a thinking being.

Kant also clarifies the relation of the 'I think' to the Cartesian cogito, and explains how the rational psychologist comes to suppose that the cogito supplies the materials for answering that question (chiefly in a dense footnote at B422–3n).

It is true, Kant grants, that something 'real is given' in the 'I think', 'something which actually exists' (B423n). But all that the 'I think' expresses is an 'indeterminate empirical intuition', of something of which we have no determinate concept – its concept is merely that 'of a something in general which does not allow of being intuited' (A400). (This something cannot therefore, Kant adds, be regarded either as appearance or as thing in itself, B423n.) Again, it is true that the cogito is empirical and a posteriori, in so far as 'I think' can only take place when some empirical representation provides it with an opportunity of employment (B423n). But the 'I think' itself precedes this empirical material, and is purely intellectual. Consequently, it does not qualify as knowledge of an empirical object. And again, it is true that my existence, because it is taken as given rather than inferred, is determined empirically and so in relation to time. But since I do not determine my existence on the basis of anything permanent given to me in inner intuition, what I do not learn thereby is whether I exist 'as substance or as accident' (B420); it is left entirely open that I am 'a predicate of another being' (B419).

The cogito does not, therefore, answer the question that rational psychology addresses. The only kind of knowledge that we can have of ourselves is empirical, and empirical investigation of the self cannot decide the kinds of matters that rational psychology is concerned with: empirical psychology is merely 'a kind of *physiology* of inner sense, capable perhaps of explaining the appearances of inner sense' (A347/B405). (Kant, incidentally, expresses doubt at A381 that empirical psychology can match empirical knowledge of the material world, and in other works – *Metaphysical Foundations of Natural Science* 471, and *CJ*, First Introduction 237'–8' – he denies it scientific status. Other remarks suggest a more favourable view: A347/B405–6, A848–9/B876–7, *Proleg* 295. This is however a separate issue.)

As has been seen, Kant's criticisms of rational psychology refer explicitly to his account of apperception, and at one level may be said to presuppose it. This does not render his critique circular, however, since the challenge that rational psychology had to meet was precisely that of justifying any more ontologically committed reading of the 'I think' than the formal interpretation that Kant showed to be warranted in the Deduction. In so far as the Paralogisms shows that rational psychology fails to meet this challenge, Kant's account of apperception is vindicated.

It should be observed, furthermore, that Kant's general account of transcendental illusion is borne out by the Paralogisms. First, it is clear that the rational psychologist supposes the categories to give us objects in the absence of intuition (A399–401). Second, rational psychology may fairly be regarded as an attempt to discover an object satisfying reason's idea of the unconditioned (A397–8), here the transcendental idea of 'the unconditioned unity of the subjective conditions of all representations in general' (A406/B432), an unconditioned ground for the synthesis of representations with the subject (A397). Because the only condition which universally accompanies representations is the 'I think', and apperception is unconditioned in the sense that it is the 'condition of all unity' (A401), reason regards the 'I think' as providing knowledge of the unconditioned ground which it seeks (A401–2). In so doing, it mistakes the 'I' for a representation of an object. In fact, all that follows from the unconditioned character of apperception is that employment of the categories is necessarily subject to the condition of apperception. Transcendental illusion regarding the self consists in an inversion ('subreption') of this relation: that is, we suppose that apperception knows '*itself through the categories*' (A402). The 'unity in the synthesis of thoughts' is thereby mistaken for 'a perceived unity in the subject of these thoughts' (A402), and the 'unity of consciousness' for 'an intuition of the subject as object' to which the category of substance may be applied (B421). This confuses, as Kant puts it, the 'determining' with the 'determinable' self, the self as condition of all judgement with the self as intuited object of cognition (A402, B406–7, B421–2).

The Antinomy I

The second form of transcendental illusion, illusion about the world, expressed in the branch of transcendent metaphysics that Kant calls rational cosmology, has a more complex structure than transcendental illusion about the self: it is two-sided, and each side of the illusion contradicts the other (The Antinomy of Pure Reason).

Cosmological illusion has its origin in reason's formation of a further set of transcendental ideas, concerned with 'absolute totality in the synthesis of appearances' (A405–20/B435–48). In contrast with the Paralogisms, where the transcendental illusion of a substantial soul is precipitated by something completely pure (the 'I think'), cosmological ideas result from reason's attempt to think an empirical object. Every appearance is, as Kant puts it, a 'conditioned': it is the way it is because of other things. As such, it implies a corresponding series of conditions (A409–11/B436–8). Reason, in pursuit of the unconditioned, accordingly forms the idea of the absolute totality of the conditions for appearances, or equivalently, in the language of the Analytic, the idea of a synthesis of appearances which is absolutely complete (A415–17/ B443–4). Thus wherever one starts in the realm of appearances – with a bread-crumb or the Himalayas – reason eventually leads to the same idea, of all of the conditions for everything empirical.

The most general and obvious cosmological idea is that of the cosmos or 'world-whole' (A408/B434). This general idea takes four more specific forms, each corresponding to a different respect in which appearances are conditioned. The aspects of appearances which provoke cosmological ideas are those in which they stand in series which start with some actually given appearance, and in which each successive member is a condition of the possibility of its predecessor – what Kant calls ascending, as opposed to descending, series (A410–11/B437–8). The series of positions of objects in space, and the series of events in time running from the present to the past, are of this kind. Reason accordingly forms the idea of the world as an absolute totality of appearances in space and time past (A411–13/B438–40). Second, every appearance is conditioned by its internal parts, which are in turn conditioned by their parts, etc., leading reason to the idea of a complete decomposition of appearances, an absolute mereological totality (A413/B440). Third, appearances stand in causal relations, giving rise to the idea of an absolute totality of their causal conditions (A413–14/B441–2). And fourth, every appearance exists contingently, which obliges reason to form the idea of an absolute totality of the existential conditions of appearances (A415/B442). Kant deals in the first instance in the Antinomy with these four ideas, without which the world would remain untotalised; later he returns to the underlying, undifferentiated idea of the world-whole.

Since the cosmological ideas require synthesis to be carried to a degree transcending all possible experience, their objects, the absolute totalities which they project, cannot be attained through experience: we cannot experience the world as a spatio-temporal totality, etc. Now, if Kant were to proceed in the way that he does in the Paralogisms, what he would have to show is that, although it is legitimate to form the *idea* of the world as a spatio-temporal totality, etc., a mistake is involved in going on to say that the world actually *exists* as such – just as he showed that it is legitimate to form the idea of the soul but not to assert its existence. The obstacle to proceeding in this way in the Antinomy is that the cosmological ideas are grounded in appearances, unlike the 'I think', which does not constitute knowledge of any sort of object, and this appears to put the rational cosmologist in a much stronger position than the rational psychologist. Kant after all acknowledged it as a principle of reason that if the conditioned is given, then the sum of its conditions (the unconditioned) is also given (A409/B436), and this principle on the face of it licenses the inference from any given conditioned to the existence of an absolute totality of conditions for appearances, as Kant notes (A497/B525).

Kant's strategy with rational cosmology consequently needs to be different. What makes it possible for Kant to pursue a critique of rational cosmology, despite its seeming well-groundedness, is the fact that transcendental illusion here assumes, as said earlier, a contradictory form: every cosmological assertion about the cosmos is counterposed by an opposite assertion enjoying an equal degree of justification in the eyes of pure reason (A406–7/B433–4). Kant's strategy in the Antinomy is accordingly not to try to show directly that reason is outside its rights in claiming the reality of its ideas, but instead to grant for the sake of argument its right to do so, and then to show that reason on that assumption contradicts itself. In this way Kant is not forced to fall back on the conclusion of the Analytic, when he denies objective reality to the cosmological ideas, but again puts this claim to the test.

The four antinomies

The contradictory structure of cosmological speculation is demonstrated in four antinomies (Antinomy, Section 2), each of which corresponds to one of the four specific cosmological ideas and consists of a pair of contradictory propositions, called a thesis and an antithesis.

In the first antinomy, the thesis maintains that the world has a beginning in time and a limit in space, and the antithesis that the world has no beginning in time and is unlimited in space

(A426–7/B454–5). The thesis of the second antinomy asserts that every composite substance is composed of simple parts which set an ultimate limit to its possible division, and that only these parts and what is composed of them exist; its antithesis asserts that no such things as simple parts exist, and that everything that exists is infinitely divisible (A434–5/B462–3). In the third antinomy, the thesis says there exists, in addition to causality according to the laws of nature, an absolutely spontaneous and 'original' causality of freedom, a cause of all causes, which originates the causality of nature; the antithesis says there is no freedom and that everything takes place according to the laws of nature, implying the infinity of the causal series (A444–5/B472–3). The thesis of the fourth antinomy affirms that there belongs to the world, either as a part of it or as its cause, a being that exists necessarily and supplies the ground for all contingent existents; the antithesis denies that there is an absolutely necessary being either within the world or outside it as its cause, and conceives the series of existential conditions as exhaustively contingent (A452–3/B480–1).

The antinomies recall the discrepancies of rationalist metaphysics with Newtonian science which preoccupied Kant early in his career (versions of them are contained in Kant's *Dissertation*). They exhibit various patterns. The most obvious is that the theses postulate limited wholes, the antitheses unlimited wholes; in the first and second antinomies, the world is represented as finite in the theses, and as infinite in the antitheses. The theses employ ideas of non-empirical objects (the world's spatial limit and temporal beginning, simple parts, a causality of freedom, an absolutely necessary being) in order to bring the world of experience to a close, whereas the antitheses represent it as a whole composed of series which are infinite or unclosed. This shows the theses and antitheses to each have a common principle: the theses rest on the principle of '*dogmatism*', because they invoke intelligible objects to explain appearances, and the antitheses on '*empiricism*', in so far as they remain 'within the world' in explaining appearances (A465–6/B493–4). This makes it natural (though the historical mapping is far from straightforward) to think of the antinomies as quarrels between rationalists and empiricists. Kant also divides the antinomies into two groups (A418–19/B446–7):

the first two are called *mathematical*, because they are concerned with quantity or magnitude, and the third and fourth *dynamical*, because they are concerned with causality and existence. (This distinction becomes important later.)

Kant's proofs of the theses and antitheses

The foundation of Kant's critique of rational cosmology consists in his attempt to demonstrate that a valid proof can be provided for each thesis and antithesis. Kant presents all of the proofs in the form of a *reductio*: they assume the opposite of what they seek to prove and aim to show that an absurdity follows. The proof of the thesis in the first antinomy (A426–43/B454–71) says: let it be assumed that the world has no beginning in time. If so, an infinite number of events have elapsed up to the present. A completed infinite series of events implies however a corresponding infinite synthesis of those events. (Because appearances are in question, their totality presupposes a complete synthesis of them.) The successive synthesis of an infinite series cannot however be completed, since an infinite length of time is required to complete an infinite task. And yet the synthesis must be complete, for if it were not, the present would not be possible. So the series of events in time must be finite; the world must have a beginning in time. The thesis' proof regarding space is symmetrical: to suppose the world infinite in space is to presuppose an infinite synthesis of its parts, which it is again impossible to complete; so the world must be limited in space.

The antithesis of the first antinomy argues (A428–9/B456–7): let it be assumed that the world has a beginning in time. If so, there was a time t at which the world came into existence, implying an immediately preceding 'empty' time t_1 in which the world did not exist. But nothing can occur in an empty time, because nothing exists in it. Since the world cannot have come into existence at any time, it must be infinite in time. Similarly for space: if the world is limited in space, then the world has a relation to the space outside it. This extra-mundane space cannot however be intuited, since it has no 'correlate' (nothing occupies it), which makes it no object of any sort (it is, as Kant puts it, an 'Unding', a non-thing). In which case, the world's relation to it is also 'nothing', i.e. cannot consist in anything. So the world cannot be limited in space.

In the second antinomy (A434–43/B462–71), the thesis is established by the following argument: if everything is composite, then nothing at all remains of composite substance once its composition has been abstracted from it. But to suppose that no subject of compositeness remains contradicts the very concept of substance. Composite substances must, therefore, be composed of simple (non-composite and hence indivisible) parts.

Yet, the antithesis argues: the claim that there exist simple parts is contradictory, since in the case of material substance (which is what is primarily in question) these would of necessity occupy space, and every space-occupant contains a manifold of constituents, which implies composition. The existence of simple beings cannot be established a posteriori, since no object of experience can testify to the reality of simple parts: the absolute simplicity of an empirically given object can never be inferred from our merely not being conscious of it as containing any manifold (inner experience cannot yield knowledge of the self as a simple substance). Substances are, therefore, infinitely divisible, and contain infinitely many parts.

The other antinomies proceed in similar terms, each cosmological claim being apparently borne out by an argument pointing to the sheer inconceivability of its opposite. In sets of comments following the proofs (the Observations on the Theses and Antitheses), Kant defends their validity, distinguishing them from other, defective or vulnerable arguments that have been offered for the same conclusions, and rebutting arguments that have been or might be given in the hope of settling the issue one way or the other. So if Kant is right, the antinomies are (for all that we have yet seen) logically unavoidable expressions of pure reason: the contradictions they comprise could not be eliminated through more rigorous philosophical analysis.

On this basis Kant is entitled to declare rational cosmology illegitimate. If pure reason in the hands of the rational cosmologist terminates in contradictions, then the only conclusion to be drawn is that there is something wrong with cosmological speculation: rational cosmology, rather than reason itself, must be allowed to destroy itself. This confirms the implication of the Analytic, that claims to transcendent knowledge in general are ungrounded.

This is enough to show that claims to knowledge of the world as a whole constitute transcendental illusion. It cannot, however, be the end of the story. It has not yet been said where exactly the fault in cosmological reasoning lies, so the diagnosis remains incomplete. Nor has reason yet been brought into harmony with itself: an alternative view of the topic of cosmology, free from contradiction, needs to be provided. Later it will be seen how Kant uses transcendental idealism to solve the antinomies.

The Ideal I

The third form of transcendental illusion is found in the doctrines of theology. Kant's critique of claims to knowledge of God's existence is arguably the most systematic and effective in the history of philosophy.

The Ideal of Pure Reason begins by considering at length the 'transcendental origin' of the concept of God, the question of how pure reason comes to have that idea (Ideal, Section 2). This sets Kant a challenge, because the concept of God, an infinite being absolutely independent from the empirical world, appears to lack any connection with possible experience; and what must at all costs be prevented is the rationalist theologian arguing that the very fact that we have the concept of God proves His existence (Descartes' cosmological argument). Kant must show that reason instead forms the idea of God through appropriating materials supplied by the understanding, as he does in the case of the other transcendental ideas. This requires some ingenuity, and the introduction of a new set of concepts.

Kant's account is, in summary, as follows. Every object of cognition can be considered in terms of the concept of possibility: it is what it is because it has some properties and lacks others, and the properties it lacks are ones that it logically could have had. So if we were to produce a *complete* specification ('complete determination') of any object we would have to go through the list of *all possible* properties. Kant suggests that when an object is synthesised, we as it were make a selection of properties out of this stock. It follows that empirical objects presuppose a kind of backdrop consisting in the totality or sum-total of possibility, this being in effect a further transcendental condition of objects (A571–3/B599–601). This source of possibility is, furthermore, according to Kant, something we can think of as an individual, as one thing, and so conceived he calls it 'the ideal of pure reason' (A573–4/B601–2; the notion of an ideal is explained in Section 1). And it is this, Kant suggests, that provides the core of our concept of God. It does so because the idea of the totality of possibility is the idea of the primordial *ground* of all things, the idea of something that *contains all reality* within itself ('*omnitudo realitatus*') and has the *highest degree* of reality ('*ens realissimum*') – the idea of the *highest being* (A574–9/B602–7).

The idea of the highest being is not the same as that of God, but the concept of God is produced from it (A580–7/B608–15). Rational theology, like all transcendent metaphysics, expresses reason's search for the unconditioned, and reason requires the existence of an absolutely necessary being (A584/B612). Since the ideas of a highest being and an absolutely necessary being are intimately related (if a highest being exists, it exists necessarily), and reason always strives to unify its ideas, the two are identified (A585–6/B613–14). The idea of a highest being is thereby caught in the web of transcendental illusion and hypostatised, i.e. treated as a transcendent thing with real existence. This entity may then be conceived as the creator of the world. This yields, once appropriate features of moral personality are added, the concept of God which figures in religious belief. The concept of God is therefore, on Kant's innovative account, not a basic given notion of the intellect, but a composite of several more primitive concepts, namely the concepts of highest being, absolutely necessary being and author of nature.

Kant distinguishes three arguments for God's existence (A590–1/B618–19), and they are the familiar ones: the ontological argument, the cosmological argument and the argument from design or 'physico-theological argument'. Each seeks to prove the existence of God under a different description and on a different basis. The ontological argument is based on a priori concepts, by means of which alone the theologian infers the existence of the highest being. The cosmological argument is based on 'indeterminate experience' or experience in general, of things as existing contingently, from which the existence of an absolutely necessary being is inferred. The argument from design is based on 'determinate experience', of the world as having an orderly constitution, which is held to establish the existence of an author of nature. Between them they cover, Kant claims, all of the possible grounds of proof of God's existence in theoretical reason.

The arguments for God's existence

Kant starts with the ontological argument (Ideal, Section 4). This argues that the concept of God includes His existence because it is that of a perfect being, and existence is a perfection; to say that God does not exist is to say that something the concept of which includes the attribute of existence lacks that attribute, a contradiction. (There are several versions of the argument; Kant appears to have in mind that of Descartes.) In Kant's terms, what the ontological argument claims is that the judgement 'God exists' is analytic: it tries to establish the existence of the highest being on the basis of what is contained in the concept of God.

Kant begins by making the plain point that to deny something's existence is not to contradict anything *in* its concept, but to say *of* the concept that it has no object, and is thus not contradictory (A594–5/B622–3). This line will, however, as it stands be dismissed by the defender of the ontological argument, Kant acknowledges, on the grounds that there is one, unique case in which this way of under-standing negative existential judgements does not apply, namely that of the highest being (A595–6/B623–4). This, it will be said, is precisely the concept of a subject 'which cannot be removed, and must always remain' (A595/B623).

Kant therefore proceeds to make his deeper, well-known criticism that existence is not a real predicate, 'not a concept of some-thing which could be added to the concept of a thing' (A598/B626). Kant of course agrees that 'exists' is a predicate in the sense of occupying grammatical predicate position, but this qualifies it only as a mere 'logical' predicate (like 'is a substance' or 'is an object of thought'). What the ontological argument requires is that existence be a 'real' (defining, determining) predicate, on a par with God's other positive attributes of omnipotence, omniscience, etc. But to think this, Kant argues, is to misunderstand the concept of existence, the content of which is exhaustively explained in the same terms as the copula in subject-predicate judgement: just as 'is' in 'God is omnipotent' serves only to 'posit the predicate *in its relation* to the subject', so in the judgement 'God is/exists', the constituent 'is/exists' serves only to 'posit the subject in itself with all its predicates ... as being an *object* that stands in relation to my *concept*' (A598–9/B626–7). If what 'exists' expresses is a relation between concepts and objects, not an attribute of objects, then existence cannot be counted a perfection, and the judgement that God does not exist does not contradict the concept of God as a perfect being: it merely denies that anything satisfies the predicate 'is a being that has all of the attributes that constitute perfection'.

As usual, Kant also formulates his criticism in terms of the distinction of analytic and synthetic judgements. In these terms, the ontological argument can be charged not merely with error but with contradiction (A597–8/B625–6): every judgement must be either analytic or synthetic; existential judgements cannot be analytic, since that would make them mere tautologies (the predicate would not add anything to the subject, which existential judgements obviously do); but if 'God exists' is synthetic, then establishing its truth requires reference to experience, contrary to the claim of the ontological argument. The ontological argument thus requires 'God exists' to be analytic and synthetic.

The cosmological argument (Ideal, Section 5) says that if anything at all, e.g. myself, exists, then an absolutely necessary being exists; therefore God exists (A604–6/B632–4, A584/B612). (It overlaps, in a way that can be confusing, with the topic of the fourth antinomy, since both are concerned with the relation of the world to an absolutely necessary being. The difference, Kant explains at A456/B484, is that the proponent of the thesis of the fourth antinomy is restricted by the cosmological context to arguing for the existence of an absolutely necessary being *qua* entity within the world; the theologian by contrast may argue for it *qua* entity distinct from the world. So the treatment of the cosmological argument in the Ideal is not a rerun of material already covered.)

Kant's principal attack on the cosmological argument is that, even if the existence of an absolutely necessary being is granted, there is no good inference to the existence of God (A607–9/B635–7): the concept of God is that of the *highest* being, and there is no reason why something less than the highest being, i.e. a limited or derived being, should not be absolutely necessary and supply the modal ground of the spatio-temporal world (A588–9/B616–17). In order to prove the existence of God, the existence of the highest being would need to be inferred from that of an absolutely necessary being. But we know already that this inference cannot be made. To make it, we would need to know that the highest being is the only thing that can be absolutely necessary, that the concept of the highest being alone is 'appropriate and adequate to necessary existence' (A607/B635). For this to be the case, however, the concept of the highest being would have to contain the concept of a necessarily existing being – which is precisely the claim of the ontological argument, and has already been refuted.

The cosmological argument is, therefore, covertly dependent on the ontological argument, and fails along with it (A607–8/B635–6). (Also, had the ontological argument succeeded, the cosmological argument would have been superfluous, for we could then have gone directly to the existence of God from a priori concepts, without need of a detour via experience in general.)

Kant also attacks the initial inference to the existence of an absolutely necessary being: it reposes, he says on a 'nest of dialectical assumptions', i.e. it violates several of the conditions for knowledge, such as the restriction of the principle of causality to the sensible world, set up in the *Critique* (A609–10/B637–8). Kant concludes that the proper role of the modal principle assumed by the cosmological argument, viz. that something must exist necessarily, is regulative (A616–17/B644–5).

The only remaining source of proof for the existence of God is the specific, a posteriori character of our experience (Ideal, Section 6). The argument from design tries to infer God's existence from the order and purposiveness which it claims to discover empirically in the world (A625–6/B653–4).

Kant, who had himself at one time subscribed to this argument, grants it intuitive force – it is 'the most accordant with the common reason of mankind' (A623/B651) – but explains its severe limitations (A626–8/B654–6). Experience cannot present us with an object adequate to the concept of God, and no principle of inference can bridge the gap between the conditioned and the unconditioned. The most the argument can show, in any case, is something about the '*architect*' rather than the '*creator*' of the world (A627/B655), i.e. something about what causes there to be order in the materials composing the world, not what brings them into existence. And what it tells us about the cause of order is, furthermore, at best, completely indeterminate: all it does is indicate an analogy between that unknown cause and human intelligence (A628/B656). Which is of course wholly insufficient for the concept of God.

This shortfalling could be remedied only by returning to the cosmological argument, and thence to the ontological (A629/B657). So the argument from design appeals covertly to the other two, failed arguments. Like the cosmological argument, it rests ultimately on the ontological argument. (Whilst emphasising its limitations as a theological proof, Kant welcomes the regulative implications of the conception of the world as a product of design, saying that it encourages us to identify purposes in natural objects and thereby represent nature as a unity: A685–8/B713–16, A698–701/B726–9, *Proleg* 357–60. Kant greatly elaborates this view in the *Critique of Judgement*.)

Kant's attempt to demonstrate that all ways to prove God's existence theoretically are barred has been widely approved by philosophers many of whom have no other sympathy with Kant's philosophy, and wish to defend atheism. Consequently it is important to appreciate two points. First, Kant concedes much more to theology than many other philosophers would allow – namely that the concept of God is, as well as intrinsically coherent, rationally necessary. His account of the transcendental origin of the concept of God serves as a subjective deduction, a proof that it is necessary for any rational being to have the concept of the highest being.

Second, Kant's case against theology turns ultimately on his claim that existence is not a real predicate. This view is enshrined in modern logic (Frege and Russell) and not often disputed. This does not, however, make it immune to criticism, and Kant's own defence of it is certainly open to challenge, for he does not show, on grounds acceptable to his opponent, that the contrary view of existence as a real predicate involves any strict incoherence. The rational theologian may simply say that existence is a real predicate, in addition to its having the positing function described by Kant, and reject Kant's assumption that analytic judgements cannot extend our knowledge as tendentious. What Kant shows is only that the view of existence as a real predicate is not obligatory, and that the Analytic offers, for anyone sympathetic with the broad philosophical outlook of the *Critique*, a superior way of understanding existential judgement.

Transcendental idealism in the Dialectic I: the dissolution of theoretical reason's contradictions (The Paralogisms, The Antinomy)

Transcendental idealism is not in the foreground in the Dialectic in the way that it is in the Aesthetic and Analytic. That is as it should be, since the critique of transcendent metaphysics needs to proceed without begging any questions. Transcendental idealism is nevertheless closely involved in this part of Kant's enterprise. As well as being, as seen earlier, integral to Kant's notion of charting the bounds of knowledge, it is shown to provide solutions to philosophical problems. The doctrine thereby receives further confirmation, and allows the critique of transcendent metaphysics to be carried to its proper conclusion. The central place in the Dialectic where this happens is the Antinomy, but the strategy of showing how long-standing philosophical problems are transformed in the light of transcendental idealism is also employed, in a marginally less explicit form, in the later parts of the Paralogisms. Here Kant applies transcendental idealism to a number of problems associated with rational psychology.

The Paralogisms II

First, Kant claims that the argument between materialism and dualism concerning the ontological status of the self or soul is dissolved (A356–60, B420, B427–8). Since the self cannot be known to be simple or to exist independently from outer objects, including the body, Descartes' arguments for dualism collapse. But the corollary of the fact that the self cannot be known to be immaterial is that it cannot be known to be material either: since I cannot affirm that I am a substance, I cannot affirm that I am a substance either identical with or distinct from my body; there cannot be any such knowledge of my relation to my body.

This follows from the criticisms of rational psychology taken alone, but transcendental idealism allows more to be said about the problem of dualism versus materialism. According to transcendental idealism, material bodies are not things in themselves but objects of outer sense, and an object of outer sense is necessarily (analytically) not an object of inner sense. A thinking subject 'inasmuch as it is represented by us as object of inner sense' cannot be 'outwardly intuited' (A357), so it cannot be material. To enquire any further about the constitution of the thinking subject would be to ask how it is independently from how we represent it, and so to ask about it *qua* thing in itself. The hitherto irresolvable dogmatic argument between dualist and materialist is, therefore, the result of their common transcendental realist assumption that soul and body are things in themselves. In the context of transcendental idealism, the question whether or not a thinking subject 'is the same in kind as matter . . . is by its very terms illegitimate' (A360).

Second, the problem of interaction, what Kant calls 'communion', between mind and body disappears in the perspective of transcendental idealism (A384–93, B427–8). The problem concerns how two things of different ontological kinds can interact. (How our minds can affect our bodies in action, and bodies affect our minds in perception.) This problem arises for dualists, and the rational psychologist is forced to address it by his commitment to dualism; it famously causes trouble for Descartes, and calls forth a variety of competing speculative theories. But Kant too needs to address it, since, though he rejects dualism, he also rejects materialism, and cannot therefore adopt the solution to the problem afforded by the materialist claim that the world is ontologically homogeneous.

Kant affirms that, if minds and bodies are things in themselves, then their interaction poses an insuperable problem: if the material world consists of things in themselves, constitutionally separate from the thinking subject, then it is indeed unintelligible that they should give rise to representations in us. But for Kant, all that the heterogeneity of mind and matter consists in is that they are two species of appearance, mind consisting of objects of inner sense and matter of objects of outer sense: they differ not 'inwardly' but in their mode of appearing. And if material bodies are mere appearances, the problem of interaction is soluble: the issue is no longer how substances of different kinds may commune, but how 'the representations of inner sense' are connected with 'the modifications of our outer sensibility' (A386). And this question can be answered: it is impossible for outer objects to so much as exist independently of our representations, and the nature of their connection has already been accounted for in the Analytic as a matter of the lawful coherence of our experience. The worry regarding how mind and body are related is thus overtaken in the perspective of transcendental idealism, which answers that mind is related to matter in the way that the thinking subject is related to outer objects, a relation explained in Kant's transcendental theory of experience.

The various theories that rational psychology proposes to explain interaction – 'physical influence', 'harmony' and 'supernatural intervention' (A389–91) – are therefore redundant. And, to the extent that the insolubility of the problem of interaction may be thought to compel us to embrace materialism, this argument for materialism has also been disposed of. (Kant grants that room is left for the thought that 'what, as thing in itself, underlies the appearance of matter, perhaps after all may not be so heterogeneous in character' from that which underlies what appears to us as mind, B427–8; but it can be no more than a thought.) The only residue of a problem that may be thought to linger is 'how in a thinking subject outer intuition . . . is possible'. But that, says Kant, 'is a question which no man can possibly answer', since it would require knowledge of things in themselves (A393).

The Antinomy II

We may now turn to the later sections of the Antinomy, where the Critical strategy of problem-resolution is spelled out in bold. Sections 3–7 of the Antinomy comprise the climax of the Dialectic, as well as being one of the most beautiful and profound stretches of argument in Kant's writings.

As noted previously, the bare conclusion that rational cosmology is illegitimate, which Kant is entitled to draw simply on the basis of its contradictory structure, leaves the antinomies unresolved. The first step towards their Critical solution consists in a deeper understanding of cosmological illusion. Why does reason shoot off in opposite directions in cosmology?

In cosmological contexts there are, Kant notes, two ways of conceiving the unconditioned (A417–18/B445–6). It can be conceived as a *particular member* of the series of conditions, one which conditions all the others, but is itself unconditioned and so closes the series. Or it can be identified with the *entire series* of conditions, in which all members are conditioned, but the whole of which is unconditioned. Obviously, the theses conceive the unconditioned in the first way, and the antitheses in the second.

This is, however, only a partial explanation of the antithetic form of rational cosmology, for it may still be asked why the fact that reason has these alternatives leads to contradictions; the existence of exclusive alternatives does not in general explain the attempt to take both. The full explanation has to do with the different demands of reason and the understanding (A422/B450), both of which are in play in cosmological speculation. In rational cosmology, unlike rational psychology, the material that reason is working with is empirical, which means that the understanding is necessarily involved. The totality that reason seeks is consequently subject to two constraints: it must harmonise with reason's own demand for totality, but also, since the totality in question involves a synthesis according to rules, with the understanding. So although seeking totality is not a task that the understanding itself engages in, reason must take up its point of view and articulate demands on its behalf. Now the problem is that the totalities demanded by each faculty are incongruent: those demanded by reason, expressed in the theses (the world's having a beginning, etc.) exceed what the understanding deems possible, and those demanded by the understanding, expressed in the antitheses (the world's being infinite in time, etc.), are inadequate to satisfy the demands of reason (A486–9/B514–17). Reason identifies the unconditioned with a particular member of the series of conditions, the understanding with the entire series, and the unconditioned cannot take both forms. The upshot is that reason cannot 'even in thought' (A462/B490) frame a consistent idea of an object, i.e. one that satisfies both its own demands and those of the understanding. The differing natures of reason and understanding are thus expressed as a conflict of reason with itself.

This explanation of the contradictory shape of rational cosmology is Critical, because it interprets a conceptual structure – which pre-Critical thought understands in terms of alternative representations of how things really are – in terms of our mode of cognition: it translates an external problem concerning the relation of ideas of reason to supposed objects, into an internal problem concerning the relations of cognitive powers (A484/B512). This strategy, whereby reason is forced to shift from being a participant in disputes to the position of umpire, and the questions of cosmology are shown to be incapable of 'dogmatic' solution, necessitating their Critical solution, Kant calls the 'skeptical method' (A423–4/B451–2).

Kant's solution to the antinomies can now be presented. What makes the contradictions of cosmology seem unavoidable is the natural assumption that *one or other of the thesis or antithesis must be true*, even if we cannot know which (A501/B529). Kant challenges this assumption. To this end he introduces a distinction between different kinds of opposition of judgements (A502–4/B530–2). A pair of inconsistent judgements forms one kind of opposition when each follows directly from the negation of the other, such that to deny the one is logically to affirm the other. We have a different kind of opposition when the negation of the one does not directly entail the other because they share a common presupposition, the rejection of which renders both judgements false. In such a case, the judgements are *contrary*, but not contradictory: *both* may logically be denied, and rejecting their common presupposition dissolves the conflict between them. Kant calls oppositions based on common presuppositions which are false *dialectical*, i.e. illusory. For example, the judgements that X has a good smell and that X has a bad smell form a dialectical opposition if X has in fact no smell at all.

Since the antinomies can be dissolved only if their theses and antitheses do not form contradictions, Kant proceeds to dismantle them on the model of dialectical opposition (A503–5/B531–3). The first antinomy comprises the judgements that the world is finite and that it is infinite. We naturally think of this as a contradiction, but, as Kant points out, both sides *assume* that the world is, as he puts it, *determined in its magnitude* – that it really does have a size. If that assumption is rejected, then it is possible to deny that the world is finite without affirming that it is infinite, and to deny that the world is infinite without affirming that it is finite: it may be affirmed both that the world is *not finite*, and that it is *not infinite*. If the world is not determined in its magnitude, the first antinomy evaporates.

Under what conditions can the assumption that the world is 'determined in its magnitude' be rejected? Kant's answer is, of course: uniquely under the assumption of transcendental idealism. According to transcendental idealism, the world *does not exist in itself* but only in so far as it is constituted in experience; so it does not exist in itself either as a finite whole or as an infinite whole (A505/B533). The solution to the first antinomy (presented in detail at A517–23/B545–51) thus consists in saying that what is given is only that the regress of spatio-temporal conditions is to be extended *indefinitely*: 'we must always enquire for a still higher member of the series, which may or may not become known to us through experience' (A518/B546), and 'should never assume an absolute limit' (A519/B547). Beyond this regulative truth, there is nothing to be said about the magnitude of the world (A519/B547).

The second antinomy receives a symmetrical solution (A505–6/B533–4; in greater detail at A523–7/B551–5). Transcendental idealism entails that the 'whole is not in itself already divided' (A526/B554). If substance is not determined in itself with respect to the number of parts that it contains, then it is false that it consists of simple parts, and false that it is composed of infinitely many parts. What is given empirically is only the *indefinite* divisibility of substance – the parts themselves are given and determined only through the object's division, which is set us as a task without any definite terminus. No more can be said about the compositeness of substance. Kant's solution to the mathematical antinomies results, therefore, in the falsity of both their theses and their antitheses. (The dynamical antinomies, it will be seen later, are solved quite differently. The rest of the present discussion is concerned only with the mathematical antinomies.)

Kant's general view, then, is that transcendental realism lies behind the assumption which generates cosmological contradiction, viz. that one or other of the thesis and antithesis must be in the right (A498–9/B526–7). By regarding the antinomies as instances of dialectical opposition, the common assumption of which is transcendental realism, the self-conflict of reason is terminated. Kant's Critical solution destroys 'the illusion which sets reason at variance with itself' (A516/B544), the underlying illusion that there *is* such a thing as the cosmos, that the world exists as a whole.

The Antinomy's proof of transcendental idealism

Finally and dramatically, Kant draws the inference reported in chapter 5:

> [The Antinomy] affords indirect proof of the transcendental ideality of appearances – a proof which ought to convince any who may not be satisfied by the direct proof given in the Transcendental Aesthetic. This proof would consist in the following dilemma. If the world is a whole existing in itself, it is either finite or infinite. But both alternatives are false (as shown in the proofs of the antithesis and thesis respectively). It is therefore also false that the world (the sum of all appearances) is a whole existing in itself. From this it then follows that appearances in general are nothing outside our representations – which is just what is meant by their transcendental ideality.
>
> (A506–7/B534–5)

As the argument may be restated: if transcendental realism is true, then the world exists as a whole. (Cosmological judgements not only presuppose but are necessitated by transcendental realism: if the world exists in itself, it cannot exist as anything less than a determinate whole.) If the world exists as a whole, then it can be proved to be both a finite whole and an infinite whole. (Because the proofs of the antinomies are valid.) Therefore, contradictions are derivable from transcendental realism. Therefore, transcendental realism is false. Therefore, transcendental idealism is true.

The proof rests on two things: the inescapability of transcendental realism's commitment to there being a truth of the matter in cosmological contexts, and the validity of the proofs of the antinomies. The first is relatively uncontroversial: in the framework of transcendental realism, things exist independently of the conditions of knowledge of them, so there can hardly be a reason for denying that all of the conditions for any given conditioned are themselves given, i.e. exist in some determinate form or other. For this reason, the transcendental realist is in no position to dismiss the cosmological questions as meaningless or ill-formed.

The second is much more doubtful. As said in chapter 5, the general view is that the proofs of the antinomies are not watertight in the way that Kant regards them as being. For one thing, they are firmly cast in his own philosophical vocabulary and contain premises directly reflecting his own philosophical views (e.g. that our ideas of totality are ideas of complete syntheses). But even if this were not the case, the problem would remain (critical commentary on the Antinomy suggests) that for each antinomy some more or less *ad hoc* set of assumptions can always be drawn up which will allow contradiction to be avoided.

The weakness of the proofs of the antinomies does not, however, necessarily debar the Antinomy from realising its objective. Transcendental idealism can still be derived from the antinomies, though less straightforwardly, so long as Kant can establish that their only possible solution is Critical. This requires reference to the methodological discussion, not yet considered, with which Kant prefaces his Critical solutions to the antinomies (Antinomy, Sections 4–5; see also *Proleg* § 56).

We may start by considering why, given that Kant's proofs are not watertight, it should not be concluded that the cosmological questions are simply unanswerable or *undecidable*. The most that is shown by the existence of cosmological disagreement, it may be held, is not that there *is* no truth about the world in itself, but that this truth cannot be *known* (by us). The transcendental realist, who separates questions of fact from questions of knowledge, may happily promote such a solution. In this light it may seem that Kant's whole argument either rests on the bare, unargued assumption that the cosmological questions must be decidable by us, or presupposes verificationism, an identification of what there can be with what we can determine, of truth with decidability-by-us. And from the standpoint of transcendental realism, such assumptions are arbitrary and question-begging.

Now if this were Kant's argument, then the Antinomy would have no impact on transcendental realism. However, the issue is not decidability as such. The problem with transcendental realism is not that it leaves us in ignorance or indecision, but that undecidability fails in *this* context to count as a philosophical solution.

Suppose there is a truth about the constitution of the cosmos, e.g. that it is finite in space and time. Were we to know this, we would know the thesis of the first antinomy to be true and the antithesis false. But we would remain unable to see how it is *possible* for the antithesis to be false: its proof, though known to be unsound, would continue to seem to establish the inconceivability of the cosmos' finitude. The antinomies would continue to 'cast us from one inconceivability into another' (A485/B513), because each cosmological assertion would continue to find 'conditions of its necessity in the very nature of reason' (A421/B449). Our perplexity would, therefore, have actually increased – 'whatever the dogmatic answer might turn out to be it would only increase our ignorance' (A485/B513) – for we would be presented with the further contradiction of believing that the antithesis is false *and* that it is inconceivable that it should not be true. (The sort of predicament we would be in if God were to tell us that in truth $2 + 2$ does not equal 4.) To put the point at its strongest, the antinomies give reason for thinking that the theses and antitheses fail to express candidate truths. Because what we can understand by the judgement 'the world is finite in space and time' is not something that we can consistently regard as conceivably true, we cannot regard it as representing a possible state of affairs; so we cannot conclude that the thesis and antithesis of the first antinomy are options between which we may remain undecided.

All that is required for this argument is that there should be, for each thesis and antithesis, *some* way of making its truth seem inconceivable, on the basis of principles which are non-arbitrary, natural to reason and demonstrably continuous with those employed in gaining empirical knowledge. In other words, Kant requires only that it be *possible* for pure reason to arrive at contradictions in cosmology, and this is something that his presentation of the antinomies, and indeed the history of philosophy, read as a record of the natural disposition of human reason, surely entitle him to assume. From the point of view of this weaker claim, it is beside the point that reason may be able to fix its assumptions in such a way as to avoid contradiction in cosmology.

What the transcendental realist would need to do, in order to turn the postulation of an unknown fact of the matter into a philosophical solution, is to supplement it with an account of *why* the truth is something that our reason cannot make properly conceivable to itself. But this is something which is prima facie unaccountable for a philosophical position which holds our mode of cognition to be adequate to the knowledge of things in themselves: in the context of transcendental realism, it can mean nothing to say that the 'limits of our reason' are too 'narrow' (A481/B509), or that 'the nature of things proposes to us insoluble problems' (*Proleg* 349). In any case, to allow that the cosmological problems should be reconsidered in subjective, reflexive terms is precisely to begin on the Critical path, which, Kant has a weight of argument to show, leads eventually to the repudiation of any fact of the matter concerning the constitution of the cosmos. (Similarly, if the transcendental realist tries to disown the cosmological problems by transferring them out of the domain of philosophy, into that of empirical science, the question is again why pure reason should not be competent to determine cosmological matters, as we naturally believe it to be, and as the validity of its principles in empirical contexts leads us to expect. Again the transcendental realist finds himself confronted by the Copernican turn.)

The inability of transcendental realism to make reason's proneness to contradiction intelligible contrasts sharply with the diagnostic power of the Critical perspective. The latter allows cosmological contradiction to be explained in no less than three, interlocking sets of terms. First, Kant shows the antinomies to be generated through different manners of conceiving the unconditioned in response to the demands of different cognitive powers.

Second, and relatedly, cosmological contradiction is shown to reflect a confusion of appearances with things in themselves. Because empirical objects present themselves as conditioned and therefore not self-subsistent, it is necessary to refer them, as the theses do, to other, unconditioned entities; but at the same, as the antitheses observe, the spatio-temporal mode in which empirical objects are given – in space and time given as necessarily extending indefinitely – precludes their being determined as standing in relation to anything unconditioned. Hence cosmological ideas 'cannot be made to agree with' their intended object (A486/B514): any defence of the theses must contradict the nature of experience, whilst any defence of the antitheses will implicitly attribute a false self-subsistence to the realm of appearance.

Third, the Critical perspective allows the failure of rational cosmology to get the world into focus to be traced back to its failure to grasp the boundedness of human knowledge, a corollary of its underlying transcendental realist conception of the world. What is needed is a way of contemplating experience as a whole which determines, rather than transgresses, the bounds of knowledge, and does not confuse them with the limits of reality. Kant's account of the cosmological ideas as having regulative import supplies just this. The theses, however, motivated by rationalism, apply the transcendental idea of the cosmos in a way which oversteps the bounds of knowledge, whereas the empiricist antitheses, failing to appreciate that experience does not bound itself, mistake the limits of experience for the limits of the world. The theses go too far and the antitheses not far enough, the error of each providing the grounds of the transcendental illusion expressed by the other. It is thereby explained why the antinomies should reveal 'a dialectical battlefield in which the side permitted to open the attack is invariably victorious, and the side constrained to act on the defensive is always defeated' (A422–3/B450).

The transcendental realist may protest that this prioritisation of a subjective problem of cognition once again manifests a Critical prejudice which he does not share. But Kant can meet this objection by arguing that the availability of a Critical solution makes it irrational to allow reason to remain in a state of indecision. Pre-Critically, there is no alternative to continuous vacillation between dogmatic assertion and counter-assertion, punctuated by 'skeptical despair' (A407/B434), because the only possible kind of solution that can be envisaged is one concerning the constitution of the object in itself. Kant, however, has demonstrated that this meta-philosophical assumption is not mandatory. Pre-Critical metaphysics *presupposes* that an object is given to pure reason, and that this *object* proposes a problem to us. But Kant has shown that questions about absolute totality are not 'imposed upon us by the object itself' (A483/B511), because absolute totality is neither an object of experience nor required for the explanation of any given appearance, and that another perspective is available in which the problems of pure reason can be solved in terms of the subject's cognitive powers. The diversity of cosmological claims springs not, like competing empirical theories, from different bodies of evidence, but from a single source (pure reason), and this undermines their claim to be possible representations of reality. It is incoherent to suppose that our cognitive powers both represent an object, the world-whole, and represent it in such a way that it necessarily appears to us as having contradictory properties: if the very same cognitive procedure (the use of pure reason, application of the principle of sufficient reason) which makes it seem as if there is an object regarding which there is something to be decided, also yields a contradictory representation of its nature, then there is the strongest reason for thinking that an illusion is involved, and that there is nothing to be decided.

Once it is recognised that, in the context of pure reason, it cannot automatically be assumed that objects, as opposed to mere ideas, are at issue, we cannot 'rightly excuse ourselves from giving a decisive answer' (A477/B505) to its questions. To 'throw the blame on the object as concealing itself from us' (A482/B510), as transcendental realism does, is to confuse rational cosmology with empirical enquiry. The claim that the cosmological questions have answers which are merely unknown to us may be denied the status of a philosophical solution, therefore, not because it leaves us in perplexity regarding the cosmos, but because it leaves us in perplexity regarding ourselves. Understood in this way, the argument of the Antinomy is clearly not verificationist: it is based, not on the undecidability threatened by the antinomies, but on the problem concerning our mode of cognition which they present us with. If Kant's argument is correct, the Antinomy vindicates Kant's call for a Copernican revolution.

It is to be noted that, had the Antinomy's argument for transcendental idealism succeeded in the way envisaged by Kant, it would have delivered Kant's problematic ontological denial – his claim that things in themselves cannot *be* spatio-temporal. The Antinomy would have shown that being spatio-temporal is incompatible with being a determinate totality. So, as well as showing that the empirical world cannot be identified with things in themselves, it would have shown that things in themselves – which must necessarily form a determinate totality – cannot be characterised by space and time. On the reconstruction given here, however, the argument of the Antinomy does not lend greater support to Kant's ontological denial than the argument of the Aesthetic: it leads, like the Aesthetic, to a conclusion about our cognitive powers, our representations of space and time, but this, for the reasons given in chapter 5, can show nothing definite about the impossibility of things in themselves being spatio-temporal.

Transcendental idealism in the Dialectic II: the problematic intelligible world (The Paralogisms, The Antinomy, The Ideal of Pure Reason)

Transcendental idealism plays a further role in the Dialectic, beyond its application to relieve theoretical reason of conflict: it safeguards ideas which have significance for morality and religion, by relocating them outside the context of theoretical reflection, in which they are endangered. The contradictions of reason which transcendental idealism here dissolves are those which exist between theoretical and practical reason (religious belief is grounded by Kant on morality and so on practical reason). This strategy is repeated several times in the Dialectic. It appears on a grand scale in the third and fourth antinomies, but is first encountered in the Paralogisms.

The Paralogisms III

Kant regards our 'resort' to rational psychology as having one chief motive: 'to secure our thinking self against the danger of materialism' (A383), a 'soulless' (B421) doctrine that destroys any hope of personal immortality. Now Kant's rejection of transcendent metaphysics, and therefore dualism, might make it seem as if the doctrine of immortality must share the same fate. Kant claims (A383–4), however, that the *possibility* – though not the fact – of personal immortality is secured by Critical philosophy. In the first place, the Paralogisms have shown that materialism cannot be known to be true. Since there can be no reason to think that the existence of thought depends on matter, there can be no reason to think that we come to an end when our bodies come to an end. Second, immortality does not presuppose dualism, as is assumed in pre-Critical philosophy: the thought that the 'I' is independent of its embodiment requires, not that its constitution be mental or 'spiritual', in the sense of being composed of the same 'stuff' as inner appearances, but simply that we be able to think ourselves beyond experience, i.e. the thought of an intelligible world. And transcendental idealism makes this thought possible.

So although the *Critique* does not give me any positive reason for thinking that I will persist after the destruction of my body – this cannot be shown on theoretical grounds, because it would require knowledge of things in themselves – Kant adds that I 'may find cause, on other than merely speculative grounds' (A383) to assume that I am immortal. This looks forward to the justification of personal immortality on the basis of practical reason in the second *Critique* (outlined at B424–6, and discussed in chapter 9). Kant defends this relocation of the grounds of belief in personal immortality by observing that the strongest consideration which leads us to suppose that our existence is independent from nature has nothing to do with speculative proofs (these 'have never been able to exercise any influence on the common reason of men', B424), but lies in our sense that our reason has a purpose pertaining to the 'order of ends' revealed in the moral law. And in this practical context, Kant states, non-empirical knowledge of the self – of ourselves as '*legislating* completely *a priori* in regard to our own *existence*, and as determining this existence', of the self as determining rather than determinable – is possible (B430–2). Morality realises the goal of rational psychology.

Rational psychology may, nevertheless, be accorded 'considerable negative value' (A382). By articulating a transcendental illusion, it provides us with positive cognition of the bounds of knowledge. In addition, it fashions a concept of the soul fit for employment in nontheoretical contexts. The conclusions of rational psychology should not, Kant says, be declared illegitimate in every sense: they are legitimate, in so far as they pretend to give us knowledge of a *concept* rather than an object. Although they give us no 'new insight', they do show that the '"I" is in concept substance, in concept simple, etc.' (A400).

The Antinomy III

The dynamical antinomies, though at one level their topics are cosmological, are similarly designed to vindicate the rational integrity of the ideas of human freedom and God.

At stake in the fourth antinomy is the idea, essential for theology but rejected in the antithesis, of an absolutely necessary being which provides the ground of the world. The third antinomy (A444–51/B472–9, A532–5/B560–3) concerns the general notion of empirically unconditioned, 'original' causality. This is employed theologically in the conception of God as prime mover (A450/B478), and it is needed also, Kant holds, and more urgently, if we are to conceive ourselves as rational agents.

The third antinomy: human freedom

Kant argues that what he calls 'practical freedom', the power of rational agency that we attribute to human beings and not to animals, presupposes 'transcendental freedom', the absolutely spontaneous, empirically unconditioned power of beginning an empirical causal series disputed in the third antinomy. (Transcendental freedom is first mentioned at A446/B474, and compared with practical freedom at A533–4/B561–2 and A801–2/B829–30.) It does so because practical freedom or rational agency is a power of acting according to judgements of what *ought* to be the case, and ought judgements have no place in the empirical world (A547–8/B575–6, A550/B578, *Proleg* 344–5):

> '*Ought*' expresses a kind of necessity and of connection with grounds which is found nowhere else in the whole of nature. The understanding can know in nature only what is, what has been, or what will be. We cannot say that anything in nature *ought to be* other than what in all these time-relations it actually is. When we have the course of nature alone in view, '*ought*' has no meaning whatever. It is just as absurd to ask what ought to happen in the natural world as to ask what properties a circle ought to have.

> (A547/B575)

Our conception of ourselves as doing things *because* there is reason to do them, manifest in our making of ought judgements, Kant is claiming, commits us to the existence of a causality other than that of nature – a causality of reason – and consequently to a conception of ourselves as transcendentally free, as entities whose wills are not determined merely by empirical causes. The moral ought brings this out most clearly (as per the example of a 'malicious lie' given at A554–5/B82–3), but Kant intends what he says here to apply to rational agency in general. It is transcendental freedom which constitutes 'the real stumbling-block' (A448/B476) in discussions of human freedom. Its denial, however, would 'involve the elimination of all practical freedom' (A534/B562), the most profound effect of which would be the abolition of the realm of 'ought' and thus the destruction of morality. Hence the inadequacy of the compatibilist conception of human freedom as merely a special form of ordinary empirical causality; this Kant rejects as a 'wretched subterfuge' which can deliver only the 'freedom of a turnspit' (*CPracR* 95–7).

   The situation is therefore as follows. The theses of the dynamical antinomies express the interests of morality and religion, and the antitheses oppose them (A466/B494, A468/B496). But even if the antitheses cannot achieve victory over the theses, the very existence of the antinomies threatens those interests, since if they are left unresolved, we cannot justifiably conceive ourselves as free or the world as grounded in God. (This is the upshot of transcendental realism, on account of its making the antinomies inescapable, A535–6/B563–4, A543/B571, *Proleg* 343.) However, it will not do to merely eliminate the conflict of reason embodied in the opposition of their theses and antitheses, as is done for the first and second antinomies. If the dynamical antinomies are solved along the same lines as the mathematical, the theses and antitheses must both be rejected as false, and the interests of morality and religion would then be sacrificed. We can, however, Kant claims, avoid this result, by providing the dynamical antinomies with a different form of Critical solution from the mathematical (A528–32/B556–60, *Proleg* 343). In the present case, he explains, it is possible for both the thesis and the antithesis to be *true*, and for transcendental illusion to be regarded as lying in their appearance of incompatibility. The reason Kant gives for the difference in form of solution is technical: it is that, in the case of the dynamical antinomies, the unconditioned whose reality is in dispute is 'heterogeneous' with the series of conditions, which is not true of the mathematical antinomies (A530–1/B558–9). What this means is best grasped with reference to the Critical solution of the third antinomy (A535–57/B563–85).

Transcendental idealism allows us to conceive empirical events in general, by virtue of their status as mere appearance, as having both empirical and non-empirical causes. An event may be caused by something which is not appearance, as well as having causes in the realm of appearance. Transcendental idealism entails this possibility (A537–9/B565–7), since it maintains that appearances are not only related to other appearances but may also be grounded, in some indeterminate fashion, in things in themselves. In this scheme, an event may be empirically unconditioned or *free* by virtue of its relation to an intelligible cause outside the series of appearances, whilst remaining empirically *determined* by virtue of its relation to empirical conditions. In this way, it is possible for one and the same event to arise from both nature and freedom, i.e. for freedom to exist alongside natural causality. Freedom and empirical determination will pertain to different causal series, and so not compete with or subtract from one another.

Kant fills out this picture by introducing the concept of 'intelligible character' (A539–41/B567–9). Anything that has causality is, he holds, governed by a 'law of causality' which constitutes its 'character', i.e. causal powers. Every appearance has, therefore, an empirical character, which is empirically conditioned, and allows its actions to be both explained and in principle predicted in accordance with the laws of nature. Now if a thing exercises intelligible as well as empirical causality, then it will have also an empirically unconditioned, intelligible character, which will belong to it *qua* thing in itself or noumenon. Since intelligible character is not subject to the condition of time, it cannot be said to change, or to begin or cease to act (A551–2/B579–80). And since its actions cannot be said to either begin or cease, they cannot be regarded as subject to the laws of nature. Nothing, of course, could be 'immediately known' of intelligible character, since what is immediately known to us is only appearance, but it could nevertheless, as Kant puts it, be '*thought* in accordance with the empirical character', meaning that we could think of a thing's intelligible character as in some way mirroring or analogous to its empirical character (A540/B568, A551/B579). Intelligible character may furthermore be thought of as determining empirical character (A551/B579). In which case, when a thing exercises causality, its intelligible character causes an event intelligibly, and also causes the thing's empirical character to cause the same event empirically. (Kant's double causality does not, therefore, imply either overdetermination, or a miraculous metaphysical coincidence which can be avoided only by postulating a pre-established harmony.)

Applied to ourselves, this model yields a double conception of human agency. A human action is, on the one hand, the free, empirically unconditioned effect of the self *qua* thing in itself (intelligible or noumenal self), and so a product of intelligible causality or causality of reason, manifesting intelligible character. And, on the other hand, it is the effect of the self *qua* appearance (empirical or phenomenal self), whereby it is conditioned and determined empirically, and manifests empirical character.

Our understanding of this structure extends as far as being able to conceive intelligible character as the explanation of empirical character, but intelligible character itself we cannot conceive of explaining (A556–7/B584–5). It goes without saying that the nature of intelligible causality is also unknowable, for we can form no determinate concept of non-temporal agency; so if this is what our freedom consists in, we have no understanding of *how* we are free (Kant makes this point clearly in the *Groundwork*, 458–9). This is, however, no objection to the conception. The important point in the present context is that the unity of nature is undisturbed on this picture, since human actions remain governed by natural law: to the extent that they are referred to agents' empirical characters, we can in principle 'predict with certainty' every single human action, because as regards empirical character in itself 'there is no freedom' (A549–50/B577–8, A553/B581).

Are we free?

Assuming this structure to be coherent, the question arises whether we have reason for thinking of ourselves as instantiating intelligible causality. Here it may be objected that we lack justification for thinking that Kant's model applies to us in a way that it does not to every other thing in the empirical world; if we regard ourselves as instantiating intelligible causality, then we should ascribe it to all natural objects. So Kant fails to distinguish our actions from the causality of stones.

Kant does not attempt to meet this challenge in full in the *Critique*, and it falls strictly outside the remit of the Critical solution to the third antinomy, which is restricted to showing only that 'freedom is at least *not incompatible with* nature' (A558/B586). In the present context Kant is concerned exclusively with relations between concepts: the reality of human freedom, and even its possibility, in the transcendental sense of real as opposed to merely logical possibility, is another matter, involving synthetic judgement (A557–8/B585–6). The Critical solution to the third antinomy merely demonstrates the compatibility of the thesis and antithesis positions: it shows that all events in nature are, as the antithesis maintains, sufficiently determined by empirical conditions, and yet that a causality of freedom may be, though not known, at least *conceived*, to that extent vindicating the thesis. This limited result nevertheless creates an opening for the real possibility of human freedom, in so far as we no longer have to fear that it is ruled out by natural causality, and indeed learn that the *non-*existence of human freedom is something that cannot be proved. (The advantage we gain is 'polemical', Kant explains, A739–40/B767–8, A753/B781.)

Though it exceeds the brief of the Antinomy, Kant does indicate some reasons for thinking that we are subjects with intelligible causality. Ought judgements, as we have seen, seem to show that we exercise a causality of reason which cannot be accommodated in the empirical world. Also, in the sphere of theoretical reason we find suggestions of transcendental freedom, for we know ourselves to be subjects of apperception, which is not empirically conditioned, and to possess faculties that give rise to pure concepts and are not objects of sensible intuition, namely our understanding and reason (A546–7/B574–5).

What this proves is, however, Kant acknowledges, very limited. It shows that our reason must *represent* itself as having a non-natural causality of its own, not that it *has* such a causality (A547–8/B575–6). Skepticism in this regard is, Kant allows, perfectly possible – what we call our freedom may, 'in relation to higher and more remote operating causes, be nature again' (A803/B851). If that is so, then we are caused to represent ourselves as free but not truly so, and the spontaneity of our apperception, along with our practical freedom, is an illusion; each of us is a 'thinking automaton', comparable to a marionette (*CPracR* 101). The most we can say, then, from the point of view of the *Critique*, is that we have some grounds for regarding it as 'at least possible' (A548/B576) that our faculty of reason possesses transcendental freedom.

A point already made, but deserving emphasis, is that transcendental idealism is *necessary* for the real possibility of human freedom. On the assumption of transcendental realism, the conditioned and its conditions – human actions and their causes – are both things in themselves and so belong to a single series (A535–6/B563–4). Transcendental realism thus unavoidably sets freedom in competition with natural causality. We can, therefore, have freedom only if we abandon transcendental realism, and our interest in freedom provides us with a further reason for doing so (*CPracR* 6, 94–8).

Kant's account of freedom evaluated

There is a fundamental interpretative question to be raised regarding Kant's account of freedom – namely, whether according to Kant intelligible causality *coexists* with determinism in the empirical realm, making his position a novel form of compatibilism, or whether it *intervenes* at points of empirical indetermination, incompatibilistically.

The bulk of the third antinomy suggests the former, but contrary indications are to be found at for example A534/B562, where it is said that transcendental freedom can be exercised contrary to the 'force and influence' of natural causes, and thereby 'begin a series of events *entirely of itself*'. The compatibilist reading makes sense of Kant's avowed intention to reconcile freedom and nature, but leaves it unclear what the *efficacy* of reason consists in; the incompatibilist reading has the opposite upshot, of granting to reason an efficacy which appears to undo the claimed reconciliation with natural causality. Kant appears to need some part of each picture in order to make freedom conceivable.

Leaving aside the difficult issue of how exactly Kant intends transcendental idealism to apply – which in any case cannot be settled without examining Kant's later, ethical writings – the *Critique* raises a more basic question concerning the strategy of investing in the noumenal. Kant's theory of freedom has seemed to many immediately objectionable on account of the metaphysical commitment it demands: philosophically defensible belief in freedom, Kant seems to be saying, involves forming concepts of the noumenal, and fixing the noumenal by reference to the phenomenal, in a way not required elsewhere in the *Critique*. For this reason, defences of Kant's ethical theory tend to either distance it from the metaphysics of the *Critique*, or reconstrue talk of the noumenal in non-ontological terms.

The justice of this response is however moot. If we knew it to be a foregone conclusion that the transition Kant anticipates making from the logical to the real possibility of freedom cannot be made, then his theory of intelligible causality would lose any attraction – the consigning of the ground of freedom to an unknowable realm would be pointless. The same would be true if we were already in possession of an adequate empirical theory of freedom. But to the extent that neither of these is the case, the application of transcendental idealism to solve the problem of freedom may be seen in the opposite light. What transcendental idealism entails we cannot comprehend regarding freedom is precisely what proves philosophically intractable in it. Kant's doctrine provides an explanation for why this should be the case, as if it had been designed with human freedom especially in view (Kant intimates as much in the Preface at Bxxvii–xxviii). Transcendental idealism translates the mysteriousness of human freedom into something at least negatively comprehensible, giving our ignorance of its nature rational form. On these grounds it may be held that the account of freedom in the third antinomy is at least on the right track, and that the next steps should be, first, to provide a deduction of freedom, and, second, to reduce the gap between freedom and nature. Kant attempts these tasks in his second and third Critiques respectively.

The fourth antinomy: God

Kant's solution to the fourth antinomy (A559–65/B587–93) mirrors his solution to the third. The idea of an absolutely necessary being is handled in the same way as the idea of transcendental freedom. Transcendental idealism allows both thesis and antithesis to be true when 'taken in different connections' (A560/B588). While the antithesis is right that everything *in* experience is empirically conditioned and so contingent, this series may yet have, as is claimed in the thesis, an empirically unconditioned, intelligible condition. This would be an absolutely necessary being lying *outside* the series of appearances and so not belonging to the world. (In this last respect Kant's solution departs from and corrects the thesis, which locates absolutely necessary being within the world, A560–1/B588–9.) Reason is allowed its idea of absolute totality, and the understanding is satisfied because everything in experience remains contingent and the regress of empirical causes is unlimited. We cannot know that an absolutely necessary being exists, but by the same token nor can we know that it does not – the antithesis is wrong to assert the non-existence of an absolutely necessary being grounding the world (A562–3/B590–1).

So the existence of God, *qua* absolutely necessary being, is at least thinkable. Again, this is on the strict condition of transcendental idealism, and all it shows is a logical, not a real possibility (so it does nothing to vindicate the cosmological argument).

The Ideal II

This implication is pursued in the Ideal of Pure Reason. The Ideal validates, as said earlier, the other idea required for God's conceivability, the idea of the highest being, thereby (like the Paralogisms) preparing the concept for employment in a non-theoretical context, and it allows it to be concluded that atheism is every bit as unjustified as the claims of theology (A640–1/B668–9). The Ideal also shows that the concept of God, once separated from the transcendental realism of rational theology, does not in any way conflict with the claims of natural science or obstruct the pursuit of empirical knowledge. In fact, to the extent that it impinges on science at all, it does so positively, on account of the beneficent regulative implications of the conception of the world as a divine artefact. It is moreover, Kant shows, as much of an expression of reason as science itself; science depends on the regulative employment of reason, so to appeal to science in support of atheism would be to cut science off from its own intellectual source.

The concepts of the soul, freedom and God therefore share a common situation, which has no parallel, and the deep peculiarity of which should be noted. They all concern an intelligible world the existence of which we have, from the point of view of theoretical reason, no warrant for either affirming or denying. (Even if things in themselves in general are known to exist, nothing follows as regards determinate intelligible entities.) This problematic intelligible world is quite unlike a hypothesis. It cannot be spoken of as something the reality of which enjoys, or lacks, any degree of probability – judgements of probable existence can be made only within the sphere of understanding, and the problematic intelligible world is an expression of pure reason entirely dissociated from understanding. We cannot, therefore, entertain towards the intelligible world the same kinds of epistemic attitudes (confidence, incredulity, etc.) as we can entertain towards hypothetical entities posited in scientific speculation or the dogmatic assertions of pre-Critical metaphysics. If any advance is to be made on the question of whether the intelligible world exists, this can be done only by tapping the resource of pure reason in ways that are independent of the theoretical concerns of the *Critique*.

In this lies one of the most profound effects of the Copernican revolution, a transformation of our conception of reality even more radical than the reconception of nature as mere appearance. It is assumed in transcendent metaphysics that what the reality of the soul, freedom and God consists in is something which it is proper for our theoretical faculty to determine. This assumption is rooted, once again, in transcendental realism: if intelligible and empirical objects are one and all things in themselves, then their common reality must be given to us in one and the same way, that is, by theoretical means. Hence the further assumption of transcendent metaphysics that knowledge of intelligible objects can be obtained by employing as far as possible the same resources as are employed in empirical knowledge – as if the reality of intelligible objects were essentially of a kind with that of empirical objects, and our epistemic relation to both sets of objects in essence the same. The Dialectic leads to the recognition that the soul, freedom and God are, on the contrary, objects the reality of which is not a matter that properly concerns reason in its theoretical mode, and that the only kind of subject for which their reality would be a theoretical matter is a subject with intellectual intuition. From this it does not follow that the soul, freedom and God do have reality, only that, if they do, then their reality is not of the kind which transcendent metaphysics supposes. The problematic intelligible world is accordingly lifted out of the range of discourse that concerns itself with questions of evidence as this notion is ordinarily understood, that is, in terms of an empirical-theoretical model. The fact that the intelligible world is not a possible object of our theoretical cognition does not, therefore, give us the slightest reason to believe that it does not exist. Kant's strategy for retrieving the problematic intelligible world from limbo – showing the reality of human freedom, and regrounding religious faith – is discussed in chapter 9.

Kant's destructive achievement

In conclusion, some brief assessment may be made of the overall force of Kant's critique of transcendent metaphysics. There can be little doubt that the Dialectic adds support to the Analytic (as well as elucidating its doctrines), and deflects the threatened 'rebound' rationalist counter-inference described at the beginning of the chapter. But to what extent has Kant conclusively discredited metaphysical speculation? As has been clear throughout, Kant's critique is not altogether independent of his own theory of knowledge and its associated metaphysics. In the context of rational psychology Kant appeals to his own analysis of apperception; what he says about rational cosmology is wrapped up with his theory of synthesis and provision of an alternative Copernican account of its contradictions; and his critique of rational theology turns ultimately on a disputable view of the concept of existence. Also, the formal errors that Kant identifies in transcendent metaphysical reasoning are visible only to someone who accepts his broad account of the relation of representations to objects, and his separation of general from transcendental logic.

This means that Kant cannot claim to have provided transcendent metaphysics with a wholly internal critique, i.e. one that meets his opponents fully on their own terms. This does not, however, render Kant's critique ineffective. Rather, what Kant's systematic, comprehensive and deeply grounded critique does is squarely relocate the burden of proof: it shows that any significant defence of transcendent metaphysics presupposes the construction of a new theory of knowledge surpassing the one expounded in the Analytic and capable of undercutting Kant's appeal to his own doctrines point by point. In particular, it would be necessary in any such undertaking to offer a superior replacement for Kant's account of intuitive and conceptual functions in cognition. It is arguable that the absolute idealists who succeed Kant manage something of the sort – the development of a new philosophical methodology – but they achieve this in large part by reworking Kant's own insights, and it would be most implausible to claim that either ancient philosophy, or the rationalist tradition which forms the historical target of the Dialectic, possess the resources for doing so.

Chapter 8

The meaning of transcendental idealism

Perhaps the most intriguing single comment made about transcendental idealism is the famous remark of Kant's contemporary Jacobi that, year after year, he had been forced in confusion to recommence the *Critique* because he had found himself unable to enter into the system of Kantian philosophy *without* the presupposition of the thing in itself, and yet, *with* that presupposition, unable to remain within it.

Jacobi accounted for his confusion by claiming to find a contradiction at the heart of the system itself. Kant asks us, Jacobi says, to think of the objects of our perception as mere subjective determinations of our being, and yet at the same time as the product of our being affected. The latter is essential in so far as transcendental philosophy wishes to stand in agreement with our fundamental conviction that our perceptions are of real things, things which are independent of our representations and present outside us; and since

empirical objects cannot play the role of things affecting us, the existence of things in themselves is necessary for transcendental philosophy to uphold the objective validity of our thought about the world. But transcendental idealism also informs us that things in themselves, and the mode in which they affect us, are utterly unknown to us – with which admission, Jacobi contends, Kant's system becomes unintelligible, for it simultaneously affirms and denies that we have access to objects that make impressions on our senses. The only route for transcendental idealism to take is to let go altogether of the presupposition of things in themselves. It thereby achieves consistency, but also, on that account, becomes an idealism of the very strongest sort, one that directly contradicts our ordinary conviction of the reality of the objects of perception, and strips our thought of objective validity.

Many later commentators have shared Jacobi's view that transcendental idealism disintegrates on examination, for the sorts of reasons just outlined. Part of the problem is that although the doctrine as stated in Kant's own terms is, in its way, clear enough, ambiguities appear when it is asked how it stands in relation to other more familiar philosophical positions, and a view of the doctrine's content then forms which leaves it exposed to a wave of objections. The view that transcendental idealism fails to achieve what Kant intended – which has recurred so regularly as to have been described as the 'standard picture' of Kant's metaphysics – has two main components. First, Kant's account of empirical objects is interpreted as assigning to them no deeply different ontological status from the purely phenomenal objects of Berkeley's idealism, making Kant's own repeated insistence on his difference from Berkeley, and on the immunity of transcendental idealism to the objections encountered by Berkeley's 'dogmatic', merely empirical idealism, ring hollow. Second, Kant is interpreted as having introduced the existence of things in themselves into his picture for reasons quite independent of the core tenets of Critical philosophy; leading to the dismissal of this claim as an ill-motivated aberration on his part. The question is whether either line of criticism of transcendental idealism is warranted.

Kant's empirical realism: the nature of appearance

The first issue, then, is Kant's proximity to Berkeley. The deep importance of this question is that – on the common assumption that Berkeley's idealism fails as a vindication of common sense, an assumption endorsed by Kant himself – it is necessary for Kant to distance himself from Berkeley; at least, if his claim that transcendental idealism agrees with our ordinary view of the reality of the empirical world, and thereby offers a satisfactory reply to skepticism, is to stand.

As said in chapter 6, the very first review of the *Critique* (in its first edition) that appeared – the Feder-Garve or 'Göttingen' review – charged Kant with advancing an idealism essentially no different from Berkeley's. That this verdict should have been arrived at is perfectly understandable. In addition to the Fourth Paralogism, there is evidence of a more general nature.

An appearance is first defined, in the Aesthetic, as the 'undetermined object of an empirical intuition' (A20/B34), and Kant most of the time refers to appearances as objects of representation ('objects of perception', B207). This allows us to think of appearances as things distinct from our representations, things that our representations are of. But Kant *also* says that they are 'the mere play of our representations, and in the end reduce to determinations of inner sense' (A101): appearances are 'nothing but representations' (A250), 'merely in us' as 'determinations of my identical self' (A129), existing 'only relatively to the subject in which . . . they inhere' (B164); outer objects are 'mere kinds of representations, which are never to be met with save in us' (A365; A384–92 contains many such statements). The importance of this is plain: if the correct reading of Kant's concept of appearance, or its ultimate sense for Kant, is that of a representation, then, given that Kant also asserts that empirical objects *are* appearances, Kant would seem to embrace a Berkeleyan, mentalistic ontology. This impression is reinforced by the apparent similarity between Kant's talk of nature as a set of rule-connected representations systematically constituted by us, and the modern phenomenalist's conception of physical objects as logical constructions out of sense experience. Kant's emphasis on the strictly transcendental sense in which empirical objects are to be identified with appearances (A29–30/B45) may suggest, but does not of itself entail, a difference of kind between his idealism and Berkeley's, for it may be asked why appearances in the transcendental sense should not also be Berkeleyan ideas. In this light, Kant's claim that transcendental idealism is, on account of its unique capacity to handle skepticism, the only way of establishing empirical realism, may appear disingenuous.

Kant's response

Kant rejected the charge of having merely rehashed Berkeley as based on a culpable misreading of his work, but nevertheless replied to it in the *Prolegomena* (see 372ff.) and second edition (where, as noted in chapter 6, it provided a motive for the substitution of the Refutation of Idealism for the Berkeleyan-sounding Fourth Paralogism). His differences from Berkeley are, Kant states, that he affirms, whereas Berkeley denies, the existence of things in themselves (*Proleg* 289), and that Berkeley reduces experience to 'mere illusion' (B71; see also B274, *Proleg* 375), as transcendental idealism does not.

Merely to assert the coexistence of appearances with things in themselves does not differentiate Kant's view of the empirical world from Berkeley's, since to postulate entities supplementary to appearances is not to augment the latter's reality. What makes the difference, Kant says, is his claim that appearances are *grounded* in things in themselves: this distinguishes Kantian appearances intrinsically from Berkeleyan ideas, by entitling Kant to say that his is not, like Berkeley's, an idealism regarding the *existence* of objects (*Proleg* 289, 293).

The second difference claimed by Kant may initially seem question-begging, and unfair to Berkeley, who after all explicitly denies that his account renders the perceptual world illusory, and argues that it leaves room for the distinction of reality and appearance. But what Kant has in mind is the difference between Berkeley and himself regarding the existence of a priori forms of experience, particularly of course, in the very first instance, the classification of space as such a form (*Proleg* 374–5). Kant's point is that for Berkeley the content of experience is not constrained by anything at all, and so is tantamount to illusion: whatever distinctions Berkeley may draw within it will not capture the true difference between veridical and illusory experience, and will not properly deserve to be described as distinctions of reality and appearance. For Kant, by contrast, experience is shot through with necessity.

There are therefore two, complementary aspects to Kant's answer to the question: by virtue of what do appearances have empirical reality? They do so by virtue of their being grounded in things in themselves, and by virtue of their necessary conformity to a priori conditions which extend as far as the Refutation's requirement of outer experience. The first source of the reality of appearances turns on the relation of experience to something outside experience, the second makes empirical reality a function of what goes on within experience. Appearances are thus grounded from two ends, and in two respects: they are grounded on the subject with respect to their form, and on things in themselves with respect to their existence.

Kant is thus entitled to claim that appearances cannot be assimilated to illusion: they are not at bottom dependent on empirical contingency, and so are not arbitrary objects, mere illusions. This is shown in the way that the a priori conditions which on Kant's account govern appearances imply the necessity of a public, intersubjective world of objects, a notion which Berkeley's idealism is notoriously incapable of sustaining.

It is, note, plausible to hold that strictly Kant does not need the connection with things in themselves in order to secure a non-Berkeleyan account of empirical reality, on the grounds that Kant's a priori conditions can do this work on their own. If so, Kant may uphold his empirical realism to someone who denies his right either to affirm the existence of things in themselves, or to speak of a relation of grounding between appearances and things in themselves.

Kant's non-phenomenalism and Berkeley's transcendental realism

Still, it may be wondered whether this is enough to create the deep difference from Berkeley that Kant wants. Despite the introduction of things in themselves as the ground of appearances, the orbit of our knowledge, the kind of objects that fall within its scope, may seem to be the same for Kant as for Berkeley – phenomenalistic objects, constructions out of purely phenomenal elements. After all, Kant is quite clear that, even if appearances are grounded in things in themselves, appearances alone are objects for us. Nor, consequently, is it clear what significance the a priori form of Kantian appearance – the transcendental object and all of the other non-empirical apparatus of the Analytic – carries in the present context: if Berkeley's idealism reduces the world to mere illusion, then arguably what Kant has provided is precisely the necessary means for distinguishing veridical sensory experience from mere illusion; the upshot being that transcendental idealism is really just a much more sophisticated and plausible version of Berkeleyan idealism.

What does establish conclusively Kant's difference from Berkeley is the consideration that Kant's ontology of empirical objects is not, and could not be phenomenalistic. This is decisive: if Kantian appearances are phenomenalistic constructions, then the description of Kant's idealism as an upgraded form of Berkeley's idealism might be apt, but if they are not, then the notion that the two idealisms are on a par should be rejected.

It is true that, for Kant, all objects lie within the framework of experience – possibilities of systematic experience provide the coordinates which fix the identity of objects (as Kant spells out in his discussion of unexperienced empirical objects at B521–3). But this does not make them ontologically of a kind with Berkeleyan ideas. Being *subject to the condition* of experienceability – that is, necessarily related in some manner to intuition – is not the same as being *composed* of experiences in any sense, particularly not of experiences in the Berkeleyan sense of elements whose mode of dependence on the subject is that of a qualitative sensory entity on a subject's consciousness of it. This could not be Kant's view. If appearances were phenomenalistic constructions, then the fundamental elements in Kant's ontology would be objects of a kind ruled out by the theory of experience in the Analytic – purely sensible objects given independently of concepts. The order of dependence in the identification of objects established in the Refutation of Idealism would then be reversed: cognition of inner experience, sensory states of the subject, would precede that of outer objects, from which subjective states would be independent.

It follows that the sense in which objects depend upon the subject for Berkeley is profoundly different from that in which they do so for Kant. The term 'subject-/mind-dependent' is in fact heavily ambiguous. For Berkeley, the fundamental mode of dependence of objects is on bare sensing consciousness. To the extent that Berkeley acknowledges cognition or judgement to be something in its own right over and above mere sensing, there is no dependence of objects upon cognition or judgement as such for Berkeley: ideas exist fully formed in being sensed. Berkeleyan subject-/mind-dependence is thus fundamentally of the sort indicated when it is observed that unfelt pain is a contradictory notion. Kant, by contrast, asserts the fundamental dependence of objects on the conditions of our cognising (judging) them. In so far as objects are for Kant dependent on intuition, this derives from the necessity of intuition for cognition, not from the nature (ontological status) of intuited objects: conceptual activity is a condition of the phenomenological presence of objects to the subject in intuition, and intuition itself is intrinsically object-directed representation, not a mere pain-like feeling of a sensory quality. The difference in mode of dependence entails a corresponding difference in the nature of the dependent objects. The understanding's employment of rules in a priori synthesis cannot, therefore, be compared with the phenomenalist's logical construction of objects.

This alone is sufficient to show that Kant's idealism is not a development of Berkeley's, but there is more to be said. The conception of appearances as phenomenalistic constructions belongs not to transcendental idealism, but to transcendental realism. To say that Berkeley is a transcendental realist – merely by virtue of his account of *esse* as *percipi*, i.e. quite apart from the role he accords to God – may seem surprising, but it can be demonstrated in the following way.

If transcendental realism consisted in a plain denial that the objects of our knowledge are subject to any sort of dependence on minds, then Berkeley would of course not be a transcendental realist. But transcendental realism is not equivalent to this denial, any more than transcendental idealism is equivalent to a blanket assertion of mind-dependence. Transcendental idealism and transcendental realism are defined by their respective affirmation and denial that our mode of cognition determines the constitution of its objects, i.e. their opposite views of the possibility of knowing things in themselves (see p. 95). Now Berkeley does hold that empirical things are constituted in themselves of phenomenalistic elements, not merely that our mode of cognition determines them to be so represented; the phenomenalistic existence of objects is for him not merely the only cognition of them available to us from the human standpoint. So, according to Berkeley, we do know things, albeit mental things, as they really are; if the objects of our empirical knowledge were to be considered from a transcendent, non-human standpoint, then what would be seen is ideas in human minds. (Later phenomenalist doctrines according to which sense-data enjoy a 'neutral', non-mental status share this transcendental realist implication.) Berkeleyan ideas, and those of empiricism in general, are therefore a limiting case of things in themselves.

The ground on which Berkeley is properly classified as a transcendental realist goes very deep. Because he holds that objects are phenomenalistic in themselves, i.e. independently of their being cognised, and that they are given to us as such, for Berkeley things owe their standing as possible objects for us, not to the relation of cognition, but to the mere fact of their 'being in our minds'. Berkeley thereby evinces the attitude towards the problem of reality which is definitive of transcendental realism: the possibility of objects is taken to be accounted for by a (presumed but unexplicated) relation to things in themselves, namely, in Berkeley's case, a relation to our minds and their phenomenalistic contents.

As regards Kant's position – quite apart from the fact that the Analytic denies the epistemological priority of purely sensible objects required by phenomenalism – no coherent marriage of transcendental idealism with a phenomenalistic ontology can be envisaged. A phenomenalistic ontology cannot be part of the basic conception of transcendental idealism, since transcendental idealism precisely eschews any foundational ontological commitments. Nor can a phenomenalistic ontology enter at any later point. A transcendental theory of experience is occupied in saying how things with being can be got to appear to us. Phenomenalistic entities are objects whose being is exhausted in their immediate sensory appearing. Consequently they are things with respect to which no distinction can be drawn between their existence as appearance and their existence in themselves. For an empiricist, this provides their philosophical attraction, but it is also the reason why transcendental idealism cannot motivate a phenomenalistic ontology: if it were conjoined with a phenomenalistic ontology, then transcendental idealism would have turned, via empirical idealism, into transcendental realism of Berkeley's sort, and the programme of transcendental explanation would have given way to ontological explanation. Purely phenomenal entities like mental images are of course admitted by Kant as contents of the empirical world (see p. 94), but they do not play any role in his account of what empirical objecthood as such amounts to. Phenomenalising empirical objects is an alternative to pursuing the transcendental question of what makes them possible for us. Sensory experience functions as a condition of possibility in Kant's transcendental explanation of objects only because objects themselves are not conceived phenomenalistically.

The strength of Kant's empirical realism, and his distance from Berkeley, should not therefore be in doubt: not only does transcendental idealism exert no pressure towards phenomenalistic idealism, it precludes a phenomenalistic ontology. Kant may accordingly claim that – once the Analytic's transcendental theory of experience, showing how and why empirical objects must be independent from empirical states of mind, is in place – the full meaning carried by 'real' and 'objective' in their commonsense application to physical objects is captured by his empirical realism; transcendental idealism does not reduce 'X exists unperceived' to any conditional formula expressing possibilities of sensation. That his own idealism entails that empirical objects are appearances solely in the transcendental sense is, therefore, as Kant says, of absolute importance.

The root of the difficulty in understanding how transcendental idealism can support anything more ontologically robust than sense-data is that we are used to thinking in terms of a pre-Critical dichotomy which obscures the transcendental meaning of Kant's statements about appearances. We are strongly accustomed to considering the issue of the reality of the external world in terms of a choice between Locke and Berkeley, between a non-mental and a mental ontology. In this light it is natural to think that Kant, since he does not come down squarely on the side of Locke, must follow Berkeley.

But in Kant's terms, to frame the issue in terms of this opposition is to presuppose the outlook of transcendental realism, and if we have trouble seeing how empirical realism can be secured on terms other than Locke's, it is because we have failed to separate empirical from transcendental realism. On Kant's account, the classification of objects into ontological kinds, non-mental and mental, is possible only once the conditions for cognition of an empirical world have been fulfilled. Since transcendental discourse is concerned with the identification of these conditions, it cannot employ concepts of these ontological kinds in completing its task.

The concept of representation itself, in transcendental discourse, does not refer to mental items in the sense of the empirical contents of minds considered as empirical particulars, but to subjective elements of cognition considered transcendentally, i.e. as making cognition of objects possible. The studied abstractness of Kant's term representation, and the wholly indeterminate character of the subjective status which it implies, are essential if his theory of experience is to be genuinely transcendental, and not implicitly assume at the outset an empiricist (or other) account of the possibility of objects. Kant's description of appearances as nothing but representations and thus determinations of the self, is not an ontological classification of any sort, and cannot be interpreted as assigning them a mental status. In this way, Kant's conception of empirical reality avoids the straight choice of Locke or Berkeley.

The two senses of appearance

There remains, as an independent matter, the question of why Kant should apparently equivocate regarding the relation of appearances to representations: why does he describe appearances sometimes as *objects* of representations (appearances$_O$) and on other occasions as themselves *representations* (appearances$_R$)? For example, the Refutation concludes that there must be 'a *thing* outside me' not 'the mere *representation* of a thing outside me', implying a contrast of outer appearances with representations; whereas throughout the Fourth Paralogism Kant talks of outer appearances as a species of representation.

The second description, it is to be noted, does not seem to be directly required by the doctrine of transcendental idealism. While it is true that appearances considered empirically, i.e. from within the human standpoint, must be conceived as appearances$_O$, it is not obvious that considering appearances transcendentally entails conceiving them as appearances$_R$: to say that the things we cognise are appearances rather than things in themselves is not, on the face of it, to say that what we cognise are representations. So the empirical/transcendental distinction does not on its own explain where the notion of appearance$_R$ comes from.

Different accounts, suggested by and appropriate to different contexts, are available to rationalise and dispel the impression of ambiguity in Kant's usage. Appearance$_O$ and appearance$_R$ may be understood as referring to the empirical object considered at different stages in Kant's analysis of the process of cognition: appearance$_R$ is the sensible appearing that provides an intuitive datum for cognition, and appearance$_O$ is the object cognised as so appearing; the two being related in that, on Kant's account, it is the fulfilment of certain further conditions – the contribution of the understanding specified in the Analytic – that converts ('objectifies') appearances$_R$ into appearances$_O$.

On another account, the difference between appearances$_R$ and appearances$_O$ is again a function of how they are considered, but this time as regards their relation to things in themselves. Prior to the introduction of things in themselves as the existent ground of the empirical realm, appearances (in so far as they fulfil the conditions of experience in the Analogies etc.) must be conceived as what our representations are representations *of*, and so are properly conceived as appearances$_O$. But after the introduction of things in themselves, this manner of conceiving appearances ceases to be appropriate, and they must then be relegated to 'modes' of the subject, i.e. reconceived as appearances$_R$. In the first context, appearances are *things*; in the second, they are appearings *of* things other than themselves, and must, because of the metaphysical heterogeneity of sensible appearings and these other, non-sensible things, be identified with states of the subject. In other words, whether empirical intuition is to be taken as delivering appearances$_R$ or appearances$_O$ depends on what else is in the picture: on whether the framework of their consideration sets them in contrast with another kind of thing that provides their ground. (There is a similarity here with Kant's treatment of apperception: just as transcendental philosophy substitutes claims about how subjects must represent themselves, for claims about the real existence of an identical subject, so it substitutes claims about how appearances must be taken, for claims about what appearances really are.)

Intersubjectivity

In conclusion, the place of intersubjectivity in Kant's account of empirical reality should be noted. That Kantian empirical reality is essentially public follows from his account of it as having necessary, a priori grounds: whatever judgements have objective validity must have validity for all subjects, and vice versa. Empirical reality is not, however, for Kant, intersubjective in the strong sense of being constituted by intersubjective interaction. Recent, 'post-Cartesian' philosophy has seen it argued that intersubjectivity (concretised in shared linguistic practice) is a condition of possibility of objectivity, but Kant's view is firmly that the intersubjective validity of judgements is grounded on the individual subject's constitution of objectivity (*Proleg* 298). The agreement of all rational subjects, the possibility of consensus, provides the 'touchstone' of a judgement's objective validity, but it is only a criterion in the sense of an external indicator, not what objective validity consists in (A820–1/B848–9). In giving priority to the subject in this way Kant remains within the 'Cartesian' philosophical tradition, despite all the deep differences from Descartes which emerge in the Refutation of Idealism and elsewhere. (Kant cannot therefore be read as anticipating Wittgenstein's private language argument. This is to be expected, in view of the relatively slight attention he pays to the issue of our knowledge of other minds; see A347/B405, A353–4, A362–3.)

The existence of things in themselves

The second component of the 'standard picture' of transcendental idealism, on account of which it encounters criticism of the sort of which Jacobi provides an early and forcible example, is Kant's affirmation that things in themselves exist, referred to in chapter 6 as a cause of much controversy.

We can begin by setting aside the objection that to affirm the existence of things in themselves is, as Jacobi suggests, to assert the plain contradiction that we have knowledge of things of which we have no knowledge. As we saw in chapter 5 (p. 99), this is met simply by distinguishing determinate (contentful) knowledge, which we lack in the case of things in themselves, from indeterminate (content-less) knowledge, which in their case we do possess. Our knowledge of things in themselves does not determine any object: we know things in themselves only in so far as we know that something not consti-tuted by the forms of our sensibility must occupy the conceptual space outside experience. Because reference to things in themselves is not underwritten by the object-individuating conditions analysed in the Aesthetic and Analytic, it is impossible to even determine whether reference to them should be singular or plural. Thus we know *of* things in themselves – of their existence – without knowing anything (synthetic) *about* them. This distinction is unformulable in many other philosophical contexts, but Kant's theory of knowledge allows him to make it coherently.

Meaning and the categories

Another, closely associated line of objection, to the effect that Kant is here in direct violation of his own strictures on meaning, should also be rejected. The concepts employed in thinking of things in them-selves as existing must of course be unschematised categories; otherwise Kant would be involved in the confusion of attempting to determine things in themselves empirically. It is alleged, however, that Kant commits himself in the Analytic to the principle that concepts isolated from sensibility are without meaning – which rules out as strictly meaningless his own claim that things in themselves exist.

In fact, Kant holds no such position on the meaning of concepts. Kant does indeed say, repeatedly and with emphasis, that apart from intuition the categories are 'without *sense*, that is, without meaning' (A240/B299), 'completely lacking in content' (A239/B298) and such-like (see also B149, A240–1/B300, B308, *Proleg* 312–13, 315). But never do these statements, taken in context, and with it borne in mind that the term 'meaning' (*Sinn*, *Bedeutung*) does not have for Kant the connotations that it has accrued subsequently in philosophy, commit him to saying that thoughts composed solely of unschematised categories have the status of nonsense. The meaning that the categories in isolation from sensibility lack is specifically cognitive, objective, determinate meaning: to say that apart from sensibility the categories are meaningless is just to say that no object can be cognised determinately by their means, that they have 'no object' (A287/B343), no 'relation to the object' (A241/B300), no 'determinate meaning' (A244) or 'relation to any determinate object' (A246; A258/B314). The restrictive principle to which Kant is committed concerns only the *application* of concepts: the categories require the mediation of sensibility, not in order to have meaning, but in order to have application to objects. That Kant *must* accord meaning of some sort to the categories taken on their own ('transcendental meaning', as he calls it at A248/B305) follows from the consideration that they are, on his account, as said in chapter 6, forms of thought or judgement *as such* and concepts of objects *in general*; they are not abstracted from concepts of empirical objects, but make an independent contribution to cognition. (Kant stresses the point in *CPracR* 54–7, where he defends explicitly the thinkability of the noumenal for theoretical reason.) If Kant held that the categories in isolation lack any sort of meaning, then he would be committed to saying that categorial meaning springs into existence at the point of interaction of understanding with sensibility, and it would be completely unaccountable how sensibility could produce this meaning *ex nihilo*, and how combining intuition with the categories makes cognition of objects possible. There would, of course, be a contradiction in asserting the existence of things in themselves, if Kant held that the categories were as peculiar to human cognition as are space and time, or if there were other reasons for thinking that things in themselves cannot conform to the forms of thought; but, as noted in chapter 6 (p. 191), nothing in Kant supports this view – transcendental ideality does not flow from the bare categoriality of objects. The thinkability of things in themselves does not, therefore, involve Kant in any contradiction.

Finding grounds for Kant's assertion

Jacobi is nevertheless right that there is a puzzle surrounding the grounds of Kant's assertion of the existence of things in themselves. Clearly this claim is not on a par with other propositions of transcendental philosophy. Unlike the conclusions of the Aesthetic and Analytic, it does not concern the structure of experience, and indeed goes beyond experience. The question is thus what supports it, if it is not the conclusion of a transcendental proof, and not to count as transcendent metaphysics. In other terms, the problem is that even if we do not need to step outside the limits of our perspective in order to *think* things in themselves, it would seem that that is precisely what is required in order for us to *know* them to exist. In the face of this riddle Kant gives us little help: again and again he writes as if it were evident that there is no alternative to assuming that things in themselves exist. But it is in fact far from obvious, as the following shows.

It is clear that there can be nothing internal to sensation considered *empirically* that implicates a relation to things in themselves, since Kant conceives sensation as preceding all representation, and in any case as known to us empirically only in so far as it corresponds to the matter of appearance. Sensation cannot, therefore, contain any a posteriori clue to our being affected by things in themselves. Also, as seen in chapter 6 (pp. 154–5), the thing in itself plays no role in the constitution of objectivity: its place is taken by the transcendental object, a concept which we employ without thereby positing the existence of anything transcendent.

A number of more likely candidates may suggest themselves as grounds for Kant's assertion. Kant may seem to be arguing that the existence of things in themselves follows from the concept of appearance: that things in themselves exist because appearances are necessarily (by virtue of their concept) *of* things which cannot be identified with appearances, and so must be identified with things in themselves (see Bxxvi–xxvii, A251–2, B306, *Proleg* 354–5). But this cannot be right, since, although Kant's concept of appearance certainly implies the *concept* of the thing in itself, and there are objects satisfying the concept of appearance, none of this implies that there are any objects satisfying the concept of the thing in itself. Any conceptual argument for the existence of things in themselves as implicated by that of appearances would, in any case, render question-begging Kant's original description of empirical objects as appearances.

Alternatively, Kant may seem to be basing the existence of things in themselves on a causal inference – from the existence of appearances as effects, to that of things in themselves as their causes (see A494/B522, A496/B524, A695–6/B723–4 and *Proleg* 314–15). This cannot be right either, however, since the assumption that appearances are effects of anything at all presupposes exactly what needs to be established. Furthermore, Kant has argued that deployment of the causal principle outside the sphere of experience is illegitimate.

An alternative tack (see *Proleg* 353–4) is to suppose that the existence of things in themselves follows somehow from the consideration that there must be an ultimate end to the explanation of things, and that the realm of appearance is not ultimately self-explanatory. Put slightly differently: that the realm of appearance does not contain the reason for its own existence, and that there must be such reason; or, that at the end of the day something must be unconditionally real, in order for anything to be conditionally real. But, on the face of it, to say any of these things would be, in Kant's terms, to base the existence of things in themselves on reason's demand for the unconditioned, or to seek to derive ontological conclusions from the principle of sufficient reason in Leibnizian fashion, and the Amphiboly and Dialectic disallow anything of the sort.

Transcendental idealism without the existence of things in themselves

In view of the obscurity which attaches to the claim that things in themselves exist, it is worth considering what would be lost by jettisoning it. Advocates of this move say that little is lost, and that the importance of the concept of things in themselves for Kant's philosophy does not require their existence. They claim that a conceptual, not an ontological, contrast of things in themselves and appearances is needed to express Kant's insights concerning the nature and scope of our knowledge. The concept of the thing in itself is interpreted as never referring, and as serving exclusively negative purposes, as if the thing in itself were a sort of 'anti-object', incorporating all of the features that would make a thing antithetical to our cognition. The concept of the thing in itself is thereby accorded the role of indirectly elucidating the concept of an object of human knowledge: it informs us about how and what we do know, by telling us how and what we cannot know. Correlatively, it is also granted a polemical use in tracing the ways in which pre-Critical conceptions of objects render them unknowable.

If this view is coherent, then, even with the existence of things in themselves subtracted from the ontological picture, transcendental idealism survives as the (still contentful and distinctive) doctrine that all that can be known to exist are appearances. And so long as the arguments presented earlier for differentiating Kant's from Berkeley's idealism are accepted, Kant's empirical realism remains as strong as can be desired, so that Jacobi is wrong that the existence of the thing in itself is required to uphold the objectivity of our perceptions.

This negative interpretation of transcendental idealism may also assume a stronger, 'atheistic' form, according to which the existence of things in themselves is not merely a matter for agnosticism, but may be positively denied, as an unintelligible supposition. This is what results if it is held that empirical objects are the only intelligible candidates for objecthood. (This position is usually argued for on the grounds that the categories cannot ultimately be distinguished in unschematised forms from their schematised versions, and that Kant is wrong to think the categories are concepts of objects in general derivable from the forms of judgement.) If this further step is taken, then the whole notion of unconditioned or absolutely independent reality evaporates, and any ontological contrast of empirical objects with other things is rendered meaningless. To say that the objects of our cognition are appearances, or transcendentally ideal, then means just that knowledge of them is possible only if certain conditions obtain: the implication that their degree of reality is inferior to that of other, actual or possible things, is blocked ('appearance' no longer means *mere* appearance).

Granting that such a position, which agrees with the analytic interpretation of Kant, may draw on some material in the Aesthetic and Analytic, it should be noted how radically it departs from Kant's intentions. It eliminates the notion that our knowledge is subject to *limitations*. Also, it contradicts Kant's intention in the Dialectic of establishing a problematic status for the ideas of reason: if the very notion of existence as an object contracts to that of empirical existence, then God and the soul cease to be candidates for real existents. The atheistic version of the negative interpretation thereby frustrates the contribution which Kant ultimately intends theoretical philosophy to make to practical philosophy, and is fundamentally dissociated from Kant's broader project of resolving the conflicts of reason (in effect, it grants victory to empiricism).

These repercussions might, for all that they contradict Kant's intentions, be welcomed. It is consequently important to observe how the atheistic interpretation also cuts itself loose from the Copernican motivation that Kant supplies for transcendental idealism. The Copernican revolution takes off from the recognition that, whatever there might be in reality, we can explain how objects are possible for us only if we forego the claim that they have reality in themselves. Relinquishing claims of access to reality in itself – in exchange for an intelligible relation to (empirical) reality, immunity from skeptical doubt and bringing reason to rest – is the bargain that reason's self-conflict, Kant argues, forces it to make. Therefore, if we now, at the end of the Analytic, declare the very notion of reality in itself to be null and void, we undo the contrast on which the Copernican revolution is premised, and the skeptic and rationalist will be quite within their rights to dispute the whole basis on which the Analytic has proceeded. Specifically, they may object that Kant's method surreptitiously presupposes verificationism, or an empiricist view of concepts. The atheistic version of the negative interpretation may be a consistent philosophical position, but it cannot lean on the meta-philosophical justification for transcendental idealism supplied by Kant. To the extent that we remain in sympathy with Kant's broader philosophical project, there is compelling reason for preferring the weaker, agnostic version of the negative interpretation.

Discarding the claim that things in themselves exist is not, therefore, disastrous from Kant's point of view, in view of the availability of the weaker version of the negative interpretation. But it should not be assumed that the case against Kant on this score is conclusive.

One way of upholding Kant's claim for the existence of things in themselves is provided by the 'two conception' view of things in themselves and appearances, to be explained later. This argues that things in themselves exist because, and simply in the sense that, they *are* appearances under another description. Another is to try to articulate on Kant's behalf a defence of its anomalous status.

Affection

Because Kant's announcement of the existence of things in themselves comes so late in the text of the *Critique* – at the end of the Analytic – it is natural to think that it must be an afterthought, a claim over and above the earlier results of transcendental enquiry, and so one that either is supposed to follow on from the analysis of experience that runs up to it, or requires additional argumentation. But it may be that this assumption is incorrect, and that the reason why the existence of things in themselves receives no explicit argument, is that it is built into the very framework of transcendental philosophy. Specifically, it may be that Kant regards it as implied by his foundational analysis of cognition.

This is indeed suggested by the statement in the first paragraph of the Aesthetic that in sensibility 'we are affected by objects' (A19/B33), which – since here 'objects' cannot intelligibly refer to empirical objects, the elementary presuppositions of which are at this point being analysed – demands to be read as referring to things in themselves. (Affection is referred to also at A68/B93, B129, B156, B207, B309, A494/B522 and *Proleg* § 32, § 36.) It may be argued that there is no intelligible alternative to this supposition. Sensation – that in us which provides for the being of appearances; what sensible and conceptual form applies to – must be conceived as having *some* ground, however indeterminately conceived. For to conceive sensation without reference to *any* ground – to suppose that the question of ground cannot arise for the matter of empirical objects – is to elevate it to self-sufficient being, and thus to accord it reality in itself. Kant's entire transcendental story would then make no sense.

To deny that sensation is an effect of things transcendentally *outside* us therefore leaves, by elimination, no alternative to saying that its ground is transcendentally *inside* us, i.e. that it is brought into existence by the subject. But to say that sensation is an effect of our transcendental subjectivity is to conceive our subjectivity as spontaneous throughout, which is indistinguishable from conceiving human subjects as non-finite, God-like creators of themselves and all their objects, again with the upshot that empirical objects become things in themselves. The Copernican revolution – accounting for objects as appearances rather than things in themselves – thus requires the data out of which our objects are constituted to be grounded on something transcendentally 'other'.

On this account, the supposition that sensation is the effect of things in themselves is necessary for Kant's fundamental analysis of cognition, and the issue of the existence of things in themselves is settled at the earliest point in setting up the basic assumptions on which the Analytic is to proceed. This explains both why Kant should write as if the existence of things in themselves may be taken for granted and not halt to argue for the claim at any point, and why he should seem to have been proposing a conceptual or causal argument for their existence. In fact, no causal inference is involved, and the description of sensation as an effect of things in themselves should not put us in mind of Locke's causal theory of perception. (Kant may of course allow for causal analyses of perception, but this sort of affection – affection by empirical objects rather than things in themselves, 'empirical' as opposed to transcendental affection – is another matter.) To say that sensation arises through our being affected by things in themselves is to say that it is the immediate subjective, pre-cognitive expression or manifestation of the subject's relation to what is transcendentally outside it. It is part of the concept of sensation in transcendental discourse that sensation is the product of our being affected by things in themselves.

In this light, it can be seen how the assertion that things in themselves exist is connected with the denial that the categories employed outside experience have determinate meaning: the former is a condition for the analysis of cognition which the latter presupposes. (To the extent that Kant is committed to anything of the sort that contemporary philosophy refers to as a 'theory of meaning', his semantic doctrines are dependent on their metaphysical context, rather than, as in much recent philosophical discussion, intended to be logically prior to any metaphysics.) The existence of things in themselves *qua* ground of appearance is the unique case in which philosophical reflection is entitled to move from the conditioned to the unconditioned, and its entitlement to do so in this instance is interdependent with its lack of entitlement in every other, more determinate context. For this reason, the claim that things in themselves exist as the ground of appearance does not license any further claims about the trans-empirical realm. All it does is express the cognitive finitude of the human subject. Our ignorance of the nature of our transcendental affection by things in themselves is an essential part of the concept, and Kant consequently agrees with Jacobi (A392–3) that the nature of the connection between the fact of the existence of things in themselves, and the fact of our being supplied with the material for constituting appearances, is something of which we have no idea. All we can say is that *unless* something existed independently of us prior to appearance, nothing would be represented and no world of appearances would be brought into being.

If the claim that things in themselves exist as the ground of appearance is in this way directly correlated with Kant's Copernicanism, and its rationale derives from the bare recognition that our cognition is conditioned and perspectival, then it does not violate any independently established Critical rule: on the contrary, it is necessary for the Analytic to run its course, and for establishing the very rule that limits our knowledge to empirical objects. Kant can consistently hold both that no reasoning that proceeds from within the empirical realm can take us outside it, and that transcendental reflection discloses the existence of things in themselves.

Things in themselves and appearances

The question that next arises concerns the nature of the relation of things in themselves to appearances. This is not exhausted by the fact that the former ground the existence of the latter by providing for the manifold of sensation to which the matter of appearance corresponds.

Appearances of things in themselves

Because, in considering our situation transcendentally, we discover that appearances are merely ideal, as well as being grounded in things in themselves, there is a sense in which appearances carry a reference beyond themselves: they are objects which for us, as it were, stand in for the transcendentally real objects which would be given to a cognitively unlimited subject – the closest we get to the things that reason identifies as its ultimate cognitive target. There is thus a sense in which appearances are, in addition to being grounded on things in themselves, appearances *of* things in themselves (Bxxvi–xxvii, B164, A252, *Proleg* 289). From this it does not follow that appearances are *representations* of things in themselves (A272/B332). That would require appearances to present things in themselves to us in the full intentional sense, i.e. make them objects for us, a claim which obviously contradicts the unknowability of things in themselves (and which Kant ascribes, as erroneous, to Leibniz, A270/B326). The relation of appearances to things in themselves is, therefore, not to be confused with the properly representational relation of appearances to the transcendental object.

Two objects versus two conceptions

To say that appearances are of things in themselves leaves undecided, however, another more fundamental question concerning their relation. Does Kant envisage things in themselves and appearances as composing two worlds, in the sense of two ontologically distinct sets of objects? Or is the language of things in themselves and appearances an expression of two points of view on a single set of objects?

On many occasions Kant talks of 'viewing the same objects from two different points of view – on the one hand, in connection with experience ... and on the other hand ... as objects which are thought merely' (Bxviii–xix[n]). This suggests that the distinction is not one of *objects*, but rather concerns the terms in which objects (those which we identify as composing a single, empirical world) may be *conceived*. Thus Kant says that the 'object as *appearance* is to be distinguished from itself as object *in itself*' (B69), and that 'if the senses represent to us something merely as it appears, this something must also in itself be a thing' (A249). The notion of a 'twofold manner of conceiving' things is of course particularly prominent in the context of Kant's theory of freedom, where the causality of the subject is 'regarded from two points of view' (A538/B566), and locutions of this sort are prevalent in Kant's ethical writings. As Kant puts in a letter (to Garve, 7 August 1783): 'all objects that can be given to us can be interpreted in two ways: on the one hand, as appearances; on the other, as things in themselves', and the contradiction involved in freedom 'falls away as soon as attention is paid to the variable meaning that objects can have'.

These statements suggest that the concept of thing in itself is intended to refer to the same objects that we know as appearances, but under a non-empirical description, i.e. to refer to the non-empirical aspect of appearances. Unlike the purely negative interpretation of the concept of thing in itself described above, this *two conception* (or 'double aspect') view resolves the difficulties associated with Kant's claim that things in themselves exist without being revisionary: it grants the concept of the things in itself a positive, referring use.

Opposed to the two conception view is the *two object* view. Kant's talk of the groundedness of appearances on things in themselves (e.g. at A695–7/B723–5) is naturally taken as talk of ontologically distinct objects, and an ontological difference provides the easiest way of understanding the doctrine that appearances are necessarily spatio-temporal and things in themselves necessarily non-spatio-temporal, as well as Kant's emphasis on their different degrees of reality.

Much can be said in defence of each. Two object theorists may claim that Kant talks as if things in themselves and appearances were two aspects of one thing, only in order to bring out their incompatibility and thereby underline the necessity of distinguishing them ontologically; and that when he speaks of appearances as if they were things in themselves under another description, he does so only in order to steer us away from identifying appearances with Berkeleyan ideas in our minds. The two object view may also be coupled with a complex doctrine of 'double affection' (elaborated by Erich Adickes), according to which the subject is originally affected transcendentally by things in themselves, and then reaffected – this time as an empirical being endowed with sense organs – by the empirical objects which are the products of the first affection.

On behalf of the two conception view, it may be observed that one cannot be sure that any of Kant's statements that things in themselves 'are not objects of our senses' (B306), that they are 'totally distinct' from appearances' (*Proleg* 318) and so on, carry a two object commitment, since the distinctness that Kant asserts may not be ontological: 'object' can be read in a purely epistemological sense. Furthermore, it may be claimed that the concept of a thing in itself as something ontologically distinct from an appearance is either merely negative and polemical, as when the objects of transcendent metaphysics are under discussion, or, when employed positively, a conceptually derivative notion reserved strictly for the exceptional context of practical reason. It has also been argued in support of the two conception view that Kant's use of the phrase 'thing in itself' (*Ding an sich*) is an elliptical form of the expression, which he also sometimes uses, 'thing considered in itself' (*Ding an sich selbst betrachtet*): 'in itself' is held to function adverbially, as qualifying how a thing is considered or conceived. But it is doubtful that 'in itself' can be treated in this way in all contexts – in the Antinomy Kant talks of 'the world in itself' (*Welt an sich*) in a way that does not lend itself readily to such a paraphrase – and in any case, the most that this philological point seems to establish is that the grammar of Kant's term does not commit him in all contexts to the two object view.

Since Kant's text itself does not decide between the two views, it is appropriate to consider the gains and losses attached to each from the point of view of arriving at a coherent interpretation of transcendental idealism.

Those who take the two object view typically (though not exclusively) go on to charge transcendental idealism with incoherence, on account of the difficulties (discussed above) allegedly surrounding the application of the categories outside experience and the notion of affection by a supersensible object. Consequently, those who defend Kant's doctrine of things in themselves (as allowing more than a polemical reading) tend to be proponents of the two conception view. The compelling reason for adopting this view, it is argued, is that, whilst supplying a direct justification for referring to things in themselves, it obviates the need for any world of ontologically distinct objects: we have already a justification for referring to appearances, from which we can derive a justification for referring to things in themselves, simply by treating these as the same objects picked out under a different description. All that is necessary is that this further description should be warranted. Kant's talk of affection boils down to the idea that we are affected by empirical things which may, along with their affecting us, be considered in a non-empirical mode. The complexities of double affection are eliminated.

Problems arise, however, in connection with this approach. In so far as it is designed to supply a justification for referring to things in themselves, the warrant for redescribing appearances as things in themselves cannot derive from a prior and independent assumption that there is, actually, a way that things are in themselves. The warrant must derive, therefore, from methodological considerations. In this vein it may be said that, because transcendental reflection considers things as they are known to us, i.e. as appearances, it obliges us to consider them also as they are in abstraction from our knowledge, i.e. as they are in themselves. But it is not clear what significance attaches to the methodological directive to consider things in abstraction from cognition, for it is not clear why subtracting relation to cognition should be thought to leave any object of thought or reference at all to be considered. Why should considering empirical objects minus cognition be any more contentful than considering them minus their existence, or considering the number 2 with its property of evenness cancelled? It might be thought that the notion of intellectual intuition answers this question, by allowing it to be said that a thing considered in itself is a thing which is intellectually intuitable. Though this is true, it fails to supply the missing warrant, because reason is still wanting for supposing that an object given to a subject of sensible intuition allows itself to be considered as an object of intellectual intuition. It is intelligible to say of an object in general – an object for a subject of some or other, undetermined sort – that it may be considered as a thing in itself, if this means merely that it is open to being determined as an object for a subject of intellectual intuition. But it is not similarly intelligible to say that an object for me – an object determined as known or knowable by a subject of sensible intuition – may be so considered. In sum, it appears that methodological considerations are sufficient to justify a non-referring use of 'thing in itself' ('objects of experience are not things in themselves'), but not a referring use.

Even if the foregoing difficulty can be resolved, the methodological approach faces another and no less serious objection. It detaches the contrast of appearances and things in themselves from that of appearance and reality: 'thing in itself' no longer incorporates the sense, clearly intended by Kant, of having greater reality than appearances (of being 'real *per se*', Bxx). The tendency of the methodological approach is to imply that 'thing in itself' just means 'thing considered apart from our knowledge of it', and while this is certainly part of its meaning for Kant, it is not all of it. Like the atheistic interpretation of transcendental idealism considered earlier, this account loses touch with Kant's view of the inferior reality of appearance.

Supplementary to these complications, it may be observed that, if there is, as suggested earlier, an alternative way of rationalising the claim that things in themselves exist, then the motivation for giving precedence to the two conception over the two object view tends to evaporate. The two object view is standardly objected to as metaphysically excessive, but given the almost vanishingly minimal contentfulness of the commitment that it involves, it is not easy to see by what measure (short of a declaration in favour of positivism) this can be so. In any case it is hard to see why any principle of ontological parsimony should be thought to have validity in the context of transcendental reflection.

A disjunctive view

This is, however, not to say that the two object view should be accepted. For one thing, it is hard to discount all of Kant's two conception talk as merely heuristic. There are, furthermore, it may now be pointed out, statements of Kant's that suggest something different from either of the two views considered so far: 'Doubtless, indeed, there are intelligible entities corresponding to the sensible entities; there may also be intelligible entities to which our sensible faculty has no relation whatsoever' (B308–9); 'the problem, namely, as to whether there may not be objects entirely disengaged from any such kind of [sensible] intuition ... is a question which can only be answered in an indeterminate manner, by saying that as sensible intuition does not extend to all things without distinction a place remains open for other and different objects' (A287–8/B344). And, from a letter (to Mendelssohn, 16 August 1783): 'this field of possible experience does not encompass all things in themselves; consequently, there are other objects in addition to objects of possible experience'. These statements, it may be claimed, do not support the two object view, so much as challenge the assumption that there is a uniform conceptualisation of the relation of things in themselves and appearances. They suggest that there are two cases to be distinguished: that of things in themselves *qua* ground of appearance (the existence of which is known, for reasons given earlier), and that of things in themselves *qua* entities satisfying noumenal concepts such as the concept of God (the existence of which is not known, the concepts of which being problematic), these objects being plainly non-identical with appearances. The former are to be conceived in two conception terms, but the latter require a two object model.

Indeterminacy

We could, then, move on to a third, disjunctive view, according to which Kant's position is that some things in themselves can be known to be ontologically distinct from appearances, and others not. There is, however, a risk here of splitting the concept of the thing in itself into two, and a better conclusion may be the following.

The difficulty of arriving at a satisfactory conception of the relation of things in themselves and appearance is due not merely to the vagaries of Kant's choice of expression, but has its roots in the difficulty we experience in handling the notion of an object in the context of transcendental reflection. Here our situation is without parallel in any empirical context where the identity of objects is in question. Consider first that it is crucial for Kant's empirical realism, that transcendental reflection should operate with an *intentional* conception of objecthood, according to which it is sufficient for something to count as an object, that it be constituted a priori and taken as such by a subject. If Kant's account of appearance left behind it no object of which spatio-temporal properties can be truly predicated – no object which is *really* spatio-temporal – then transcendental idealism would be landed with the claim that awareness of appearances is equivalent to distorted awareness of reality. Its claim would be that objects which are not spatio-temporal necessarily appear to us as if they were, i.e. as they are not, and so are necessarily *mis*apprehended by subjects of our sort. Even more problematically, it would follow that appearances are deemed objects only from the human standpoint, and that really – in the perspective of transcendental reflection – there are none such, but instead only false ways in which things appear. As it might be put, it would follow that there only *appear to be* appearances. In order for the objectual conception of appearances from the human standpoint to be underwritten, transcendental reflection must, therefore, endorse an intentional conception of objecthood, and it is of course this conception which is set out (with specific reference to objects of spatio-temporal intuition) in the Analytic.

This allows empirical judgement to be conceived as objective judgement of the real properties of things (appearances), but it creates complications for the two conception view, since things in themselves are not objects in the intentional sense. In order to think of appearances and things in themselves as both objects, and of them as both aspects of one and the same object, a different, non-intentional conception of objecthood is required. A non-intentional sense of object is required for the very concept of a thing in itself. Now transcendental reflection is perfectly entitled to avail itself of this conception, but it makes the identity asserted by the two conception view curious in so far as, first, the objects that are said to be identical are objects in deeply different senses; and, second, neither of the senses in which appearances and things in themselves are each objects, seems to be the same as that in which there is one object of which they are both aspects. There is, then, a difficulty implicit in the very formulation of the two conception view, namely that the identification of appearances, which are objects in the intentional sense, with things in themselves, which are objects in some other sense, cannot, it seems, be made perspicuous. The heterogeneity of senses of object in play in transcendental reflection does not, however, favour the two object view either: given that appearances are objects in a deeply different sense from things in themselves, the sense in which they may be conceived as 'two objects' is equally obscure.

The perplexity into which we are led regarding the identity of objects in transcendental reflection points to a third view, namely that transcendental reflection is incapable of making out determinately the relation between appearances and things in themselves. That we are neither obliged to reduce the concept of things in themselves to that of a non-empirical aspect of appearances, nor entitled to claim that appearances and things in themselves are necessarily non-identical, is, it may be argued, both fitting with Kant's own variable manner of conceiving things in themselves, and a proper consequence of the limits of our knowledge. Though transcendental reflection reveals that things in themselves exist as the ground of appearances, it does not allow us to say that they either are, or are not the 'same things' as appearances. To do so, we would need to be able to say what, outside the empirical sphere, counts as a distinction of objects, and what as a distinction of aspects of one and the same object; and what counts as a distinction of objects in an ontological sense of 'object', and what in an epistemological sense. That would presuppose some grasp, which we cannot have, of the principles of individuation of things in themselves. In thinking of things in themselves, we do not therefore think of anything whose relation to appearances we can determine: the most that can be said is that some contexts (such as human freedom) suggest more strongly the one manner of conceiving their relation than the other.

This explains why the opposition of two object and two conception views should result in a stalemate. Because the sense of 'object' is not fixed in any single way, the two object theorist can always appeal to a sense of object in which appearance and thing in itself cannot be the same thing, and the two conception theorist to a different sense of object, one which makes it superfluous to talk of two worlds. Each can regard the other as operating with a conception of objecthood which misrepresents the ontological facts. The argument could be settled if, and only if, either side could demonstrate that the other's way of conceiving the identity of objects is mistaken. But this would presuppose, as said above, a grasp of objecthood which is only available from the transcendent perspective which transcendental idealism denies us. That transcendental reflection should lack the resources needed to settle the argument is thus no accident.

On these grounds, it may be concluded that there is nothing at issue between the two views from the perspective of a finite cognitive subject engaged in transcendental reflection: aside from special contexts like human freedom, it is a matter of indifference whether one says that there is one world conceived in two ways, or two worlds.

The transcendental ideality of the self

Kant, as we have seen, holds that transcendental ideality extends to the self, as much as it does to things distinct from it. Kant's sharp distinction of two aspects of self-knowledge, inner sense and apperception, the latter affording no determinate cognition of the self, is carefully designed to serve his thesis that we do not know ourselves as we are in ourselves. This claim nevertheless encounters special difficulties – ones which do not attend the case for transcendental idealism in general – and these have led some to think that in this instance the restriction of our knowledge to appearances collapses (bringing down, it is urged, Kant's metaphysic as a whole).

Basically there are two problems. First, it would seem that by Kant's own account we have much knowledge of a determinate but non-empirical kind about the self, suggesting that here at last we must regard ourselves as penetrating to the nature of something as it is in itself. We know, for instance, how the self is structured in terms of its faculties, that it executes various orders of synthesis, and everything else that falls under the heading of 'transcendental psychology'. So even if the Paralogisms succeed in showing that rational psychology fails to attain knowledge of the self as a thing in itself, and Kant's own account of apperception avoids that commitment, Kant may still seem to have done the same job as rational psychology, by a different, transcendental route.

Second, the argument which Kant makes prominent in defending the ideality of the self (given in the second General Observation on the Aesthetic at B66–9, and §§24–5 of the B Deduction, B152–9) encounters difficulties. It says that self-knowledge cannot be of something transcendentally real, because it presupposes affection (passivity); knowledge of the self as a thing in itself is reserved for a subject of intellectual intuition, which, being free from sensibility, would not affect itself in any way (its self-intuition would be 'self-activity only', B68). The problem here is that, due to the famous peculiarities of self-knowledge, the sense in which it is true to say that self-affection takes place seems sufficiently different from outer affection to cast doubt on the conclusion.

The first problem can be handled by insisting on the distinction, made quite explicit in the Deduction and Paralogisms, between the self *qua* transcendental subjectivity or condition of objects, and the self *qua* thing in itself or noumenon. Both are non-empirical, but it is to the former that Kant means to ascribe a priori synthesis, and it stands on the edge of experience rather than its far side. It remains fixed at that limit because in transcendental philosophy we conceptualise our subjectivity exclusively with reference to the possibility of objects. To know of the transcendental self that it synthesises etc. is, therefore, to know it only *qua* synthetic source of the structure of experience, and not to know the non-relational ground, if there is such, of this synthetic activity (for which intellectual intuition would be required). It is not, therefore, to know the self as it is in itself.

So, although it is broadly true that there is an asymmetry between what we know transcendentally of the self and of other things, this should not be confounded with the contrast between knowledge of appearances and of things in themselves. Ultimately, all it amounts to is the fact that the subject has priority in the subject–object relation, that the supreme condition of this relation is itself subjective. This is what makes it seem as if, and it supplies the only good sense in which it is true that, our knowledge of the self goes deeper than our knowledge of anything else.

The second problem arises because of the undeniable deep differences between inner and outer sense. Inner sense has no manifold of its own (Bxxxix[n]): its 'material', Kant says, consists only of intuitions of outer objects (B67), and the intuiting of these does not appear to involve sensation or any analogue thereof. Self-consciousness precludes the distinctness of consciousness and object found in outer perception, or the same sort of passivity. This makes it hard to see how an ideality-implying story may be told about inner sense. Kant can justifiably maintain that in order for inner intuition to yield self-knowledge – in order for the inner flow of representations to be cognised, and the self determined as empirically real – it is necessary that conceptual content be introduced into inner intuition. As Kant puts it in the Deduction, the understanding with 'its original power of combining the manifold of intuition' must 'determine' inner sense 'inwardly', inner sense being 'affected thereby' and a 'combination of the manifold' produced in it (B153–5). This action of the understanding's may indeed be described as self-affection, and Kant may claim that his theory of self-knowledge is at least as effective as any other in dispelling the air of paradox which surrounds this notion (B155–6). But what he postulates here is an affection in which a manifold (of inner sense) is rendered determinate with respect to its form (time), not one in which a manifold is created and initially receives form.

This means that it is not enough for Kant to rehearse the argument of the Aesthetic, by appealing directly to the temporality of self-experience, to found the transcendental ideality of the self. It might have been thought that Kant could simply argue: the possibility of objects in general presupposes transcendental conditions, which in the case of inner objects is supplied by time, and time, as a form of sensibility, must be considered transcendentally ideal; ergo the self, which is known only in time, is transcendentally ideal. (Kant may seem to be arguing like this in the Aesthetic's discussion of the transcendental ideality of time, A32–6/B49–53.) But the argument does not succeed, because even if the Aesthetic has proven that *outer* objects are transcendentally ideal with respect to their temporality, it does not follow that it has done the same for *inner* objects. It needs to be shown, not merely assumed, that self-knowledge presupposes sensibility in a sense relevantly similar to outer perception, and this presumption is undermined by the differences between inner and outer sense. For the same reason – the want of any clear justification for treating the inner on the same terms as the outer – no ground in the Analytic for regarding the self as transcendentally ideal is forthcoming.

This is not to say that the immediacy of our relation to our mental states, or the fact that we are unable to insert a wedge between how we experience our mental states (their *percipi*) and how we suppose them to be (their *esse*), as we can in the case of physical objects, *entails* the transcendental reality of our mental states; all that follows from these considerations is that it is an objective truth that our experiences have temporal form, i.e. the empirical rather than transcendental reality of our selves *qua* temporal. Rather the point is that a question-mark hangs over the application of the general argument for transcendental idealism to inner objects: why should the self's own states not be precisely objects that can be given *without* the mediation of transcendental conditions? In which case their temporality (though not that of outer objects) will characterise them as they are in themselves.

At this point, it is worth observing that, so long as the question of the self's transcendental reality or ideality is so far merely undecided, Kant need not pursue the matter, because by his own lights he can rely on his moral theory to decide the issue. As he writes in the second Critique: 'the strange though incontestable assertion of the speculative [i.e. first] *Critique, that even the thinking subject is* in inner intuition *a mere appearance to itself*, gets its full confirmation in the *Critique of Practical Reason*, and that so thoroughly that one would have to arrive at it even if the former had never proved this proposition at all' (*CPracR* 6; Kant looks ahead to this result at B430–2). However, to the extent that the *Critique* is meant to pave the way for Kant's practical philosophy, making its acceptance easier, it ought to say something to make us positively favour the thesis that the self is transcendentally ideal.

The self in the system of experience

Progress can be made by considering the place of the self in Kant's theory of experience as a whole. In the Analytic we learn that knowledge of my own existence in time presupposes the construction of a single system of experience in which my representations are conditioned by outer objects. Now such a system is possible only if my representations are, if not fully subject to the same a priori principles as outer objects, then at least partially integrated with them. It is necessary, therefore, that inner objects be accorded the same, intra-worldly status as outer objects, and since the latter are mere appearances, so too must be states of the self. (It is at this point of reconceptualisation, and not before, that the subject acquires *psychological* properties, in the familiar empirical sense.) So, although the transcendental ideality of the self does not follow from self-affection merely *qua* action of the understanding, it does follow from the objectification of the self in the empirical order which that action entails. This also explains why Kant should suggest at one point (B67) that transcendental ideality transfers itself from the materials of outer sense to those of inner sense: it does so, not because awareness in general necessarily takes on the qualities of whatever it is awareness of, but because both sets of objects have to be locked into one and the same system of appearances.

Finally, the importance of this whole issue should be underlined. If we have knowledge of the self as it is in itself, then transcendental philosophy is transformed into determinate knowledge of a really existing object: transcendental knowledge of our mode of cognition, of the conditions and structure of experience, becomes equivalent to knowledge of the structure and powers of the self. In that case, the Copernican strategy of explaining objects in terms of our mode of cognition amounts to explaining objects in general in terms of one privileged real object, the self, which has the role of providing a fundamental *ontological* condition for all other objects. Kant's transcendental theory of experience would then be a form of transcendental realism (albeit a novel one). Confining self-knowledge to the self *qua* appearance is, therefore, an essential concomitant of Kant's Copernican programme.

(In this context, it is worth remarking that Kant has very little to say on the question of the status of our knowledge of our mode of cognition, and of how we come to know the propositions of transcendental philosophy, issues often brought under the heading of 'meta-critique'. His idealist successors, as will be indicated in chapter 10, made much of the absence from Kant of any metacritical theory.)

Entering into, and remaining within, the Kantian system

We have seen that Jacobi's contention that the Kantian system incorporates a paradox is not justified. There is no contradiction in saying that the objects of our perception are inside us in the transcendental (and no other) sense, and that they presuppose something outside us (in the transcendental sense), of which we can have negative and existential (but no other sort of) knowledge; we can know ourselves to be affected by something unknowable. And Jacobi is also mistaken in supposing that our fundamental conviction of the objectivity of our perceptions is contradicted by Kant's account of empirical reality.

Kant's picture appears paradoxical to Jacobi because he does not hold apart the two levels, empirical and transcendental, and consequently mistakes the relation between things in themselves and appearances for a relation within the empirical realm. This leads him to regard Kant's doctrine of things in themselves as if it combined Locke's doctrine of substance with a Berkeleyan denial that there can be reference to anything outside our ideas – as if it were the product of superimposing Berkeley's theory of existence and meaning on Locke's causal-representative theory of perception. In fact, as we have seen, the thing in itself is not introduced by Kant to rectify an otherwise Berkeleyan conception of objects; its contribution to Kant's empirical realism is not as crudely direct as Jacobi supposes. That things in themselves exist as the ground of appearance is a special transcendental proposition, and to make this claim is to go as far as the bounds of knowledge but not beyond them. Jacobi would be right if, in order to cognise the bounds of experience, it were necessary to take up a second perspective, a perspective on our perspective, but this is not necessary; reference to things in themselves can be made from the edge of our perspective. What allows, and indeed forces, us to move to this edge is the consideration that, as Kant puts it, experience has bounds but does not bound itself – as shown by the fact that our thought extends beyond the confines of our cognition.

The peculiarity of our cognitive situation, according to Critical philosophy, is that we can grasp the perspective which conditions our knowledge only by referring to a point of view outside it, of which we can form a conception, but which we cannot occupy. This reference is expressed in the presupposition of things in themselves. To represent our situation in this perspectival manner will appear incoherent so long as we operate within the terms of transcendental realism, which supposes that the correct philosophical picture of human cognition must be, like reality itself, free of any perspectival character. Kant's philosophy, however, is meant to be perspectival in a sense in which transcendental realism is not.

What at root separates transcendental idealism from its critics is thus a meta-philosophical difference. Transcendental realism holds that human knowledge can account for itself, and in so doing knows reality: it assumes that the fundamental conditions of human knowledge are identical with constituents of reality, and that there is nothing necessary for cognition that cannot itself be cognised. Transcendental realism takes up, so to speak, the point of view of reality, and tries to dissolve our perspective on reality into the structure of reality itself, subsuming the subject–object relation into reality's relation to itself. Thus it holds that there is nothing ultimately perspectival about our cognitive situation. Transcendental idealism, by contrast, holds that cognition is subject to conditions that cannot themselves be cognised in the same sense in which objects are cognised, and so that human knowledge can account for itself only by referring outside its sphere. Hence Kant's perspectival picture of our cognitive situation, and the contrast it draws between elucidating the conditions that make objects possible for us, and identifying the fundamental constituents of reality. The propositions of transcendental philosophy must consequently all be understood as expressing *necessities of representation*: all have the form, 'We must represent its being the case that . . .'. On this account, philosophical knowledge does not comprise knowledge of objects – of their general features and so of reality – but only of the conditions of knowledge of objects. It is knowledge only of the 'shape' of our perspective. The notion of perspective implies a devaluation of our knowledge, but in Kant this takes place solely with respect to the global ontological status of the objects of our cognition: the human perspective itself, which fixes our world, is itself fixed. For this reason – even though no insight into the grounds of this fixity, beyond the unity of apperception, is possible for us – the upshot of Kant's perspectivism is the precise opposite of relativism.

Jacobi's protest that transcendental idealism is confused is warranted, in so far as it registers the genuine peculiarity of its commitment to the inescapably perspectival character of our cognitive situation. There is a difficulty in *entering into* the Kantian system, in so far as it contradicts the expectation that our cognitive situation will be elucidated in a non-perspectival manner. This difficulty is, however, acknowledged and explained within the system itself, in terms of the task of thinking the perspective that constitutes our identity as subjects. And because the difficulty is dissolved on the inside of the Kantian system, Jacobi should have found no problem in *remaining within* it.

Chapter 9

The complete Critical system (The Canon of Pure Reason)

If we recall the philosophical task set in the Preface, it is clear that, for all that Kant has achieved by the end of the Dialectic, the problem of metaphysics remains in a crucial respect unsolved. The original problem was that despite the fact that the severity of philosophical disagreement renders any claim to metaphysical knowledge hollow (dogmatism is unacceptable), metaphysical knowledge is at once a deep need of human reason (indifference is unacceptable), and presupposed by morality and the rationality of cognition (skepticism is unacceptable). Kant has shown one kind of metaphysical knowledge to be possible, which is enough to save the conception of cognition as a rational phenomenon, and of ourselves, correlatively, as rational beings, against Hume's contention that this conception must be surrendered in the light of the limits of our knowledge. But Kant has yet to solve the remaining conflict between the impossibility of knowledge of a supersensible reality proven in the Dialectic, and the need for transcendent metaphysics

307

which is imposed by both our natural disposition to metaphysics ('our inextinguishable desire to find firm footing somewhere beyond the limits of experience', A795/B823), and the requirements of morality. As said in chapter 1 (pp. 16–18, 22), it is Kant's view of morality as standing in need of metaphysics that makes Hume's abandonment of metaphysics and reason in favour of Nature ultimately unacceptable to him. Since the motivation for Kant's philosophy was at the very outset bound up in this way with the fate of morality, transcendental philosophy is not secure until it has settled the conflict of morality – and religion – with the scientific world-view.

In the Preface Kant told us that, although the *Critique* will not supply a theory of morality, it contains an essential preparation for a proper grounding of morality (Bxxv), which will in turn provide the correct, rational foundation for religion – Kant's claim being to have 'found it necessary to deny *knowledge*, in order to make room for *faith*' (Bxxx). In a section bearing the unpromising title 'The Canon of Pure Reason', buried away in the Transcendental Doctrine of Method, Kant presents the final part of his strategy for solving the problem of metaphysics: a demonstration that Critical philosophy can, through its vindication of the metaphysics of experience and criticism of transcendent metaphysics, bring harmony to reason and validate the moral order. In so doing the Canon provides a prospectus of the future development of Critical philosophy and a preliminary outline of the Critical system as a whole, the groundplan of which is identified with the answering of three questions (A804–5/B832–3):

1 What can I know?
2 What ought I to do?
3 What may I hope?

The first of these has been answered in the main body of the *Critique*. Kant's answers to the second and the third are sketched in the Canon.

'What ought I to do?' The moral law

That Kant is in a position, by the end of the Dialectic, to achieve the vindication of morality and religion promised in the Preface is on the face of it far from obvious. Whatever may have been gained by Kant's anti-atheistical defence of the concept of God, the prospect of religion resting on anything more than an arbitrary leap of faith appears extremely dim. Nor is it evident that Kant can make much sense of moral value. He cannot allow morality to depend on knowledge of God or a transcendent realm of any sort: the *Critique* plainly destroys the basis on which Judaeo-Christian morality conceives us as immortal souls subject to the law of God. And Critical philosophy cannot allow that morality has its source in the direct, a priori apprehension of universal moral truths, since it destroys the epistemology required by such a view of moral knowledge. Furthermore, the Analytic defends an exclusively Newtonian conception of the natural order, of which moral value is no essential part. This appears to leave the moral good to be somehow constructed out of natural facts. But by reducing nature to a formal unity exhibiting a merely mechanical causality, Kant has eliminated any objective basis for thinking of ourselves teleologically, as having natural purposes to fulfil, and so blocked the robust characterisation of human beings at the foundation of Aristotle's virtue ethics.

It would seem, then, that the only possible conception of morality available to Critical philosophy is utilitarian or subjectivist, an ethical theory in some way based empirically on the desires and feelings of human beings: since the metaphysics of the *Critique* reduces all knowable facts to empirical facts, and these are exclusively non-normative, the reality of morality in any other form seems precluded. The consequences for aesthetic value, it may be added, are presumably similar. And yet it was precisely with a view to avoiding a Humean ethic of sentiment, and reconceiving morality on the deeper and firmer lines outlined by Rousseau, that Kant undertook the *Critique*: so if the only morality that can be built up from the materials bequeathed by it is utilitarian or Humean, there would be a heavy irony, in so far as Kant, having argued vigorously against empiricism in his theoretical philosophy, would have condemned himself to an empiricist conception of moral value – morality, and human value generally, would be a function of our preferences and feelings, and have no more than a contingent, a posteriori foundation. Kant's claim for the moral significance of the *Critique* appears extremely puzzling so far. And, more generally, the landscape of the *Critique* appears bleak from the point of view of meaningful human activity: even though its world is constituted by our minds, we cannot feel immediately at home in it in any deep sense. It is thus not unintelligible that one of Kant's contemporaries (Jacobi) should have charged Kantian idealism with tending to nihilism.

A Copernican revolution in ethics

But, if Kant is correct, to suppose all this is to repeat the central, transcendental realist error which the *Critique* criticises: that of looking to objects for sources of justification, rather than to the subject. On Kant's account, to look to the world – either empirical or trans-empirical reality – for a ground of value and foundation for morality, is to look in the wrong place, and the defect of all previous accounts of morality is precisely that they have sought to found morality either in transcendent objects like God ('rationalist' ethics) or empirical objects such as ourselves considered as natural beings ('empiricist' ethics). The key to a correct conception of morality lies in a second Copernican revolution, this time concerned with *practical* reason. Whereas ethical primacy had previously been granted to some or other conception of the Good, Kant accords it to the subject's power of willing.

Human action is first and foremost, Kant assumes, an exercise of reason. This means, in the first place, that reason plays a necessary part in the realisation of whatever ends are proposed to us by our empirical natures, i.e. by our experience of objects as providing us with incentives to act. To the extent that we pursue such ends – ones determined by what Kant calls 'inclination' – reason does not set any ends of its own: it is merely, in Hume's phrase, the slave of the passions. Now if Kant's account of morality were symmetrical with his account of theoretical knowledge, then a view of practical reason as subordinated to ends set by nature (inclinations) would define the limits of the involvement of reason in human action. Since in the theoretical sphere the legitimate role of our intellectual faculties is restricted to unifying and giving form to empirical material, symmetry would imply that the most that reason can do in the practical sphere is create means–end unities (judge what must be done in order for particular inclinations to be satisfied), and organise our inclinations into coherent plans of action (judge which inclinations cohere with which others, and determine their order of priority).

On Kant's account, however, this limited conception of practical reason is false, for practical reason is capable of determining itself to act independently of inclination, and when it does so (and under no other conditions) it determines itself *morally*. Kant's argument for this claim is extremely complex and only hinted at in the Canon. Interpolating, therefore, from the later works on ethics where it is developed (the *Groundwork of the Metaphysics of Morals* and *Critique of Practical Reason*): Kant starts with ordinary moral consciousness, the primary and outstanding characteristic of which is that moral laws 'command in an *absolute* manner' and not merely 'hypothetically', i.e. they claim validity without supposition of empirical ends – unlike the pragmatic 'rule of prudence', which derives from the motive of happiness and tells us merely what we must do *if* we wish our inclinations to be satisfied (A807/B835; see also A800/B828). This assumption, Kant holds, can be supported by appeal to the 'moral judgement of every man', and is clearly expressed in the ordinary concept of duty: if it is my duty to φ, then I am obligated to φ whatever consultation of my desires instructs me to do. Now if the moral law is in this fashion necessary, then it must also be – for familiar Kantian reasons – a priori. The same result is dictated, Kant argues, by another central fact of ordinary moral consciousness, namely that we regard the moral worth of an individual as determined solely by the quality of their will, and as a good that is independent of anything else, and that nothing else can compare with – an 'unconditional good'. This compels, Kant maintains, a conception of action which bestows moral worth on action which is performed for the sake of duty independently of inclination, and a consequent conception of the motive of duty as consisting in respect or reverence for the moral law, a law which again must be a priori.

There must therefore be – if morality is not to be a chimera – some principle of action which is a priori and constrains all rational agents irrespective of their contingent empirical constitution. The only principle that can satisfy this condition of apriority and strict universality is, Kant argues, the categorical imperative, variously formulated as the principle that 'I ought never to act except in such a way that I can also will that my maxim [the reason or ground of my action expressed in a generalised and impersonal form, as a rule to which I can appeal in justification of it] should become a universal law' (*Gr* 402–3); and (equivalently, Kant argues) as 'So act that you use humanity, whether in your own person or in the person of any other, always at the same time as an end, never merely as a means' (*Gr* 429). To the extent that an agent determines himself in the light of this principle he will be, Kant points out, autonomous or self-legislating, since the law that guides his actions will be one that derives from his own nature *qua* rational agent, and one that he has prescribed to himself without being determined to do so by nature (in a broad sense inclusive of his own empirical constitution). Now evidently, such extra-natural self-determination – called by Kant 'pure practical reason' – is possible only if human agents possess the kind of freedom that Kant calls transcendental, as opposed to merely practical.

The immediate difficulty, however, with grounding morality on transcendental freedom is that the concept has been shown to be problematic. Kant's solution is to say that the question of whether we really do possess the transcendental freedom which morality requires 'is a question which in the practical field does not concern us', and 'does not come within the province of reason in its practical employment': 'it is a merely speculative question, which we can leave aside so long as we are considering what ought or ought not to be done' (A801–4/B829–32). As this point is developed in the *Groundwork*: 'in a practical respect' rational beings must be assumed to be 'really free', and since 'all laws that are inseparably bound up with freedom' are just as valid for a 'being that cannot act otherwise than *under the idea of freedom*', as they are for a being whose freedom is provable for theoretical reason, assuming freedom from a practical point of view escapes from the onus of having to 'prove freedom in its theoretical respect' (*Gr* 447–50), though it of course requires freedom to be theoretically conceivable. Because the idea of transcendental freedom lies ready, pre-prepared by theoretical reason, we are fully entitled to regard our moral consciousness as an expression of reason's capacity for self-determination, i.e. of pure practical reason: this unique a priori 'fact of reason' provides the equivalent of a deduction of the moral law.

Now transcendental freedom presupposes, Kant argued in his Critical solution to the third antinomy, the metaphysics of transcendental idealism; in no other way is it thinkable. Though not explicit in the Canon, in the *Groundwork* and second Critique Kant affirms that morality must be regarded as presupposing and giving application to the – again, from the theoretical point of view, problematic – concepts of noumenal selfhood and agency. The moral law thus supplies me with an awareness of self which is in one respect the same as that claimed by rational psychology, in so far as it reveals my consciousness of my existence to contain 'a something a priori' which relates me to 'a non-sensible intelligible world'; although it does not allow me to claim any more determinate knowledge of myself, and the meaning that categories such as causality possess when employed in the moral-practical context is strictly analogical (B430–2). (The view of metaphysics as an expression of moral consciousness again articulates an idea Kant first presented in *Dreams*.)

At this point, the meaning of Kant's statement in the Preface that the positive value of the *Critique* lies in its contribution to morality (Bxxiv–xxv, Bxxviii–xxix) becomes clear: without the transcendental idealism implied by its criticism of metaphysics, the possibility of human freedom could not be upheld, and because morality 'necessarily presupposes freedom (in the strictest sense) as a property of our will', morality would then 'have to yield to the mechanism of nature' – practical reason's transcendence of the bounds of sensibility would be destroyed. Transcendental idealism is essential to release morality from the dependence on the speculative employment of theoretical reason which has previously been its lot. Although Critical philosophy does not prove human freedom, it at least allows it to be thought, and this is all that morality, due to its essentially non-theoretical nature, requires.

Kant's moral theory reveals, in the shape of the categorical imperative, an a priori structure of action analogous to the a priori structure of experience, the difference being that whereas the latter is necessarily realised in the phenomenal world and appears to us as what *is* the case, the former appears to us primordially as what *ought* to be the case, and coincides with what is the case only in so far as our actions do in fact proceed from the moral law; its realisation in the phenomenal world is practically necessary, but from the theoretical point of view contingent. The world 'in so far as it may be in accordance with moral laws' – as it can be as a result of the free actions of rational beings, and as it ought to be in the light of the moral law – Kant calls 'a *moral world*' (A808/B836). The moral world is the Critical descendant of the spirit world hypothesised in Kant's pre-Critical *Dreams of a Spirit-Seer*. In such a world, the will of each rational being is placed under laws that bring it 'into complete systematic unity with itself and with the freedom of every other'. The idea of a moral world, though purely intelligible (for it contains no reference to anything empirical), is in the first instance simply this sensible world viewed 'as an object of pure reason in its practical employment', i.e. as something that can be brought about through action. It is therefore a 'practical idea', i.e. an idea that can and ought to influence the sensible world, bringing it into conformity with itself. In the *Groundwork* the moral world is redescribed as a 'kingdom of ends', and in other writings Kant argues that its realisation requires liberal and republican principles of political organisation.

The practical fulfilment of reason

Pure reason is therefore capable of doing in the practical sphere precisely what it cannot in the theoretical: in the latter it is restricted to regulative employment, but pure practical reason is constitutive and its principles have objective reality; so 'it is in their practical, meaning thereby their moral, employment, that the principles of pure reason have objective reality' (A808/B836; as Kant claimed in the Preface, Bxxi–xxii). The idea of a moral world gains objective reality not by referring to an object of intellectual intuition – which is what would be required for the ideas of theoretical reason to gain objective reality – but by referring to the sensible world as an object of pure practical reason. When practical reason is exercised non-empirically, its objects are ones that the subject creates: its concepts 'at once become cognitions and do not have to wait for intuitions to receive meaning', because 'they themselves produce the reality of that to which they refer', namely a morally good determination of the will (*CPracR* 66).

Because pure reason does in the practical sphere what only a divine, intuitive intellect could do in the theoretical, viz. create its own objects, it is possible for the pure reason of a subject with a non-divine, discursive intellect to achieve in the practical sphere what it cannot in the theoretical.

The moral order, though an order to be constructed in this, the phenomenal world, and not one belonging to some transcendent world, has its reality in the noumenal world in the sense that reference to the noumenal is implicit in moral judgement (via the concept of transcendental freedom). And since noumenal reality is, as conceived by theoretical reason, the realm of the unconditioned, there is consequently a sense in which through morality we make contact with transcendent reality, and the desire to know the supersensible that the *Critique* shows to be doomed to frustration in the field of speculation receives an oblique fulfilment – not in the form originally envisaged, but none the less in a way that can give satisfaction to our reason as a whole. This coincidence of the presuppositions of morality with the unconditioned demanded by theoretical reason is not fortuitous: at a deep level they are united by their common reference beyond empirical reality.

'What may I hope?' From morality to God

In the final section of the Ideal of Pure Reason, Kant classifies theology into kinds on the basis of the grounds adduced for the existence of God, and indicates that there is one remaining ground that has not yet been considered, namely the causality of freedom and the moral order that corresponds to it (A632/B660). A possible window onto the existence of God thus remains open. Kant's exploration of it takes the following form (sketched at A589/B617). Suppose we have, as Kant takes himself to have shown, practical knowledge of moral obligation, and that this knowledge is rationally necessary. Now if it can be demonstrated that this knowledge presupposes the existence of God, then it will follow that we are entitled to postulate the existence of God on grounds of rational necessity supplied by practical reason. That is, we would be entitled to base belief in God's existence on what *ought to be* – on the existence of obligation – rather than on what *is*. This would amount to *moral theology* (as distinct from theological ethics, for which God's existence is a presupposition).

The highest good

To show that belief in God's existence is a presupposition of morality, Kant turns to the relation of morality and happiness. It follows from Kant's analysis of morality that the motive of happiness is no part of the moral motive, and that in no sense does happiness constitute or ground the moral good. Happiness is nevertheless, Kant holds, a necessary object of will for any finite, sensible agent, and as a natural end of humanity it must be considered in itself a good, though not a moral one. Now Kant locates a problem – an antinomy of practical reason, no less. There is no a priori guarantee that the moral law will not conflict with the pursuit of happiness, or even require that all hope of happiness be forsaken. Now if it were the teaching of Critical philosophy that human agents are in reality purely noumenal beings – that phenomenal existence is an *illusion* – then the Stoic doctrine that we should pursue the moral good with indifference to the prospect of happiness would be rationally acceptable. But on Kant's account the sensible side of humanity is not an illusion, but essential to its reality. Sensibly derived motivation cannot, therefore, be denied a rational claim on us, as the 'voice' of our own nature attests (*CPracR* 127); to suppose the contrary, Kant condemns as misanthropy.

This means that, in the absence of any mediation of the conflict of the respective claims of morality and happiness, practical reason is torn between these two principles, and we are faced with an 'apparent conflict of practical reason with itself' (*CPracR* 115). It follows that the ultimate or complete good for human beings – what Kant calls the 'supreme good' in the Canon, and the 'highest good' in the second Critique – is not moral perfection independent of happiness: it must comprehend happiness. But, Kant argues, the highest good also cannot be a mere agglomeration of moral perfection and happiness; a merely accidental unity would, on account of the lack of a necessary connection between its parts, fail to provide practical reason with a coherent and unitary object of will, and the antinomy would not be overcome. The highest good must consequently be happiness 'united with worthiness to be happy', i.e. a unity of moral worth and happiness in which the former grounds the latter. This alone will provide a coherent end for practical reason, overcoming its antinomy by allowing happiness to be aimed at through the attainment of moral worth.

Given this conception of the highest good, the moral law may be reformulated as, '*Do that through which thou becomest worthy to be happy*' (A808/B836), for it is now conceived as identifying the 'necessary conditions under which alone this freedom [of a rational being] can harmonise with a distribution of happiness that is made in accordance with [moral] principles' (A806/B834).

The transition to God

Now it must fall within the scope of what can be (rationally) hoped, that this distribution may actually be realised: otherwise practical reason has nothing that it may conceive itself as bringing about through its own exertions – the highest good cannot function as an object of will – and relapses into antinomy. Reason is therefore called upon to supply some set of theoretical judgements which will rationalise the hope which is presupposed by the exercise of pure practical reason, and this is the point at which, Kant argues, the doctrines of the existence of God and immortality of the soul reveal their rational necessity (A809–11/ B837–9). In our idea of a moral world, happiness is distributed according to desert, because freedom is there the direct cause of the distribution of happiness. Such a system of 'self-rewarding morality' is however only an idea, and in the world of appearance neither nature nor the causality of our actions secures a distribution of happiness proportional to desert. A necessary connection between morality and happiness securable in the phenomenal world by ourselves alone cannot be affirmed. Consequently it needs to be assumed that there is a '*Supreme Reason*' (God) which causes happiness to be distributed according to its desert, and the world in which this takes place must be assumed to be 'a consequence of our conduct in the world of sense', that is, 'to be for us a future world' (an idea presaged by the claim in *Dreams* that the virtuous man will hope for an afterlife). Thus reason 'finds itself constrained to assume' an 'intelligible world, under a wise Author and Ruler', 'together with life in such a world, which we must regard as a future world' (A811/B839). Without 'a God and without a world invisible to us now but hoped for', the 'glorious ideas of morality' would be 'objects of approval and admiration, but not springs of purpose and action' (A813/B841), and the moral law would have to be regarded as an empty figment (A811/B839).

In this light, morality may be reconceived as the will of God accompanied by a system of divinely administered rewards and sanctions, but on the strict condition that we should not 'look upon actions as obligatory because they are the commands of God', but 'regard them as divine commands because we have an inward obligation to them' (A819/B847). The ultimate ground of this moral theology is that the 'rational faith' which it enjoins is necessary in order for us to 'fulfil our vocation in this present world'; the moral argument for God's existence is a 'transcendental' argument (A589/B617), because it is concerned with conditions of possibility (of a morally good will). The conflict of reason with faith is now superseded, matters of faith having been brought within the scope of reason, and yet in a way that preserves the (Pietist) conception of faith as an expression of the self deeper than the intellect. Far from being nihilistic, it is fair to say of Kant that the 'secret of his philosophy is the unthinkability of despair' (T. W. Adorno).

Theoretical reason can assent to the hope-delivering, theoretically formulated propositions of practical reason because, Kant maintains, the concepts employed in formulating them are, like transcendental freedom, problematic (theoretical reason has nothing to say against their objective reality), and because the context in which they are to be affirmed is exclusively practical (theoretical reason cannot proceed to employ them as if they were justifiable on theoretical grounds). Though a rational agent's affirmation of the objective reality of God and a future life on practical grounds is a case of genuine belief, it is not, Kant emphasises, equivalent to theoretically founded belief: the existence of God and the immortal soul is only 'postulated', belief in them is only 'moral belief', and the certainty of moral belief rests only on subjective grounds of moral sentiment (it 'springs from the moral disposition itself', *CPracR* 146). Consequently I should say not '*It is* morally certain that there is a God etc.', but '*I am* morally certain, etc.' (A829/B857).

The Dialectic's denial of the possibility of theoretical knowledge of God and the soul is not, therefore, contradicted in Kant's moral theology, and has indeed proved necessary for the practical vindication of our ideas of God and the soul (taking one step back has allowed us to take two steps forward). For, had God and the soul been objects of theoretical knowledge, appeal to them would have been incompatible with the autonomy of morality (*CPracR* 146–8), and they would not have been available to play the role of postulates in the practical context. The deep rationale for Kant's idea that practical reason can lead to conviction in the existence of God lies, once again, in the transcendence of the bounds of sensibility immanent in moral consciousness: by attaining the unconditioned in the practical sphere, pure reason puts itself in a position – it gains the right – to affirm the reality of the unconditioned in forms conceived by theoretical reason.

The unity and ends of Reason

Kant thus erects on the basis of pure practical reason what he calls a 'practical-dogmatic metaphysics'. In so doing he draws on a set of doctrines concerning the nature of reason, independently of which his reasoning is not fully intelligible. Spelling these out also brings into view the humanist vision expressed in the Critical system.

The primacy of practical reason

In the first place, Kant's extraction of the postulates of God and immortality from moral consciousness presupposes a doctrine that he formulates as 'the primacy of practical reason'. Questions of primacy arise in transcendental contexts when two or more cognitive powers, operating independently of one another, lead to different results – as when practical reason requires for the resolution of its antinomy that the objective reality be affirmed of ideas (God and the immortal soul) to which theoretical reason, left to its own devices, would not ascribe objective reality. To accord primacy to practical reason means to grant it the right to settle matters in such contexts, to allow its 'interest' to take precedence over that of theoretical reason. (This right is limited, of course, by the condition that theoretical reason should not thereby be brought into conflict with itself: practical reason could not require theoretical reason to assume the existence of something that it judged impossible.)

The notion that practical reason has legitimate priority in this sense over theoretical reason is essential for Kant's theories of morality and religion, and yet, as he acknowledges (*CPracR* 143n, 144–6), the doctrine may seem strange, if not irrational, in so far as it implies that considerations stemming from the will may dictate what we hold to be true. The appearance of irrationality in Kant's reasoning is removed by making explicit further elements of his conception of reason.

Unity and teleology of reason

Though they are necessarily represented by us as distinct powers, theoretical and practical reason are ultimately, Kant insists, but *one* reason, and their operation must consequently be integrated. The demand for their integration must be taken as absolute, because if it is not met, it will be possible for pure reason to conflict with itself, which would mean abandoning the very notion of rationality. The unity of reason is 'the condition of having reason at all' (*CPracR* 120). The notion of reason as a necessary unity was put in place as far back as the Preface to the *Critique* (Axiii). For Kant it derives not from the (transcendental realist) thought that avoidance of contradiction is a desideratum because it is a condition of the representation of reality, but from the (Copernican) need of the subject to be able to hold on to the notion of rightness of judgement and the correlative conception of itself as a rational being.

If reason must be unified, the question arises on what basis this is to be done, what principle is to supply its required unity. Here transcendental idealism proves essential to Kant's argument. In the perspective of transcendental realism, theoretical reason is chained to the function of representing reality, which means that it must be granted primacy. (More precisely, the issue of the unity of reason cannot arise for transcendental realism in the form in which it does for Kant, since the very notion of rationality will be analysed by the transcendental realist in terms of the representation of reality, reducing all questions of the unity of reason to questions of correct representation.) Transcendental idealism, equipped with a different conception of cognition, eliminates this ground, previously regarded as decisive, for according pre-eminence to theoretical reason. In its place, a new perspective opens up. If our rational powers are not to be thought of fundamentally as answerable to something other than and independent from themselves, then they can, and must, be thought of as answerable to themselves.

The notion that our rational powers are to be considered teleologically, and that they carry their ends within themselves, emerges time and again in the *Critique*. First, it is involved in the doctrine of the regulative role of reason, which is couched in terms of reason as setting ends for the understanding. Second, in the Antinomy (Section 3, A462–76/B490–504) Kant weighs the claims of the theses and antitheses in terms of the ends of reason which they further. He asks 'which side we should prefer to fight on', 'if we consulted only our interest' (A465/B493), and observes that the theses accord with reason's practical ends and its interest in unity, whereas the antitheses, by robbing us of the 'foundations of morals and religion', cause practical reason 'irreparable injury', and frustrate the demand for unity of reason. Third, in the Canon Kant says that all the interests of reason are directed to answering the three questions of what we can know, ought to do and may hope, and he accordingly raises the question of the ultimate end of reason. (That reason must have one ultimate end follows from the necessity of its unity, together with that of conceiving reason teleologically.) Kant argues that – in view of the conclusion of the Dialectic, that pure reason when employed theoretically fails to yield knowledge – it may be inferred that the ultimate aim of reason is not theoretical but practical. With respect to the three objects 'which possess interest' for reason (A796/B824) and comprise the 'proper object' (B395n) of metaphysical enquiry – namely freedom, God and immortality – the interest of theoretical reason is 'very small', since these ideas contribute nothing to the explanation of appearances, and are 'not in any way necessary for *knowledge*'. But the existence of these objects is – Kant's theories of morality and religion establish – of very great practical significance. Hence it is reasonable to suppose that nature's purpose in constituting our reason in such a way that we are drawn to speculate about freedom, immortality and God, is to confront us with 'the problem *what we ought to do*, if the will is free, if there is a God and a future world' – that is, to direct us to moral ends. Kant thereby adds another level to the explanation of transcendental illusion: reason's extension of itself outside the empirical sphere is undertaken at the behest of practical reason ('theology and morals were the two motives, or rather the two points of reference, in all those abstract enquiries of reason to which men came to devote themselves', A853/B881).

That the subject's powers must be regarded teleologically – as having ends and interests – provides the key to Kant's argument for the postulates (*CPracR* 121). Because questions about which power of the subject has primacy are questions concerning the relative strengths of their interests, and all questions of interest are practical questions, it follows that questions of primacy are properly questions for practical reason to resolve. Consequently the unity of reason must lie in a principle of practical reason. On this ground theoretical reason is rationally required to accept whatever assumptions are necessary for resolving the antinomy of practical reason (providing these do not lead it to conflict with itself).

The ultimate end of reason is not, therefore, to gain knowledge, but to will the highest good. The highest good furnishes an end set by pure reason that subsumes all other ends and gives them systematic form. It thereby satisfies reason's 'architectonic' interest (explained in the Architectonic of Pure Reason, following the Canon), its need to regard 'all our knowledge as belonging to a possible system' (A474/B502). In the system sought by reason, 'the manifold modes of knowledge' are brought 'under one idea' in such a way that the whole determines, in teleological fashion, the relations of all its parts, as in an organism, and the parts are derived 'from a single supreme and inner end, through which the whole is first made possible' (A832–4/B860–2). (Rational systematicity and teleological organisation are equivalent for Kant.) Because the ultimate end of reason as a whole lies in the moral vocation of humanity, theoretical enquiry itself now stands under moral conditions: mathematics, natural science and empirical knowledge in general receive their ultimate point from their contribution to the highest good (A850–1/B878–9). Furthermore, just as there is an ultimate end for us to realise and to which all our other ends are subordinate, so creation must be regarded as having its final end in man as a moral being: the final, unconditioned purpose of creation – a description which nothing natural could satisfy, all things within nature being conditioned – is man considered as noumenon, transcendent of nature outside and inside himself. The natural world thus assumes a purposeful aspect as setting the scene for man's pursuit of his moral vocation, and is subsumed under the ends of reason. Finally this moral-teleological perspective is consummated in theology: the moral employment of reason requires that the world 'be represented as having originated from an idea', and so leads to 'the ideal of supreme ontological perfection', i.e. God, 'as a principle of systematic unity' of ends. (Kant adumbrates his moral teleology and associated 'transcendental theology' at A815–16/B843–4; it is set out properly in the *Critique of Judgement*, §§82–7, where it incorporates the moral argument for the existence of God.)

The place of Critical philosophy itself within the scheme of reason's purposes is not adventitious. As Kant indicates in the very last section of the *Critique*, the History of Pure Reason, the Critical 'path' becomes visible once sensualism and intellectualism, dogmatism and skepticism and all the other antinomial philosophical positions have run their course and been worked through. The systematicity and methodological order which Critical philosophy brings to the creations of reason – which were originally crude and have evolved culturally under pressure from moral interest, Kant says (A817/B845) – is the culmination of a long history of attempts to articulate the idea of philosophy (A834–40/B862–8). The history of philosophy, on a Kantian interpretation, exhibits a narrative in which reason is first divided from and then reunited with itself. At the outset reason forms, on account of its practical interest, the concepts of God, freedom and immortality. Once introduced, these concepts of the unconditioned are taken up by theoretical reason, which (rather than restricting itself to the task of regulating the understanding) attributes theoretically knowable reality to them. Practical reason is thus originally responsible for leading theoretical reason astray into the hubris of transcendent metaphysics. Theoretical reason, however, then comes to pose the greatest threat to practical reason, as its lawless speculations lead it to formulate the atheistic and morality-devastating doctrines of determinism, naturalism, materialism, empiricism, etc. Critical philosophy arises in response to the conflicts of reason thereby generated, and it seeks to undo the original error whereby practical reason inadvertently led theoretical reason to undermine it, thus securing for practical reason its 'rights of possession' (A776/B804). In this way metaphysics makes its contribution to 'the true and lasting welfare of the human race', just as Kant declared, many years before the *Critique* was written, it is obliged to do.

Through his practical philosophy, Kant not only deflects the Counter-Enlightenment claim that we need to turn our backs on reason in order to hold onto our faith, but also meets the challenge to the Enlightenment set by Rousseau's complaint that human civilisation and the exercise of reason bring neither happiness nor virtue. Whether reason and culture directly promote happiness is, for Kant, properly irrelevant to their estimation, since happiness, deferred to the context of the highest good, is no longer to be conceived as their immediate purpose. And with regard to virtue, Rousseau's charge is met by the identification of morality with autonomy, which guarantees that reason *per se* – pure practical reason, as opposed to whatever empirical use has contingently been made of reason – is beyond criticism, and that the individual remains capable of pursuing the task of achieving moral worth.

Kant's moral theory yields also a solution to the problem of theodicy. How this world rates on the scale of worst possible to best possible – its intrinsic badness or goodness – is, in Kant's terms, a question with no theoretically determinable answer. What reason has instead to determine is that we should become morally better and hence worthier of happiness. In the light of this task facing us, the course of human history – the outward development of humanity as such, as opposed to the inner moral development of individuals – assumes a new aspect. Whether history actually evidences progress and provides ground for optimism is again not a determinable matter of fact (in this respect Kant denies the Enlightenment its self-satisfaction). The true philosophical question is what view of history coheres regulatively with our task of practical advance – what rational hope we may entertain with respect to history. And here, Kant argues, there is room for us to envisage that the suffering and sacrifices of generations have not been in vain, because the forces of nature which shape human society (at bottom, man's mix of sociability and unsociability) are leading humanity, as it were providentially, towards the full development of its capacities and a just legal-political order.

The Critique of Judgement

The unity of practical and theoretical reason that Kant demonstrates in the second Critique, which carries all these ramifications, does not, however, bring the Critical system to a close. In the Introduction to the *Critique of Judgement* Kant acknowledges that an 'immense gulf' continues to separate freedom and nature – what lies inside and what outside man – in so far as their respective domains of legislation remain quite discrete ('just as if they were two different worlds', *CJ* 176). The unity of reason has so far been conceived in restricted terms, according to Kant, and this is unsatisfactory, given that the moral law and the laws of nature must be presented 'ultimately in one single philosophical system' (A840/B868). In order to deepen the unity of reason, Kant undertakes in the third Critique an examination of the faculty of judgement, specifically judgement in teleological and aesthetic contexts. It is the latter which is crucial for Kant's concluding the Critical enterprise. Again the form of Kant's analysis is Copernican: judgements that objects are beautiful do not attribute to them some real property, but express a pleasure induced by their purposive agreement with our cognitive powers; aesthetic experience too presupposes autonomy on the part of the subject. In a complex fashion such judgements refer, Kant argues, through their manifest-ation of an a priori purposiveness of the natural world for the subject, to a new conception of the supersensible – one that allows theoretical and practical reason, and their corresponding realms of nature and freedom, to be unified.

Beauty occupies, therefore, a supreme mediating role in the Critical system. Its privileged position is firmly conditional on its status as 'the symbol of the morally good' (*CJ* 59), and thus on moral consciousness. The sublime, also, is understood by Kant as essentially a moral experience (*CJ* 28–9). As ever, it is the moral law that provides the conduit through which value flows into the world. The Critical interpretation of aesthetic experience thus renders it congruent and essentially connected with rational consciousness – contrary to the Counter-Enlightenment and romanticism, according to which the two are at variance and aesthetic value is incomprehensible by reason. In the aesthetic context, as in all others, the Copernican revolution – first in theoretical philosophy and then in ethics, the first making the second possible – is the key to Kant's articulation and defence of the humanism of the Enlightenment.

Chapter 10

The reception and influence of the *Critique*

It would be hard to exaggerate the importance of Kant's philosophy; hardly any major philosophical movement since the end of the eighteenth century can claim to have shielded itself from his influence. Kant rewrote the history of modern philosophy in a way that made it impossible to conscientiously revert to earlier modes of philosophising. The *Critique* swiftly brought rationalism to a halt, and after Kant empiricism has displayed a nervousness regarding its foundations and been forced to assume more sophisticated forms. With the single exception of Hegel, no later philosophical system equals in stature Kant's attempt to weld together the diverse fields of natural science, morality, politics, aesthetics and religion into a systematic, overarching epistemological and metaphysical unity. Moreover, in contrast with many other great philosophical systems, Kant's is one that it has continued to seem possible, to some degree, to endorse as a whole, as opposed to an edifice that

has most to offer through being dismantled. Hence the continuing controversy concerning the exact nature of Kant's achievement.

The developments that have come out of the *Critique* reveal much about the work's content. This chapter is intended to give a sense of their richness and variety, and to trace the principal routes by which Kant's ideas have exerted their influence.

The immediate reception of the *Critique*

The reception of the *Critique* in the years immediately following its publication saw it rapidly installed at the centre of German philosophical interest, and gaining a reputation that was soon to spread abroad. The first wave of critical responses to the *Critique* highlighted the aspects of Critical philosophy that were to give Kant's readers most difficulty, and pointed in many of the directions subsequently taken in post-Kantian philosophy.

Some endorsed and undertook to propagate the Critical philosophy. Most prominent of these was K. L. Reinhold (1758–1823), whose expository *Letters on the Kantian Philosophy* aimed to provide Kant's ideas with an improved presentation. Reinhold's acceptance of Kant was not unqualified, however, and his initial popularising task – in which he had Kant's approval, and was entirely successful – was soon followed by a much more ambitious project. This was related to the fact that Kant had not developed his philosophy on the basis of any single first principle: while there is a highest principle *within* his philosophy – the transcendental unity of apperception – it is by no means a ground from which the other elements in his system can be derived. Reinhold thus decided that Critical philosophy stood in need of a firm foundation: since it was not all derived from a single idea, it did not fulfil Kant's own conditions for a science (set forth at A832–4/B860–2). Reinhold's 'philosophy of elements' aimed to supply the missing foundation, in the form of a single, apodictic, Cartesian-style first principle concerning representation in general. Reinhold's 'principle of consciousness' was intended to prove the existence of a unified faculty of representation. This was something which Kant had always denied could be known: his statement at A15/B29 that sensibility and understanding 'perhaps spring from a common, but to us unknown, root', was intended to draw a line under the topic, not encourage speculation about it. (Kant maintained a diplomatic silence on Reinhold's later efforts.) Reinhold's view that Kant's philosophy as it stood failed the test of systematicity was shortly to be taken up by other philosophers of greater stature, the absolute idealists.

Explicit, and increasingly heated, criticism of Kant came from several quarters. As said in chapter 8, the *Critique* was charged in the very first ('Göttingen') review of it that appeared (1782) with merely rehashing Berkeley's idealism. The review's authors, Christian Garve (1742–98) and J. G. H. Feder (1740–1821), were Lockeians, to whom the Critical philosophy was evidently unacceptable. Others attacked the *Critique* with a view to defending their Leibniz–Wolffian inheritance. Mendelssohn, the last systematic exponent of rationalist epistemology, defended the ontological proof against the 'all-destroying' Kant. J. A. Eberhard (1739–1809), who founded a journal devoted to attacking Kant's philosophy (and aiding recovery from the 'stupor' induced by it), claimed that Kant had made no advance on and only erroneous deviations from Leibniz. Eberhard's criticisms spurred Kant to produce a lengthy polemical response (*On A Discovery*, 1790), and this work, if the *Critique* had not already done so, sealed the fate of rationalism. In an account of German philosophy written in the first half of the nineteenth century, Heine describes the *Critique* as 'the sword that slew deism in Germany' and Kant as 'the arch-destroyer in the realm of thought'. It would be more philosophically accurate to say that deism, or the Leibniz–Wolffian system as a whole, had been divided up and transformed into a theory of reason's regulative employment, and a metaphysics of practical reason, but Heine's remark captures how Kant was commonly perceived.

Criticism of Kant came also from the very different quarters of the Counter-Enlightenment. This tendency had its roots before Kant but gathered pace alongside the Critical philosophy, which served it as a prime target. Jacobi, as has been seen (pp. 269–70), made the specific objection that things in themselves render transcendental idealism contradictory, but his more general claim was that the same moral should be drawn from an examination of Kant's philosophy as, he maintained, should be drawn from Hume's criticisms of metaphysics – namely, that our intellect is impotent in grasping reality or supporting any of our beliefs, for which feeling is required, and that religious belief consists in simple faith. Whereas conservative critics like Eberhard regarded Kant as misrepresenting the truth about reason, Jacobi paid Kant the no less unwelcome tribute of developing reason consistently but to the point of nihilism, thereby reducing to absurdity the Enlightenment claim for reason's autonomy.

Jacobi was not alone in regarding Kant as having inadvertently provided fuel for skepticism. That Critical philosophy merely enabled skepticism to assume a new and more sophisticated form, Kant's own anti-skeptical endeavours resting on merely dogmatic foundations, was argued by Kant's critic G. E. Schulze (1761–1833). Another philosopher, Solomon Maimon (*c*.1755–1800), attempted to show that – due to Kant's uncompromising heterogeneity of sensibility and understanding – all of the old problems of skepticism reproduce themselves in the context of Kant's Copernicanism: that is, even when it is granted that objects must conform to our cognition, knowledge remains unsecured. Maimon concluded that, in order to avoid skepticism, recourse must be had to epistemological materials of the very kind that Kant had sought to discredit in the rationalists. This was another important lesson soon to be taken up by the absolute idealists.

Hamann and Herder – like Jacobi, central figures in the reaction against Enlightenment – also engaged in criticism of Kant, Hamann writing a brief *Metacritique of the Purism of Reason* (1781) and Herder an extremely lengthy *Metacritique of the Critique of Pure Reason* (1799). Their 'metacritical' attack was directed at Kant's very conception of his project, rather than its specific results. Hamann claimed that the misguidedness of Kant's undertaking is demonstrated by the fact that, in order for the isolation of pure reason to be consistently carried through, reason would need to be purified of all linguistic elements, since language has necessarily a sensory aspect. However, this would of course leave nothing behind. Language is 'the only, the first and the last instrument and criterion of reason, with no other credentials but tradition and usage'. Kant's distinction of sensibility and understanding, Hamann asserted, rests on an 'arbitrary, improper and self-willed divorce of that which nature has joined together' in a primordial unity of which language is the central manifestation. Herder similarly inveighed against Kant's hypostatisation of reason, claiming that there is no such thing as 'the faculty of reason' to be made an object of investigation, in contradistinction to the whole, historically contextualised human organism. Kant's failure to grasp the methodological primacy of language, according to Hamann and Herder, leads to the word-jugglery, the 'metagrobolising' of transcendental philosophy.

Absolute idealism: Fichte, Schelling and Hegel

Many of the earliest responses to the *Critique* show Kant being misconstrued for want of a proper appreciation of the transcendental turn – justifying his claim that the work stood in danger of being misunderstood, not refuted (Bxliii). But the same cannot be said about the philosophers composing the intensely fertile period in German philosophy that followed Kant, known as the age of German idealism or post-Kantian idealism. Under this general heading, J. G. Fichte (1762–1814), F. W. J. von Schelling (1775–1854) and G. W. F. Hegel (1770–1831) belong together, as composing what is referred to as absolute idealism; Arthur Schopenhauer (1788–1860), a slightly later philosopher, defended a version of idealism closer in some respects to Kant's.

The absolute idealists grasped fully the significance of Kant's Copernicanism, but regarded Kant as having only set in motion a transformation in philosophy that remained to be completed, as if the *Critique* were only a preface to the revolution that it had announced. Their 'completion' of Kant began by overturning a sizeable number of Kant's doctrines, and resulted ultimately, in Hegel, in a philosophical standpoint at one level flatly opposed to that of Kant. The process through which this occurred fell into a number of stages, beginning with Fichte. Fichte's revisions of Critical philosophy were made in Kant's own name, under the pretext of fidelity to the 'spirit' rather than the 'letter' of Kant's philosophy, just as Reinhold had claimed to be only fulfilling the standard of systematicity that Kant had set himself. Schelling pursued the avenue of post-Kantian thought opened up by Fichte, and Hegel, whose criticism of Kant's system is the most sustained and comprehensive, represented himself as having far surpassed Kant.

The sources of absolute idealism did not lie in philosophy alone. It coincided with the flourishing of romanticism in Germany, from which it drew inspiration (Schelling and Hegel in their youth were close friends of the poet Friedrich Hölderlin, 1770–1843). Romanticism placed spiritual, quasi-religious demands on the intellect which a philosophy of finitude such as Kant's seemed to frustrate, and which absolute idealism sought to meet through a drastic revision of Kantian doctrine, Hegel indeed claiming explicitly that religion is subsumed in his own philosophy (Kant's philosophy, by contrast, he characterises as merely the Enlightenment 'reduced to method'). One particularly clear example of the felt need for a development of idealism that would restore lost unity to the human being is the great work of Kantian inspiration, *On the Aesthetic Education of Man in a Series of Letters* (1795) by Friedrich Schiller (1759–1805). Schiller did not make a definite substantial contribution to Kantian philosophy, so much as illustrate how Kant's harsh duality of nature and reason, of inclination and duty, might be wrestled with and mediated in order to yield a deeper unity, and correspondingly richer image of potential human fulfilment than Kant had allowed to be conceivable in earthly existence.

The transformation of Kantian into absolute idealism was bound up with a number of far-reaching criticisms of Kant. A recurrent theme in the writings of Fichte, Schelling and Hegel is the rejection of the thing in itself as either gratuitous or incoherent, for the sorts of reasons described in chapter 8 (pp. 280–4, 292). At the same time, Kant seemed not to have succeeded in banishing skepticism from philosophy; on the contrary, for Hegel at least, transcendental idealism's reduction of the objective world to 'man's own perspective and projection', and Kant's prohibition on determining theoretically the objective reality of our ideas of the soul and God, qualify as firmly skeptical conclusions. The main lines of absolute idealist criticism of Kant tended, however, to focus on meta-philosophical ('metacritical') issues revolving around the need for systematicity and first principles, or at any rate comprehensiveness. In the light of these desiderata, Kant's analysis of cognition immediately appeared vulnerable. Kant, so it was claimed, presents the distinction of sensibility and understanding as if it were something that is merely come across and does not require investigation, a point that Hegel put polemically by saying that Kant's method here becomes merely 'empirical'. What is wanted instead, it was claimed, is an a priori derivation of the distinction between the receptive and spontaneous faculties of the subject, and similarly for space and time and the categories. The complaint that Kant had failed to ground the faculties had a further aspect. It seemed to mean that, according to Kant, our cognitive power as a whole is nothing but a collection of disjointed faculties – a 'sack full of faculties', as Hegel put it – and thus that the unity of subjectivity reposes on sheer contingency. To the absolute idealists this seemed unacceptable: the unity of our faculties, they supposed, cannot be merely aggregative – it must itself have a rational character that can be grasped philosophically. In the same vein, it could be claimed that Kant had failed to establish the unity of theoretical and practical reason in a satisfactorily strong sense: because they had not been derived from a single source, the gulf between nature and freedom remained untraversed. And in broad terms, Kant's whole procedure of prefacing a theory of knowledge with a self-critique of reason seemed fraught with paradox: how can there be a knowing (of reason) before any knowing (of objects)? How indeed can reason engage in any activity, including critique, if it avoids all presupposition?

In this way, in response to these various (forceful though not conclusive) criticisms, it becomes possible to see how the character of Kant's idealism is open to being totally transformed. If the thing in itself is incoherent or nullifies the value of the Copernican revolution, this problem can be overcome by supposing that the 'matter' of empirical objects, the content of our representations, has its source in the subject as much as their form. That is to say, form and content merge, leaving no residue of ungrasped reality, with the result that the objects of our representations need no longer be demoted to 'mere appearance'. Kant's sharp distinctions of intuition and concept, and general and transcendental logic, are thereby undermined, and unconditional or absolute reality becomes identical with what is encompassed in thought. From which it is but a short step to saying that all knowledge must be, at root, *self*-knowledge. What may also be claimed is that intellectual intuition, far from being a mode of cognition which we do not possess, supplies the single fixed point hitherto missing from Kant's system, and the model of all genuine cognition. If Kant's brute distinction of sensibility and understanding is unacceptable, it can be remedied by supposing them to have a common source in a single, unified faculty of representation, the discovery of which restores unity to reason and subjectivity. The option then presents itself of regarding the subject, not as merely constituting the world with the aid of forms that are *given* to it, but as itself *making* the forms with which it makes the world. In addition, with the abolition of any philosophically principled limit to knowledge, all reason for denying objective validity to the speculations of pure reason vanishes, and the way is open to treating what Kant rejects as dialectic in positive terms, as more than merely regulative. Such, in very rough terms, is the shared outlook of absolute idealism which Fichte, Schelling and Hegel formulate in different ways.

Fichte agreed with Kant's results, but without accepting his derivation of them. In particular, Fichte affirmed that all objects of our knowledge are dependent on the non-empirical subject, but held that this dependence must go deeper than Kant had supposed. The self which, as Kantian apperception, merely *conditions* all objects with respect to their conceptual form, is transformed by Fichte (in his major work, the *Wissenschaftslehre*, 1794) into an absolutely unconditioned *productive* ground of all things. Thus, where Kant conceived self-consciousness merely as the capacity to refer all representations to an identical subject of which we have no determinate concept and therefore no knowledge, Fichte describes the self as 'positing' itself (as a self) and a fortiori having complete knowledge of itself. The foundation of all knowledge is an act of self-positing with which the self is identical. As pure activity, the self-positing self is also identical with its freedom. Since in this act the 'I' must be conscious of itself immediately and yet non-sensuously, self-positing is at the same time intellectual intuition of the self. Everything set over against the self, the domain of the not-I, is, according to Fichte, equally the product of an act of (self-limiting) positing on the part of the self, which it undertakes in order to provide itself with a scene of action and platform for moral self-realisation. Kant's first Critique is, as it were, absorbed into his second: nature is united with freedom by virtue of its subordination to practical reason. Subject and object are, on Fichte's account of the genesis of the self's objects, transcendentally identical, in the sense of being united in the absolute self.

It is to be noted that in Fichte idealism is founded (as it is in Schelling and Hegel) on the spontaneity rather than receptivity of the subject, and so without appeal to the Aesthetic's doctrine of sensibility. Aside from supplying idealism with its needed single first principle, Fichte regarded his idealism – by virtue of the primacy it accords to self-activity over representation – as supplying a true unity of theoretical and practical reason, and a firmer foundation than Kant had provided for freedom and everything resting on practical reason, viz. God and the moral law.

Schelling's philosophical system is rendered somewhat indistinct by his constantly changing statements of it, and the history of philosophy has tended to reduce his significance to that of a transitional figure in the development from Fichte to Hegel. Schelling's achievement in his earlier works at any rate (*Ideas for a Philosophy of Nature*, 1797, and *System of Transcendental Idealism*, 1801) was to have articulated – or at least recognised the need for – a more complex and explanatory conception of the absolute than is found in Fichte. Schelling shared Fichte's view that Kant's fruitful turn towards the subjective could be consolidated only by extending the role of the self, but sought to overcome the outstanding defect, as he saw it, of Fichte's system: its inability to account, by means of 'positing', for the external natural world. In order to 'get back to objectivity', Schelling developed first a 'philosophy of nature', which tries to show that free self-conscious subjectivity is grounded in nature, teleologically conceived, and later a 'philosophy of identity' in which subject and object figure as equally the products of self-division within a primordial, absolute unity. The subordination of objects to the subject announced in Kant's Copernican revolution is thus replaced by their joint subordination to a third term, the Absolute, in which they are united, and it becomes a matter of indifference whether we conceive the subject–object relation subjectively or objectively, derive nature from the self or the self from nature.

Just as Schelling started as a disciple of Fichte, Hegel began his philosophical career under the wing of Schelling, and in his case too the intellectual debt is massive. Hegel, however, both reconceived the absolute, and undertook to provide – what Fichte and Schelling had, by comparison, barely sketched – a systematic deduction of the objects of knowledge.

On what is the more common interpretation of Hegel's philosophy (which elicits even more controversy than that of Kant), the identity of Kant's philosophical subject is changed in a way that parallels Schelling's innovation: what Hegel calls *Geist* (Spirit), a genuinely universal, impersonal subject of thought that has priority over the plurality of personal or individual self-consciousnesses and an intimate relation with man's social existence, takes over the role of the 'I' of apperception. On a slightly different interpretation, Hegel's key innovation consists in reversing the relation between thought and subjectivity in such a way that the concepts which constitute reality are no longer representations in the subject but rather entities with a real, semi-platonic status, to which subjectivity is subordinated; human theoretical knowledge then becomes a matter of discerning (rather than, as in Kant, bringing about) the relation of concepts to objects. On the first reading, Hegel's move is to distinguish subjectivity as such from the subjectivity of individual thinkers. On the second, it is to distinguish thought as such from subjectivity *tout court*, and to replace subjectivity with conceptuality as the ground of philosophical explanation and reality itself. On both interpretations it is clear why Hegel should entitle his own idealism 'objective' and Kant's merely 'subjective', even 'psychological'.

Unlike Kant, Hegel conceives the constitution of being by thought in historical terms, as a developmental movement, identifiable as Spirit's gradual achievement of complete self-consciousness. The task of philosophy is accordingly, for Hegel, to express the system of concepts progressively realised in natural and human history, the dynamic logic of the 'self-moving Concept'. This requires an encyclopaedic review of human consciousness, inclusive of art, religion and philosophy, throughout all its phases. In so doing philosophy articulates the Absolute; the Absolute is the exhaustive, unconditioned and self-grounding system of concepts made concrete in actuality, the world of experience. What Hegel may be seen to be offering with this conception is a set of terms on which everything within the transcendental perspective – which in Kant is accorded only objectivity-relative-to-the-subject (a worthless status, in Hegel's view) – can be raised to unrelativised, absolute objectivity. Since on this account there is no longer room for so much as the thought of anything in principle unknowable lying on the far side of the subject and its representations, the thing in itself disappears for Hegel, as it does for Fichte and Schelling, and the Critical, knowledge-limiting aspect of transcendental philosophy is jettisoned. Where Hegel departs from Fichte and Schelling is in repudiating their aim to locate a single fixed point from which the philosophical system unfolds. For Hegel there is no exit from the circle of conceptualisation, and what Fichte and Schelling had tried to put at the transcendental origin of thought is relocated by Hegel at its end: the Absolute is where thought must terminate, not what it proceeds from.

In Hegel's perspective, Kant's Dialectic acquires a new significance. The conflict of reason with itself observed by Kant is held by Hegel to be nothing peculiar to the ideas treated in the Antinomy: it is a necessary feature of all thought that it generates contradictions and is driven to go beyond them. Reason's capacity to overcome its antinomies is, Hegel claims, guaranteed by its awareness of its own discord, which compels it to produce new concepts – and thereby new objects – in which former contradictions are resolved. Antinomy is thus what determines the evolution of increasingly complex and comprehensive forms of rationality. Kant's verdict in the Antinomy should therefore, in Hegel's view, be reversed: the ideas of reason must have reality, precisely because they are *reason*'s, and it is the understanding, a faculty which Kant falsely absolutised, which is defective, and whose forms must be subjected to criticism and revision. The verdict of the trial in the *Critique*, that pure reason has only subjective validity, is for Hegel invalidated by Kant's empiricist prejudice in favour of 'possible experience' as arbiter of philosophical disputes; this mere dogma is, Hegel believes, all that lies behind Kant's claims for the superiority of Critical over speculative philosophy. The speculation of pure reason is thus reinstated by Hegel.

It is evident that, by the time we reach Hegel, idealism has acquired a completely new character. Whereas philosophical reflection in Kant remains within the 'egocentric' vantage point familiar from Descartes, philosophy in Hegel appears to move onto a plane of autonomous conceptuality outside the orbit of any individual knowing subject.

In an attempt to summarise the development from Kantian to absolute idealism, one may say that it turns fundamentally on the absolute idealists' belief in the need to find a way of eliminating the ultimately perspectival character of Kant's transcendental picture. As noted in chapter 8, Kant's theoretical philosophy tells us how we must *represent* our cognitive situation, but not how things are, or how we are, outside our perspective; nor does it explain why this, rather than some other sort of perspective, should be *our* perspective. Dissatisfaction with this aspect of Kant explains why the theme of 'subject–object identity' becomes so important in absolute idealism, to the extent of coming to be regarded as the goal of philosophy as such (Hegel calls it 'the only true and philosophical' idea). Kant having taught that all knowledge and reflection is conditioned by and internal to the sphere of subject and object, which we cannot step out of, the absolute idealists sought to find a way of conceiving this sphere as more than just our perspective. The human perspective would then, they supposed, cease to be a *mere* perspective – it would become something *absolute*, the God's-eye point of view, the point of view of reality on itself, and the line separating the sphere of subject and object from what lies outside it could be rubbed out.

The notion of subject–object identity is extremely strong. It means not just that there is in all relating of subject to object something formal or structural which they share, nor just that this shared form or structure provides the ground of their connection – both of which thoughts are already in Kant – but that subject and object are *parts* of a unified *whole*, a whole which *precedes* and is *more than* the sum of its parts. If this could be demonstrated, then the subject–object relation would cease to be the medium through which we gain knowledge of objects: it would become the ground of all reality, and all cognition would become the self-knowledge of the subject–object whole.

The identity could not, however, the absolute idealists appreciated, be merely asserted, in the dogmatic fashion of previous philosophy, such as the monism of Benedict Spinoza (1632–77). It would have to be shown from the inside that the human perspective is unlimited or (in Hegel's terminology) infinite. Doing this is obviously no trivial matter. If we are to think the subject–object relation as an essential whole, then we, as subjects, need to grasp the distinction of subject and object in terms *other* than those in which it *presents* itself to us; we need to grasp it as not 'just distinct aspects of my subjective viewpoint' but rather as 'objectively posited' (Hegel). In other words, we need to be able to think the subject–object relation itself in terms which are not merely subjective. And yet we must be led to this thought – to the 'speculative' standpoint – from inside our perspective; otherwise we break the fundamental rule of transcendental philosophy. As Schelling put it: 'transcendental philosophy would be completed only if it could demonstrate this *identity* [of subject and object] – the highest solution of its whole problem – *in its own principle* (namely the self).'

Whether or not transcendental philosophy ever achieved such completion in the terms that Fichte, Schelling and Hegel set themselves, the standard Kantian criticism of absolute idealism is, perhaps not surprisingly, that it amounts to a reversion to pre-Critical, dogmatic metaphysics. In the earliest years of absolute idealism – in 1799 – Kant himself publicly disavowed Fichte's 'totally indefensible' system as having no relation to Critical thought, castigating him for attempting to 'cull' a real object out of mere logic (Open Letter on Fichte's *Wissenschaftslehre*, 7 August 1799).

This estimate is, however, certainly unjustified. Whilst it would be an exaggeration to say that there is a logically necessary line of development running from Kant to the later idealist systems (a picture tendentiously fostered by Fichte, Schelling and Hegel in succession), there is a relatively perspicuous philosophical route leading from the one to the other, as has been indicated. Absolute idealism is no simple regression to pre-Kantian philosophy: even though it denies that the objects of our knowledge are mere appearances, and so holds them to be things as they really are, it does not revert to a pre-Critical transcendental realism; when it lifts the restrictions on knowledge imposed by Critical philosophy, it takes Kant's teachings into account. It seeks to employ the transcendental perspective to render the very idea of a constitution independent of subjectivity and thought nonsensical, and thereby transcend the distinction of appearances and things in themselves – it, as it were, attempts to bring transcendental idealism full circle into identity with transcendental realism. Of course, in Kant's terms, this is impossible, because he regards transcendental idealism and transcendental realism as contradictories which exhaust the field; but the absolute idealists took themselves to have attained a higher level of philosophical reflection than Kant's, from which his opposition of transcendental idealism and transcendental realism could be regarded as merely provisional and not exhaustive.

Nor was absolute idealism without any foundation in Kant's own writings. Kant had described the *Critique* as only a 'propaedeutic' to the system of pure reason (A11/B25), and though the import of this lone remark was unclear (Kant later withdrew it), he had also talked in the *Critique of Practical Reason* of 'the expectation of perhaps being able some day to attain insight into the unity of the whole pure rational faculty (theoretical as well as practical) and to derive everything from one principle', as nothing less than an 'undeniable need of human reason' (91). The absolute idealists interpreted this as a necessary condition for the success of transcendental philosophy, rather than (as Kant probably intended it) a mere regulative ideal for philosophical enquiry. Further, it could be pointed out that Critical philosophy had developed in Kant's own hands in the direction of greater systematicity and a correspondingly deeper unity of reason. The third Critique, which the absolute idealists regarded as at least as important as the others, was read by them as relaxing the anti-speculative stance taken in the first. And, though they did not know it, the absolute idealists' view of the proper trajectory of transcendental philosophy is supported by the unpublished writings of Kant's final years, the fragmentary notes and jottings subsequently collected as his *Opus Postumum*. These strongly suggest a philosophical transition in the making. They show Kant at least experimenting with a revision of transcendental idealism in which the self would posit itself, theoretical reason would share the autonomy of practical reason, and the thing in itself would become a mere correlate of the subject's self-positing, a 'cipher' rather than an existing being.

The facts of Kant's own development aside, absolute idealism may be defended as striving to elucidate what remained insufficiently clarified in Kant's philosophy. Specifically, Kant leaves unanswered questions concerning the nature of transcendental subjectivity (How is it possible for the 'I' to accompany all of my representations? What is the 'I'? What does its spontaneity consist in?); the status of transcendental 'brute facts' such as the dualism of sensibility and understanding, and the forms of our sensibility (Why is our intellect discursive? Why is our intuition sensible? Why does our intuition assume the forms of space and time?); and the very possibility of transcendental philosophy (How is it possible for the subject to achieve knowledge of its transcendental operations, of the conditions of experience and limits of knowledge?). To the extent that their systems provided answers to these questions, the absolute idealists may be held to have shown that there are alternative ways of thinking out the Copernican project to Kant's. And if the unclarities in Kant's position actually amount to tensions or contradictions which cannot be resolved in his terms – as the absolute idealists believed – then their unravelling of the threads delicately woven together in Critical philosophy is justified, and the door is open to claiming absolute idealism as the only consistent form of Copernicanism, the necessary result of following through Kant's insights. It is thus pre-eminently to absolute idealism that it is appropriate to look in the history of philosophy for a critical perspective on Kant, and the justice of its development is a question of the highest importance for any with an interest in Kant's philosophy.

Schopenhauer

Also highly significant from this point of view, but set apart from the current of idealism just described (which he reviled), is the philosophy of Schopenhauer, as set forth in his *The World as Will and Representation* (1818, 2nd edn 1844). Schopenhauer regarded himself as having delivered the truth in Kant's teachings from the mists of absolute idealism. Despite many deep differences – Schopenhauer refuses any distinction of objects from representations, gives his idealism a physiological twist and employs the principle of sufficient reason in place of transcendental proof – Schopenhauer does remain in one fundamental respect true to Kant: the empirical world, what he calls the 'world as representation', has for him too non-ultimate reality. Where Schopenhauer departs most dramatically from Kant is in his claim to have discovered, by means of 'a way *from within*' overlooked by Kant, the nature of the thing in itself: our immediate, non-representational awareness of ourselves as striving bodily agents must, Schopenhauer claims, be deemed awareness (albeit inadequate) of our selves as things in themselves. The identity of will and thing in itself in our own case can be generalised, Schopenhauer holds, to all of nature, and since, he further argues, individuation pertains only to the domain of representation, it follows that reality consists in a single undifferentiated Will, of which empirical reality is the appearance.

There is therefore in Schopenhauer a double metaphysic: an idealism regarding the world as representation is laid alongside a realism regarding the world as will, preserving Kant's bifurcation of appearances and things in themselves. Schopenhauer's world-will may recall the absolute of Fichte, Schelling and Hegel, but there is at least one profound difference between the two monistic conceptions: Schopenhauer's view of will as intrinsically blind directly contradicts the absolute idealist view of reality as inherently rational and purposive.

Kant and twentieth-century philosophy

In the latter half of the nineteenth century, Kant's ideas underwent a large-scale revival in Germany. The general tendency of this movement, known as neo-Kantianism, was to emphasise the epistemological dimension of Kant's philosophy, its significance for empirical science. After the First World War neo-Kantianism found itself rivalled and displaced in Germany by phenomenology, one of the most original and influential philosophical developments of the twentieth century.

Phenomenology may be regarded as having returned to the idealist aspect of Kant's philosophy and carried forward the thinking of the nineteenth-century post-Kantian idealists. Its founder, Edmund Husserl (1859–1938), stressed the source of phenomenology in Descartes, but his mature 'transcendental phenomenology' owes far more to Kant, and Husserl affirmed its inseparability from transcendental idealism. Using the concept of intentionality, taken from Franz Brentano (1838–1917), Husserl recast Kant's conception of transcendental subjectivity. The subject of apperception is reconstrued by Husserl as a transcendental constituting *consciousness*, and Kant's problem of the possibility of objects becomes accordingly the 'problem of transcendence', of explicating the relation of consciousness to the objects that are transcendent of it. The natural world is regarded by Husserl as a realm of objects existing as the correlates of acts of consciousness, in a manner extremely similar to Kant's account of the empirical world as a realm of appearance.

The Kantian character of phenomenology after Husserl is obscured by the fact that its main practitioners – Martin Heidegger (1889–1976), Jean-Paul Sartre (1905–80) and Maurice Merleau-Ponty (1907–61) – were either indifferent or hostile to the task of providing a rational ground for knowledge claims. This of course marks a deep departure from Kant, but in another respect post-Husserlian, 'existential' phenomenology is the result of a thoroughly Copernican endeavour to distance philosophy (further than Husserl had done) from the outlook and preoccupations of traditional epistemology. This is a central element in Heidegger's attempt, in *Being and Time* (1927), to approach ontology on the basis of an interpretation of the fundamental structures of human being or 'Dasein'. Heidegger carries the Copernican revolution beyond cognition, as Kant understands it, by tracing the subject into the realm of everyday practical existence. In his controversial book, *Kant and the Problem of Metaphysics* (1929), Heidegger aligns Kant's investigation into the possibility of metaphysics and the a priori with his own conception of ontological enquiry. Sartre, emphasising by contrast Kant's opposition of freedom and nature, constructs in *Being and Nothingness* (1943) a conception of the world premised on the reality of human freedom, an undertaking which derives straightforwardly from Kant's practical philosophy. The mode of being of human subjects, what Sartre calls the For-Itself, is accordingly ascribed the key properties of a noumenal agent, and the position on value that Sartre comes to partially recapitulates Kant's. In Merleau-Ponty's *Phenomenology of Perception* (1945), Kant figures explicitly as a proponent of the 'objective thought' that Merleau-Ponty criticises. None the less, the movement towards 'pre-objective being' which Merleau-Ponty advocates in place of objective thought – an attempt to disclose a realm of world-constituting conditions centred on the perceiving body – is clearly transcendental in character. In these respects, because of its sustained commitment to the perspectival character of all knowledge, a non-naturalistic and non-substantial conception of the subject, and its programme of tracing objectivity to its sources in subjectivity, phenomenology remains true to the spirit of Kant, and directs his idealism in the opposite direction from the absolute idealists.

Kant's influence, mediated by that of Hegel and Marx, is manifest in the Critical Theory of the Frankfurt School which flourished in Germany in the interwar years and subsequently in the United States. In this tradition of social and political thought, Jürgen Habermas stands out as closely aligned with Kant by virtue of his defence of the legacy of the Enlightenment, in opposition to the presently well-consolidated post-modern movement in philosophy. Habermas upholds a universal, formal conception of rationality, founded not on Kant's subject of apperception but on intersubjectivity. Communication, Habermas maintains, presupposes certain specific norms which have transcendental status, constitute the rationality of discourse and social interaction and provide the basis for morality and critique of existing social practices. These norms, the object of 'transcendental pragmatics', are, Habermas claims, independent of any metaphysical grounds.

Kant's philosophy has not similarly inspired any major philosophical developments in the English-speaking world. This goes back to its initial reception in Britain. Introducing Kantian ideas to England was largely the work of S. T. Coleridge (1772–1834), who saw in it, among other things, a means of combating the reductionist associationist psychology of the time. The fiercely romantic application that Coleridge made of transcendental philosophy would, however, doubtless have been rejected by Kant himself as a recrudescence of the mystico-obscurantism to which the *Critique* had been meant as an antidote. The effect of the romantic advocacy of Kant was to make it all the easier for J. S. Mill's (1806–73) empiricism to ignore Kant and predominate in England in the nineteenth century, championing the intellectual forces which Coleridge deplored. Only in the latter half of the century did Kant's ideas take hold, through the Hegelian school of the British Idealists, especially T. H. Green (1836–82), and even then only under the shadow of Hegel's critique of Kant.

The rapid rise of analytic philosophy in Britain after the turn of the century brought this brief period of Kantian prestige to an end. Analytic philosophy arose in conscious reaction to British Idealism, in opposition to which its founding fathers, G. E. Moore (1873–1958) and Bertrand Russell (1872–1970), laid down a number of fundamental, anti-Copernican tenets. These included the concept of direct epistemic relations, unmediated by any Kantian transcendental conditions, and a sharp distinction between acts of judgement, conceived as subjective psychological events, and objects of judgement, inclusive of propositions, conceived as independently existing abstract entities – in opposition to Kant's unitary conception of judgement, which from the Moore–Russell standpoint appears psychologistic and confused. The proper method of philosophy was defined by a commitment to analytical investigation of the formal structure of sentences, informed by mathematical logic. In this picture no room is left for synthetic apriority. (Logical positivism, the next major development in analytic philosophy, reaffirmed and made much of the pre-Critical bifurcation of knowledge.) Roughly the same set of views prevails in the third great contributor to the analytic approach, Gottlob Frege (1848–1925), despite a more sympathetic attitude to Kant, whose apriorism and anti-naturalism he shared. Thus in Moore, Russell and Frege, philosophy is wedded to a conception of philosophical logic as more fundamental than epistemology, and to a semantic approach which makes meaning the central concept of philosophy, and its analysis the central mode of solution to philosophical problems. The antipathetic view of Kant which this implies is reflected in the analytic interpretation of Kant.

Ludwig Wittgenstein (1889–1951) is usually numbered among the founders of analytic philosophy, but the case of his relation to Kant is more complex. The strand in Wittgenstein that analytic philosophy has tended to concentrate on is his case for the priority and publicity of linguistic meaning, to which extent Wittgenstein's outlook is opposed to the broadly Cartesian approach of Kant. Wittgenstein's private language argument is generally counted as a transcendental argument, but only in the analytic sense. But there is also in Wittgenstein, both early and late, a strong Kantian element. This came less from Kant himself than from Schopenhauer, in whose thought Wittgenstein allowed himself to become immersed. Wittgenstein's *Tractatus* (1921), in describing the logical structure of any possible language, retreads the path of laying out the transcendental conditions of thought, and makes of language itself something transcendental. Although in Wittgenstein's later philosophy (in the posthumously published *Blue and Brown Books*, 1958, and *Philosophical Investigations*, 1953), language is brought down to earth and embedded in ordinary human activity, a kind of transcendental idealism persists: Wittgenstein's 'we' – that in which Wittgenstein's forms of life and language games inhere – functions as the collective analogue of Kant's transcendental subject.

In view of their deep methodological and metaphysical differences, it is somewhat surprising that the writings of contemporary analytic philosophers should none the less be thick with approving references to Kant. This is due in part to their no longer accepting in full the doctrines that founded analytic philosophy (although, it should be added, the strong naturalist programme initiated in the States by W. V. Quine has more recently given analytic philosophy quite different reasons for rejecting Kant). It also owes a great deal to Strawson's appropriation of Kant in the name of 'descriptive' (as opposed to 'revisionary') metaphysics – metaphysics that merely describes our existing conceptual scheme – which has led to a school of philosophy based in Oxford that continues to thrive, interesting itself in transcendental arguments and applying Kantian ideas to the philosophy of mind. Something analogous to Strawson's Kantianism in theoretical philosophy appears in practical philosophy with John Rawls' Kantian liberalism, arguably the most important development in political philosophy in the second half of this century. Kant's influence also manifests itself – often here joining forces with Wittgenstein or traditional pragmatism, which had itself taken some lessons from Kant's Analytic – in the various forms of 'anti-realism' or 'internal realism' currently explored in analytic philosophy. In the work of Michael Dummett, Donald Davidson, Hilary Putnam and Crispin Wright, attempts are made to define a notion of rational belief supplanting traditional realist conceptions of truth, and a conception of objectivity which is free of commitment to transcendental realism and at the same time avoids the familiar pitfalls of verificationism, logical positivism and other descendants of classical empiricism.

In conclusion, it may be noted that there is, alongside the continuity of Kant's influence, one striking and very deep discontinuity in the reception of his ideas. For absolute idealism, making sense of Kant meant pushing his idealism further, a task which his doctrines of the subjectivity of space and time and the existence of things in themselves were judged to impede. In contemporary analytic philosophy, and many other subsequent appropriations of Kant, the very same key doctrines are objected to and subjected to reconstruction, but for exactly the opposite reason, namely that they are considered metaphysically extravagant. This swing from regarding transcendental idealism as insufficiently idealistic to excessively so exemplifies, in Kant's terms, the difficulty of bringing human reason to rest, and reminds us that the aim of the *Critique* was to discover a point of equilibrium for reason by determining once and for all the possibility of metaphysics.

Whether or not Kant achieves that goal, it is possible to claim on his behalf that transcendental idealism remains distinguished by its unique capacity to harmonise the scientific image of the world with our pre-scientific conception of ourselves, and, more broadly, that the Critical system effects the most comprehensive reconciliation of the different strands within Enlightenment, which continues to define our intellectual horizon, that we possess.

Bibliography

For detailed commentary on the text of the *Critique*, see N. Kemp Smith, *A Commentary to Kant's 'Critique of Pure Reason'*, 2nd edn (London: Macmillan, 1930), and H. J. Paton, *Kant's Metaphysics of Experience: A Commentary on the First Half of the 'Kritik der reinen Vernunft'* (London: Allen & Unwin, 1936), 2 vols (Paton extends only to the end of the Analytic). Kemp Smith's interpretation and Paton's endorsement of Kant have both been much criticised, but they are classics of Kant commentary which contain much insight and are enormously helpful in opening up the text.

The quotation on page vi from Gottfried Martin is from *Kant's Metaphysics and Theory of Science*, trans. P. Lucas (Manchester: Manchester University Press, 1955), p. 181. The quotation on that page from F. W. J. von Schelling is from *System of Transcendental Idealism (1800)*, trans. P. Heath (Charlottesville: University of Virginia Press, 1993), p. 168.

1 The problem of metaphysics

A detailed account of the German philosophical background up to and including Kant is contained in L. W. Beck, *Early German Philosophy* (Bristol: Thoemmes Press, 1996), pt III. On the Counter-Enlightenment, see I. Berlin, 'The Counter-Enlightenment', in *Against the Current: Essays in the History of Ideas* (London: Hogarth, 1979). Kant's essay 'An answer to the question: What is Enlightenment?' (1784), is found in his *Practical Philosophy*, trans. and ed. M. Gregor (Cambridge: Cambridge University Press, 1996).

E. Cassirer, *Kant's Life and Thought* (New Haven: Yale University Press, 1981), is an integrated biography of Kant and account of his philosophical development. Kant's pre-Critical writings on metaphysical subjects are collected in Immanuel Kant, *Theoretical Philosophy, 1755–1770*, trans. D. Walford (with R. Meerbote) (Cambridge: Cambridge University Press, 1992). For an account of Kant's pre-Critical period, see F. Beiser, 'Kant's intellectual development: 1746–1781' (concentrating on metaphysics and method), in P. Guyer ed., *The Cambridge Companion to Kant* (Cambridge: Cambridge University Press, 1992), and M. Friedman, *Kant and the Exact Sciences* (Cambridge, Mass.: Harvard University Press, 1992), Introduction (concentrating on the theme of Leibnizian metaphysics versus Newtonian science).

The Leibniz–Clarke correspondence referred to on page 5, is found in G. W. Leibniz, *Philosophical Papers and Letters*, ed. L. Loemaker (Dordrecht: Reidel, 1979), pp. 675–721. The quotation from David Hume on page 6, is from *An Enquiry Concerning Human Understanding* (1748), sect. XII, pt III; p. 165 of the 3rd edn by P. H. Nidditch (Oxford: Oxford University Press, 1975). The quotation from Kant on page 10 is taken from Ernst Cassirer, *Kant's Life and Thought*, trans. J. Haden (New Haven: Yale University Press, 1981), p. 18. The work by Alexander Baumgarten referred to on page 10 is *Metaphysica* (Halle, 1739). The work of G. W. Leibniz referred to on page 11 is *New Essays on Human Understanding* (1705), trans. Peter Remnant and Jonathan Bennett (Cambridge: Cambridge University Press, 1981). The works of Kant referred to on page 12 are *Metaphysical Foundations of Natural Science* (1786), in Kant, *Philosophy of*

Material Nature, trans. James Ellington (Indianapolis: Hackett, 1985), *Religion Within the Boundaries of Mere Reason* (1793), in Kant, *Religion and Rational Theology*, trans. and ed. Allen Wood and George di Giovanni (Cambridge: Cambridge University Press, 1996), and *Toward Perpetual Peace* (1795) and *The Metaphysics of Morals* (1797), in Kant, *Practical Philosophy*, trans. and ed. M. Gregor (Cambridge: Cambridge University Press, 1996). The quotation on page 13 is from J. G. Herder, *Briefe zu Beförderung der Humanität, Sämmtliche Werke*, ed. Bernhard Suphan (Berlin: Weidmannsche Buchandlung, 1881), vol. 17, p. 404. The quotation from David Hume on page 22 is from *A Treatise of Human Nature* (1739–40), bk I, pt IV, sect. VII; pp. 268–9 of the edition by L. A. Selby-Bigge (Oxford: Clarendon, 1975).

2 The possibility of objects

P. F. Strawson's analytic interpretation of Kant is explained more fully in *The Bounds of Sense: An Essay on Kant's 'Critique of Pure Reason'* (London: Methuen, 1966), ch. 1. What I have called the idealist position is more loosely defined, and meant to cover a family of different views of Kant. One particularly well-developed version is set out in H. Allison, *Kant's Transcendental Idealism: An Interpretation and Defense* (New Haven: Yale University Press, 1983), chs 1–2. Other attempts to say what Kant's Copernicanism consists in are R. Pippin, *Kant's Theory of Form: An Essay on the 'Critique of Pure Reason'* (New Haven: Yale University Press, 1982), ch. 1, R. Aquila, *Representational Mind: A Study of Kant's Theory of Knowledge* (Bloomington: Indiana University Press, 1983), ch. 1, and E. Bencivenga, 'Knowledge as a relation and knowledge as an experience in the *Critique of Pure Reason*', in R. Chadwick ed., *Immanuel Kant: Critical Assessments* (London: Routledge, 1992), vol. 2.

The quotation from P. F. Strawson on page 31 is from *The Bounds of Sense: An Essay on Kant's Critique of Pure Reason'* (London: Methuen, 1966), p. 15. The quotation from Dieter Henrich on pages 31–2 is from *Aesthetic Judgement and the Moral Image of the World* (Stanford, Calif.: Stanford University Press, 1992), pp. 3–4. The work by John Locke referred to on page 45 is *An Essay Concerning Human Understanding*, ed. Peter H. Nidditch (Oxford: Clarendon, 1975).

3 How are synthetic a priori judgements possible? (The Introduction)

Criticism of Kant may be found in J. Bennett, *Kant's Analytic* (Cambridge: Cambridge University Press, 1966), §§2–4, and R. Robinson, 'Necessary propositions', in T. Penelhum and J. J. MacIntosh eds, *The First Critique: Reflections on Kant's 'Critique of Pure Reason'* (Belmont, Calif.: Wadsworth, 1969). In Kant's defence, see H. Allison, *Kant's Transcendental Idealism: An Interpretation and Defense* (New Haven: Yale University Press, 1983), pp. 73–80, L. W. Beck, 'Can Kant's synthetic judgements be made analytic?', in R. P. Wolff ed., *Kant: A Collection of Critical Essays* (New York: Anchor, 1967), and A. Melnick, *Kant's Analogies of Experience* (Chicago: University of Chicago Press, 1973), Appendix, 'Syntheticity'. Kant defends at length the analytic/synthetic distinction and his conception of synthetic apriority against a rationalist critic in his essay 'On a Discovery According to Which Any New Critique of Pure Reason Has Been Made Superfluous by an Earlier One', Section Two, 226–51, in H. Allison ed., *The Kant–Eberhard Controversy* (Baltimore: Johns Hopkins University Press, 1973), pp. 139–60; Allison analyses the issue, ibid., pp. 46–75.

The quotation from David Hume on page 52 is from *An Enquiry Concerning Human Understanding* (1748), sect. IV, pt I; p. 25 of the 3rd edn by P. H. Nidditch (Oxford: Oxford University Press, 1975).

4 The sensible conditions of objects (The Aesthetic)

On Kant's analysis of cognition, see H. Allison, *Kant's Transcendental Idealism: An Interpretation and Defense* (New Haven: Yale University Press, 1983), pp. 65–8, or at greater length, 'The originality of Kant's distinction between analytic and synthetic judgements', in R. Chadwick ed., *Immanuel Kant: Critical Assessments* (London: Routledge, 1992), vol. 2, pp. 325–37. The relation of Kant's theory of knowledge to rationalism and empiricism is well explained in L. W. Beck, 'Kant's strategy', in T. Penelhum and J. J. MacIntosh eds, *The First Critique: Reflections on Kant's 'Critique of Pure Reason'* (Belmont, Calif.: Wadsworth, 1969). Kant's arguments for the apriority and intuitivity of space and time are analysed in H. Allison, *Kant's Transcendental Idealism*, pp. 82–94, D. P. Dryer, *Kant's Solution for Verification in Metaphysics* (London: Allen & Unwin, 1966), pp. 169–78, R.-P. Horstmann, 'Space as intuition and geometry', *Ratio* 18, 1976, 17–30, and A. Melnick, *Kant's Analogies of Experience* (Chicago: University of Chicago Press, 1973), pp. 7–30.

5 Transcendental idealism

Kant's case for the transcendental ideality of space and time is criticised in P. F. Strawson, *The Bounds of Sense: An Essay on Kant's 'Critique of Pure Reason'* (London: Methuen, 1966), pp. 51–62, 68–71 and P. Guyer, *Kant and the Claims of Knowledge* (Cambridge: Cambridge University Press, 1987), ch. 16. For a defence, see H. Allison, *Kant's Transcendental Idealism: An Interpretation and Defense* (New Haven: Yale University Press, 1983), pp. 98–114. On the proof in the Antinomy, see below under chapter 7.

The quotation from Adolf Trendelenburg on page 107 (from his *Logische Untersuchungen*, 1862, p. 163) is taken from M. J. Scott-Taggart, 'Recent work on the philosophy of Kant', in *American Philosophical Quarterly* 3, 1966, 171–209 (p. 184).

6 The conceptual conditions of objects (The Analytic)

Giving an overview of the Analytic, see A. Melnick, *Kant's Analogies of Experience* (Chicago: University of Chicago Press, 1973), pp. 30–57.

Locating faults in the metaphysical deduction, see J. Bennett, *Kant's Analytic* (Cambridge: Cambridge University Press, 1966), ch. 6, and P. F. Strawson, *The Bounds of Sense: An Essay on Kant's 'Critique of Pure Reason'* (London: Methuen, 1966), pp. 74–82. See also G. Bird, *Kant's Theory of Knowledge* (London: Routledge & Kegan Paul, 1962), ch. 7, and H. Allison, *Kant's Transcendental Idealism: An Interpretation and Defense* (New Haven: Yale University Press, 1983), ch. 6.

The literature on the Transcendental Deduction is extensive. Strawson's interpretation (*The Bounds of Sense*, pp. 89–117) is referred to in much of it, as is that of Bennett (*Kant's Analytic*, chs 8–9). Of particular importance are D. Henrich, 'Identity and objectivity: an inquiry into Kant's Transcendental Deduction', trans. J. Edwards, in *The Unity of Reason: Essays on Kant's Philosophy* (Cambridge, Mass.: Harvard University Press, 1994), a detailed reconstruction of the argument, and 'The identity of the subject in the Transcendental Deduction', in E. Schaper and W. Vossenkuhl eds, *Reading Kant: New Perspectives on Transcendental Arguments and Critical Philosophy* (Oxford: Blackwell, 1989), concentrating on apperception. Also by Henrich, see 'The proof-structure of Kant's Transcendental Deduction', in R. Walker ed., *Kant on Pure Reason* (Oxford: Oxford University Press, 1982), on exegetical issues, and 'Kant's notion of a deduction and the methodological background of the first *Critique*', in E. Förster ed., *Kant's Transcendental Deductions: The Three 'Critiques' and the 'Opus Postumum'* (Stanford, Calif.: Stanford University Press, 1989), on the Deduction's methodology. See also H. Allison, *Kant's Transcendental Idealism*, ch. 7, R. Pippin, *Kant's Theory of Form: An Essay on the 'Critique of Pure Reason'* (New Haven: Yale University Press, 1982), ch. 6, and P. Guyer, *Kant and the Claims of Knowledge* (Cambridge: Cambridge University Press, 1987), pt II. The regressive interpretation of the Deduction is expounded in K. Ameriks, 'Kant's Transcendental Deduction as a regressive argument', *Kant-Studien* 69, 1978, 273–87, and R. Walker, *Kant* (London: Routledge & Kegan Paul, 1978), ch. 6. On the transcendental object, see H. Allison, 'Kant's concept of the transcendental object', *Kant-Studien* 59, 1968, 165–86.

For a clear exposition of the Schematism, see H. J. Paton, *Kant's Metaphysics of Experience: A Commentary on the First Half of the 'Kritik der reinen Vernunft'* (London: Allen & Unwin, 1936), vol. 2, bk VII. Pursuing the issues it raises, see H. Allison, *Kant's Transcendental Idealism*, ch. 8, R. Pippin, *Kant's Theory of Form*, ch. 5, and P. Guyer, *Kant and the Claims of Knowledge*, ch. 6. Guyer reads the Schematism as recommencing the argument of the Analytic. Heidegger's interpretation of the Schematism, in *Kant and the Problem of Metaphysics* (1929), trans. R. Taft, 4th edn (Bloomington: Indiana University Press, 1990), §§19–23, is intriguing and contentious.

For detailed studies of the Analogies, see A. Melnick, *Kant's Analogies of Experience*, chs 2–3, and P. Guyer, *Kant and the Claims of Knowledge*, chs 8–11. See also P. F. Strawson, *The Bounds of Sense*, pp. 118–52, R. Walker, *Kant*, pp. 98–105, H. Allison, *Kant's Transcendental Idealism*, chs 9–10, and G. Buchdahl, *Kant and the Dynamics of Reason: Essays on the Structure of Kant's Philosophy* (Oxford: Blackwell, 1992), ch. 9. Strawson and Walker argue that Kant inflates his legitimate conclusions; Melnick and Allison pay close attention to the theme of transcendental time-determination. Buchdahl argues against the supposition that the second analogy is concerned with knowledge of causal laws. There are helpful remarks on the System of Principles as a whole, including the Axioms, Anticipations and Postulates, in E. Cassirer, *Kant's Life and Thought* (New Haven: Yale University Press, 1981), pp. 174–93.

The view that the Refutation of Idealism proves knowledge of things in themselves may be found in H. A. Prichard, *Kant's Theory of Knowledge* (Oxford: Clarendon, 1909), pp. 319–24. On the Refutation, see H. Allison, *Kant's Transcendental Idealism*, ch. 14, M. Baum, 'The B-Deduction and the Refutation of Idealism', *Southern Journal of Philosophy* 25 (Supplement), 1986, 92–9, and M. Gram, 'What Kant really did to idealism', in J. N. Mohanty and R. Shahan eds, *Essays on Kant's 'Critique of Pure Reason'* (Norman: University of Oklahoma Press, 1982). P. Guyer, *Kant and the Claims of Knowledge*, pt IV, argues that the Refutation is independent of transcendental idealism.

For consideration of Kant's reply to the skeptic in broader terms, and of Kant's transcendental method in relation to modern transcendental arguments, see B. Stroud, *The Significance of Philosophical Skepticism* (Oxford: Clarendon, 1984), ch. 4, and 'Transcendental arguments', in R. Walker ed., *Kant on Pure Reason*. A. C. Genova, 'Kant's notion of transcendental presupposition in the first *Critique*', in R. Chadwick ed., *Immanuel Kant: Critical Assessments* (London: Routledge, 1992), vol. 2, is a penetrating analysis of Kant's method of transcendental proof.

The quotation from G. W. F. Hegel on page 133 is from *(Encyclopaedia) Logic* (1817), trans. W. Wallace (Oxford: Clarendon, 1975), §42.

7 Unknowable objects (The Dialectic)

Criticising Kant's theory of reason and the associated architectonic of the Dialectic, see J. Bennett, *Kant's Dialectic* (Cambridge: Cambridge University Press, 1974), ch. 12. On the regulative role of reason in science, see G. Buchdahl, *Kant and the Dynamics of Reason*, chs 7–8, and S. Neiman, *The Unity of Reason: Rereading Kant* (Oxford: Oxford University Press, 1994), ch. 2.

The Paralogisms chapter is discussed in H. Allison, *Kant's Transcendental Idealism: An Interpretation and Defense* (New Haven: Yale University Press, 1983), pp. 278–87. Two detailed studies are K. Ameriks, *Kant's Theory of Mind: An Analysis of the Paralogisms of Pure Reason* (Oxford: Clarendon, 1982), especially chs 1–2 and 4, and C. Thomas Powell, *Kant's Theory of Self-Consciousness* (Oxford: Clarendon, 1990), chs 2–4. Ameriks argues that Kant's own position on the self remains heavily rationalist; Powell clarifies Kant's arguments and doctrines, and defends their consistency.

S. Al-Azm, *The Origins of Kant's Arguments in the Antinomies* (Oxford: Clarendon, 1972), contains helpful historical clarification of the Antinomy. On the weaknesses of Kant's proofs in the first and second antinomies, see N. Kemp Smith, *A Commentary to Kant's 'Critique of Pure Reason'* 2nd edn, (London: Macmillan, 1930), pp. 483–92, and J. Bennett, *Kant's Dialectic*, chs 7–9. Kant's handling of their relation to transcendental idealism, more specifically, is criticised in P. Guyer, *Kant and the Claims of Knowledge* (Cambridge: Cambridge University Press, 1987), ch. 18, and P. F. Strawson, *The Bounds of Sense: An Essay on Kant's 'Critique of Pure Reason'* (London: Methuen, 1966), pt III, ch. 3. Also of interest is Hegel's very different criticism of the Antinomy, in *(Encyclopaedia) Logic* (1817), trans. W. Wallace (Oxford: Clarendon, 1975), §48. Taking more favourable views of the Antinomy's attempted proof of transcendental idealism, see H. Allison, *Kant's Transcendental Idealism*, ch. 3, E. Bencivenga, *Kant's Copernican Revolution* (Oxford: Oxford University Press, 1987), ch. 6, and C. Posy, 'Dancing to the Antinomy: a proposal for transcendental idealism', *American Philosophical Quarterly* 20, 1983, 81–94.

Difficulties in Kant's treatment of theology are identified in J. Bennett, *Kant's Dialectic*, ch. 11. A. Plantinga, 'Kant's objection to the ontological argument', *Journal of Philosophy* 63, 1966, 537–46, illustrates how Kant's verdict on the ontological argument may be resisted. Defending some important elements in Kant's case, see W. Baumer, 'Kant on cosmological arguments', in L. W. Beck ed., *Kant Studies Today* (La Salle, Ill: Open Court, 1969). A. Wood, *Kant's Rational Theology* (Ithaca: Cornell University Press, 1978), is an excellent study of the topic as a whole.

S. Körner, 'Kant's conception of freedom', *Proceedings of the British Academy* 53, 1967, 193–217, exposits Kant's theory of freedom and proposes a way of avoiding its noumenal commitments. Indicating some of the theory's difficulties and ambiguities, see J. Bennett, *Kant's Dialectic*, ch. 10. Two impressive interpretations of Kant's account of freedom, defending its coherence, are A. Wood, 'Kant's compatibilism', in A. Wood ed., *Self and Nature in Kant's Philosophy* (Ithaca: Cornell University Press, 1984), and H. Allison, *Kant's Transcendental Idealism*, ch. 15, and *Kant's Theory of Freedom* (Cambridge: Cambridge University Press, 1990), pt I.

8 The meaning of transcendental idealism

Jacobi's essay 'On transcendental idealism' is found in F. H. Jacobi, *The Main Philosophical Writings and the Novel,* Allwill, trans. G. di Giovanni (Montreal and Kingston: McGill–Queen's University Press, 1994), pp. 331–8. The 'Feder-Garve' or 'Göttingen' review (1782) is translated in R. Walker ed., *The Real in the Ideal: Berkeley's Relation to Kant* (New York: Garland, 1989), pp. xv–xxiv. The 'standard picture' of Kant as a Berkeleyan and phenomenalist, with all its imputation of confusion, is set out in H. A. Prichard, *Kant's Theory of Knowledge* (Oxford: Clarendon, 1909), ch. 4; the view is restated in P. F. Strawson, *The Bounds of Sense: An Essay on Kant's 'Critique of Pure Reason'* (London: Methuen, 1966), pt IV. Opposing it, see G. Bird, *Kant's Theory of Knowledge* (London: Routledge & Kegan Paul, 1962), ch. 1, and H. Allison, *Kant's Transcendental Idealism: An Interpretation and Defense* (New Haven: Yale University Press, 1983), chs 1–2. Further key differences with Berkeley are pinpointed in R. Walker, 'Idealism: Kant and Berkeley', and other papers in R. Walker ed., *The Real in the Ideal.*

The incoherence of the thing in itself is argued in G. Schrader, 'The thing in itself in Kantian philosophy', in R. P. Wolff ed., *Kant: A Collection of Critical Essays* (New York: Anchor, 1967), and P. F. Strawson, *The Bounds of Sense*, pt IV. The issue of the meaning of the categories is dealt with by J. P. Nolan in 'Kant on meaning', *Kant-Studien* 70, 1979, 113–21. The negative interpretation of transcendental idealism is found in H. E. Matthews, 'Strawson on transcendental idealism', in R. Walker ed., *Kant on Pure Reason* (Oxford: Oxford University Press, 1982), and A. Melnick, *Kant's Analogies of Experience* (Chicago: University of Chicago Press, 1973), ch. 4. Seeking to elucidate Kant's commitment to the existence of things in themselves, in different ways, see H. Allison, *Kant's Transcendental Idealism*, ch. 11, R. Aquila, 'Things in themselves and appearances: intentionality and reality in Kant', *Archiv für Geschichte der Philosophie* 61, 1979, 293–308, K. Fischer, *A Critique of Kant* (1883), trans. W. Hough (London: Sonnenschein, 1888), ch. 1, N. Rescher, 'Noumenal causality', in L. W. Beck ed., *Kant's Theory of Knowledge* (Dordrecht: Reidel, 1974), M. Westphal, 'In defence of the thing in itself', *Kant-Studien* 59, 1968, 118–41, and R. Pippin, *Kant's Theory of Form: An Essay on the 'Critique of Pure Reason'* (New Haven: Yale University Press, 1982), ch. 7. Allison defends the two conception view, drawing on G. Prauss' influential *Kant und das Problem der Dinge an sich* (Bonn: Bouvier, 1974) (no translation available); Aquila and Fischer take the two object view. E. Adickes' important and frequently cited *Kant und das Ding an sich* (Berlin: Pan, 1924) (no translation) sets out the doctrine of double affection. For an account of transcendental idealism as essentially a metaphysical doctrine, see H. Heimsoeth, 'Metaphysical motives in the development of critical idealism', in M. Gram ed., *Kant: Disputed Questions* (Chicago: Quadrangle, 1967). In direct opposition, G. Buchdahl offers a non-ontological, Husserlian account of transcendental idealism in *Kant and the Dynamics of Reason: Essays on the Structure of Kant's Philosophy* (Oxford: Blackwell, 1992); ch. 1 explains his general approach, and chs 5–6 concentrate on the concept of affection.

On the transcendental ideality of the self, see H. Allison, *Kant's Transcendental Idealism*, ch. 12, and K. Ameriks, *Kant's Theory of*

Mind: An Analysis of the Paralogisms of Pure Reason (Oxford: Clarendon, 1982), ch. 7.

9 The complete Critical system (The Canon of Pure Reason)

A selection of Kant's writings important for grasping the unity of the Critical system would include: *Groundwork of the Metaphysics of Morals*, sect. III; *Critique of Practical Reason*, bk II, 'Dialectic of pure practical reason'; *Critique of Judgement*, Introduction, §§28–9, §59 and §§82–91; and 'Idea for a universal history with a cosmopolitan purpose', in Kant, *Political Writings*, ed. H. Reiss, trans. H. Nisbet (Cambridge: Cambridge University Press, 1970). The moral-religious vision of Rousseau's that so influenced Kant is set forth in 'The creed of a Savoyard priest', in *Émile* (1762), trans. B. Foxley (London: Dent, 1974), pt IV.

An outstanding account of Kant's moral theory is given by D. Henrich in 'The moral image of the world', in *Aesthetic Judgement and the Moral Image of the World* (Stanford, Calif: Stanford University Press, 1992), and 'The concept of moral insight and Kant's doctrine of the fact of reason', in *The Unity of Reason: Essays on Kant's Philosophy* (Cambridge, Mass.: Harvard University Press, 1994). The rationale for Kant's formalist ethics of autonomy is explained in J. Silber, 'The Copernican revolution in ethics: the good reexamined', in R. P. Wolff ed., *Kant: A Collection of Critical Essays* (New York: Anchor, 1967). On Kant's moral theology and issues relating to it, see L. W. Beck, *A Commentary on Kant's 'Critique of Practical Reason'* (Chicago: University of Chicago Press, 1960), pt III, G. Buchdahl, *Kant and the Dynamics of Reason: Essays on the Structure of Kant's Philosophy* (Oxford: Blackwell, 1992), ch. 15, and R. Sullivan, *Immanuel Kant's Moral Theory* (Cambridge: Cambridge University Press, 1989), chs 8 and 15. Locating Kant's theory of morality and religion in the context of his innovatory conception of reason, see S. Neiman, *The Unity of Reason: Rereading Kant* (Oxford: Oxford University Press, 1994), O. O'Neill, *Constructions of Reason: Explorations of Kant's Philosophy* (Cambridge: Cambridge University Press, 1989), pt I, and R. Velkley, *Freedom and the Ends of Reason: On the Moral Foundation of Kant's Critical Philosophy* (Chicago:

University of Chicago Press, 1989). On the role of the aesthetic in the Critical system, see K. Düsing, 'Beauty as the transition from nature to freedom in Kant's *Critique of Judgement*', *Noûs* 24, 1990, 79–92.

G. Deleuze, *Kant's Critical Philosophy: The Doctrine of the Faculties*, trans. H. Tomlinson and B. Habberjam (London: Athlone, 1984), offers a short and incisive synopsis of the Critical system.

The quotation from Theodor W. Adorno on page 318 is from *Negative Dialectics*, trans. E. B. Ashton (London: Routledge & Kegan Paul, 1973), p. 385.

10 The reception and influence of the *Critique*

The immediate reception of the *Critique* is charted in detail in F. Beiser's fascinating *The Fate of Reason: German Philosophy from Kant to Fichte* (Cambridge, Mass.: Harvard University Press, 1987). On this early period, see also G. di Giovanni, 'The first twenty years of critique', in P. Guyer ed., *The Cambridge Companion to Kant* (Cambridge: Cambridge University Press, 1992), and T. Rockmore, *Before and After Hegel* (Berkeley: University of California Press, 1993), ch. 1. Relevant primary texts are collected in G. di Giovanni and H. S. Harris eds, *Between Kant and Hegel: Texts in the Development of Post-Kantian Idealism* (Albany: State University of New York Press, 1985).

Criticism of Kant by the post-Kantian idealists may be found in J. G. Fichte, *The Science of Knowledge* [*Wissenschaftslehre*] (1794), trans. and ed. P. Heath and J. Lachs (Cambridge: Cambridge University Press, 1982), First and Second Introductions; F. W. J. von Schelling, *On the History of Modern Philosophy* (1856–61), trans. and ed. A. Bowie (Cambridge: Cambridge University Press, 1994), pp. 94–106, 'Kant'; G. W. F. Hegel, *Faith and Knowledge* (1802), trans. W. Cerf (Albany: State University of New York Press, 1977), sect. A, 'Kantian philosophy', *Phenomenology of Spirit* (1807), trans. A. Miller (Oxford: Clarendon, 1977), Preface and Introduction, *Lectures on the History of Philosophy* (1833–6), trans. E. Haldane and F. Simson (Lincoln: University of Nebraska Press, 1995), vol. 3, pt III, sect. III, B, 'Kant' and (*Encyclopaedia*) *Logic* (1817) trans. W. Wallace (Oxford: Clarendon, 1975), ch. 4, sect. 2, 'The Critical philosophy'; and A. Schopenhauer, *The World as Will and Representation* (1844), 2 vols, trans. E. Payne (New York: Dover, 1966), vol. 1, Appendix, 'Criticism of the Kantian philosophy', and vol. 2, ch. 18, 'On the possibility of knowing the thing in itself'. For a brief history of post-Kantian idealism, see W. Windelband, *A History of Philosophy* (1901) (New York: Harper, 1958), vol. 2, §§41–3.

An excellent reconstruction of the philosophical development from Kantian to absolute idealism may be found in R. Pippin, *Hegel's Idealism: The Satisfactions of Self-Consciousness* (Cambridge: Cambridge University Press, 1989), pt I; Pippin indicates the relevant issues left unresolved by Kant in *Kant's Theory of Form: An Essay on the 'Critique of Pure Reason'* (New Haven: Yale University Press, 1982), ch. 8. Also illuminating is D. Henrich, 'Fichte's original insight', trans. D. Lachterman, in D. Christensen ed., *Contemporary German Philosophy* (University Park: Pennsylvania State University, 1982), vol. 1. Hegel's critique of Kant is analysed in K. Ameriks, 'Hegel's critique of Kant's theoretical philosophy', *Philosophy and Phenomenological Research* 46, 1985, 1–35, and S. Priest ed., *Hegel's Critique of Kant* (Oxford: Clarendon, 1987).

J. Habermas situates his Kantianism without metaphysics historically in *Postmetaphysical Thinking*, trans. W. Hohengarten (Cambridge: Polity, 1992), pt I. On Wittgenstein's Kantianism, see J. Lear, 'The disappearing "we"', *Aristotelian Society Supplementary Volume* 58, 1984, 219–42, and H. Schwyzer, 'Thought and reality: the metaphysics of Kant and Wittgenstein', *Philosophical Quarterly* 23, 1973, 193–206. The relation of Kant to analytic philosophy is discussed by P. Hylton in 'Hegel and analytic philosophy', in F. Beiser ed., *The Cambridge Companion to Hegel* (Cambridge: Cambridge University Press, 1993). Two recent works testifying to the continuing influence of Strawson's interpretation of Kant are Q. Cassam, *Self and World* (Oxford: Oxford University Press, 1997), and J. McDowell, *Mind and World* (Cambridge, Mass.: Harvard University Press, 1994).

An interesting set of reflections on post-Kantian developments and the concept of a Copernican revolution in philosophy is K. Hartmann, 'On taking the transcendental turn', *Review of Metaphysics* 20, 1966, 223–49.

The work by K. L. Reinhold referred to on page 328 is *Briefe über die Kantische Philosophie*, 2 vols (Leipzig, 1786–87), reprinted Leipzig 1923, ed. R. Schmidt. The quotation from J. A. Eberhard on page 329 is taken from H. Allison. *The Kant–Eberhard Controversy* (Baltimore: Johns Hopkins University Press, 1973), p. 15. The quotations from Heinrich Heine on page 329, lines 24–5, are from *Religion and Philosophy in Germany: A Fragment*, trans. J. Snodgrass (Albany: State University of New York Press, 1986), pp. 107, 109. The work by J. G. Hamann referred to and quoted from on pages 330–1 is *Metacritique of the Purism of Reason* (1781), in R. Gregor Smith, *J.G. Hamann: A Study in Christian Existence with Selections from His Writings* (London: Collins, 1960), pp. 213–21. The work by J. G. Herder referred to on page 330 is *Eine Metakritik zur Kritik der reinen Vernunft* (1799), in *Sämmtliche Werke*, ed. Bernhard Suphan (Berlin: Weidmannsche Buchandlung, 1881), vol. 21. The quotation from G. W. F. Hegel on page 332, line 12 is from *Lectures on the History of Philosophy* (1833–6), trans. E. Haldane and Frances Simson (Lincoln: University of Nebraska Press, 1995), p. 246. The work by Friedrich Schiller referred to on page 332 is *On the Aesthetic Education of Man in a Series of Letters* (1795), trans. and ed. Elizabeth Wilkinson and L. A. Willoughby (Oxford: Clarendon, 1967). The quotation from G. W. F. Hegel on page 332 is from *Faith and Knowledge* (1802), trans. H. S. Harris and W. Cerf (Albany: State University of New York, 1977), p. 74. The quotation from G. W. F. Hegel on page 333 is taken from Dieter Henrich, 'On the unity of subjectivity', trans. Guenter Zoeller, in *The Unity of Reason: Essays on Kant's Philosophy* (Cambridge, Mass.: Harvard University Press, 1994), p. 46. The work by J. G. Fichte referred to on page 334 is *The Science of Knowledge* [*Wissenschaftslehre*] (1794), trans. and ed. P. Heath and J. Lachs (Cambridge: Cambridge University Press, 1982). The works by F. W. J. von Schelling referred to on page 335 are *Ideas for a Philosophy of Nature* (1797), trans. Erroll E. Harris and Peter Heath (Cambridge: Cambridge University Press, 1988), and *System of Transcendental Idealism* (1801), trans. Peter Heath (Charlottesville: University of Virginia Press, 1993). The quotation from G. W. F. Hegel on page 338 is from *Faith and Knowledge* (1802), trans. H. S. Harris and W. Cerf (Albany: State University of New York,

1977), p. 94. The quotation from G. W. F. Hegel on page 339 is from *Faith and Knowledge* (1802), trans. H. S. Harris and W. Cerf (Albany: State University of New York Press, 1977), p. 76. The quotation on page 339 from F. W. J. von Schelling is from *System of Transcendental Idealism* (1801), trans. Peter Heath (Charlottesville: University of Virginia Press, 1993), p. 12. The work of Arthur Schopenhauer referred to on page 341 is *The World as Will and Representation* (1st edn 1818, 2nd edn 1844), 2nd edn trans. E. Payne, 2 vols, (New York: Dover, 1966). The works of Martin Heidegger, referred to on page 343, are *Being and Time* (1927), trans. John Macquarrie and Edward Robinson (Oxford: Blackwell, 1962), and *Kant and the Problem of Metaphysics* (1929), 4th edn, trans. R. Taft (Bloomington: Indiana University Press, 1990). The work of Jean-Paul Sartre referred to on page 343 is *Being and Nothingness: An Essay on Phenomenological Ontology* (1943), trans. Hazel Barnes (London: Methuen, 1958). The work of Maurice Merleau-Ponty referred to on page 343, is *Phenomenology of Perception* (1945), trans. Colin Smith (London: Routledge & Kegan Paul, 1962). The works of Ludwig Wittgenstein referred to on page 346 are *Tractatus Logico-Philosophicus* (1921), trans. D. Pears and B. McGuiness (London: Routledge & Kegan Paul, 1961), *The Blue and Brown Books: Preliminary Studies for the 'Philosophical Investigations'* (Oxford: Blackwell, 1975), and *Philosophical Investigations*, trans. G. E. M. Anscombe (Oxford: Blackwell, 1976).

Index